A HISTORY OF SIXTEENTH-CENTURY FRANCE, 1483–1598

A History of Sixteenth-Century France, 1483–1598

Renaissance, Reformation and Rebellion

JANINE GARRISSON

Translated by Richard Rex

St. Martin's Press   New York

Originally published by Editions du Seuil, Paris, as two books:
Royauté, Renaissance et Réforme, 1483–1559 (1991) and
Guerre civile et compromis, 1559–1598 (1991).

First published in the United States of America in 1995

Printed in Malaysia

ISBN 0–312–12612–3

Library of Congress Cataloging-in-Publication Data
Garrisson, Janine.
A history of sixteenth-century France (1483–1598) : Renaissance,
Reformation, and rebellion / Janine Garrisson ; translated by
Richard Rex.
p. cm.
Originally published in French as two separate books: *Royauté,
Renaissance et Réforme, 1483–1559,* and *Guerre civile et compromis,
1559–1598.*
Includes bibliographical references and index.
ISBN 0–312–12612–3
1. France—Civilization—1328–1600. 2. Renaissance—France.
3. Reformation—France. 4. France—History—War of the Huguenots,
1562–1589. I. Title.
DC33.3.G36   1995
944' . 028—dc20   94–47567
                                                          CIP

Contents

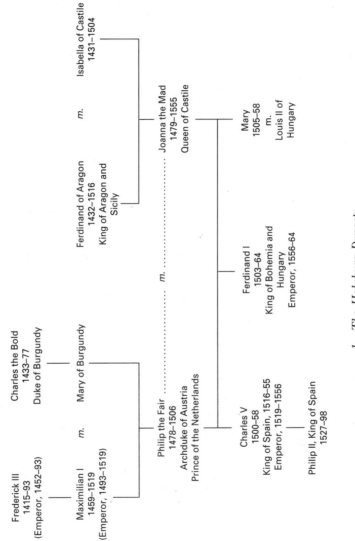

1 The Habsburg Dynasty

Frederick III
1415–93
(Emperor, 1452–93)

Maximilian I
1459–1519
(Emperor, 1493–1519)

m.

Charles the Bold
1433–77
Duke of Burgundy

Mary of Burgundy

Ferdinand of Aragon
1432–1516
King of Aragon and
Sicily

m.

Isabella of Castile
1431–1504

Philip the Fair
1478–1506
Archduke of Austria
Prince of the Netherlands

m.

Joanna the Mad
1479–1555
Queen of Castile

Charles V
1500–58
King of Spain, 1516–55
Emperor, 1519–1556

Ferdinand I
1503–64
King of Bohemia and
Hungary
Emperor, 1556–64

Mary
1505–58
m.
Louis II of
Hungary

Philip II, King of Spain
1527–98

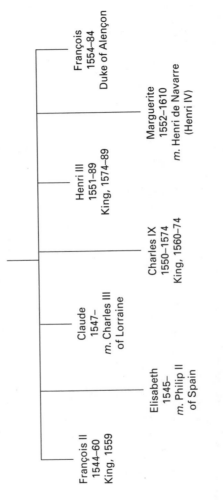

Henri II, King of France from 1547 to 1558
m. Catherine de Medici

François II
1544–60
King, 1559

Elisabeth
1545–
m. Philip II
of Spain

Claude
1547–
m. Charles III
of Lorraine

Charles IX
1550–1574
King, 1560–74

Henri III
1551–89
King, 1574–89

Marguerite
1552–1610
m. Henri de Navarre
(Henri IV)

François
1554–84
Duke of Alençon

2   *The Later Valois (simplified)*

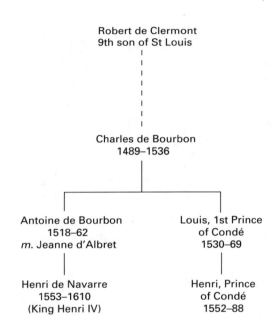

Robert de Clermont
9th son of St Louis

Charles de Bourbon
1489–1536

Antoine de Bourbon
1518–62
m. Jeanne d'Albret

Louis, 1st Prince
of Condé
1530–69

Henri de Navarre
1553–1610
(King Henri IV)

Henri, Prince
of Condé
1552–88

3   The House of Bourbon, Leaders of the Protestant Party

x

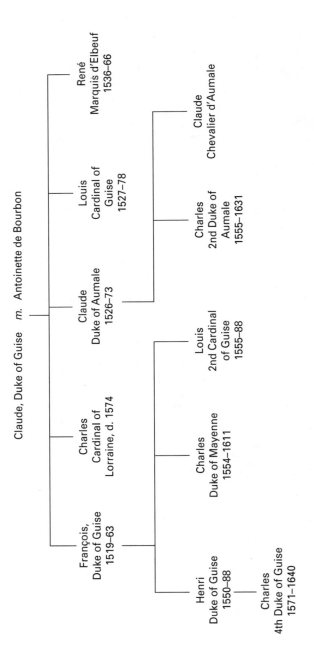

Claude, Duke of Guise   *m.*   Antoinette de Bourbon

François, Duke of Guise 1519–63

Charles Cardinal of Lorraine, d. 1574

Claude Duke of Aumale 1526–73

Louis Cardinal of Guise 1527–78

René Marquis d'Elbeuf 1536–66

Henri Duke of Guise 1550–88

Charles Duke of Mayenne 1554–1611

Louis 2nd Cardinal of Guise 1555–88

Charles 2nd Duke of Aumale 1555–1631

Claude Chevalier d'Aumale

Charles 4th Duke of Guise 1571–1640

4   *The House of Guise (simplified)*

Part I

The Kingdom and its People

Introduction

The kingdom of France in 1483 occupied an area little different
from that assigned to Charles the Bald as Western Francia by the
Treaty of Verdun in 843. To the north-east, the rivers Escaut and
Meuse formed the border with the Netherlands and the Empire,
while the eastern limits were marked by the Saone, the Rhône,
and the Alps. The Mediterranean shore and the Pyrenees constituted a long southern frontier interrupted only by the county of
Nice and the enclave of Roussillon. Although the realm clearly
prefigured the 'Hexagon' of modern France, it was no less clearly
far smaller, covering little more than 450 000 km². It formed a
reasonably coherent and defensible whole, but was not without
weaknesses. None of the great frontier rivers represented an
impassable obstacle to an invading force, and this fact helps
explain the policy of prudent expansion to the north and east
pursued by monarchs from the time of Louis XI. The French-
speaking duchy of Lorraine, which stood between France and
the Empire, enjoyed close relations with the former, thanks to its
duke's descent from King René of Anjou. The duke's two
brothers, Claude (Count of Guise and Aumale) and Jean (later
Cardinal of Lorraine), entered the service of the French kings in
the early sixteenth century. Claude became a naturalised Frenchman in 1506, and in 1513 married Antoinette de Bourbon (sister
of the great Constable), thus establishing a dynastic connection
with a noble house of royal blood. Louis XI took a particularly
close interest in the duchy of Savoy, placed like Lorraine between
the kingdom and the Empire. He sought to bring it into the
kingdom through marriage alliances, but the dukes wavered between their two powerful neighbours. But marriage alliances

3

remained the main element of Valois policy towards the Alpine principality. Another buffer-zone, Comté – the Franche-Comté of today – had remained in the hands of Mary of Burgundy when the Burgundian state collapsed after the death of Charles the Bold in 1477, and had subsequently descended to the Habsburgs. This strategically vital territory was a special target of French ambition, like Burgundy itself, which had, however, fallen to the French Crown upon the duke's death. Burgundy remained a particular bone of contention during the Habsburg–Valois conflict, and was often invoked as a *casus belli.* When French dreams of Italian hegemony faded under Henri II, the main lines of foreign policy were laid down for a century or more: over and above dynastic and opportunistic alliances, to push forward the vulnerable eastern and northern frontiers and thus loosen the Habsburg stranglehold imposed by Germany and Spain. And this France was, nevertheless, the wealthiest and most populous state in Europe, and the one with the most coherent political geography.

This favourable situation at the heart of Europe was compromised by internal weaknesses which would disturb modern commentators, to whom unity is the cornerstone of a stable political structure. For the sovereign did not exactly control the whole of the land known as France. Avignon and the Comtat Venaissin belonged to the papacy, while the town of Orange and its environs owed allegiance to the house of Orange-Nassau. Calais had long been in English hands. And the great territorial fiefs whose lords paid homage to the kings of France were veritable outposts of autonomous jurisdiction descended from the feudal period. Not only Brittany, but, at the heart of the realm, the hereditary possessions of the Bourbon dynasty (le Bourbonnais, la Marche, le Forez, and the Auvergne) were governed in effect as independent states. Beneath their dukes, each had its court, chancery, and fiscal administration. Judicious marriages secured Brittany for the French kings, but the Bourbon domains were acquired only by dint of François I's notorious destruction of the Constable. The lands of King René of Anjou fell to the Crown painlessly, made over to Louis XI by the last heir. It is in this perspective that we should view the attitude of the French kings towards the activities of the Viscounts of Béarn, who were also the kings of French Navarre. The kings of France had to combat Spanish designs on this little Pyrenean enclave while simultaneously restraining the propensity of its rulers to pursue an independent policy. The marriage of Jean d'Albret to Catherine, sister and heiress of François Phébus, head of the house of Foix, and thus Viscount of Béarn and King of Navarre – a marriage encouraged by Louis XI – reduced the risks and contributed to the consolidation of the Midi under a single feudal dynasty. Another marriage a few years later, between Henri d'Albret and Marguerite d'Angoulême in 1527, further tightened the ties of these provinces to the kingdom as a whole.

Even apart from these remnants of feudalism, diversity was the rule in the kingdom of France. The very language of the monarch – the dialect of the Ile-de-France – was restricted to an aristocratic and bourgeois elite. Even in official documents, whether private or public, this language vied for place with Latin, which remained the preferred medium of the intellectual elite well into the seventeenth century. In the provinces, French and Latin were confined to the ruling classes. Most people spoke only their native Breton, Picard, Provençale, or whatever. The king's subjects were not only unable to understand each other's dialects: they were often unable to grasp what their rulers were saying. Weights and measures varied not simply from one province, but from one town to the next. The law which governed the dealings of people and property in the south, profoundly influenced as it was by Roman law, was a written code; but in the north it was largely customary and oral. This varied from village to village, although one can identify certain broad families, such as the customs of Paris or of Normandy. These were the concern of the jurists, who strove to record them in order to clarify and rationalise them, a task which lasted well into the sixteenth century. Even the direct tax, the *taille*, the very sinews of central power, displayed no uniformity in its incidence or collection. Depending on whether they lived in the north or the south, taxpayers were assessed for the *taille* on the basis of their landed property as valued in local registers, or else on their income as calculated by local commissioners. The fiscal and legal privileges enjoyed by members of orders and corporations further complicated the picture.

Even greater difficulties were posed to a central power anxious to extend its control over the country as a whole by the local rights and liberties inherited from the medieval period. These added a further level of diversity to the conditions of individuals and institutions, devolving power and decision-making to a remarkable degree. The liberties of the provinces preserve their jurisdictional position as it had stood before their integration into the kingdom. The provincial estates, such as those of Brittany, Provence, Languedoc, and Burgundy – to name only the most illustrious – continued to flourish. These administrative and fiscal institutions, which represented the three orders of society (clergy, nobility, and commonalty), served as a point of contact between central power and local interests, and themselves exercised considerable local authority. The towns, whose constitutions were infinitely various, enjoyed within their walls almost total autonomy. Their magistrates wielded enormous powers, regulating trades and crafts, controlling the forces of law and order, and levying local taxation. In the countryside, the seigneurs – great or small, lay or clerical – exercised over peasants and villagers feudal powers which often seemed to their subjects more immediate and compelling than those of the Crown.

This dispersal of centres of power and decision-making was further compounded by the delays and difficulties of communications, which at once reinforced regional variations and justified the political and social division of the country into small and autonomous units. The parish, the town, and the province filled the geographical and intellectual horizons of the French. Individuals were defined by their parish and diocese, or occasionally by their province: the kingdom was a nebulous concept. The very name 'France' signified, in the provinces, nothing more than the Ile-de-France. 'France' in its modern sense was a concept confined to the intellectual and political elite. The poets and propagandists of the early sixteenth century made the term more familiar to their readers, and later in the century it became widespread – paradoxically at the very moment when the Wars of Religion were tearing the country apart.

The way in which Louis XI and his councillors governed in the aftermath of the Hundred Years War provided the model that was to be followed by all his successors from Charles VIII to Henri II. He sought to concentrate power in a few hands, to bring all business, however trivial, under the immediate eye of the monarch, and to maintain continuous liaison with the provincial governors, the civic aldermen and consuls, and the magistrates of the sovereign courts – in short, with all the local agents of power. From Louis XI onwards, the incessant correspondence between monarchs and their local representatives in the towns and provinces testifies to their single-minded determination to be present everywhere. The same intention underlay the torrent of edicts, decrees, and ordinances which flooded out from the King's Council, making the royal will a reality even for the humblest cogs in the administrative machinery of the realm.

Striving to uphold their position as the supreme source of authority for each and every subject, the kings fostered with a sure instinct and a shrewd political intelligence that religion of monarchy which constituted the only bond of unity among Frenchmen. The anointing which made the bearer of the Crown into a thaumaturgic king remained the ultimate weapon in the armoury of royal symbolism. And, again following the example of Louis XI and his perennial journeyings around the realm, the kings made sure that they manifested themselves in person to their subjects. Although there was a sort of divine aura about the power they wielded, they did not wish to hide it under a bushel. On the contrary, they diligently constructed the stage on which to display it. Pursued in order to elicit that consent at which all political authority aims, it was an essential part of the art of government. Images of the king in majesty were set up one after another: splendid processions, châteaux, works of literature, sumptuous festivities, and striking judicial appearances gradually drove home the message about unique and indivisible sovereignty. Dependent powers which existed as emanations of the supreme power gradually lost their distinctive images. Gentlemen, officeholders, prelates, and artists were all alike submerged in the 'service of the king' and all alike came to bask in the reflected glory of the Crown.

The intention was to impress upon the French imagination images of kingship in majesty which were in fact inseparable from a harsher reality, that of the king in his traditional role as warrior, warlord, and conqueror. Wars, especially those waged by François I and Henri II, became a way of strengthening the bonds between the king and his subjects – one thinks in particular in this context of the trauma which followed the capture of François at Pavia. Above all, they provided the chance for the king to tighten his control of the country under the pretext of the defence or expansion of the realm.

'Mother of arts and arms and laws, thou France' – these proud words from the pen of Du Bellay appeared at a time when the carefully planned task of reducing the country to obedience under a supreme authority was well under way. The architects of this work, acting in collaboration with the elites of the kingdom, were to a certain extent Charles VIII and Louis XII, but above all François I and Henri II.

1 Peasant Life

The People of France

After the long period of demographic decline induced by the disasters of the fourteenth and fifteenth centuries, the later fifteenth century witnessed a dramatic resurgence of population that was obvious even to contemporaries. The Burgundian chronicler Jean de Clercq went to the heart of the matter in 1466: 'From Easter until the middle of August there were more marriages in the towns and villages of Artois and Picardy than the older folk can recall ever having seen before, or having heard of from their forebears.'[1] Other commentators remarked on the effects of this demographic blossoming, waxing lyrical over the reclamation of land for cultivation and the buoyancy of trade and industry. Claude de Seyssel, Louis XII's official panegyrist, welcomed the rise in population as the engine of economic growth: 'with the people increase also goods, revenue, and wealth'. Leaving aside his flattery, we should nevertheless recall that, if Louis himself was hardly the stuff of greatness, at least he presided over demographic and economic expansion.

Putting figures on these subjective judgements is a tricky business. There were no censuses at this time, nor – until the reign of Louis XIV – an adequate level of registration. Occasional statistical surveys undertaken for tax purposes give us some solid information, but they are not enough to chart population changes with precision. One is left with only the general indicators of demographic recovery: the reclamation of land, the expansion of towns, and the repopulation of deserted villages. Even so, some historians have tried to put figures on the demographic trends.

They reckon the French people at about 16 million in 1515, 17 million in 1547, and perhaps 20 million around 1560 – that is, back to the level of the late thirteenth century before the Hundred Years War, the Black Death, and the famines. This steady recovery was due primarily to a high birth-rate – around 40 births per thousand – itself reflecting a fall in women's age at marriage (in the seventeenth century, a rise in the age of marriage was the major brake on birth-rate) which maximised their effective fertility. But a lower mortality-rate in a kingdom now mercifully free from foreign and civil conflict was also an important factor. Thanks to persistent good weather, food was available in sufficient and often abundant quantity to support a population whose previous spurts of growth had met prompt Malthusian checks. The famines which were to set in with the 1520s were still far off. And epidemics were less frequent, though still capable of occasional virulence. Under François I and Henri II, as Emmanuel Le Roy Ladurie has observed, epidemics were more widely spaced, perhaps as a result of the quarantine measures adopted in some towns.[2] A decline in the incidence of leprosy reinforced this admittedly limited trend.

The consequences of demographic recovery were immediately apparent in social and political terms. The gaping holes left by the ravages of the fourteenth and early fifteenth centuries were filled by internal migration. Poorer regions, where populations soon outstripped limited resources, exported their surplus population to more favourable areas, where labour was in demand thanks to the effects of war or disease. Recent research has shown how the peasants of Rouergue left their inhospitable land for the greener grass of Quercy,[3] while those of Poitou and the Vendée made for Guyenne and the Garonne. Languedoc drew men down from the Massif Central and from as far afield as Brittany,[4] though Bretons tended mostly to migrate to Normandy. With labour mobility, land reclamation, and the resurrection of deserted villages, the increase in the level and mobility of the population around 1500, as the horrors of the past faded, restored the means of production as well as the numbers of producers.

The recovery manifested itself above all in a phenomenon which did not escape contemporary attention – 'the triumph of the town'. For the 'beautiful sixteenth century' – which one ought to date 1460–1520, when the wounds of former hard times were healed and prosperity was brought in the wake of a diversifying and growing economy – gave birth to the world of the town. Rising food production could support a non-agrarian population, even if many urban centres contained many countryfolk. The interplay of peasant immigration, foreign migration, and demographic growth swelled the numbers of townsfolk. Recent research on towns all points in one direction. As Richard Gascon puts it: 'The urban thrust began around the middle of the fifteenth century, accelerated steadily from 1470 to 1540, and culminated in the decade preceding the outbreak of the civil wars. This long phase of growth saw the populations of towns double or even triple in some cases.'[5]

The new importance of the town within the kingdom calls for particular attention. Following the approach of Bernard Chevalier, let us take a sort of cross-section of French urbanisation around 1538, when growth was steady.[6] A population assessed for tax purposes at 200 households – and probably numbering some 800 to 1000 inhabitants – in effect marks the boundary between a village and a town. Small towns ranged from 200 to 600 households, the middling from 600 to 2500, and large towns from 2500 to 12 500. The greatest towns, numbering over 100 000 households, were scarcely to be found in France. Chevalier suggests the following profile for French urbanisation: about 200 small and middling towns; 47 large towns; and in the highest class, Paris alone. Some statistics enable us to see the implications of urban expansion more clearly. Paris, according to contemporary observations, was thronged with people. Richard Gascon has estimated some 200 000 inhabitants around 1330, and 400 000 around 1550 – figures which suggest not just a remarkable recovery from the fourteenth-century collapse, but a considerable increase. Lyon too exhibited great vitality, rising from perhaps 20 000 in 1450 to 40 000 around 1500, and reaching 70 000 or 80 000 by 1550. Similar patterns can be seen in such provincial capitals as Toulouse, Bordeaux, and Rouen, which rose from 20 000 each around 1450 to 40 000, 50 000, and 60 000 respectively by 1550.

Historians disagree about the character of this urban renaissance. Gascon attributes it unhesitatingly to a spectacular increase in total urban population, whereas Chevalier maintains that there was little overall change between 1300 and 1600 other than the swings and roundabouts of circumstance. Nevertheless, even he concedes that 'the town stamped itself upon society without having achieved statistical preponderance'. This is hardly the place to try and resolve this knotty problem, but a number of recent local studies, such as that of Alain Croix on Nantes and its hinterland, and Hugues Neveux's general survey in the *Histoire de la France urbaine*, point towards a 'genuine demographic increase'.[7] This meant a degree of urbanisation hovering around 8 to 10 per cent in 1500, and breaking the 10 per cent barrier by 1550 – still way below Flanders, where perhaps 30 per cent of the people lived in towns, but almost comparable to Italy.

The important thing to note, apart from the strictly demographic facts, is the uneven distribution of towns around France. The map drawn by Gascon on the basis of the 1538 returns for the *solde des hommes de pied* shows that the urban concentrations lay in the Paris basin (where Paris itself weighed heavily), along the Garonne from Bordeaux to Toulouse, in the mid-western region dominated by Poitiers, Limoges and La Rochelle, and the areas around Lyon and Dijon.[8] Elsewhere towns were thin on the ground, with yawning gaps in the Alps, the Landais, the Pyrenees, the Auvergne and Brittany. In fact, nothing would be more surprising to the modern observer than the small numbers of people who lived in towns, perhaps between 1.7 and 2 million in the early sixteenth century. Negligible in our eyes, these numbers nevertheless seemed immense to contemporaries, and the towns enjoyed an importance out of all proportion to their numerical significance – a fact to which we shall return in the next chapter.

The World of the Countryside

The bulk of the French people lived in the countryside, whether in isolated farmsteads, small hamlets, or sizeable villages. Some 85 to 90 per cent of the population depended directly on the land, and agriculture was the basis of national prosperity. It provided not only food, but also the raw materials of the major industry (textiles) – flax, hemp and wool – as well as the staples of foreign trade – corn, spirits and salt. From the late fifteenth century, peasants turned themselves more and more into craftsmen, spinning and weaving in their cottages during the slack months of the agrarian year to supply flax, hemp and wool to the merchant-craftsmen of the towns.

Nevertheless, what society above all required of the land and its workers was daily nourishment – which was indeed primarily bread. Agriculture in the Middle Ages, as in modern developing countries, provided above all else cereals, most of them suitable for baking. Wheat for white bread, and barley, oats, rye, buck-wheat and *méteil* (a mixture of wheat and rye) covered the fields. Local conditions determined the choice of crop: the colder lands of acidic soil lent themselves to buckwheat, the sandy soils of Brittany to rye; *méteil* grew well on the light soils of the Midi, and wheat reigned, though not supreme, in the Paris basin. The cereals for sale in the urban markets tell us what bread the townsfolk ate: in Paris, wheat, rye, barley and oats; in Toulouse, corn, rye, oats and millet provided the flour for bakers and for such consumers as owned an oven.

Preoccupied though they were for the most part with the production of cereals, the peasants nevertheless found time to grow other crops and rear livestock. With no animal or chemical fertilisers, it was essential to allow the land regular fallow periods, and the agricultural system recognised this. North of the Loire, fields were left fallow every third year, bearing a winter cereal and then a spring crop (oats) in the other years. In the Midi, the time-honoured Mediterranean two-year cycle prevailed. But with fields sown every other year, this meant that in any given year only half of the available land was productive, compared with two-thirds in the north. The poorer cultivation ratio of southern lands was matched by a relative technological backwardness which further reduced yields. The rolling fields of the Parisian basin were tilled autumn and spring by ploughs with iron blades, drawn for the most part by horses rather than oxen.[9] In the south, flimsier ploughs barely scratched the surface for sowing: 'the typical plough of the south,' observes Le Roy Ladurie, 'drawn by ox, mule, or even by hand, was a cheap wooden device, always breaking, and easily repaired or replaced'.[10] The edge, or at best the blade, might be of brittle iron, so that the peasant's toil was interspersed with regular visits to the blacksmith to repair or sharpen the strip of metal. The implements used for hoeing and weeding, botched up from tempered wood, were of doubtful utility. And the farming methods themselves limited the chances of bumper harvests. Crops were sown too close together and were reaped with poorly sharpened sickles or scythes which showered grain on the ground. Of course we must qualify this picture: Jean Jacquart has shown that the peasants of Hurepoix had in their ploughs a highly effective tool. But they did not know how lucky they were compared with their counterparts in Brittany or Quercy.

Cereal yields were thus, inevitably, poor, and hardly increased between the Middle Ages and the eighteenth century. Neverthe-less, the agrarian output of the kingdom was – weather, war and plague permitting – enough to feed some 20 million people in 1550. In the seventeenth century, Vauban tried to put some fig-ures on productivity. He reckoned that for every unit of wheat sown, poor lands would yield 4.5 units, and good land 5.5 units, which works out at about 9 hundredweight per hectare from the former, and 11 hundredweight from the latter. His figures were indeed a little sketchy, but they could hardly be otherwise. At Hurepoix in Picardy, good lands could bear 15 or even 16 hun-dredweight in good years, while in Quercy the peak was 10 hun-dredweight, and in the Languedoc a mere 7.5 hundredweight. Overall productivity was thus limited, but there were consider-able variations according to time and place.

The fallow and waste lands were hallowed features of the un-changing agrarian scene. The uncultivated land, which included scrub, bush, and woodland, was a pillar of country life, providing grazing for pigs and sheep, as well as timber, wild orchards, mushrooms, root crops, and game. Much has been written on the importance of scrub in the peasant life of Brittany, as also on common rights in land not under active cultivation.

The third domain of peasant agriculture was the garden, a patch of free soil which the peasant and his wife would seek to enrich with household, human and animal waste. Gardens were large, often over a hectare, even three hectares on the poor soil of the sharecropping farms of Poitou, and did not count for purposes of taxes tithes or rents. Tended with care thanks to their man-ageable size, they produced vegetable or textile crops, and be-came a sort of laboratory in which peasants could experiment with tomatoes, cucumbers, pumpkins, artichokes or melons, with new crops of all sorts from Italy, Spain, or the Americas.

In the later fifteenth and early sixteenth centuries a number of innovations were introduced into the virtually subsistence agri-culture of France. They were, for the most, patches of specialised production. Thus the woad cultivated around Albi, the Ariège valley, and the Lauragais for the Toulouse market made that provin-cial capital an international city. From 1460 to 1560 Toulouse and its hinterland enjoyed enormous prosperity. It must have required great courage and determination for an Albigensian peasant to abandon his traditional agricultural routine and exchange subsistence cereal production for woad. He had to move to a three-year rotation (woad, fallow, and wheat), and growing the woad made huge demands on his time and skill. The topsoil had to be hoed free of clods before sowing, and sowing itself required great care. From the appearance of the first shoots until the harvest he waged a constant and exhausting battle against weeds: five months of unremitting manual labour. Once harvested, the leaves had to be carefully washed before being sent to the woad mill to be reduced to 'cocagnes' (little balls of woad extract), and even then it took a fermentation process to convert the raw material into the product sought by the dyers of western Europe.[11]

Elsewhere in the kingdom, the revival of agriculture was accompanied by the introduction of other non-cereal crops: growing demand stimulated hemp production in Britanny, for example. But above all there was a boom in the wine trade. Of course, farmers everywhere in the Middle Ages tended a few vines for domestic consumption. But vineyards now began to expand dramatically in Burgundy, the Ile-de-France, Languedoc, the Bordelais, and along the Atlantic littoral from Nantes to La Rochelle. Languedoc saw in addition the spread of the olive, whether concentrated in groves or scattered among the fields. Fiscal records suggest that the olive was in this area the third most important crop after cereals and grapes. A little further north, the chestnut tree played the role of the olive in the pattern of land use.

The revival, growth and diversification of agriculture was not a uniform process, but set in at different times in different regions. Fortunately, the period as a whole was free from those climatic catastrophes which could spoil harvests and induce local or widespread famine, catastrophes so familiar to the peasantries of the preceding and succeeding eras. The political climate was equally favourable. Apart from the League of the Common Weal under Louis XI and the Breton Revolt under Charles VIII, domestic peace prevailed, sparing farmers the devastations and exactions of soldiers. Even taxes, except under Louis XI, remained tolerable, at least until the 1520s. So the French countryside enjoyed from 1450 until the 1520s, and in some places even until 1550, a period of sustained prosperity. The peasantry, few enough at first, recovered to its thirteenth-century level, and each family had some land, even if only a smallholding. The peasants obtained from their seigneurs or landlords favourable terms for the lands they rented. Sharecropping terms were generous, with the labourers able to retain two-thirds of their produce. And leases were similarly easy, while agricultural wages were buoyant. Proprietors reluctant to work the land themselves had to attract manual labour to restore their domains. This led to a general rise in living standards, and to positive affluence in the upper ranks of the peasantry. All the contemporary evidence for daily life points the same way: the rebuilding and extension of farms, the increase in furniture and goods listed in *post mortem* inventories, and the greater availability of education for boys from the countryside.

The peasantry, as we have said, was for the most part proprietary. Some lived on holdings as large as 15 or 20 hectares in the north, or 25 to 30 in the Midi. Others, less well endowed, managed on between 3 and 10 hectares in the Parisian basin, or about 20 in the south, hiring from noble, ecclesiastical or even bourgeois domains. They might be tenants in Normandy and the Parisian basin, or sharecroppers in Brittany, Aquitaine, Languedoc, Provence, the Auvergne, and Burgundy. Even the vast bulk of the peasantry had smallholdings of anything up to 5 hectares. To make ends meet they dabbled in brewing, cottage industries, or perhaps sharecropping. The 'beautiful' (if short) sixteenth century allowed them to get by – though rarely to get rich, as they had nothing to sell but their labour. But their position was not as parlous as it was to become later.

The revival and development of the countryside profited above all the non-farming proprietors even though, early in the period, they had to make certain sacrifices. Recovery of fortunes was frequent among the seigneurial classes. The seigneur distributed vacant tenancies in order to lure manual labour from other provinces, with such success that Hugues Neveux proposed the theory of a 'rise of the gentry' from about 1450 which sustained the fortunes of the class for a further three centuries. Seigneurial entrepreneurs took care to reorganise their lands before farming them out, creating coherent and manageable agricultural units. On the poor soil of Poitou this led to the formation of sharecropping units barely distinguishable from middle-sized tenancies.[12] A postponement to accounting days of tenants' dues, whether payable in cash, kind, or labour, accompanied the revival of the seigneurs, and at first, between 1450 and 1470, the lessor did not make excessive demands. He became more demanding as waste lands receded, harvests rose, and buildings were improved. The prices of tenancies rose, chiefly through new tax assessments, but so did the prices of domain land. Domain lands, the full and unshackled property of the seigneur, were consolidated, though less than has been believed (so, at least, local studies suggest). More significantly, it was exploited, often by leasing or sharecropping, in a more systematic fashion.

This brings us to the arrival in the countryside of strangers to the rural environment. From the mid-fifteenth century, at the time of the great revaluation undertaken by lay and clerical seigneurs, amateurs arrived from the towns in large numbers. Yvonne Bezard tells us that of the 150 *censitaires* of the Bishop of Paris in 1491, 22 lived in Paris itself, employed as merchants, advocates, solicitors, or councillors of Parlement.[13] Elsewhere, craftsmen, shopkeepers, and magistrates of small towns and villages took leases in order to exploit them by sharecropping or sub-letting. The famous movement of the 'land grabbers' first emerged in this crucial phase of the fifteenth century, and it gathered momentum at the expense of the peasant proprietor throughout the sixteenth century, fuelled by the profits of trade and industry, and encouraged by the disintegration of peasant landholdings. For, as we will see later, from the 1520s the conditions of peasant life worsened dramatically, leading to the disposal of leases and freeholds.

For the moment, however, recovery and plenty enriched the life of those who worked the land. The rural community, clustered at the heart of a lordship, around a village or hamlet, and coinciding almost invariably with a parish, constituted a corporate person recognised by both custom and Roman law as well as by the Crown. It was represented by rural consuls (in the Midi), or a syndic or a proctor, who might well also serve as the churchwarden or churchwardens, thus emphasising its essential identity with the ecclesiastical unit. As Jean Jacquart puts it, the community had its own parliament: the assembly of household heads drew together those who lived on the land, and included widows. The seigneur himself might preside, or perhaps the parish priest, a notary, or some other local notable. Its role, which remained substantial until the end of the sixteenth century, had two major aspects. One was strictly economic, the management of the land. In the open field systems of the Parisian basin, economic individualism was an impossibility: the community took decisions about crop rotation, the dates of haymaking and harvest, and the use of common pasture and woodlands. Elsewhere, the date of the vintage was agreed in common, as were questions of moving between mountain and valley pastures. But the assembly also had a social role: selecting a syndic to represent common interests to the seigneur; appointing the schoolmaster, the midwife, and the village constable. The community also constituted the basic unit for the royal or provincial agents (depending on whether the *taille* was fixed by royal *élus* or by local estates) who had to allocate the burden and collect the revenue of taxation.

In the later fifteenth century, and even more in the sixteenth, the rural community played a part in the life of the nation and the great issues of the day. The codification of customary law which so preoccupied the government and the lawyers could not be achieved without the aid of the peasant assembly. There the elders hammered out an initial version of the customs before the royal commissioners. This fundamental unit of early modern France was more than capable of defending itself against injustice and the infringement of its rights. The peasant revolts, such as those of the Pitauds under Henri II, or those of the later sixteenth century, were engendered in these local assemblies. In calling themselves 'people of the communes' or 'of the common estate', these movements emphasised their roots in the rural communities. Towards 1555, the rural consuls of remote parishes in the Vivarais, Guyenne, and Languedoc wrote letters (or had them written) to Geneva begging for a pastor trained in the sound Calvinist school; sometimes they were simply seeking the return of a local parish priest who had gone over to heresy and left to undergo theological retraining in Geneva before becoming a licensed minister. Rare as these expressions of popular Protestantism were, they testify none the less to the vigour of communal society in the parochial or seigneurial village.

Men for the War

The good times that began under Louis XII, when food production kept pace with the growing population, came to an end in the 1520s. A rigid system of production, incapable of sustained growth, set strict limits to demographic increase. Although the birth-rate remained high, net growth was halted by famine and epidemics. The kingdom was struck by widespread famine thirteen times between 1520 and 1600, and even local shortages killed their tens of thousands. French history in the sixteenth and seventeenth centuries is dotted with subsistence crises induced by successions of poor harvests themselves precipitated by the hazards of the weather. And the weather was at its most inhospitable in the closing decades of the century, during the 'little ice age' evoked by Emmanuel Le Roy Ladurie: cold winters and wet summers with unseasonable frosts delayed germination, destroyed seedlings, and made crops ripen late or rot early.[14] The worst crises of the century occurred in 1529–30, 1538–9, 1562–3, 1573–4, 1585–8, and 1593.

Uncertain Bread

It is worth examining a little more closely the social consequences of the famines whose workings have been so painstakingly laid bare by economic historians. A famine induced by two or three bad harvests had immediate effects in the countryside. Squeezed until the pips squeaked by inflexible demands for rent, the peasant kept for his own use but a small fraction of what he produced. The corn was scarcely in before the agent of the parish priest or the bishop arrived to claim his share – one sheaf in every twelve, or one in eight in the Midi. While mules, horses, or oxen turned the millstone to grind the corn from the chaff, the landlord or his bailiff looked on eagle-eyed, counting the sacks before taking their share in accordance with the lease. Or else, in the north, the producer took some of his corn straight to the nearest market in order to raise cash to pay his year's rent. And throughout the realm peasants had to sell a further share of their crop in order to pay, the king's taxes. Once the seedcorn too had been set aside, there was precious little left to feed the family – so much the less if the harvest was bad. If a peasant had enough land of his own to work, he could hold out through two or three bad years. But if, as was usually the case, he had only some small plot, he had to borrow money against his food or even his seedcorn in order to pay his taxes. Before long he would fall behind with his payments, and would be compelled to surrender some of his land to the moneylender. The same syndrome is common enough today in such peasant societies as India or Pakistan. After exhausting the resources of his land – making bread of grass, bark, or fern–

the destitute peasant, racked with hunger, would take his family off to town, hoping to sell any livestock still surviving and to scratch a living from charitable doles, casual labour, or begging.

But it was never long before dearth and famine breached the city walls. The women were the first to see the danger signals: steeply rising prices for bread or grain. In a matter of days wheat, oats and rye – in fact, any cereal – would double, triple or quadruple in price, soaring beyond the average budget. Day-labourers and journeymen, craftsmen, and even the lower ranks of the magistracy and the merchants, were reduced to subsistence level by the ineluctable need for daily bread. On the other hand, those with reserves of capital made huge purchases, and those with large stocks of grain hoarded them jealously, aiming to sell at the peak of the market.

During the period before the new harvest was gathered in, that is to say during spring and summer, the situation in towns worsened considerably. Municipal authorities did their utmost to keep the markets supplied. In Parlement cities, the Parlement would pour out decrees forbidding the hoarding of grain, even ordering house-to-house searches. In Paris itself, the royal city whose huge population made it especially volatile, the authorities bought in grain from better supplied provinces, and even from abroad. Royal edicts forbade the export of French corn, and provincial estates issued similar prohibitions within their jurisdictions. But to little effect outside Paris, where famine was experienced less than elsewhere (except when Henri III and then Henri IV besieged the city in 1589–90). Hospitals clogged up with the sick as people who were reduced to eating anything first contracted gastric afflictions and then starved to death. Women became too weak to conceive, and those already pregnant lost their babies. Parish priests registered the deaths, perhaps adding a sorrowful comment if the deceased was a parishioner. But many vagrants, strangers to the town, would not even be recorded in the register: anonymous, they were thrown without ceremony into a common grave or left dead in a ditch by a road.

Crisis mortality cut swathes through the population, certainly accounting for over a million deaths. And it left its mark on the age distribution, as in this year or that the birth-rate slumped. But life went on, and the gaps were soon filled, so that for a century or more the population was roughly stable at the level it had known around 1340, on the eve of the Black Death, namely some 18 million. Even the wars made little impact on the human capital which made France the most populous nation of Europe. This 'full world', constantly replenished by the high birth-rate, nevertheless felt the full force of those periodic subsistence crises characteristic of rigid rural societies.

The Condition of the Peasantry

From about the 1530s, the countryside entered a curious state in which overpopulation and subsistence crises combined to upset the equilibrium which had been established with some difficulty in the previous century.

In the early sixteenth century, the peasants – the vast majority of the population – held the bulk of the land of the kingdom. There were substantial holdings on which seigneurial rights weighed more or less heavily according to the region. North of a line drawn from Bordeaux to Geneva seigneurial rights were heavy but, except in Burgundy, Brittany, and the Auvergne, they did not reduce peasant income as much as has often been suggested. The *cens*, the traditional tribute to the seigneur, was by now largely symbolic. But the feudal obligations to provide labour, transport, or fodder weighed heavily on those who worked the land. The sire de Gouberville, who held demesne land in the neighbourhood of Cherbourg, arranged to have the land which he set aside for his own use harvested by his villeins, thus exploiting his right to their labour; and he got a good price for leasing out the manorial mill where his seigneurial subjects were obliged to take their grain. However, the lands which he worked in this way provided largely for his own household consumption. Lordship here was thus sometimes burdensome, and often vexatious. But in the Midi it was far lighter, and sometimes nonexistent, for freeholders were more numerous. Le Roy Ladurie has calculated that, around 1480, a hectare of land in the area of Montpellier would pay rent of about 6 *sous* a year, a trivial sum rendered derisory by inflation: by 1570, it represented less than 1 per cent of the gross harvest.

Though the peasants were all landholders, they were by no means all of the same kind. To the extent that one can make sense of a complex system which, contrary to what is commonly thought, was changing throughout the century, one can identify three main categories. Small proprietors were by far the most numerous. Possessed of one or two hectares, they had to hire their labour out to make ends meet, working as unskilled labourers paid in cash or kind, or dabbling in cottage industry or sometimes in sharecropping. The researches of Jean Jacquart on Hurepoix and of Pierre Goubert on the Beauvaisis have shown that, in these regions, three-quarters of the peasantry belonged to the ranks of the small proprietors.[15] The crisis hit them hard, especially after 1560, driving them into debt and, as they found themselves unable to cling onto their land, into vagrancy.

The middling proprietors tended to own between 3 and 10 hectares in the Parisian basin, or between 7 and 20 hectares in the Aquitainian or Mediterranean Midi, and would hold perhaps another 10 or 20 hectares as tenants or sharecroppers. To work this little bundle of land they would have some draught animals and a plough of some kind. They could make a living if the weather brought them good harvests, but as the climate worsened from the 1520s, and then the troubles broke out in the latter half of the century, they too fell into debt and saw their holdings fall piece by piece into the hands of buyers who for the most part did not work the land themselves.

Finally there was the small group of substantial peasantry, owning perhaps 15 to 20 hectares in the Parisian basin, or 25 to 30 in the Midi (where they were known as 'pagés' or 'ménagers', i.e. husbandmen). For the most part well off, occasionally even rich, these farmers were immune from poor harvests, for they always covered themselves. They often had a lucrative second string to their bow, perhaps trading as merchants. Dealing in corn and cereals, they could even profit from the high prices in periods of dearth. Or by running an inn, a tavern, a kiln, or a mill, they could lord it in a fashion over their less fortunate neighbours. Or again, manufacturing linen or woollen cloth in their home, they might trade in a local or even regional market, or deal with a merchant from the town. This rural bourgeoisie had a good business sense, and rented demesne land and seigneurial rights from landlords, or went into tithe-farming for monastic or episcopal proprietors, or simply for the local parish priest. These proprietors would keep draught animals, oxen and horses in their cattlesheds or stables, and would even hire them out. They had little hesitation in educating their sons, in the village school at first, and later at college in town, following the proven route to social advancement which might enable their descendants to leave the land.

This schematic picture of peasant society can hardly take account of the regional disparities found all over the country. France was a kingdom whose geography and history had combined to produce a host of distinctive regions between which the status and condition of the peasantry varied widely: from the established farmer of Beauce, whose sideboard proudly displayed his pewter pots, to the poor Breton sharecropper under the yoke of an always demanding and often impecunious squire. Broad generalisation is the only realistic alternative to a village-by-village description.

The developments of the sixteenth century, as we have said, were far from favourable to peasants, at least of the humbler and middling sorts. 'Rural proletarianisation' is hardly too strong a term for a process whose various but interactive causes reinforced each other in a sometimes tragic way. The overpopulation of the countryside led to a fragmentation of landholdings in regions such as Normandy and the Parisian basin, where partible inheritance prevailed. In the Midi, however, the influence of Roman law kept for a son (usually the eldest) the lion's share of the inheritance, which was eroded only a little by dowries for daughters and token provision for younger sons. Indebtedness led to the sale of plots. Through a well-oiled process familiar in our own times in developing countries, the peasant was forced to borrow grain for consumption or seedcorn, and cash to pay his taxes, using his land as security. Once the arrears built up, the lender foreclosed in order to recoup his outlay.

Peasant indebtedness was considerably aggravated by the disastrous effects of the wars of religion. The comings and goings of soldiers, whether Catholic, Protestant, or simply mercenary, left in their wake a trail of rape, pillage, murder, devastation and extortion. There is a touching sincerity about the lamentations which characteristically abound in the contemporary narratives. Claude Haton, the parish priest of Provins, took to describing both Protestant and Catholic gentlemen as 'gentils-pilhommes' ('gentle-highwaymen'). Pierre de L'Estoile, known for his close interest in the gossip of the city and the Court, nevertheless tells also of the excesses of the soldiery in Champagne and Picardy, and around Blois.[16] The peasants, oppressed beyond the limits of endurance, occasionally rose up, as in the Dauphiné during 1579, or in Périgord and the Limousin during 1594, refusing to pay taxes no matter who was demanding them. Or else, broken by their privations, they went to swell the bands of vagrants and vagabonds from whom the unending war recruited its cannon-fodder.

The Redistribution of Property

The sale and even the abandonment of land led to major changes in the distribution of property. Large properties accumulated in the hands of the 'land grabbers'. The nobility, as long as they were not themselves hard up, bought farmland and woodland. At the highest levels of society, the great dynasties did not let their State responsibilities obstruct serious land accumulation. Anne de Montmorency kept a close eye on his vast estate, whose annual revenue in the early 1560s was around 140 000 *livres*, representing a capital value of about 3 million – considerably more than the 250 000 *livres* capital at the disposal of his father, Guillaume, in 1522. At a more modest level, the provincial gentry were also consumed with land hunger. Gilles de Gouberville's account-book testifies to his patient accumulation of land.[17] On the poorer soil of Poitou, the sixteenth century saw the gentry sound the retreat of the feudal system: they inexorably took land out of traditional tenure and liquidated smallholdings in order to put together larger units which could reach as much as 100 hectares.[18] These new holdings were then put out to a tenant or sharecropper who, depending on the scale of the holding, might be a veritable agricultural entrepreneur, lording it over a flock of peasants, smallholders, or wretched landless labourers. The region around Niort, Parthenay, Cholet, and Bressuire thus saw the rise of a gentry which remained in control of the land until 1789.

From early in the century the urban bourgeoisie were investing in land the profits they derived from trade, office, and usury. To some extent the nobility were selling their lands and leases, but probably not as much as was once thought. It was above all the peasants who were driven to sell by debt and foreclosure. Royal officials were greedy even for the tiniest plots. The Parisian official elite patiently gathered in tenancies and even lordships around the capital,[19] and the councillors of the sovereign courts in Aix, Bordeaux, Grenoble, Rennes, Rouen and Toulouse did not lag behind. In the towns and villages, notaries, advocates and proctors wove legal webs in which poor peasants became inextricably entangled. Between 1527 and 1529 the proctor of the Dijon

Parlement bought 22 plots of land from 10 vendors, accumulating an estate of some 60 hectares. Tradesmen, from the wealthiest merchants to the humblest grocers, bought land as insurance against the ups and downs of trade. Vezian d'Anthenac, a woad-merchant from Toulouse, finished with 8 hectares of land from a series of 12 deals in 1553. This process operated at all levels of society, and craftsmen frequently called on the notary to seal up a purchase of land from some peasant ruined by social, economic, or demographic crisis.

Thus the French countryside underwent significant changes in the sixteenth century, slowly at first, then quickening during the decades of the troubles. The middling peasant proprietors were gradually squeezed out, their holdings broken down into a host of plots of less than a hectare, or else amalgamated into larger blocks in the hands of wealthy townsfolk. And even the small plots were vulnerable. The last resort of the wretched peasant, they too ended up being sold in their turn, leaving their erstwhile owner with three choices: to hire out his labour, to take to the roads, or to join the ranks of the Catholic or Protestant forces.

The Rise of Peasant Poverty

The disintegration of the traditional peasant world allowed the townsfolk to break into it. The new proprietors, whether gentry, officials, or tradesmen, regarded their land as an investment which had to yield a return. Outside the Parisian basin, where tenancy was the rule, they preferred to put out their lands to sharecroppers under agreements which divided the fruits of the land and specified payment in kind, labour, or carriage. But while, in the fifteenth and early sixteenth centuries, sharecropping terms had been good for cultivators because proprietors were keen to get a return from their land and manpower was short, the scales shifted against cultivators as the sixteenth century wore on, and their opportunities for betterment and social advancement dwindled. Around 1600, the famous Protestant agronomist Olivier de Serres offered clear and crisp advice to those who wished to maximise the return from their lands. He told them to divide the yields strictly and equally, leaving the cultivator to cover from his share such expenses as the wages of labourers hired for sowing, weeding and harvesting, the raising of livestock, and the maintenance of the plough.

Despite the disintegration of State authority, which intensified after the rise of the League in 1585, the burden of royal taxation was undiminished. The *tailles* doubled during the Wars of Religion, even if they were not always collected by the agents of the Crown. And, alongside royal officials, agents of the rival parties descended upon rural communities with their own demands. The more or less incessant fighting put additional strains on peasant budgets, whether for the defence of the village or for the feeding and lodging of troops from the regular or irregular forces. And war disrupted the markets and fairs, brought pillage and devastation, and thus helped push up prices. Of course this benefited farmers with a marketable surplus, but few of them were that fortunate.

Nevertheless, all was not black in this gloomy scene. The general disorder caused delays in the payment of rents, and sometimes of dues. But the authorities intervened, when and as far as they were able, in defence of existing rights. The Parlements of Paris and Toulouse endorsed the claims of the Church when peasants, not always under the influence of the Reformation, withheld their tithes in 1560, 1561, 1562, and until 1567. And the hard times brought on by bad weather, overpopulation, and the consequences of war were good times for landowners who, whether nobles or not, were in a position to dominate the growing rural proletariat. The gentry, weakened by the Hundred Years War but more or less rebuilt by the end of the fifteenth century, now began to prosper. Its social and economic influence survived, if it did not actually flourish, under the strains of civil and religious turmoil. In the Ile-de-France, as Jean Jacquart has shown, it even underwent substantial restructuring. In Poitou, the accumulation of lands took place through the play of the feudal retreat around the fief: the noble now became the owner of his old tenancies, and his former tenants found themselves reduced to sharecroppers. And even if the masters of grazing and ploughland felt the impact of poor harvests in the shape of lower income in kind (or even in cash if their land was rented out), they had other resources. But the peasants had nothing else to fall back on. Only those with adequate holdings (about 15 hectares in the north, or 25 in the south) were able to survive a year or more of poor harvests without borrowing. Such tenants or husbandmen were increasingly set apart from the wretched have-nots, forming a kind of rural bourgeoisie between the worlds of the city and the country. In Poitou they might be the general managers of some great landowner, be he a nobleman, merchant, or officeholder. In the Parisian basin, they might be the farmers of some vast estate, adding to the income from their own land the profits from collecting church tithes, trading in corn or cattle, or exploiting forges or kilns, etc. Often enough they expanded their own landholdings at the expense of the impoverished peasants of their village.

By the end of the sixteenth century this bourgeoisie tended to dominate rural society, which, however, had had some fine moments during the wars, when solidarity in the face of soldiers or brigands had been imperative. But rural society was manipulated to the advantage of the new masters of the land, who were seeking to expand or consolidate their domains at the expense of the ancient common rights of the peasantry. They whittled away at common grazing, the legacy of primitive agrarian communism. At first forbidden in certain areas, such as meadows, olive groves, vineyards, orchards, it soon faced hedgerows, fences, and ditches enclosing the ploughland. Although the process did not progress as rapidly and decisively as in England, it was nevertheless under way from the reign of Henri IV. Nor were the new landowners, whether town or countryfolk, reluctant to encroach on common land. Woodland, moorland, and waste land were taken from the impoverished communities by seizure, trickery, or purchase, thus depriving the poor and not-so-poor peasants of a traditional supplement to their resources.

Thus the peasant world, which had been relatively stable from 1480 to 1520, disintegrated. The rise of a new class of landless labourers marked the break with the old system. These men worked on the great estates or else hired their labour to sharecroppers for seasonal employment in sowing, haymaking, harvesting, or grape-picking. Sharecroppers already had more good fortune, for to become one required capital in the form of cash, corn, or cattle. However, the hazards of farming could reduce both labourers and sharecroppers to penury. When that happened the mountain folk descended into the plains, for example from the Cévennes down into Languedoc, or from the Dauphiné into the Rhône valley. Others left the kingdom completely, heading for Italy or Spain, like the peasants of the Aude region who emigrated to Catalonia, far from poverty and the ravages of war.

Peasant Revolts

The general impoverishment did not proceed without protest and revolt. As in Guyenne during 1548, the peasants could rise against their oppressors. In the 1560s tithe revolts accompanied the advance of the Reformation. In 1579–80 the Dauphiné was swept by a peasant rising in which the 'Carnival at Romans' was but one of several tragic episodes. 1590 saw the rising of the 'Gauthiers' of Perche and the Norman Bocage, while in 1592 the people of the plains of Comminges combined in the league of the 'campanères' (or 'countrymen'). And in 1594–5 rebellion swept across a vast area of Quercy, Marche, the Agenais, and Saintonge, a region which in the following century was to see many further such explosions on a local or regional scale.[20] With the benefit of hindsight, these risings look more like assaults on those immediately responsible for peasant distress than resistance to the fiscal power of the Crown. Tithe strikes were a feature of the Garonne valley and Languedoc, where ecclesiastical dues weighed particularly heavily on harvests, sometimes verging on 12 per cent of the grain crop.[21] Nor were they unknown in Saintonge and Normandy. Some commentators, following Monluc, have argued that the Protestant pastors attempted to mount the bandwagon by preaching against the tithe. But one can credit the faithful of the rural parishes with enough intelligence to see that their church dues were not always promoting the Kingdom of God. Le Roy Ladurie, in evoking this resistance to the ecclesiastical levy, weighs its effects against the revenues of the institution, but the Church, in the immense flood of grievances and complaints which it presented to the King's Council after 1598, shamelessly exaggerated the losses and damages incurred during the Wars of Religion. Grievances against the tithe did not blind peasants to their other oppressors. Royal taxation headed the list of grievances for peasants and townspeople alike when they rose in the Dauphiné in 1579. Although they addressed their grievances to the provincial estates in traditional fashion, their revolt took on the violent aspect of a *jacquerie*.[22] They called for greater justice in the allocation of the *taille*, demanding in particular that nobles should pay the *taille* on land which they did not hold by feudal tenure and that the records of taxes levied over the past 20 years should be checked by accountants appointed by the third estate of the provincial assembly. They protested, in passing, against the burden of supporting the numerous garrisons in that strategic region, the administration of the *gabelle* by agents from outside the province, and the way in which seigneurial dues and rights were exacted. The protesters also demanded that the supplementary taxes required by the king should not be levied without the consent of the people. In 1594–5 the 'Tards Avisés' or Croquants protested not only against royal taxation but also against the exactions of the nobility (whether Catholic or Protestant), refusing to work on their lands. Like their counterparts in the Dauphiné, they formed a 'third estate of the countryside', appointing an advocate who presented their grievances on the desk of the estates of Périgord. Henri IV, anxious to pacify the uprising, wrote off arrears of the *taille* in May 1594, requiring in return that the Croquants lay down their arms. But they remained in the field until 1595, to be wiped out on 26 August by a force of provincial gentry at Saint-Crépin-d'Auberoche (in the present-day department of the Dordogne).

The Witch Craze

The witch craze that convulsed France, like much of Europe, in the later sixteenth century offers further evidence for the breakdown in rural society. Of course the phenomenon studied in several works by Robert Muchembled was deep-rooted and complex, but in this period it took on a special importance for both countryfolk and civic elites.[23] Witches and cunning men, initiated into the secrets of white magic, folk healers endowed with mysterious powers by the community, had lived and worked in the community for centuries, feared and yet approached for aid, marginalised yet still familiar figures. Little by little they were turned into scapegoats, made responsible for the evils of the times, authors of misfortunes which the traditional mind could explain only in terms of fate or divine vengeance and chastisement. Witches therefore became scapegoats who had to die for the sake of the parish, village, or township. But it needed a spark to inflame opinion against them. This came from the city, where, since the late fifteenth century, lay and clerical intellectuals had set about exposing the malevolent efforts of satanic powers, whose agents were above all women, to subvert the order of earth and heaven. The spark was a book, the *Malleus maleficarum* ('hammer of witches') compiled in 1486 by Henrich Institoris and Jacob Sprenger, whose 25 editions between 1486 and 1600 testify to its wide readership. Consulted by civil and ecclesiastical judges before and during witch trials, it was indeed a witch-hunters' handbook, identifying the Satanic votaries whom they felt an urge to destroy in order to dispel the threatening shadows and leave the field clear for their young reason and superior culture.[24] But other factors are necessary to explain the intervention of judges from the cities in the traditional world of nature, where hitherto the peasants had carried on as they pleased: the desire of the elites who were now invading the countryside to bring to heel and dominate by force the dark and irrational powers always present in everybody, powers with which the countryfolk had for centuries been familiar; the desire of physicians and agents of royal justice to seize control of the mysterious reality which teemed beyond the city walls, so as to install their own lore and law there. In short, the bourgeois, equipped with the *Malleus*, appeared and initiated denunciation. And in the act of accusation, the accusers experienced the fierce pleasure of defending their space, closing ranks against a common enemy, and bridging the gulf that separated the cocks of the walk from the day-labourers, a gulf which henceforth cut through the social fabric of the countryside.

Pinned down by that involuntary but damaging alliance, the witch could hardly avoid the fate laid down by the *Malleus*, death by purifying fire. But she did not go down without in her turn seeking some revenge on those who had brought her low: friends, neighbours and relatives, she had seen them meet a man, a fox, or some dark animal in a field; she had seen them secretly touch a child who had died suddenly; she had seen them slip into the stable where a few days later some wretched animal had died. And so the judge would return to the village for a fresh round of interrogations and arrests, to complete the fine proceedings of which every magistrate on every bench in the kingdom dreamed. Neurotic relationships and an unhealthy alliance between town and country sent victims by hundreds to the stake. The outcome of this unequal contest between culture and nature, though it could not rebuild the conclusively broken primitive solidarity of the rural community, was that the citizens who hunted the witches to death basked in the complacent certitude of having defeated the agents of an irrational and magical 'anti-world', and of having extinguished all traces of mysteries, instincts, dark beliefs, and atavistic wisdom. The man of the city henceforth stood, free from past ties with the natural world and illuminated by the harsh light of precartesian rationality, as a merciless destroyer of those who owed obedience to other forms of knowledge.

2 Urban Life

The World of the Towns

In the late fifteenth and early sixteenth centuries, the towns, whether walled or not, played a social role out of all proportion to their geographic or demographic extent. Governed by corporations of municipal magistrates (the names varied – consuls, jurats, or aldermen), they enjoyed a genuine autonomy. Magistrates were selected according to many different systems, but the assembly of heads of household rarely played an important part, although direct universal suffrage remained the rule in a few small towns. More commonly, the power of election rested with a council which appointed the various municipal officers. In the Midi a collegiate system prevailed, with social or professional groups each nominating one member to the town council – such groups included the nobles, the advocates, the scriveners, the merchants, and the craftsmen. Sometimes the suburbs might also nominate a representative. Lyon operated such a system, with a civic assembly, comprising one or two members from each craft guild, which each year elected six new councillors who, with the six appointed the previous year, constituted the consulate. However the civic magistrates were elected or selected, they always came from the urban aristocracy, the 'senior pars'.[1] Towards the end of the fifteenth century this gave rise to local conflicts, especially in the Midi, as demands were made for the broadening of electoral colleges. Riots broke out at Agen in 1481 and 1514 as the artisans called for a place on the town council, and Cahors experienced similar agitation in the same period. But peace was restored when the elite accepted a workers' representative.

32

The jurats, consuls or aldermen were responsible for the allocation and collection of royal taxes, urban administration and policing, the fixing of prices and the supervision of the market (especially in cereals, whose plentiful supply was the guarantee of civic peace), and, where relevant, defence and the maintenance of the walls. In some cases they exercised powers of high justice. It is hardly surprising that neighbouring nobles sought to strip them of this particular mark of power and prestige, for municipal office conferred (at Toulouse, Angers, Angoulême, Cognac, Lyon, and elsewhere) noble status. Those of noble birth might scorn it, but it stood upwardly mobile families in good stead. Municipal office was generally monopolised by men drawn from a narrow range of occupations: merchants, notaries and advocates, goldsmiths, innkeepers, wealthy craftsmen, doctors and apothecaries. Often enough the same few families kept a stranglehold on municipal office for generations.

At the end of the fifteenth century, urban autonomy was growing ever more vigorous. Louis XI interfered frequently and often arbitrarily, but did little more than scratch the surface of local privilege. François I and Henri II looked to the towns as sources of revenue, but had no desire to encroach upon their traditional liberties. The most important towns in the kingdom were in any case already under the royal thumb, and constituted the basis of the monarchical apparatus which, as we shall see, expanded so dramatically in the early sixteenth century. Sovereign courts such as Parlements, *chambres des comptes* and *chambres des aides* were established or strengthened in the provincial capitals. The machinery of the 'financial State' was set up in many towns of high or middling rank; and a little later, in 1552, the *présidiaux* came to be added to the bailiwick or seneschal tribunals to enmesh the whole kingdom in the net of royal jurisdiction. Royal officeholders and agents often sat on town councils, imposing de facto restraint if not actually dominating them. More widely, where municipal and royal institutions stood alongside, the former rarely maintained its integrity, whether relations were strained or relaxed. Where civic magistrates came up against councillors of Parlement, they could not but give way: the jurats of Bordeaux and the *capitouls* of Toulouse were like little boys beside the officers of the sovereign courts, and hardly dared act without their consent. While François I and Henri II felt that this barely veiled control was adequate, in the later sixteenth century, especially under Henri IV, the monarchy made a concerted attack upon civic liberties.

Towns as Economic Centres

The towns underwent, or rather led, an economic boom in the later fifteenth and early sixteenth centuries. Peace and relative freedom of movement fostered change on every scale. The demographic boom stimulated demand and provided labour, although wages, initially generous, were under pressure from excess labour by the 1520s. Circumstances outside the kingdom also encouraged growth: the voyages of discovery opened new markets and brought new products, while the Spanish conquistadors brought back masses of American gold and silver which then spread throughout western Europe.[2] The price inflation experienced in France as elsewhere during the sixteenth century was an incentive to entrepreneurs and indeed to all those with something to sell. The inhabitants of the towns profited to varying degrees from this intense economic activity.

Craft industry was always the main form of urban economic activity. The master-craftsman sold his products, be they necessities or luxuries, from the workshop in which they were made. Working with a number of apprentices and journeymen, who often formed part of his household, he would probably be a member of some trade guild (although, despite the best efforts of Louis XI, this was far from always the case). The master-craftsmen played a major role in urban life. They sat in the civic assembly, served by turns in the magistracy, and took their places in those processions by which the community expressed its vision of itself. However, while some traditionally wealthy trades continued to flourish – stationers, for example, and clothiers, jewellers, goldsmiths and silversmiths – master-craftsmen in general experienced a marked decline in standards of living during the second half of the sixteenth century, accompanied by a loss of status within their towns.

On the other hand, the merchants displayed a remarkable dynamism. In considering them, we must distinguish them according to the scope of their commercial horizons. Those whom contemporaries described flatly as 'merchants' tended to deal in anything saleable within their immediate vicinity: cloth and clothing (textiles were the consumer goods par excellence of the time),

jewellery, paper, horses, or grain. What matters is that these goods
might come from anywhere in France – lace from Brittany, broadcloth from Normandy or Paris – or beyond – velvet from Genoa
or silk from Milan. They would be retailed anywhere within a
radius of 20 kilometres from the town where they arrived wholesale. The customers were found at all social levels, from the peasant
in search of seedcorn to the gentleman after a pair of spurs. Nor
did this kind of trade exhaust the energies of men who can best
be compared to those who kept 'general stores' in the old West,
or to those Chinese merchants found throughout South-East Asia
and even in Africa. They lent money to nobles, clergy, and farmers.
To farmers they might also lend corn for sowing or consumption. If the borrower defaulted, they would foreclose on the
mortgage and add another piece of land to their assets. These
merchants diversified into tithe-farming, with their cut enabling
them to build up grain reserves against times of shortage, when
their stores became veritable treasure-troves bringing their owners
eight-, nine-, or ten-fold returns on their outlay. The merchant
thus fits Marc Bloch's picture of the land-grabber. The plots acquired through foreclosures, added to those acquired through
patient purchases, gradually built up into significant properties.
This pattern endured for centuries, but for further detail the reader
is referred to the major synthesis provided by the *Histoire de la
France rurale*.[3] Let us for now follow the merchant's path up the
social scale. The acquisition of land was the traditional starting-
point on the road to nobility, especially as the lands acquired
were often seigneurial. It also brought economic security. Trading was always a risky business. Most sales were made on credit –
a practice which opened doors normally closed to the unpolished
burgher, bringing contact with noblemen and churchmen. As he
rose in status, the merchant took his place among the civic magistrates. In the sixteenth century, lawyers and merchants carved up
urban government, gradually squeezing out the craftsmen. A successful merchant might be able to contract a socially advantageous marriage for himself, but more usually he fulfilled his
ambitions through his children. For them, life led through school
to university and the law, with a career in the judicial or financial
service of the Crown as the goal. Alternatively, the Church held
tempting prebends, rich plums which the prudent parent could
reserve in advance for a son to take up on reaching the requisite
educational attainments and canonical age.

Another kind of entrepreneur, with a broader view, was the merchant-venturer of the sort that had appeared in the great textile centres of Flanders and Tuscany as early as the thirteenth century.[4] These men would secure the rights to the entire output of a number of town or country craftsmen, providing them with raw materials and perhaps also with the tools of the trade, and then marketing their products through a national or even international network. The producers thus tended to become dependent on these capitalists, tied to them by advances made in cash or kind. Breton lace, Norman broadcloth, muslin from Reims, unfinished woollens from Lodève, Béziers and Carcassonne, and finished woollens from the Black Mountains were brought by the merchant-venturers for sale in the huge international fairs of Lyon or the regional fairs at Parthenay, Beaucaire, Fontenay-le-Comte and elsewhere. Italy, the Levant, the Barbary Coast and Spain bought high-quality French textiles at low prices. Like their local counterparts, these big merchants played a full part in civic life, bought lands (even entire seigneuries), and sent their sons to school. Sometimes they were patrons of the arts, able to afford silver tableware, a mansion in town, or even a château. Through their own marriages and those of their children they were assimilated to the nobility, above all in backwoods provinces such as Gascony and the Rouergue.

Even further up the scale from the local traders and the merchant-venturers we can identify a group with horizons so broad as to deserve the name of businessmen. The term is by no means univocal. There were big differences between a woad-magnate in Toulouse, a banker in Lyon, and a Norman entrepreneur like Jean Ango. Yet as a group they represent a new kind of man, one whose 'bold temperament was equal to the risks of business and of life'. They were the aristocracy of commerce. France may not have had its Fuggers or Welsers, those German capitalists who were bankers to princes, but there were still some astonishing success stories. Richard Gascon maintains nevertheless that the great French export trade to Italy, Spain and the Mediterranean was dominated by foreigners, who profited from taking to their home countries the products brought together by French merchants. These foreigners were 'masters of the market in quality cloth, spices, and metal goods'. Some of them were easily assimilated: 'soon came the crowning glory of their career, appointment to the civic magistracy and other offices; and, for the richest and most ambitious, recognition and favour from the royal court'. Others, less well known, remained cloistered in their ghettos, with their own church and their own religious calendar, living closer to the other foreign communities than to the natives of the town. In Lyon, for example, the German quarter was next to the Italian, which was in turn next to the Spanish.

At the very highest levels of commerce, then, the French were not major players. But some of them came close, especially in the banking sector. The basic activity of the merchant-banker was the provision of letters of credit, which did away with the onerous and perilous business of transporting large quantities of cash over long distances, facilitated foreign exchange, and profited the banker, who of course charged in cash for the service. The risks were high. Those who advanced huge sums had to fear not only the perpetual monetary tinkering of the French monarchs, but also the hazards of agricultural production (which could upset the entire internal market), civil disorder, and of course war. Large-scale trade could not function without the banking advances which provided letters of credit. Gilles Caster has shown how the Toulousan woad-magnates, Jean Bernuy, Pierre d'Assézat and Jean Cheverry, who organised production from sowing to sale, encountered financial problems which only the flexibility of letters of credit could resolve. Lyon – which, thanks to Louis XI, had replaced Geneva as the hub of the Rhine–Rhône trading axis – established an indisputable French supremacy in this area. At its annual fairs, the market in financial paper was so perfectly oiled that it scarcely developed any further throughout the entire Ancien Régime. The merchant bankers came there from throughout the kingdom and beyond, as the biggest deals could only be managed at the Lyon fair.

Credit was available not only for major international traders but also for major luxury consumers. Gentlemen, churchmen and courtiers spent huge sums in keeping up appearances, and regularly had recourse to the bankers of Lyon, Paris and Rouen, as well as to their humbler counterparts in provincial centres and lesser towns. In return, the moneylenders managed seigneurial and ecclesiastical revenues, which allowed capitalism to penetrate even the most traditional social mechanisms.

In addition, credit was extended to the State. And here we find the merchant-banker in his most influential, as well as his most hazardous, role. In this period of inflation in both power and the public display of power, princes could not rely on their ordinary revenues (from Crown lands) or even on their extraordinary revenues (from taxation) to cover expenditure: they had to borrow. One form of royal borrowing was to farm out tolls, customs, and other indirect taxes. The financier advanced in cash a discounted sum which he then recouped through levying the tax on the ground. Thus Julien Ruiz of Nantes 'farmed revenues of every kind'. He was, it is true, a merchant-banker of exceptional standing. On a more humble level, merchants in market-towns included among their multifarious activities the farming of municipal taxes, advancing cash sums to the corporation in exchange. But credit extended to royalty took on other forms which involved equally large sums. Louis XII and François I looked to the bankers of Lyon to finance their Italian campaigns on the security of the administrators of the royal finances. These agents, Semblançay in particular, paid dear for the entanglement of their private affairs in those of the State. From 1536, the Lyon money market found itself ever more deeply embroiled in the toils of a monarchy which indulged in profligate short-term borrowing at rates of up to 16 per cent per annum, or 4 per cent a quarter. 'They mobilised', in the words of Richard Gascon, 'in the service of the State not only the personal capital of the bankers but also that of their depositors.' The 1558 setback to the 'Grand Parti' – the association of creditors created to manage the expansion of the royal debt – was only superficial, as loans were converted into shares in royal revenues. But though the bankers got themselves out of a hole, the bonds which they issued to tap private capital fell disastrously in price, ruining many of their creditors. But for all that, this period saw the Crown take the first steps on the route which led into the hands of the moneylenders, who henceforth intervened in the machinery of public finance and became the beneficiaries of the public purse.

This same phenomenon could be seen in Normandy, albeit to a lesser degree. The example of Jean Ango remains the most spectacular. The scion of a Rouen merchant dynasty which had moved to Dieppe in the sixteenth century, he diversified the family business, moving into tax-farming, privateering, and exploration. For France played its part in the thrust which took Europeans into a wider world. François I himself went shares with the Norman capitalist in an expedition to seek a North-West passage to China and Indonesia. On one occasion he visited Ango at his famous manor of Varengeville. As for Semblançay, the intermingling of private and public affairs pioneered by Admiral Chabot ended in the latter's trial, when interesting revelations hinted at the malpractices of which Chabot was guilty, in involving the government too obviously (by means of royal ships and licences) in the adventures of the Norman capitalists. Jacques Cartier, the sailor of Saint-Malo, also received the king's financial support for his expeditions, which led to the discovery of Canada. But in this case the motives were more pure, with the profit motive hardly figuring. Even so, the tireless Cartier failed to establish a colony beyond the seas, and remained a long-term creditor of the Crown, which was unable to pay him the sums promised to cover the expenses he had already incurred.

All these men, be they bankers, adventurers, or international merchants, pursued a matrimonial strategy designed to lever them into the ranks of the nobility. They sought equality with the highest placed men of affairs and the greatest of the *noblesse de robe*. They were active in civic life. In the striking case of Lyon, the sixteenth century saw the merchants displace the lawyers as the dominant group. In Toulouse, d'Assézat and Bernuy willingly assumed civic office, as did the Forbin and Riquetti families at Marseille. Like their humbler counterparts who dealt in cloth and grain, they bought up seigneuries, inheritances and tenancies, which they exploited vigorously. In time their sons or grandsons came to hold the highest public offices. Chancellor Duprat was the son of a merchant and banker who had been consul of Issoire. Guillaume Briçonnet's brother was a leading businessman. The Bernuy family, which once dominated the Toulouse woad trade, moved instead into office-holding: Jacques, son of the fantastically wealthy Jean Bernuy, became *Président des Enquêtes* in the Toulouse Parlement in 1544. And the d'Assézat who were leading councillors there were undoubtedly nephews of Pierre, the famous merchant. Pierre Cheverry rounded off his business career with the post of *général des finances* in the Languedoc. And the son of Jean Ango happily combined royal service with his offices and revenue farms, and even combined the post of Governor of Dieppe with active participation in joint-stock companies involved in piracy, cod-fishing, and other trading ventures.

These aristocrats of business, no less than their humbler local counterparts, expressed their financial power in stone. Mansions in town and châteaux in the country provided work for local architects, sculptors and painters. Richard Gascon maintains that, in Paris at least, the libraries of the merchants were more impressive than those of the lawyers, the royal servants, and the churchmen. As for elsewhere, it is hard to believe that Ango, Ruiz or Cheverry did not collect books.

Whatever their status, merchants did not maintain traditional relations with God or the Church. Of course, in many merchant families, such as the Duprat in the late fifteenth or the Bernuy in the early sixteenth centuries, or among the less chic businessmen of the Rouergue, traditional religious attitudes flourished. They set up their sons as bishops or canons, left huge sums for masses or for the poor, or had themselves buried in religious habits.[5] However, individualism, the awareness of a wider world, the lust for profit and the taste for risk, were traits that sat ill with traditional religious practice and the demands of the Church. The Church condemned lending at interest, which was therefore disguised with ingenious contracts. But could these contracts soothe a bad conscience or avert damnation? At the beginning of the sixteenth century, Antoine Brenquier, a merchant and consul of Rodez, stood at the head of a list of usurers compiled by the saintly bishop François d'Estaing: a mere sidelight perhaps, but also a sign of profound mutual incomprehension. More individualised approaches to the sacred, however, were available. Jean Ango, a friend of Marguerite de Navarre, was drawn to the *devotio moderna.* In 1537, Guillaume Masenx, a merchant of Gaillac for whom all was fair in making money, was present at some notable's house together with some 'ministers'. Who were they? Where did they come from? Nobody knows – but the businessman called them 'ministers'. The proximity of Lyon to Germany favoured the spread of Reformed religion in commercial circles. At Toulouse the woad-magnates dabbled in the new religious currents: Pierre d'Assézat and Pierre Cheverry went over to Calvinism.

Commerce in the sixteenth century was a source not only of wealth and social mobility but also of spiritual curiosity. It was undoubtedly a source of power in the towns for those who conducted it, and an engine of growth for the towns themselves.

Towns as Intellectual Centres

Great or small, towns possessed the institutions which dispensed knowledge: schools, colleges, and universities. Can one detect an expansion of educational provision in France towards the end of the fifteenth and in the early decades of the sixteenth centuries? A rather timid affirmative can draw some support from the wealth of modern research into this period, one of the turning-points of modern history. The scholarly debates which rage around the origins of the Reformation can now be supplemented by that provoked by Pierre Chaunu over the expansion across the kingdom of the cultural elite – even if that elite remained a minority. The possessors of this skimpy or generous intellectual baggage put forward from that time a view of the world and of the social order which was different from that of their ancestors. Was this because hitherto the teaching of reading and writing had been virtually (though never totally) a monopoly of mother Church? The question could perhaps be put another way: did the prosperity of France in this forty-year period see an increase in literacy?

The little schools where children learned to read, write and count are hard for the historian to come to grips with. Yet, transient and various as they were, they certainly existed. Sometimes the parish priest would teach for money. In well-to-do families, a tutor might be hired: it happened more frequently than one might imagine. A merchant of Lectoure was having his children educated privately around 1510. In Quercy, one of the most backward provinces, even the larger villages were having schoolmasters appointed by their consuls from the 1450s, as were the equally backward Forez and Rouergue.[6] Elsewhere, song schools and the schools run by minor clergy provided pious children with elementary instruction. There is undoubtedly an element of truth in the remark of the Venetian ambassador Marino Giustiniano, made in 1535, that 'there is nobody in France, no matter how poor, who cannot read and write'.

The colleges provided the equivalent of today's secondary education. Whether they were modelled on the colleges of the Brethren of the Common Life or on the Strasbourg Gymnasium, or whether they continued the medieval practice of mixing together pupils of all levels under a single teacher, these establishments were flourishing. Towns desired them and founded them, sometimes seizing control of them from the church authorities. Most major cities had at least one. Some, like the college of Guyenne at Bordeaux, enjoyed a degree of fame. Those of Paris were far superior to their provincial counterparts, tempting merchants and lawyers elsewhere to send their sons to study in the capital despite the greater – and constantly increasing – expense.

The universities attracted students from all over the kingdom and beyond. The university of Paris, the crucible of Christian humanism and evangelism, remained the most prestigious. Those which taught law – Roman and canon law were of course the only types studied academically – were well attended. Although in the absence of detailed research we cannot put a figure on it, subjective testimony makes it clear that there was a considerable increase in attendance at the law courses of Orléans, Bourges, Toulouse, and Poitiers. Even in the fifteenth century, the universities had begun to lose that exclusively clerical character which they owed to their ecclesiastical origins and to the academic dominance of canon law and theology. They were becoming to a large extent instruments of the temporal power – nurseries for servants of the State. The new university foundations of Aix (1409), Poitiers (1431), Valence (1432), Caen (1452), Nantes (1460), Bourges (1464), and Bordeaux (1473) were all inspired by political considerations of princely prestige or administrative requirements. They delivered bachelor's, master's, and doctoral degrees which qualified their recipients for the priesthood, teaching, medicine, or royal office. Whatever their defects and reputation, they provided their clients with passports to social advancement. The practical proof of this can be seen in the distribution of the fifteenth-century foundations, which saw at least one in every Parlement's jurisdiction. Moreover, these production-lines for clerics and lawyers were also centres of social cross-fertilisation, conferring on those who attended not merely degrees, but a broader mental horizon.

Towns clearly offered a potential market for the printing trade. However, the initial impact in France of the 'Gutenberg galaxy' was rather low key. The tables compiled by Lucien Febvre and Henri-Jean Martin show that before 1500 France was, in this area, an underdeveloped country in comparison with Germany, Italy and Spain. But despite the delay, the masters of the new craft gradually began to respond to the call of noble and ecclesiastical patrons and of new markets. Jean de Rohan installed two printers in his Breton château in 1484, while the abbots of Cluny and Cîteaux also summoned printers from Germany. And, at least at first, the proliferation of theological works, sacred texts, and devotional manuals furthered the catechetical aims of the Church.[7]

The new trade prospered above all in the great university towns.

Paris had its first press as early as 1470, installed in the Sorbonne itself. Its masters, a pair of Germans, soon opened an important branch outlet at the sign of the Golden Sun in the *rue Saint-Jacques*. The major judicial centres soon had printing-shops too, for lawyers rivalled clerics as bibliophiles. The great palaces of justice in Paris, Rouen and Poitiers had well-equipped bookshops soon enough. Nor did the commercial centres lag far behind. Lyons, whose commercial role developed so dramatically in the later fifteenth century, obtained its first press in 1473 thanks to the entrepreneurial skills of Barthélemy Buyer, who financed and probably selected the first publications. The geography of French printing around 1500 thus offers a fair reflection of the kingdom's urban framework. The main centres were Paris, Lyon and Rouen, followed by Poitiers, Toulouse, Caen, Tours, Orléans, Rennes, Nantes, Albi, Grenoble, Provins, Troyes, Dijon, Châlons-sur-Marne, Angoulême, Limoges and Angers. On a humbler level, presses sprang up in less famous centres such as Cluny, Uzés, Périgueux, Tréguier, Bréhaut-Loudec and Narbonne, reflecting the movements of itinerant printers, the whims of wealthy gentleman-scholars, or the catechetical preoccupations of zealous churchmen.

Before 1500, according to Febvre and Martin, the book was essentially a commodity: publishers responded to consumer demand, which was predominantly for religious works. They produced the Bible (in Latin or the vernacular), the *Imitation of Christ*, the Fathers of the Church, the *Golden Legend*, or devotional manuals like the *Art of Dying Well*, often illustrated with woodcuts. Even allowing for the preponderance of clergymen among the literate population, it is easy to appreciate from this profusion of pious publication that the elite was profoundly concerned with the afterlife. Across Europe as a whole, nearly half of all books published before 1500 were religious. Some 30 per cent were literary, while the remainder were divided between legal and technical subjects. These figures are equally true of France alone. In France, as elsewhere, the Latin classics were an important sector of the market: Virgil, Ovid, Juvenal, Terence, Plautus, Seneca and above all Cicero, the most widely printed classic of the fifteenth century. France in fact outstripped other countries in printing Cicero. The vernacular classics of medieval courtly literature – the *Roman de la Rose* and *La Conquête du Grand Charlemagne* – were also soon in print. And one should not forget that the literary sector included a large number of basic Latin grammars.

Febvre and Martin produce some staggering statistics for European printing before 1500, testimony to the insatiable cultural appetite of the time: between 30 and 35 thousand printings of some 10 to 15 thousand separate titles can be identified in the second half of the fifteenth century. Actual production must have been even greater, as many editions have doubtless disappeared without trace. Assuming an average print-run of about 500 copies, some 20 million books must have been printed before 1500. In appreciating the significance of these figures, we should bear in mind two things: the population of Europe was considerably smaller then than now; and the literate population even more so. The impact of restricted literacy was of course tempered by the characteristic strengths of an oral culture. When reading was so frequently public, whether as the traditional medieval 'lectio', as the Sunday reading in church by the priest, or as reading aloud in the evenings at home, a book could leave powerful traces in memories schooled in a culture of oral tradition. If, even today, a particular copy of a book reaches on average some four readers, how many more non-readers must have been reached by each copy in the later fifteenth century!

After 1500, as we shall be seeing again later, the book left an indelible mark on people's minds. Total production grew by leaps and bounds, and its pattern changed. The relative importance of devotional works declined, while the philosophical and literary sectors expanded. This can be seen from Table 1, based on figures for Parisian printing compiled by Febvre and Martin. In the course of the sixteenth century the book was to become not only a weapon in ideological and religious conflict, but also a manifestation of an intellectual awakening and of new cultural approaches born of social change and a widening of the elite.

Table 1   Book production in early sixteenth-century Paris

Year	Total production	Devotional works	Classical and humanist texts
1501	88	53	25
1515	198	105	57
1525	116	56	37
1528	269	93	134
1549	322	56	204

The advent of the printer–bookseller in the town led to the emergence of social groups hitherto unknown. In the peace of the cloister, medieval scribes had slowly copied out traditional texts: the great publishers of the sixteenth century appeared as heroic figures of a world in intellectual ferment. Their fifteenth-century predecessors, usually Germans, had worked with basic equipment, adapting themselves to the needs of local markets at the behest of some noble or clerical patron, their limited production remaining within traditional parameters. But within a couple of generations, printers were stamping their own cultural, philosophical, and religious preferences on the product. Sacred texts in Latin, Greek and Hebrew were published by men like Robert Estienne and his son Henri at Paris; Chrisopher Plantin at Paris, Caen, and Antwerp; and Sebastian Gryphius at Lyon. Gryphius published Rabelais alongside Marot, Erasmus alongside the Latin classics. Printers founded commercial dynasties, passing on sophisticated equipment to sons or nephews so that they could continue the production of ancient texts in fine editions, and engage in the debates of the time. The career of Robert Estienne (1503–59) was an intellectual odyssey. He ended his days a refugee in Geneva, having published a Hebrew Bible which breached Catholic regulations by including uncanonical books. The printers' employees, journeymen or apprentices, constituted an industrial elite. They could all read. For the most part newcomers to the towns where they worked, they were not integrated into the artisan traditions. And this combination, as Natalie Zemon Davis has shown in the case of Lyon, gave them a real class-consciousness which led them to organise and even to strike in vindication of their grievances. Such men swelled the ranks of the Reformers.

The towns saw the development of the 'newsletters', flysheets informing the public about the great events of the kingdom and the Continent. Often enough these widely circulated and cheaply produced sheets, illustrated with arresting woodcuts, were attempts by those in power to silence false rumours or reap the full glory of some minor triumph.[8] The triumphs of Charles VIII and Louis XII in Italy, the births of dauphins, the visits of foreign sovereigns (notably that of Charles V in 1540), and splendid royal entries into great cities, such were the staple of these transient chronicles. The famous Placards of 1534 participated in the nature both of these newsletters and of the countless polemical flysheets that flooded out in the wake of the Tumult of Amboise in 1560. Intended to be read aloud, these leaflets poured out from the presses of the major towns. Jean-Pierre Seguin has identified in the reigns from Louis XII to Henri II some 116 such items produced in Paris, 70 in Rouen, 42 in Lyon, and 7 in Toulouse, among others. But the place of imprint tells us nothing about their impact, as they circulated throughout the kingdom in the baggage of salesmen, satisfying the thirst for information of the highest and lowest in society.

Towns as Social Centres

The towns, which were centres for the circulation of the written word, also resounded with the voice of the preacher. Preachers could be heard in the churches or in the squares, in the town hall or the market place, dominating the crowd from the vantage of their wooden scaffold or stone pulpit. The preachers summoned by civic magistrates to mark the great feasts of the Church calendar (above all the seasons of Lent and Advent) belonged for the most part (60 per cent) to the orders of friars. The Dominicans or Friars Preachers held pride of place, followed by the Franciscans and then by the Carmelites and Augustinians. Usually graduates in theology, they preached in an accessible French, although some celebrated preachers like Gerson and D'Ailly drafted their sermons in both Latin and French. 'The common people, great or small', officials, merchants and craftsmen, women as well as men, standing, or seated on benches or on the ground, listened eagerly to preachers and were carried away by their words. And they could be stirring words, building up the sense of community and solidarity by identifying visible or invisible enemies: the devil and his demons, the heathen Turks, or Jews, or – in time – heretics. Above all, they aroused in their hearers the longing for perfection and holiness, in flight from sin and in obedience to the commandments of the Church. Preachers sought to root out the individual and collective sins which might bring down divine vengeance upon the community. They were capable of bringing crowds to life and manipulating them.[9] For one example, let us look neither at the great names of the early fifteenth century, like Gerson and D'Ailly, nor at those of the early sixteenth century, like Olivier Maillard or Jean Vitrier, but at the Dalmatian Franciscan Thomas Illyricus,

who made a preaching-tour through south-western France between
1518 and 1520, taking in Bordeaux, Agen, Condom, Nérac,
Montauban, Toulouse, Foix, and many other centres. Like all his
colleagues, he was interested above all in the towns, as were the
towns in him. He certainly drew the crowds. At Condom, on the
feast of All Saints 1518, the Franciscan church was not big enough
to hold them, and they had to use the meadow beside the hospital. At Montauban a pulpit had to be set up in the cemetery. At
Toulouse, in November, the Franciscan church overflowed, so they
moved out into the *Place Saint-Georges*. Like all preachers, Thomas
worked on his sermons. He wrote everything down, even his stage-
directions for delivery. Here for example is the preparation for a
sermon preached in 1521 on the Holy Name:

> As soon as I ascend the pulpit, I make the sign of the cross,
> join my hands, and raise them to head-height. I pause in silence
> for about the length of a Credo. Then I strike up an anthem,
> and, falling to my knees, call on the name of Mary with an Ave
> Maria. After the Ave Maria I recite the Veni Sancte Spiritus to
> myself. At last, rising, after a moment's silence I announce the
> theme and add, 'In the name of Jesus and of his mother Mary
> and of all the company of heaven, may the peace of Jesus Christ
> be upon us. Amen'. I then launch into the exordium and pro-
> ceed with the sermon.

The stage-directions continue throughout the sermon in order
to bring the text to life, though they are put into the third person for the aid of subsequent users:

> The Holy Name of Jesus is the Gateway to Heaven, o wretched
> soul! (very loud). The Most Holy Name of Jesus is the Gateway
> to Heaven! Do you want to find rich pastures in the next life?
> Then enter by the gateway that is Jesus. You will find it when
> you renounce your vices and your sins. (Weep here and raise
> the voice in as mournful a tone as possible: a sermon which
> does not arouse contrition is no use at all. . . . Then show the
> crucifix to the people until the end of the sermon. . . . Extend
> your arms in the form of the cross, pass a rope around your
> neck; take up the crucifix again and, beating your breast, cry
> with tears choking your voice) Cry out, wretched souls! Beg
> 'mercy, my Lord! mercy, mercy, mercy'. (Give the blessing and

leave the pulpit immediately. If you wish your ministry to bear
fruit, avoid the society of men, and above all of women).

A master alike of words and gesture, Thomas Illyricus was
thoroughly versed in the art of persuasion. The content of his
sermons was traditional in every respect. He sought to free his
hearers from the slavery of sin – concentrating especially on gamblers. He explored the currents of devotion to Christ and Mary,
characteristic, as we shall be seeing again, of late medieval piety.
Finally, like his Parisian colleague Jean Vitrier, he made no attempt to gloss over the shortcomings of the clergy and their abuse
of their spiritual power.[10]

The average Christian of the time, according to Hervé Martin,
might hear some 800 sermons in his life. One can hardly doubt
that they stirred the hearts and minds of listeners avid for emo-
tionally charged religious rhetoric.

Literate or illiterate, intellectual or not, the townsman did have
something other than the traditional story-teller and the unskilled
efforts of the parish priest to listen to: the theatre was an inte-
gral part of the urban environment. All sorts of performances,
from farces to mystery-plays, entertained urban populations in the
second half of the fifteenth century, especially in the commer-
cially and industrially booming towns between the Loire and the
Seine, between the Seine and the Saône, and along the Rhône.
The judicial centres were the homes of satire, where the youths
of the legal profession exposed the follies of all and sundry. Their
scripts often carried political messages or aimed shafts at the great
ones of the world, the royal councillors. More frequently, they
forcefully revived the traditional carnival themes of inversion, of
fools and idiots in control of power and money. Farces, usually
short pieces, tended to caricature the traditional urban stereotypes:
greedy craftsmen and shopkeepers, lewd priests and monks, ar-
rant rogues, naive and gullible peasants, and grotesque braggarts
and bullies. These comic performances likewise represented an
ethic of inversion, presenting to the spectators, in place of the
accepted norms of social behaviour, norms based on cunning,
trickery, and brute force. Complacent in its coarse amorality, farce
was impossible to take seriously. Satire, in contrast, based as it
was on a critical world-view, and purveyed largely by the younger
members of the bourgeoisie, students, and junior lawyers, often
aroused official ire. In 1486 Charles VIII gaoled an author and

four amateur actors for a comedy which compared him to a spring clogged with grass, weed and debris – in other words, surrounded by evil councillors. François I did the same to three actors in 1516 who dared to say on stage that 'Mother Folly presides at court, pilling, polling, and robbing all round.'

The mystery plays, with their religious themes, belonged to an ancient dramatic tradition. Their lengthy scripts, often ten thousand lines or more, could take days or even weeks to perform. Produced by town or guild corporations in honour of their patron saints, action-packed, lavishly staged, and with crowds of performers, they were expensive to put on. So such works as the famous *Mystère de la Passion*, composed by Arnould Gréban in 1450, were staged only rarely. In the words of the poet Jean Bouchet, who saw the Passion at Poitiers in 1486, 1508 and 1534: 'I have seen these mysteries three times, enough to content me for a lifetime.' The authors or adaptors of these texts were not always of impeccable orthodoxy: questionable propositions could slip into their verses here and there. So there might be a risk of mortal sin for the spectator, wary or not. In 1548 the Parlement de Paris signed the death-warrant of the mystery plays by banning a performance of the *Vieil Testament*. In an age of doctrinal controversy, public declarations about the faith could not be left to the common people, 'to those ignorant of their ABC'. It was a matter for the educated, for the literate and the qualified whose special province it was. Henceforth, to paraphrase Antonin Artaud, doctrine was not absorbed by osmosis, but was instilled by a clergy specially trained for the task.[11]

As a centre of culture, learning, information, and collective action, the town of the fifteenth and sixteenth centuries, like the town of today, was rich in possibilities and opportunities for the meeting of minds and the interchange of ideas. The peasant, for all that he might broaden his experience in the rural parish, the local market, or even the regional fair, was never really on home ground there as he was in the village assembly or the parish festival, the gatherings which genuinely breached his isolation.

From the later fifteenth century, inns, taverns and public houses shared in the general urban prosperity fuelled by the growing circulation of labour and goods. In the centre or on the outskirts, these establishments housed travellers, fed locals and visitors, and gathered together around a bottle men of every social category. Here one could chatter or argue to one's heart's content.

How many accusations of heresy were lodged on the basis of alehouse gossip! Richard Gascon has estimated that Lyon saw a fivefold increase in the number of alehouses between 1515 and 1545. Many a similar tale might be told elsewhere, seeing that vineyards were springing up ever more thickly around such centres as Paris, Orléans, Reims, Gisors, Bordeaux and Cahors. As a forum for discussion, conviviality, and even violence, the tavern was a fixed point in the social frame of reference. The home was not so welcoming that it could accommodate the merchant and the artisan, the journeyman and the petty court functionary. They looked elsewhere for warmth, nourishment, gaming-partners, and conversation. Between 1470 and 1520, good harvests meant cheap wine for all. This widened the opportunities for socialising and for exchanging ideas, especially radical ideas on society and religion. Little wonder that the alehouse became, in the eyes of civil and ecclesiastical authorities alike, an outpost of hell and a den of all that was opposed to the Church. But for the ordinary townsfolk it represented an opportunity to let their hair down and sometimes to broaden their horizons.[12]

The outward appearance of the town hardly changed at all in the sixteenth century. Often encompassed by walls, it was a hotchpotch of houses, a web of streets and confined spaces occasionally enlightened by the green of a cathedral close. Not even the inhabitants gave a thought to airing it, planning it, or cleaning it. The squalor in which they choked while the open country spread out beyond their gates offers a curious contrast to the lively forces which clustered and flourished in this confined world.

In these four or five decades the town evolved all these individual and collective potentialities. A degree of education or wealth acquired here made it possible to surmount any social hurdles within a couple of generations. Thus the elite was constantly renewed with new blood and new ideas. The common people, despite the trammels of traditional urban and guild structures, were not isolated from these social developments any more than they were from the circulation of new words and ideas. The town was the melting-pot in which new ways of seeing and understanding both this world and the next were forged.

But the pot in which these new ideas and understandings simmered and bubbled was perhaps more of a pressure-cooker, and it was soon to reveal the growing tensions of a society in crisis. Their population-density led to intolerable poverty once the climate deteriorated in the 1520s and 1530s. The diseases contingent upon overcrowding, together with scarcity and famine, brought social tensions to light. In due course these tensions would snap, setting journeymen against masters, whole communities against tax-collectors, and poor against rich amid subsistence crises. But the town was also to set the stage for other confrontations, as those who adopted new religious teachings and practices squared up against those who remained loyal to the old ways and beliefs. The urban space thus became the forum in which the spectacle of open heresy meant for some the advent of liberation, and for others the arrival of the perhaps half-expected enemy within.

The Deterioration of Social Relations in the Towns

The people of the towns were almost as hard hit as those of the country in the course of a century which saw overpopulation, inflation and subsistence crises combine to bring about the proletarianisation of the labourer and sometimes of the artisan too. This was not a smooth but an episodic development. From the 1490s to the 1520s, inflation was gradual, which in fact encouraged both manufacturing and trade, which were responding to the opening of new markets at home and abroad. Producers enjoyed a decent standard of living whether they were entrepreneurs, artisans, or mere apprentices or journeymen. But their situation worsened from the 1530s as successive harvests failed, inducing a sharp rise in grain and bread prices and a consequent decline in real wages. Nevertheless, industrial growth continued, even if it slowed appreciably after 1570 as wages fell, under the impact of unemployment and huge price increases.

Besides these macroeconomic developments, significant changes were under way in the organisation of production. A sector characterised by the methods of commercial capitalism appeared and even flourished. The entrepreneur or merchant–manufacturer provided craftsmen, who might well be peasants, with materials and even tools for them to work at home. He then gathered in the finished product for sale in national or international markets. For peasants, this kind of cottage industry was a financial lifeline, forming, as Pierre Goubert has shown, their main occupation after agriculture itself. But for the artisans in the towns such employment represented a loss of independence as they found themselves becoming wage-labourers at the entrepreneur's beck and call. Often enough they found themselves inextricably bound to the entrepreneur by an accumulation of debts comparable to that by which so many poor peasants were ruined. Thus the silk-weavers of Lyon, once master craftsmen, fell into the hands of the entrepreneurs, who alone disposed of the capital necessary to purchase expensive raw materials like gold, silver, and silk thread used in the production of the luxury fabrics which enchanted painters.[13] Similar changes occurred in the Norman cloth trade, the production of says (a serge-like mixture of silk and wool) at Amiens, and the Breton linen industry. In the industries organised along these lines, growth continued until about 1570, when a slump was induced by the civil and religious turmoil and by the impoverishment of town and country alike. Thus in the Amiens region some 6000 workers were producing between 40 and 50 thousand says. Some 8000 silk-weavers were employed in the Tours region around 1550, while Lyon at about the same time had 5000 employees in the silk industry. Printing, an industry whose development we considered above, required a heavy investment in machines, paper, type, and blocks, as well as the highly skilled labour of well-paid typesetters and proofreaders. So book production tended to be concentrated in a few cities, such as Paris, Lyon, and Rouen, which could distribute books throughout and outside the kingdom.

Nevertheless, apart from these proto-capitalist developments, industrial production was for the most part carried on by craftsmen who, whether they belonged to a free trade (*métier libre*) or to a sworn craft guild (*métier juré*, the less widespread system), worked in a family workshop with the assistance of apprentices and journeymen. But it would be a mistake to underestimate the self-sufficiency of the villages and the countryside in such things as the spinning and weaving of clothes and household linen, ironwork, masonry, baking and tiling.

The two main economic problems of sixteenth-century France, inflation and overpopulation, induced tensions in the traditional and precapitalist systems of social relations. Of course profits could still be made, and social advancement remained possible as success in trade and industry led sooner or later to the purchase of office and of noble estates or other land, thus making possible a lifestyle insulated from the hazards of trade. High prices were good for those with something to sell, be they farmers with a surplus, entrepreneurs with capital and those all-important raw materials, or highly skilled craftsmen like jewellers, furriers, or silversmiths. But the vast majority of workers, whether they were master craftsmen or hired hands, experienced increasing difficulties from the 1530s.

Wage-labourers did not face severe problems until the later 1560s. The turning-point was around 1570. Not that their real wages increased much – the expansion of the labour supply meant that employers did not have to give much ground, although wages followed prices after a fashion. Many labourers were paid partly in kind (with food, clothing and shelter), topped up with cash. They were, of course, hit hard by the increasingly frequent subsistence crises, for the master craftsman, unable to cover the rising costs of feeding them, could always discharge them in the knowledge that they would be easy to replace later. Under normal circumstances, remuneration in kind protected journeymen and wage-labourers from inflation. Unemployment was the more serious threat. And the real deterioration in their conditions set in only after 1570, when real wages began to fall and unemployment rose.

Crisis, Unemployment and Labour Disputes

For many labourers and craftsmen the deterioration in their living standards in terms of both remuneration and security could not be offset by working longer hours. The Catholicism which pervaded society imposed the strict rhythm of its sacred calendar. Sundays and holy days were days of rest: workshops and yards were closed, with a consequent loss of wages. On average there were about five working days a week, though this does not allow for the seasonal impact on, for example, the building industry. When the printworkers went on strike at Lyon in 1539, one of their demands was that the workshops should remain open for work on holy days.[14] Without trying to tell how much this owed to religious ideals (the printworkers of this time were particularly favourable to the Reformation) and how much to financial worries, we can still observe the emphasis that was placed on the profusion of Catholic feast days.

The gradual deterioration in the living standards of labourers, and often of their employers too, accelerated sharply after 1570. The experience of Lyon, which Richard Gascon has studied in great detail, was typical of many other French industrial and commercial centres. Gascon's investigation of prices and wages between 1535 and 1600 has shown that after 1570 wages constantly lagged far below the cost of living, in a manner unprecedented except in 1563 and 1566. Hired hands and unskilled labourers were harder hit than the journeymen, who were to some extent protected by remuneration in kind. Table 2 shows, for the different categories of worker, how many years in each quarter-century saw wages fall below the poverty line, that is, where they barely sufficed, if at all, for the purchase of daily bread.

Table 2   *Wage levels of different categories of worker*

	Journeymen	Unskilled	Hired hands
1475–99	0	1	5
1500–24	0	0	12
1525–49	0	3	12
1550–74	0	4	20
1575–99	1	17	25

The consequences of this increasing impoverishment for French society were both serious and enduring. Labour disputes of an almost modern kind broke out at the start of this process in towns where there was a labour elite with a keen sense of its rights. The strikes of the journeymen printers of Lyon and Paris are typical in this regard. At Lyon, the printing capital of France, the printworkers (compositors, printers, proofreaders etc.) formed a secret society called the 'Tric'. Like a traditional confraternity, it had statutes and elected leaders, and was held together by a mutual oath and a promise to down tools if a member had cause to complain against his master. A special needs fund was also set up. The great strike broke out in 1539 for very specific reasons.[15] The journeymen were aggrieved by poor food (an important part of their real remuneration), the increasing numbers of apprentices being taken on (which prejudiced their own chances of finding work), and the enforced closure of workshops on religious feast days. It was a long strike, and when the special needs fund was exhausted, the journeymen applied for assistance from the *Grande Aumône*. Sure of their rights, they summoned their employers before the seneschal's court. The seneschal condemned the strike in principle but awarded an increase in their remuneration in cash

or kind. Appealing to the Parlement, the journeymen of the Tric
had the limited satisfaction of seeing their employers ordered to
reduce the numbers of apprentices. Fearlessly pursuing their cause
to the King's Council, the printworkers found their case brusquely
dismissed, and were then denounced as rebels and sent back to
the Seneschal of Lyon for sentencing. The strikers were duly condemned to prison, banishment, or even in some cases death.
Underlining this repressive and authoritarian response, the Edict
of Villers-Cotterêts contained the following article: 'We forbid all
masters, journeymen and servants in any trade whatsoever from
forming any combination or association large or small . . . and
from consulting with each other about the conditions of their trade.'

   This royal measure, which could not but seem a direct response
to the journeymen printers, repressed many labourers' associations which had been formed around the same time as the Tric.
Restricted to labourers, these associations were very different from
the traditional trade guilds or corporations, which gathered together
in an old-fashioned harmony (which no longer really existed) all
those engaged in a single trade, from masters to apprentices. These
secret societies have inevitably left little in the way of records,
although they are known to have existed not only in Lyon but
also in Toulouse, Paris and Poitiers (where the town council banned
an association of young joiners in 1538).

   The doctrines of the Reformation soon penetrated the tense
and anxious world of the craftsmen and their servants. Historians
of Protestantism, among others, have waxed lyrical over the
woolcarders of Meaux, the printers of Lyon, and the saddlers of
Paris, who made up the earliest congregations of religious dissidents, singing their psalms in the streets and later taking communion under both kinds. Some have therefore been led to
exaggerate the numbers of ordinary people in the Calvinist ranks,
thus failing to appreciate the preponderance of notables. Others
have suggested that the Reformation responded more directly to
the concern of the lower orders with social justice than did the
traditional Church. But in fact the importance of craftsmen and
journeymen in the French Reformation was rarely disproportionate to their place in the population as a whole. On the contrary,
they were over-represented in the ranks of the Catholic League.
That said, the desire of the journeymen to be allowed to work on
Catholic feast days has been seen, for example by Natalie Davis
in her study of Lyon, as a sign of Protestant sympathy. But she

has also shown that those workers initially attracted by the new faith were prompt to leave it as they tired of the intrusiveness of the Consistory and the restrictions of the *Discipline ecclésiastique*.[16]

The Petrification of the Guild System

On a general level, the sworn guild system (which, we should remember, covered only a few trades) underwent two major developments in the sixteenth century. The first saw sworn guilds gain ground at the expense of the free trades through the pressure that the Crown and the civic authorities exerted on the ordinary labourers. Civic authorities were especially keen to extend the sworn guild system, as sworn guilds afforded them opportunities for personal gain and social control. The Crown, for its part, was concerned with standardisation and discipline, and aimed at bringing into the sworn guild system all those trades which had hitherto remained free. Edicts were promulgated for this purpose in 1581 and 1597, but to little effect: most trades remained free until the Revolution. With respect to the guilds, as in many other areas, the Crown broke its own laws. With one hand kings insisted on incorporating all 'mechanicals' into sworn guilds, yet with the other they sold 'letters of mastery', that is, licences granting the status of master craftsman without the need to go through apprenticeship and journeymanship or to meet the other requirements which sworn guilds made of those who wished to go into business on their own account. In addition, royal privilege excluded 'workers following the Court' from the constraints of sworn guild membership: they too were allowed to proceed directly to master's status. That said, those who benefited from this privilege tended to be artists rather than artisans, the sculptors, painters, engravers, clockmakers, goldsmiths, and perfumers accommodated by Henri III and Henri IV in the grand gallery of the Louvre.

The second development which took place within the sworn guilds had serious implications for the world of manual labour in sixteenth-century France. For such guilds ceased to be flexible bodies in which promotion from journeyman to master craftsman followed smoothly in the medieval fashion. The pressure on incomes meant that journeymen found it hard to accumulate the capital required to purchase a workshop and the necessary equipment, a problem which affected free trades and sworn guilds alike.

And in the sworn guilds there was a further obstacle in the shape of the formal requirements made of aspiring master craftsmen. For their part, established master craftsmen were anxious to pass on their businesses to their sons, and thus tightened social rigidities within the guilds. Through their representatives on the governing bodies they required ever more costly and elaborate 'masterpieces' from aspiring journeymen. For the Parisian dyers of silks and linens, the preparation of a masterpiece took a journeyman ten days – during which he received no wages. Other requirements added to the difficulties. The journeyman was obliged to give a banquet for his future colleagues, to give presents to the governing body, to donate a piece of silver to the guild, and to pay entry fees. As the century wore on and wages came under increasing pressure from the rising cost of living, fewer journeymen could hope to cross the threshold. As the gulf between workers and masters widened, the former saw their promotion blocked by a lack of capital and a pervasive nepotism that condemned them to be journeymen all their lives.[17] The other side of the coin was that the guild masters became a closed elite. Dispensed from the requirements of apprenticeship and the masterpiece, and enjoying far less burdensome conditions of entry, sons easily succeeded their fathers. Similar advantages were available to artisans who married the boss's daughter – or widow. So, while the lot of most manual labourers grew increasingly hard, the elites of the rich and long-established guilds (such as the goldsmiths, furriers, or silk-weavers), at least in certain cities such as Paris, became exclusive castes wielding great influence within cities through their places on municipal tribunals and in civic administration. Claude Marcel, for example, a prominent goldsmith and Parisian officeholder, enjoyed the confidence of Catherine de Medici and was Mayor of Paris from 1570 to 1572. After the Edict of Saint-Germain in 1570, by which the regime made peace with the Huguenots, Marcel soon emerged as the leader of those who had benefited from the confiscations of Huguenot property in the previous decade but were now obliged to make restitution. He and his followers, hardline Catholics to a man, were opposed to any reconciliation. Marcel himself bears a heavy responsibility for the Massacre of Saint-Bartholomew and the subsequent looting.[18]

But outside such mercantile elites, the pauperisation of 'mechanical' labourers went on. Only relative among such artisans as retained their independence, it was severe among the other artisans as well as among journeymen, unskilled labourers and hired hands, and it inevitably entailed a loss of social standing. This can be appreciated from their declining political role in the towns. Although they still took part in general assemblies, they appeared less and less on town councils. Decision-making was being taken out of their hands by an urban elite of wealthy merchants, advocates, notaries and officeholders. In Lyon, while one or two leaders from each guild sat in the general assembly, the new trades had no places, or at least obtained places only very late, by 1568. Elsewhere, craftsmen were being explicitly excluded from municipal political office: from 1512 in Nevers, 1530 in Sens, and 1595 in Reims.

It is hardly surprising that at much the same time the ruling elites in the towns developed a lofty contempt for 'rude mechanicals', be they masters or wage-labourers. But did this reflect disdain for the new poor, or fear of the disorder which might arise from their growing numbers? In any case, the lower orders dismissed as 'riff-raff' in so many contemporary texts were brusquely excluded from the social map by the jurist Loyseau, whose *Traité des ordres* was published at Paris in 1610. The treatise offered a panorama of society as it wished to see itself, classifying the people of France by honour and birth. Arriving at last at the manual labourers, Loyseau explained that they could not aspire to any special recognition because 'We commonly call "mechanical" anything that is vile and lowly. Artisans, who are indeed "mechanical" in the strict sense, are therefore to be reckoned vile and lowly people.'

The Marginalisation of Female Labour

This social disqualification of the world of peasant and artisan labour was a particularly heavy blow for women. Apart from their role in housekeeping and bringing up children, women had also engaged in their own right in artisan labour during the Middle Ages. But the sixteenth century saw a marginalisation of women in the world of work, against a wider background also generally unfavourable to women. This background was a patriarchal system of which the king, father of his people and alone competent to judge what was good or bad for them, was the epitome. The justification of royal authority blended with the juristic tradition of Roman Law, for example in the writings of Tiraqueau and Dumoulin, to reduce women to marital subordination and juridical incapacity. Civil and religious society, whether Catholic or Protestant, was deeply interested in the subject of marriage, at once a political necessity, an economic reality, and a means of human fulfilment. Henceforth, women were to play within marriage the secondary role of spouse and mother, and were to be excluded from occupations deemed incompatible with their family obligations. In this matter as in others, economic developments weighed more heavily than ethical or political considerations. To get things in perspective, one must go back several centuries into the Middle Ages, when women were able to work in their own right in mixed or even exclusively female guilds, sometimes of great reputation. Girls as well as boys could enter apprenticeship, acquire professional training, and become masters of their craft – hence the use of words like 'apprentesses', 'journeywomen', and 'mistresses' to match their masculine counterparts. As 'mistresses of their craft', women took part in guild assemblies and exercised supervisory and other guild functions, at any rate in the exclusively female guilds.[19]

But the sixteenth century saw several developments which contributed to the marginalisation of female labour. The new silk industries at Lyon and Tours evolved a degree of division of labour which disadvantaged women. They were set to winding and twining thread while the weaving of whole cloth was restricted to men. Women were effectively excluded from the printing trade by their lack of education, which had not been a disadvantage in the almost wholly illiterate society of the Middle Ages. Even the system of cottage industry in the countryside saw the peasant or labourer work on the loom in his house or shed, while his wife devoted her spare time to spinning. But this was not her only labour, for she also played a full part in sowing, haymaking, harvesting, pruning and grape-picking. Pictorial evidence reminds us insistently of the communal nature of rural labour. But while in the twelfth and thirteenth centuries men and women worked in the fields for the same pay, differentials began to emerge in the fourteenth century, with a woman receiving only three-quarters of a man's wage, and widened in the fifteenth century, when her pay fell to barely half a man's.

The process of marginalisation was more rapid in the urban context. What with the economic crises and the excess of labour supply over available jobs, work became identified with man's work. A process akin to that which prevented labourers from ascending the guild hierarchy prevented the wives or daughters of deceased master craftsmen from following in their footsteps. The guild elite put obstacles in their way. And there was no appeal, for at the same time such women as still succeeded in becoming mistresses of their craft found themselves losing their rights to attend guild assemblies. Women were even being driven out of their traditional specialities: weaving gold thread, working precious stones and even various kinds of needlework were henceforth male preserves. Many of the free trades were also ceasing to be mixed. Only the linen, ribbon and lace trades remained open to both sexes. On the roster of Parisian guilds, the only all-women guilds remaining at the start of the seventeenth century were the flower-sellers, the linen-workers and the flax- and hemp-workers. And early in that century a dispute broke out between the men's and women's linen guilds, with the former seeking to impose male supervisors on the work of the latter. But in 1641 the women's guild won their case for female supervision of standards within their trade, except that one of the two sworn mistresses had to be unmarried. Alongside their accelerating loss of juridical identity, women in the world of work saw themselves deprived by unfavourable economic circumstances of their professional independence and of proper recognition of the value of their labour. Outside the home they were henceforth restricted to thankless, underpaid, second-rate and often piecemeal work. They would labour for several centuries under the disadvantages imposed by the triumph of a patriarchal system and by a disastrous social and economic crisis.

Tensions and Outbursts in the Towns

The harsh developments of the sixteenth century, which reduced master craftsmen to wage-labourers, deprived journeymen of prospects for advancement, and depressed real wages to the point where they barely, if at all, met the cost of living, were not accepted without protest. The peasants, as we have seen, took arms against taxation, tithes, seigneurial dues, and the excesses of soldiers. In the towns, men and women used a different vocabulary of protest when, say, new taxes penalised the main product of their region, when royal power encroached upon municipal privilege, or when the price of bread became prohibitive. Richard Gascon sees the 1520s and the 1540s as the most troubled period in the history of sixteenth-century French towns. This begs comparison with the towns of Castile, Valencia, Germany and the Netherlands, which were likewise convulsed with public disorder in the same period. The *Grande Rebeyne* which broke out at Lyon in 1529 was captured for posterity by the physician Symphorien Champier, at that time a town councillor there. The common people took over the city, forcing those in authority to take refuge in the monastery of Saint-Jean. They looted the homes of the rich, and sold off the stock of the public granary as well as the grain reserves of a rich abbey on the banks of the Saône.[20] With the local authorities thus in abeyance, it fell to the King's Lieutenant to restore order. He stiffened the resolve of the consuls and with their aid put together a force which regained control of the situation. This rising of the lower orders was severely punished, but it shook the Lyon elite to the core. Indeed, this famine-inspired riot had an impact on a national scale. The Bordeaux rising of 1548 was a rather different affair, for the common people of the city rose in sympathy with the Pitauds, the peasants who were ravaging the south-west in reaction to the increase in the *gabelle*. It was a violent and bloody business, with 20 deaths in the city on 21 August 1548, among them the king's representative, Tristan de Moneins. The violence focused on those who, in one capacity or another, profited from the *gabelle*, whether as commissioners, tax-farmers, managers, or security guards. The government was seized with panic as the cry 'Long live England' went up, and the Constable Montmorency suppressed the rising with pitiless brutality.[21] The rising at Romans in 1579–80 involved what the elite dreaded most, an alliance between the urban poor and the peasants, and it seems to have taken on a new social dimension. Reinforced by an alliance with the peasantry, the populace of Romans rose up against the greedy and profiteering urban oligarchy and gave power instead to a commune composed of 'the vilest and most seditious artisans'. This rebel government held power for a year thanks to the paralysis of royal authority in the face of its national problems, but it was overthrown when, on the night of Carnival in 1580, the civic notables massacred the ringleaders with the assistance of the King's Lieutenant Mongiron, who had just defeated the peasants. The growing tensions between rich and poor, the increasing frustrations of manual labourers excluded from civic government, the demands for a fairer distribution of wealth and taxation within the towns, all emerge clearly in the placards posted by the rebels, in their slogans, and in the rituals of inversion performed during the bloody Carnival.[22]

Do the violent outbursts which punctuated the already tumultuous life of the towns in the later sixteeenth century – for example, those against the Huguenots in 1562 and 1572, and against Henri III in 1588 – reflect underlying social conflicts, a deep-rooted malaise induced by the deterioration in the general standard of living? Perhaps hatred of the rich was intensified when the rich were, in addition, heretics, who could be blamed for bringing down the vengeance of God. The looting of houses during August 1572 in Paris and the other cities convulsed by the Massacre of Saint-Bartholomew certainly offers some support for this view. But more simply, these murderous explosions indicate a general disposition towards violence that found scope for expression in the civil and religious turmoil of the later sixteenth century. On the other hand, one might suggest that the massive adherence of the towns to Protestantism, however short-lived it may have proved, reflected a desire on the part of both the elite and the common people to restore a communal solidarity that had been smashed by economic crisis and the burdens of a centralising State. The dramatic rise of the League reflects even more faithfully this desire to return to a lost harmony. Whether Huguenot or Leaguer, the towns of the later sixteenth century were convulsed by religious passion, the traditional expression of social dislocation.

The Authorities and the New Poor

The spread of poverty on all sides, above all in the towns, where the poor were only too visible, was a cause of constant concern to the authorities. And the process was aggravated by the very civil wars which it nourished, although its roots were set down around 1530, when the population edged past the subsistence level. In Lyon some 10–15 000 people, about a fifth of the population, were living below the poverty line by 1590. The monarchy was impotent in the face of this rising tide of poverty and hunger. The ordinance of Moulins (1566) obliged every town to feed its own poor, although this aimed more at maintaining public order by stopping vagrancy and vagabondage (at least on paper) than at alleviating poverty as such. And the King's Council made the Marshals responsible for pursuing vagrants and sending them to the galleys or else to forced labour on royal fortifications. But poor relief was left entirely to local authorities. Lyon had already led the way in 1534 by establishing the *Grande Aumône*, for here, as elsewhere, traditional ecclesiastical provision could no longer keep up with increasing need. Poverty was now a social problem, indeed everybody's problem, and the town council took it in hand. After the *Grande Rebeyne* of 1529 and a severe famine in 1531, the authorities in Lyon decided to levy a rate on well-off citizens in order to establish a relief fund (which was supplemented by ecclesiastical contributions). This permitted the distribution of food and money to the needy every Sunday on the basis of an official list, which authorised the issuing to recipients of a document which was a sort of passport to charity.[23] Public begging was forbidden as no longer appropriate, and in effect so too was private almsgiving. If 'sturdy beggars' did not wish to be run out of town, they had to labour on public works like road-cleaning and ditch-digging. The wandering poor who came to the city were given a one-off dole and sent on their way. But in taking responsibility for poor relief, Lyon found itself obliged to try to tackle poverty at its root. Two orphanages were established in addition to the existing Hôtel-Dieu run by the clergy for the sick. Orphans were taught to read and write, and the brighter boys were then given free college education while the rest were put to apprenticeship. The girls were found positions as servants or silk-workers, and were provided with a dowry to help them find husbands. The Lyon system, based on humanist thought about poverty, was a model for other cities; and similar charitable institutions, run by laymen, were set up at Paris (in 1544), Dijon, Troyes and Amiens. From 1560–61, in those towns which went over to the Reformation, civic and church authorities cooperated closely in the systematic response to poverty. At Nîmes, Montauban and La Rochelle, the entire system was financed by the 'poor box', funded by the Huguenots through collections, donations and legacies. Deacons and elders reported to the Consistory on the poor in their districts; and the Consistory then decided on the appropriate amount and duration of relief. At Nîmes the municipality appointed a surgeon to tend the poor, while the church paid a schoolmaster to teach needy children. At Montauban the sick poor were tended without charge. And at Orthez poor schoolchildren were provided by the Academy with free shoes, clothes, reading and writing books and medical care.

These lay-run charitable institutions led to new attitudes towards the poor in society at large. This is not to say that the traditional view of the poor person as 'another Christ' ('alter Christus'), which allowed almsgiving to enter into the accountancy of 'good works', was instantly displaced. It survived a long time yet among those Christians who inveighed against the officials responsible for expelling, and later for confining, mendicants. But society was changing, and the elites were assimilating an ethic of earthly labour and social utility. Had not Erasmus, at the beginning of the century, railed against the ignorance, arrogance and idleness of the mendicant friars?

The Spanish humanist Juan Luis Vives drew up in 1527 his treatise *De subventione pauperum*, in which he censured indiscriminate individual almsgiving. Some years later, Calvin dismissed beggars who reached out their hands in the streets as 'petty brigands'. The explosion in the numbers of poor people on the streets of Europe's towns suddenly brought the problem home to municipal and national authorities, who suspected them of carrying disease and causing trouble. Hence arose the concern with the rational organisation of charity and thus the intervention of the laity in an area traditionally reserved to the Church. The new Lutheran and Calvinist churches, following through their doctrine of justification by faith alone and sharing contemporary ideas on the necessity of work, were in complete agreement with the thinking of the secular authorities. A distinction came to be drawn between the 'deserving poor' (widows and orphans, the unemployed, the sick and disabled) and the rest ('sturdy beggars', the idle, vagrants and masterless men), in order to discourage the kind of indiscriminate almsgiving that might only encourage vice. With regard to the deserving poor, society regarded the education of children as essential in order to break the vicious circle of poverty and ensure that everybody had the opportunity to find work suitable to their talents. But this change in coping with poverty was accompanied by the emergence of a more ambiguous attitude to the poor. The very fact that the poor were now registered and recorded meant that they were henceforth classified and categorised, set apart from the rest of the population. And so in Amiens, during the famine of 1573 which drove hordes of craftsmen and textile workers to the *Bureau des pauvres*, the town council demanded that the bishop forbid marriage among the labouring classes for men under 25 and women under 18, in order to prevent the poor multiplying too rapidly. Above all, fear of the poor gripped the hearts of the rich, for the poor, to the extent that they did not conform to the normal rules of society, represented something dangerous and disturbing. In this context we should note the vogue in sixteenth-century Europe for books which flatly or ironically denounced the wiles of beggars who presented honest folk with imitation ulcers or feigned disabilities. Such texts sought to expose the workings of their underworld organisations and to interpret their secret jargon, thus in effect turning them into a counter-culture which threatened normal society. The *Liber vagatorum*, compiled towards the end of the fifteenth century and first published in Germany in 1509, enjoyed great success and ran into many editions (one of them with a preface by Luther). It catalogued the various types of beggars, exposing the little ruses and lies with which they angled for pity. This beggar literature was a veritable genre, represented by *The Fraternitie of Vacabondes* in England, and by the picaresque novels in Spain. The genre was not quite so rich in France, but cheating beggars filled the eighth chapter of Nicolas du Fail's *Propos rustiques* (1547), were prominent in Ambroise Paré's *Livre des monstres et des prodiges* (1573), and were the subject of the *La vie généreuse* (Lyon, 1596). This last work was a spectacular success, passing through several editions until in 1627 it became part of the stock-in-trade of Nicolas Oudot, the publisher of the 'Bibliothèque bleue' of Troyes, and thus became a cottage classic.[24]

For all the distrust and the literary warnings the management of poverty in the towns and on the streets remained largely ineffective. Municipal charities and Protestant institutions which dealt with poverty as a social reality undoubtedly played an important part, but the old habits of individual almsgiving were too deep-rooted to die so soon, even if they did fade away in the seventeenth century, especially among the educated classes. At that point, the elite began to envisage the complete exclusion of the poor from society by locking them away. Lyon, unsurprisingly, was once again to the fore of this development, with the first general hospital being established there in 1614.

Peasants who fled to the towns in times of famine never returned to their land. Unemployed journeymen, unskilled labourers and hired hands tramped the roads and begged, ready for any adventure. Whatever their birth, without work they found no place when people were in abundance and social structures were petrifying.

In Spain and Portugal, where economic conditions were no better, the colonies provided a perpetual outlet for ambitions and yearnings after glory, riches, power and discovery to flower or fade. But there was no such outlet for the French, whose land remained confined to its traditional limits throughout the century. The expeditions of Jacques Cartier in Canada (1534–5), of Villegagnon in Brasil and of Jean Ribault and Goulaine de Laudonnière in Florida (1562 and 1565) proved to have no future, at least in the cases of Brasil and Florida. The latter add grist to our mill in that they were encouraged by the Admiral Coligny, a Protestant convert who thus hoped to secure a safe haven for his co-religionists, to nibble away at the vast colonial possessions of the Iberian kingdoms, and even to turn these humble expeditions into colonial and expansionist enterprises in which Huguenots and Catholics might stand shoulder to shoulder against the common enemy – Spain.

For Coligny, even if he thought in essentially baronial terms, nevertheless saw to what extent the kingdom was a powder-keg ready to explode. But the worst happened and, during 40 years of religious and civil turmoil, the French devoted their unemployed energies and their unsatisfied yearnings to mutual slaughter. The civil conflicts were fuelled by an almost inexhaustible supply of cannon-fodder. The young, or at least those whom the sources call young ('sons of family', 'children', 'young journeymen') were especially violent participants in the debates of the day. They were to be found active on both sides during the days of butchery, as at Meaux, Troyes, Sens and Toulouse in the massacres of Huguenots in 1562, in the slaughter of papists at Nîmes on Michaelmas 1567, and above all during the Massacre of Saint-Bartholomew in 1572, when chroniclers were horrifed at the sight of boys hurling unweaned infants into the purifying Seine. In her colourful style, Natalie Davis has pointed out the prominence of teenagers in these religious riots, and has even suggested that the youth clubs in the towns and villages served as starting-points for both Catholic and Protestant outbursts.[25] The explosive increase in the French population was, together with the economic crisis, responsible for these juvenile excesses. But the adults did not lag behind. After 1559 almost anybody could put together a gang, call himself a captain in the cause of one or other church, and roam the country. Like pirates or mercenaries they fought on one side or the other during the 'official' campaigns, but in the short-lived intervals of peace they holed up in a village or a mountain fastness and engaged in banditry and terrorism. Such were Captain Fabre, a peasant from Corbières, Captain Baccou, the son of a blacksmith from Rouergue, the cobbler Montendre who became a sergeant, the hosier from Nîmes who proclaimed himself sergeant-at-arms, and Ensign Caput, a carpenter who served the ex-goldsmith Pierre Céllerié. Such men found in the wars an escape, a way of life, even a career, which the petrifying society of later sixteenth-century France otherwise denied them.

Over and above these petty adventurers with resounding titles, who convinced themselves, on whichever side they stood, that they were defending true religion, real and battle-hardened leaders were available in abundance. The Treaty of Cateau-Cambrésis, agreed between France and Spain in 1559, demobilised, as we know, thousands of gentlemen and even more soldiers. Plenty of people of goodwill appreciated at the very time what implications this held for the future of France. More than 40 years of foreign war, of regular pay and frequent plunder, had accustomed gentlemen and commoners alike to the warrior's life. It was hard for them to settle back down to a civilian existence. So when the factions began to take up arms, there they were ready to serve. Fighting was their trade.

Part II

The Renaissance Monarchy

3 Passions in France

The Desire for the Next World

In the last decades of the Middle Ages, as Europe dressed its wounds, recouped its losses, rebuilt and augmented its economic capital, religious life was enriched by a new range of collective and individual experiences. This diversification derived from new movements in society, from the emergence of a broader elite, and from the demand for ever greater certainty about the next world.

The scars which the fourteenth century had inflicted upon popular religious sentiment had by no means faded away. Anxiety about death and about life after death weighed heavily on Christians in search of solace for their inward uncertainties. Yet if they certainly were 'a people troubled about salvation', they were also a people both inventive and energetic in the pursuit of remedial and preventive spiritual medicine. To some extent the Church acquiesced in this or even encouraged it by proposing remedies of her own. The invention of Purgatory, on which the system of indulgences rested, led to the kind of spiritual balance-sheet on which the merits of Christ, the Blessed Virgin, and the saints were set against the punishments due for sins. Thus the indulgence, which originated as a release from canonical penances imposed in this life, came to be applied also to punishments reckoned due in the next. The Masses which testators wanted sung after their death bear witness to their anxiety for the repose of their soul, an anxiety which was the livelihood of hordes of chaplains in cathedrals and parish churches. The Masses numbering 1565 over 18 years, paid for in advance by a wealthy widow of Grignan in 1450, must have made the career of some lucky priest.[1]

This kind of spiritual book-keeping originated in the busy world of the town, with its concern for the precise measurement of time, space, money, labour and goods. It bespeaks the new social and economic dimensions of urban existence. But it can also be seen in noble wills throughout Guyenne, Provence and the Dauphiné, which specify in minute detail staggering quantities of *post mortem* intercession.

The religiosity of this anxious but imaginative age multiplied the channels of mediation between heaven and earth. The luxuriant growth of the cult of the saints, a deep-rooted phenomenon upon which Protestants heaped scorn, offered comfort by humanising the sacred and bringing it physically close to the believer. The cult was expressed in the veneration of holy relics; and monasteries and churches therefore hoarded these precious assets, which drew in crowds of devout pilgrims. Confraternities focused their activities on a patron saint; books like the *Golden Legend* acquainted the believer with the earthly deeds of his heroes; painted or sculpted images depicted the saint in the very act of charitable or miraculous intervention. And each saint had his speciality: St Roche, St Sebastian and St Anthony gave protection against the plague; St Christopher against the hazards of travel; and St Apollinus against toothache.

But the most fervent devotions were those directed towards Christ and his Mother. The cult of the Virgin, already rampant, grew ever stronger and took on new forms. The 'stations' of Our Lady multiplied and gave rise to minor paraliturgical ceremonies like the Salve Regina (still used in France today). The persona on whom devout sensibility was thus focused embodied contradictory characteristics. The Woman of Sorrows, with her dead son's body across her knees, was a participant in his sacrifice: the Pietà brought her close to believers just as it brought home to them the Five Wounds of Christ. A more tender image was that of the contented yet composed young mother carrying the baby Jesus in her arms, often enough with her own mother, St Anne, joining this cosy maternal scene. In another role, she was protective, sheltering believers, as she had her own child, beneath her cloak. There was a more abstract dimension to her cult in the doctrines of the Annunciation and the Immaculate Conception, symbolised in art by the fifteenth-century allegory of the Unicorn. Finally, she was depicted in the full glory of her Coronation amid choirs of angels and saints in heaven. Altar-pieces, windows, hangings, statues and paintings emblazoned these images in churches and chapels across the realm as they were rebuilt after the conclusion of the Hundred Years War.

There was a similar tension between joy and pity in the images of Christ himself. His Nativity, and his childhood in the Holy Family, were constant themes of the art, poetry and drama of the time (the oldest collection of Christmas carols dates from the later fifteenth century). On the other hand, the Passion, the crisis of his life, focused Christian sentiment upon the bitterness of his sufferings. The blood of suffering and redemption flows with terrible realism on depictions of the Crucifixion or the Passion, to signify his saving death and proclaim eternal life. Artists frequently portrayed Christ, crucified or not, pouring out his blood as on a wine-press or in a fountain, symbols of the sources of life. The devotion of the Stations of the Cross was gradually taking shape, a testimony, like the *devotio moderna*, at once to the growing taste for spiritual exercises, the love of detailed enumeration, and the emergence of a more internalised and individualistic piety. It was for similar reasons that the Rosary, thanks to Alain de La Roche, took on its definitive form at this time. At a simpler level, the same considerations explain the popularity of the Five Wounds, a devotional image disseminated by printing.

While death remained at the heart of popular religious preoccupations, people's attitude towards it was changing. The destruction and physical corruption of the flesh signified the transience of human life. That artists dwelt on it so much was certainly a reflection of widespread attitudes: perhaps of grief at leaving a life one loved, or else of fear of what lay beyond. The image of the *danse macabre*, the dance of death that, without respect of persons, led all to their inevitable end, was one of the most pervasive images of the age: some 54 examples survive from the fifteenth and sixteenth centuries, while preceding ages had not produced any. The diffusion in print of the *artes moriendi* presented Christians with a view of the instant of death as decisive for all eternity: in that instant the soul was a battlefield, with ghastly demons screaming and clawing on one side, on the other the cardinal virtues and the guardian angel, the passport to a heavenly home. Nor was Hell ignored by sculptors, painters and poets. The refined tortures awaiting the reprobate were set down in grizzly detail, and offered scope alike for the melancholic and the fantastic imagination, as in the *Garden of Delights* of Hieronymus Bosch.

Philippe Ariès has talked of 'one's own death' in discussing this new attitude to death.[2] Late medieval man, the literate and wealthy man of the town, grieved over the thought of leaving the earth and the good things he loved so dearly, and over the body that had or would let him down. He viewed his departing as an individual and unique event, peculiar to himself alone. Hence arose the teaching of the *artes moriendi* that the Last Judgement was no longer delayed until the end of time, but took effect for each soul at the moment of death in the decisive choice between virtue and vice. The funeral pomp and crowds of mourners and poor folk that accompanied the corpse to burial made the same point, for burial was no longer in some common grave but in an individual tomb.

These religious developments did not proceed everywhere at the same rate. In the countryside life still followed its medieval rhythms. It was the towns that led the way in this field as in so many others. It was the towns that gave birth to the more individual relationship with the sacred. The *devotio moderna* was utterly dependent on the book. Its system of pious and sometimes mystical exercises in prayer and meditation were rooted in devotional reading. This school of piety, which originated in Flanders, produced 'the age's greatest work of consolation', the *Imitation of Christ* of Thomas a Kempis, a canon regular in the house of Mont-St-Agnes at Zwolle.[3] He created an astonishing work even if he was merely the scribe of the four-volume Bible in which the *Imitation* is found (some scholars maintain that Jean Gerson was the original author of the *Imitation*). Whoever wrote it, the *Imitation* is a sublime moral treatise which calls the reader to detachment from the things of this world and invites him to find through a constant dialogue with Christ a purer life of inward peace. This ideal is to be attained through an intimate relationship between Christ and the soul which to some extent marginalises the institutional Church. To tell the truth, when one considers that this more personalised piety flourished so shortly before the Protestant Reformation, it is tempting to see it as verging on heresy. In the *devotio moderna*, Christians discovered a spiritual way suited to their world and daily concerns. Concentrating on the personal relationship with God, they were drawn away from communal religion. Questioning the value of the intercession of the saints (in the manner of Marguerite de Navarre, Erasmus, or Rabelais), concentrating their energies upon the sacrifice of Christ, and striving to live by the Gospel, their ties to the Church were subtly weakened. In the period 1486–1540, the Church could welcome and even encourage these new tendencies, as she could always eradicate them by her condemnation. Since Catholic and Protestant reform sprang from the same soil, it is futile to try to define a boundary between a Catholic and a Lutheran or Calvinist spirituality for the period before institutional decisions were taken about what and how to believe. Take, for example, the following extracts from Marguerite de Navarre's *Dialogue en forme de vision nocturne*, probably written in 1524:

> Do not live as the pagans do,
> Who think that through meritorious works
> They have won paradise by right.
>
> If you do not wish to clothe youself with faith
> And God has you in indignation,
> Running to the saints will be going too far astray.
>
> But as for you, whatever you say or do,
> Rest assured that you are free
> If you possess the love and grace of God.[4]

Here already are justification by faith in place of justification by faith and works, Christ as the sole Redeemer, and faith as the free gift of God. Twenty years later, even a well-born lady would have gone to the stake for such statements. The *devotio moderna*, a form of interior piety refined from the flamboyant religiosity of the fifteenth and sixteenth centuries, was the preserve of the cultural elite. The humanists and the literate, such as the members of the Meaux circle, sought to simplify the relationship between man and God by raising it to a higher plane of understanding and sensibility. The Jesuits, as we shall see, also took into account the aspirations of those to whom they ministered. The Reformers radicalised these tendencies, relocating them in a system based on the absolute subjection of the elect to the God who had chosen them.

The close of the Middle Ages and the early decades of the sixteenth century were a time of bold intellectual exploration. Between the lust for life and the fear of death, between an astonishing inventiveness and a burden of tradition, between the new certainties of youthful vigour and the inherited irritations of institutional restraint, it was a time for enthusiasm, passion and hope.

Humanism and the Renaissance

To begin by attempting to define and differentiate these fluid terms, we might simplistically propose that humanism refers to the world of literature while the Renaissance refers to that of the fine arts. But this will not quite do, as we write so often of the 'literary Renaissance' or of 'Renaissance philosophy'. So perhaps it might be better to seek a common denominator in the leading figures of the movements, defining the 'Renaissance man' or 'humanist' as one who saw himself as the author of a new world. This world was contrasted with the old world of the Middle Ages, yet with no sense of a tragic break. Philosophers, grammarians, geographers, artists, poets and moralists were conscious of their part in an intense cultural efflorescence and turned their backs on the recent past calmly and without rancour. Instead they placed themselves against a historical background of their own construction, that of pagan antiquity. They saw themselves as the heirs of that ancient culture, which they experienced not as past but as a dimension of the present. The evangelism of the humanists was in a sense a realisation of the Gospel analogous to the realisation of classical themes and models in the literary Renaissance.

The humanists of the Renaissance shared one great passion which united them across all divisions of time and space: man. Man was their special concern. 'I have read in the works of the Arabs,' wrote Giovanni Pico della Mirandola at the start of his oration *On the Dignity of Man* (1486), 'that in all the world there is nothing more remarkable than man' – a sentiment on which he dilated at length in that 'manifesto of militant humanism':

> At last the Great Artisan decided that man, to whom he had been unable to give any distinctive quality, should share in all the qualities peculiar to each of the other creatures. He thus made man a creature of indeterminate nature and placed him at the centre of the cosmos, saying: 'I have given you, Adam, neither a particular place nor a peculiar form or function, so that you may according to your own judgement take whatever place, form and function you desire. . . . I have placed you at

the centre of the cosmos so that you may more easily observe what is in the world. You are neither of heaven nor of earth, neither mortal nor immortal, and so, making of yourself what you will, you may take whatever form you prefer. . .' How great is the generosity of God the Father, how high and marvellous the happiness of man! To him alone has been given the power to have whatever he pleases and be whatever he chooses.

Man at the centre of the universe, the glorious epitome of all creation, was the focal point on which all humanist concerns converged. Now the knowledge and learning of the ancients, hitherto forgotten or corrupted, returned in all their former glory. The innovators of the fifteenth and sixteenth centuries based their educational and spiritual enterprise on the reappropriation of classical antiquity. Their teaching can be summed up in the words universalism, optimism and elitism. Universalism, in that they held each person to be an embodiment of the fullness of humanity: 'I am a man, and think nothing human foreign to me' – the words of Terence, resounding triumphantly across the centuries, might stand as the motto of the humanists. Optimism, in that they held each individual capable of improvement. Education and culture were the means to this end, together with the social status they enjoyed or acquired, and the astonishing age in which they lived. Elitism, because the humanists thought that there was no salvation without education. Their position in the age-old debate between nature and nurture modified that of the Middle Ages as their ethics laid greater emphasis on individual well-being and they made culture the dominant end of human existence. Humanity would progress and improve thanks to the efforts of the intelligentsia. As Bartholomew Latomus said in his inaugural lecture at the Collège de France:

We all hope to see in a short while a general alteration – a new era of peace between nations, order in society and religious harmony: in a word, the blessings of a good life and of every kind of prosperity.

With their confidence in a future to be brought about by the cooperative efforts of countless individuals, and a passionate concern for the things of this world which revealed an essentially lay perspective, the humanists were already liberated – in part – from the religious tensions focused on the afterlife. How could it have been otherwise? For although the men of the Renaissance sought to renew the world of antiquity, they could not in fact live here below like their pagan heroes, for whom there was no Christian hope of heaven. However, many humanists aimed at a synthesis of the teachings of Plato and Christ, founding it on a belief in the immortality of the soul and a concept of virtue as a participation in the divine being. The humanists, almost mad with hope for a new world – 'the world stirs as though waking from a deep sleep', Erasmus wrote – formed a group held together not only by powerful ideas but also by shared experiences. The nation, even the nation of their birth, meant little to them, as they formed an international community. In Latin they shared a common tongue, and in the great universities – Padua, Alcalá, Paris, Oxford, Louvain and Bologna – a common home. Vast networks of correspondence linked them, and the great humanist printers and booksellers who shared their world-view gave them a platform. They even shared a pilgrimage: the return 'ad fontes' in Italy.

Yet the humanists were not an entirely homogeneous group. There were marked differences from one generation to the next, as they faced up to different social problems. The fifteenth century was an age of trail-blazing led by four adventurous Italian pioneers: Nicholas of Cusa (1401–64), Lorenzo Valla (1406–57), Marsilio Ficino (1433–99), and Giovanni Pico della Mirandola (1463–94). Valla aimed to produce more accurate versions of Aristotle, remaining loyal to the strict principles of his philosophy. Nicholas of Cusa pushed orthodoxy to its limits in his search for an all-embracing philosophical system, even proposing a union of different religions around some fundamental principles and the notion of one God worshipped in different ways. Ficino and Pico emphasised the grandeur and the freedom of a race which could choose its own place in creation. The generation which flourished in the first third of the sixteenth century was made up of writers from a wider range of nations: the Spaniard Juan Luis Vives (1492–1540), the Englishman Thomas More (1478–1535), the Dutch Erasmus (1469–1536) and, from France, Jacques Lefèvre d'Étaples (1450–1536), Guillaume Budé (1467–1540) and Marguerite de Navarre (1492–1549), to name but a few.

In the later 1530s, French humanism underwent a metamorphosis. The spirit of the age was no longer favourable to liberty, and people went to the stake for what they had said or written. Rabelais and Marot had to demonstrate their Catholic and royal credentials, Ronsard took the more lucrative side, and Calvin joined Farel in exile at Geneva. As the century wore on, intolerance tightened its grip. Some stars shone briefly here or there, men like La Boétie, Montaigne, Bodin, or Castellion, but the age of hope had passed.

For the humanists, new horizons of thought and action opened out on every side. Some of them pursued ideals of universal scholarship, and were by turns philosophers, mathematicians, doctors, grammarians or poets, without ever joining the professional ranks of any discipline. Others pursued more practical aims as royal councillors or diplomats. Thomas More, Machiavelli and Guillaume du Bellay held public office, as did Montaigne later. But it was in writing that most of them sought fulfilment. Several genres held a particular attraction for them: social comment and criticism, education, political thought, and above all classical scholarship. These vast fields of endeavour were further enlarged by that of religion as the Christian humanists sought to renew the Church. Humanist critics like Erasmus and Rabelais poked fun at pedantry and social absurdities, playing variations on such traditional themes as the silliness of the Sorbonne, the mediocrity of monks, and the vanity of courtiers. Humanists and preachers alike gave monks, priests, cardinals and popes such a drubbing that they proved easy pickings for Luther and Calvin.

The importance of education was a commonplace, as the formation of youth offered the only guarantee of survival for the intellectual innovations which the humanists were bringing about. And so, vast numbers of humanists tilled this field, producing textbooks and handbooks to help young aspirants join the ranks of the humanist literati. Erasmus himself composed in 1530 a textbook, *De ciuilitate morum puerilium*, which was a bestseller for nearly two centuries. Vives concerned himself with the education first of girls and then of women, before, in 1531, compiling his *De Disciplinis* for the benefit of all mankind. And when Rabelais outlined Pantagruel's intellectual formation, he was in effect codifying a humanist programme of moral, physical, and intellectual education. In his Abbey of Thélème as elsewhere, the basic principles of humanist pedagogy were clearly set down: the natural environment in which people would grow like plants in the sun was a cultured environment which would furnish knowledge to stock minds and undertake the moral upbringing of 'free and well-born' youth.

Schools sprang up all over Italy and then Europe to put these educational theories into practice. A new kind of college was developed by the Brethren of the Common Life in their establishments at Zwolle and Deventer in the Netherlands. Each age-group was put in a separate class, and each class followed a curriculum of a suitable level. The lowest classes (the eighth, seventh and sixth) studied 'grammar' – basic spoken and written Latin. The fifth form proceeded to logic, and the fourth and third to rhetoric. Finally, in the top two classes, the pupils moved on to moral and natural philosophy. This graded curriculum inculcated a profound knowledge of Latin language and literature, as its lessons were all taken from classical texts. The pupils studied with the aid of textbooks, and the foremost humanists were not ashamed to produce these aids: Erasmus himself edited authors such as Seneca, Cicero, Pliny the Elder, Livy and Terence for their benefit, besides translating from the Greek of Aristotle, Ptolemy, Demosthenes, Xenophon and Euripides. He compiled for them his *Adages*, a storehouse of classical sayings, proverbs and axioms on which generations of students depended. The distinguished Flemish humanist Josse Bade produced a Latin grammar, as the Italian Valla had done before him. And Robert Estienne compiled a celebrated dictionary, the *Thesaurus latinus*.

French colleges soon began to remodel themselves along the lines laid out by the Brethren of the Common Life or the Strasbourg Gymnasium. The Parisian Collège de Montaigu (where Ignatius Loyola and John Calvin were for a while fellow-students) adopted the new system, as did the college at Nîmes, the Collège de Guyenne in Bordeaux, and the Collège de la Trinité at Lyon. From 1561, starting at Billom in the Auvergne, the Jesuits covered France with a network of similar establishments, while the Huguenots followed suit, albeit on a more modest scale. For the system not only imparted solid classical scholarship but was also well adapted to shaping the consciences of youth. Although in some respects these colleges marked the passing of humanist aspirations to universality, they certainly did fulfil the humanist aim of forming a moral and intellectual elite. Pupils were taught public speaking – the Jesuits even taught them to act in plays – and the art of discussion as well as dancing and the handling of weapons. Henceforth there was a strict demarcation between the elementary schools of reading, writing and arithmetic, and the more modern establishments to which few children from humble background could aspire. From this time on, pupils worked individually with their own textbooks and exercise-books, carrying out written and oral exercises. The old arts faculties, where instruction was given in lectures which the students had to repeat, had had their day. The colleges replaced them with an entirely new curriculum and an entirely new method of delivering it. The cultural revolution of the humanists was located at this level too.

The huge efforts made by those generations of scholars to revive classical thought in its entirety indeed deserve to be called a cultural revolution. The humanists strove to purify the Latin tongue from its medieval corruptions, and to this end poured forth dictionaries, grammars, treatises and stylish, accurate translations. Greek, little known and never systematically taught in the Middle Ages, posed few problems for the restorers of classical literature. They compiled dictionaries and grammars for the convenience of students, and, more importantly, translated Greek texts into Latin or even the vernacular. It is to the men of the Renaissance that we owe our knowledge of the writings and thought of the Greeks and Romans, and more – for oriental languages, especially Hebrew, did not escape their appetite for learning.

Their 'heroic passion for learning' – rivalled only by their passion for teaching – extended into all sorts of areas. Medicine (above all anatomy), geography, the natural sciences and botany were studied not only through such classical authorities as Hippocrates, Galen, Ptolemy, Pliny and Aristotle but also through original research. Oronce Fine (1494–1555) of Briançon, a professor in the Collège de France, devised a system of cartographic projection in the form of a heart, which was essentially that used by Abraham Ortelius in his *Theatrum orbis terrarum* (Antwerp: Plantin, 1570), a collection of 53 maps drawn by French and Italian mapmakers and annotated by Ortelius himself. Although little progress was made in the natural sciences, there was nevertheless a genuine concern to attain a realistic representation of nature, evident in the superb engravings and illustrations of sixteenth-century books. In the field of astronomy, Renaissance scholars largely marked time, content for the most part simply to edit or translate such ancient authors as Ptolemy. The Copernican revolution made little immediate impact on the scholarly world: the *De revolutionibus orbium coelestium* (Nuremberg, 1543) aroused no furore, although

Copernicus hedged his bets with regard to official teaching by presenting heliocentrism as nothing more than a hypothesis. Later in the century his ideas were to strike chords in a few men of science, notably Giordano Bruno and, of course, Galileo, through whom the scandal was ultimately to break in 1617. But the scholars of the Renaissance remained in an Aristotelian universe with an immoveable earth at its centre. Even the intelligent and cultured Melanchthon was content to follow Luther's blunt rejection of Copernicanism.

Why did this vast movement of free thought not bear fruits of peace, toleration, and respect for others? Instead, the 1540s saw intellectuals forced to align themselves, not only in France but throughout Europe, with groups which they themselves were actually helping to regiment. And, it must be said, the humanists themselves contributed to the concentration of political power. Not only Machiavelli, but, within France itself, Budé, Bodin and Montaigne presented an authoritarian monarchy as the only guarantee of civil order and tranquillity. Artists too, as we shall see, put their talents at the service of the cult of monarchy. And the literate public of scholars, philosophers, translators and writers, and officials, henceforth tended to toe the party line, which certainly did no harm to their careers. Christian humanism, as we shall see shortly, retreated from doctrinal and liturgical radicalism as the churches hardened their lines against each other and squeezed out alternatives.

It was almost as though the sudden prospect of unbounded human freedom was so dazzling that men had to hurriedly don dark glasses. Or again, that faced with this diverse, prolific, and vibrant intellectual movement (one which some humanists even spiced with mystical, magical, and esoteric learning), people took fright and retreated into closed mental systems behind clearly drawn lines.

The Checkmate of Christian Humanism

Humanism, imbued though it was with pagan antiquity, nevertheless had a strongly Christian component. The same care which Renaissance scholars brought to classical texts was devoted to the recovery of the pristine text of the scriptures. There was a trend towards translating from the original Greek or Hebrew, whether into Latin (as with Erasmus's *Novum Instrumentum* of 1516) or the vernacular. Lefèvre d'Étaples published a new Latin edition of St Paul in 1512, followed by French translations of the New Testament in 1524 and the Old Testament in 1530. Religion, for the Christian humanists, meant believing in and living up to divine teaching. Theology was simply the study of Revelation. 'To explain doctrine' was the sole aim of Lefèvre and his followers. By comparing the various versions they identified the errors, omissions and interpolations in the official text of the Bible, Jerome's Vulgate. A revision was imperative, and they set about the task with alacrity. Lefèvre published five versions of the Psalms in parallel text, and Erasmus consulted manuscripts in places as various as Louvain, Basle, Paris and London in order to establish an accurate text of the New Testament. He commissioned further researches in England and Spain, and in Rome he himself gathered and collated texts. At last, after five years of detailed preparation, the work was published, with a dedication to Pope Leo X which emphasised that it had been undertaken with a view to 'the renewal of the faith of Christ.'

Religion, Erasmus wrote, 'is not so much a theory as a way of life', 'the pure worship of God and the observance of his commandments..' 'Where there is love,' wrote Lefèvre, 'there is true religion.' The Christian humanists lamented that theology was no longer the clear and plain exposition of divine teaching. For century after century the scholastics had buried it with syllogistic analysis under a heap of pointless and insoluble questions about 'substance and accidents', the nature of angels, and man's state of grace before the Fall. The humanists held them in contempt, dismissing them as 'theologisers', dunces and 'sophists.' In the *Praise of Folly* (1509), Erasmus scorned them as 'noxious weeds'. Rabelais, whose religious sensibility drew him towards evangelism – that is, Christian humanism – detested the doctors of the Sorbonne with their baggage of sterile scholasticism.

The whole ecclesiastical establishment was called into question. If the *Praise of Folly* portrayed the folly of kings and courtiers, it also dwelt on that of priests, monks, bishops, cardinals and popes in loving detail. 'Today all is topsy-turvy', Erasmus wrote of the bishops, 'for these shepherds feed none but themselves.' Nobody has fewer cares than the popes, he wrote, 'because they reckon they have done enough for Christ if they turn out in their ceremonial and almost theatrical regalia, glorying in titles like

Beatitude, Reverence, and Holiness, and playing the bishop only in benedictions and excommunications'.

The Christian humanists yearned and strove for renewal within the Church. In their view the hierarchy of popes, bishops and priests had but one basic task: the propagation of the faith. To preach and keep the Gospel ought to be, as in former times, their chief concern. Ecclesiastical power should be paternal rather than magisterial, for the truth of scripture should be proposed rather than imposed. The kingdom of God was not to be brought about by condemnations, excommunications and interdicts, but by teaching.[5] The Church, whose hierarchical organisation was not called into question by these evangelists, had strayed from her original calling, and ought to return to it, reforming hearts and souls through moral discipline and restoring Christ by means of the Gospels.

Keen, like many Renaissance scholars, to put their ideals into practice, a group of Christian humanists based at Meaux endeavoured to reform their diocese along evangelical lines. The effort was led, from 1521, by the bishop, Guillaume Briçonnet, who gathered there a brilliant team including Lefèvre d'Étaples, Gérard Roussel, François Vatable, Michel d'Arande, and Guillaume Farel. In 1523 they were joined by Pierre Caroli and several others. All were thoroughly versed in sacred and secular scholarship: all knew Greek, and some even Hebrew. Most of them were priests, although Farel remained a layman despite regularly preaching sermons. The renewal drive was founded on the reform of religious houses within the diocese, by which monks were compelled to live according to their monastic rules. Priests were obliged by episcopal order to reside in their parishes close to their flocks. Briçonnet held a visitation of his diocese to get to know its people and their needs. He held annual synods at Meaux, bringing together the parish priests with the friars and licensed preachers. At these synods (especially those of 1519 and 1520), he emphasised the moral responsibility of priests for their flocks, including the sinners and those who omitted their Sunday obligations. He emphasised also their vocation to proclaim the Gospel, above all through regular Sunday sermons. Preaching lay at the heart of the Meaux renewal programme. For the Christian humanists, the function of the Church was to bring the Bible to the people; and the spoken word was for them the best means of doing so. The diocese was therefore divided into first 26 and later 32 sections, and a licensed preacher was assigned to each in order to bring the nourishment of God's word to even the most remote corner of the diocese.[6]

For all the good intentions, the Meaux circle was unable to pursue its programme of inner renewal for long. Undermined by doctrinal disagreements between its members, it received crippling blows from higher Church authorities. Briçonnet and his team had friends in high places: Marguerite de Navarre and, through her, François I. And in 1517 Leo X himself had been so favourable to the bishop's projects as to issue indulgences with which to reward the devotion of his flock. But the Sorbonne was on the alert. Anxious at the spread of Lutheranism, the Sorbonne had, on 15 April 1521, condemned 104 propositions extracted from the Reformer's works, and on 14 August they censured one of Meaux's licensed preachers, Martial Masurier. His crime (trivial enough in twentieth-century eyes) was to have argued in a public sermon that the single figure venerated throughout the western Church as Mary Magdalene was in fact a conflation of three distinct individuals: Mary of Bethany, the sister of Martha and Lazarus; Mary of Magdala, from whom Jesus had expelled the seven devils; and the sinner who had anointed the feet of Jesus in the house of the pharisee. Lefèvre himself had published polemics to the same effect in 1519, sparking off a fierce controversy. The Sorbonne's condemnations raised some weighty questions. Was freedom of interpretation permissible? And even if it was, was it also permissible to set such matters before a laity unaware of the inconsistencies, however minor, of the Scriptures? The authorities answered no in both cases, and the Sorbonne called on the Parlement de Paris to take steps against Lefèvre as a heretic, ruling out in advance any other interpretation of the condemned thesis. Thanks to the intervention of the king, Lefèvre was left undisturbed for the moment. But the watchdogs of orthodoxy were still keeping their eyes on Briçonnet's colleagues. Pierre Caroli was censured by the Sorbonne in 1524 for asking his parishioners to bring vernacular copies of Paul's Epistles to his sermons as well as for enouncing various other suspect propositions. Two other preachers were dealt with for similar offences. And 1525 was a harsh year for the Bishop of Meaux. With the king a prisoner of the Emperor, and amid widespread economic hardship, a veritable frenzy of orthodoxy gripped the government, the Sorbonne, and the Parlement. The Meaux circle, in the person of Briçonnet himself, provided a convenient scapegoat. His trial before Parlement began in June 1525, and lasted until November 1526. He was held responsible for the words of his preachers, and was also charged with publishing the Bible in French for his flock and with replacing Franciscan friars with outsiders as his licensed preachers. Above all, he was blamed for the appearance of open Lutheranism in his diocese. On 3 October 1525 Parlement issued a warrant for the arrest of Pierre Caroli, Gérard Roussel, Jacques Lefèvre, Martial Masurier, Michel d'Arande and others. The Meaux circle dispersed, some fleeing to Strasbourg and others finding refuge with the Queen of Navarre, while others less fortunate were condemned to the stake or to life imprisonment. Thus, in 1526, was a *via media* turned into a dead end.

But the collapse of the Meaux circle also owed a lot to the diverse religious preferences of its members. These intellectuals, intoxicated by the new horizons opening before their eyes, were not all headed in the same direction. Here lay the greatest danger for the Church. For the spirit of the Renaissance had left them at once more sure of themselves and, paradoxically, more vulnerable in that self-confidence. The period 1520–25 was no longer one of complete freedom: the impact of Luther had sent out shockwaves which led to a hardening of attitudes on all sides. As the limits of free expression contracted, the Meaux circle found itself in a difficult position. Lefèvre was attacked in 1521 for exegetical theories originally propounded in 1516. Meanwhile, Luther's teachings contained enough of the leaven of the humanists to tempt some of them into a wholehearted commitment to what was now defined as heresy. Farel and Caroli abandoned the Roman Church, the former to end up some years later as the leader of the Reformed community of Geneva, and the latter, having become a pastor among the Swiss, to abjure his errors at Lyon in 1537 and then to return to them again. Briçonnet had shown his personal horror of heresy as early as 1523, by revoking the licences of preachers suspected of Lutheranism. But, to judge by the proceedings in the Parlement de Paris, his diocese nevertheless seemed remarkably susceptible to the new doctrines from Germany. But had the preachers of Meaux really rendered the soil particularly favourable? Or was the diocese unusual only in falling under the close inspection of the Parlement in its role as watchdog of orthodoxy?

The end of the Meaux experiment, marked by the dispersal of

its personnel and by the orthodox position taken up by its bishop (who continued to exercise a vigorous ministry in his diocese), itself marked the deathknell for hopes of bringing about in France a modern Church, closer to the teaching of the Gospels, dedicated to bringing the Scriptures to the people, ready to root out internal abuses, and taking up the remedies proposed by the humanists. There was, it is true, an institutional reform of the Roman Church in France, well able to provide answers to the religious questions of the faithful. But the Church which emerged from this process was an armed camp, not the community of pious folk envisaged by Lefèvre and Erasmus.

The Catholic Reform

Catholic reform was not a creature of the sixteenth or even of the fifteenth century. One must go back to the fourteenth century to find the wellsprings of this broad reformist current. The thought of Jean Gerson (1363–1429) contained most of the reforming themes and schemes to be taken up by theologians and scholars of succeeding generations. This is hardly the place to embark on a thorough investigation of the ideals and achievements of this great chancellor of the University of Paris. But a brief sketch is possible and illuminating.[7]

Gerson was above all a mystic, his desire for God, nourished by Scripture, drawing him to the heights of divine knowledge. And he wished to make this privilege available to all, illiterates as well as scholars, women as well as men: 'Some will profess their astonishment that, in handling such an elevated matter as the contemplative life I should write in French rather than Latin, and for women rather than men – but not unsophisticated people, and especially not my dear sisters.' In his concern to raise the moral standards of the people he penned numerous little tracts like the *ABC des gens simple*, the *Science de bien mourir*, or the *Manière de conduire les enfants à Jésus-Christ*, as well as brief treatises for the political education of the dauphin Charles VIII. At the same time, he laboured for an inner renewal of the Church, reckoning that this could be achieved only through the education of the young, not yet tainted with the vices of their elders, and more intellectually malleable. This is one of the threads that runs through the whole history of Catholic reform.

The reform movement gathered force in the later fifteenth century thanks to the economic boom. As agriculture revived, the Church once more enjoyed the ample revenues of old. Linked as they were to tithes or ground-rents, they were the foundation on which a host of chapels, churches and religious houses were raised. This was the heyday of late Gothic flamboyance, with its intricate curves and tracery, and its prolific decoration which covered without obscuring the basic architectural features of vaulting arches and high windows. Huge numbers of churches were built or rebuilt in this distinctive style, which prevailed into the sixteenth century and beyond. Many of them were in Paris, testifying to the wealth, power, and religious zeal of the clergy.[8] In Normandy and Brittany, Champagne and Picardy, Tours and Lyon, new buildings reared skywards, their construction often extending until the later sixteenth century. In the late fifteenth and early sixteenth centuries, the clergy followed the lead of the monarchy in enlightened artistic patronage. The Cardinal of Amboise built the Château de Gaillon in the Seine valley, showing all the Italianate taste of a Renaissance prelate and politician. Bishops and abbots commissioned altarpieces and tryptychs from painters, and from sculptors they sought tombs, tabernacles, statues and rood-screens. It is unfortunately not possible to catalogue these works any more than their patrons or artists, but they bear eloquent witness to the power of a Church in glorious resurgence.

Reform had obsessed the clerical elite for generations. The general councils of Constance and Basle early in the fifteenth century set the agenda, but even by the end of Louis XI's reign there was little to show for it.[9] The movement gathered fresh momentum under Charles VIII when the ideal of 'reformatio' resurfaced in the Estates General of 1484. The third estate joined the clergy in adding to their list of grievances the abuses connected with the reservation and commendatory tenure of benefices, and sought to ensure regular provincial church councils. The uncompromisingly Gallican spirit of the Estates was entirely welcome to Charles, who responded by summoning an assembly of prelates at Sens to set about the reform of the Church. In July 1485 this assembly set forth a comprehensive programme which gave priority to restoring monastic discipline, revitalising the clergy, and curtailing the fiscal abuses encouraged by the papacy. Their decrees were full of pious intentions which, in the event, were frustrated by the opposition of Pope Innocent VIII, jealous of

'his honour and his rights'. But a movement had been inaugurated which attracted the support of an elite of humanists, churchmen and lawyers. In Paris a reformist circle gathered around the
person of Jean Standonck, master of the Collège de Montaigu,
who combined ascetic Flemish mysticism with a fervent charity
towards the poor and a Renaissance passion for scholarship. Like
Gerson before him, he employed all the means at his disposal to
spread his ideas – preaching, writing and lecturing. Appointed
Bishop of Sens in 1497 despite the opposition of the all-powerful
Guillaume Briçonnet (uncle of the Bishop of Meaux of the same
name), he was given a wider field in which to disseminate the
devotio moderna he represented. And in other parts of the kingdom similar circles gathered around figures who, though less
eminent than Standonck, nevertheless strove for the reform of
the Church in their capacity as bishops, abbots, or royal officials.
Nobody imagined that reform could proceed without the support of the king. On the contrary, Charles VIII's old Chancellor,
Rochefort, having carried through various political reforms, reckoned that ecclesiastical reform was also the king's responsibility.
Himself won over to reformism, Charles convoked an assembly
of prelates at Tours in 1493. This gathering candidly catalogued
prevalent abuses: immorality, simony, the abuse of indulgences,
venality in worship, 'girovague' monks, and the scandal of ignorant and depraved preachers and vicious priests. These problems
could be remedied by determined action, but the machinery was
lacking or was itself crippled by abuses. Synods and councils were
not held. Free episcopal elections had been displaced by papal
or royal nomination. And the canons stipulating the intellectual
and moral qualifications of beneficed clergy were widely disre-
garded. The remedy proposed by the Tours assembly was a return to the ancient laws, customs and discipline of the primitive
Church. Reform meant not changing the institution, but recovering its pristine state. The Tours programme looked to national
and provincial councils or to the general chapters of monastic
orders for the substance of reform, to the papacy for sanction,
and to the monarchy for implementation.

Reform did indeed get under way in the localities, even though
royal support was interrupted by the exigencies of the Italian Wars.
In such dioceses as Langres, Nantes, Troyes, Paris, Chartres and
Rodez, bishops held synods, promulgated disciplinary legislation,
held visitations, and supervised the provision of the apparatus

for worship and the repair or construction of churches. Increasing contact with parish priests and vicars allowed them to spread the reformist message in the parishes. Their efforts were supported by the people, whose intense religious concerns we have already observed. The wave of confraternities founded in the closing decades of the fifteenth century, dedicated to the Rosary, the Passion, or Corpus Christi, testifies to the devotional cooperation between clergy and laity.

Was it because of episcopal vigilance (though this remained occasional, as many bishops continued to accumulate non-resident benefices), a widespread religious zeal, or simply an economic recovery that the priesthood became at this time a socially respectable and financially rewarding career?[10] Whatever the explanation, the fact is clear enough: there was an enormous increase in clerical ordination. In the case of the diocese of Sées (Normandy), Imbart de la Tour found 840 ordinations in 1470, 902 in 1490, and 1196 in 1514. Similar increases have been observed in the cases of Avignon, Rodez, Rouen and Toulouse. For some reformers, there were simply too many priests. But in practical terms, prescinding from the explanations just offered, the abundant supply of priests was a response to a huge demand fuelled by the proliferation of endowed masses for departed souls and by the obligation of absentee clergy to hire curates to perform their duties.

The bishops, who were taking the lead in the reform effort well before the Council of Trent, were not unconcerned with the moral and intellectual qualifications of their clergy. Some, like François d'Estaing and Georges d'Armagnac at Rodez, even took part personally in examining candidates for ordination. And the level of the beneficed clergy was certainly rising. They were often graduates, even bachelors or doctors in divinity or canon law. But the measurable intellectual improvement among the beneficed cannot conceal the deficiencies of the curates and stipendiaries who were so often hired to perform the duties of their absentee masters. In the diocese of Beauvais in 1551, only one beneficed priest in five resided with his flock. The rest were either studying at university, serving as canons in the cathedral, or residing in another parish. And the complaints about the inadequacies of the clergy uttered by bishops, intellectuals or layfolk all tended to concentrate on this hired clerical proletariat.

In seeking to reform their dioceses, the bishops placed particular importance on the discipline of religious houses. For it was here that the crying abuses were to be found – or at least the most cried about, for the intellectual climate was generally hostile to monasticism. Jean Simon, Bishop of Paris, tried to enforce the observance of the monastic rules in the convents of his diocese, and at times had to gain entry by force in order to introduce reliable nuns as his agents. He was especially concerned to restore discipline in the abbey of Saint-Victor. The Cluniac order set about reforming itself. Their abbots, who were among the few still to be elected by the monastic community in accordance with the Rule of St Benedict, implemented a series of measures passed by the order's general chapter between 1481 and 1486. Silence, fasting, and common life were restored, commendatory tenure of office was banned, structural repairs were set in hand, and the whole programme was supervised by means of regular visitations. The monarchy supported their efforts. Even better, under Louis XI the pope extended to the Cardinal d'Amboise legatine powers which made him the supreme ecclesiastical authority in the land. Before long, other monastic congregations were following the Cluniac lead in internal reform: Cîteaux from 1493, and Prémontré from 1498.

But it was among the friars that reform made the most dramatic progress. It began spontaneously, but Cardinal of Amboise sought to see it through, starting in Paris. The Franciscans resisted his intervention, and the Dominicans engaged in a trial of strength which ended in their expulsion and replacement by a reformed congregation. The inflexible will of the Cardinal did not shrink from the use of force. But he did not always have to resort to it. In Provence and the Amiens region things went much more calmly. The provincial Parlements supported his draconian reforms, which often involved the expulsion of recalcitrants from their priories. Convents too felt the rigour of the Cardinal's reforms. The *Grand Conseil* and the Parlement de Paris willingly cooperated, providing him with the warrants and authority 'to correct and punish monks and nuns, . . . to reduce them to a stricter observance of their rules, to coerce the recalcitrant, . . . and to suspend or even dismiss heads of houses'. A few years of the Cardinal's 'ecclesiastical dictatorship' sufficed to see the majority of convents visited, morally reformed, and structurally restored.

François I sought to complete the task thus begun. Having secured papal authorisation for bishops to reform convents, he gave a new impetus to reform through the legate Cardinal Charles de Luxembourg, whose two-year mission of visitation and investigation brought reform to the monasteries of Normandy and Meaux in 1517, and those of Toulouse in 1518.

Needless to say, this immense effort did not achieve reform at a stroke. Monks and friars did not become saints overnight, and many monasteries continued to wallow in worldliness. The contemplative orders experienced a decline in vocations, although the friars, who continued to enjoy the patronage of princes and urban elites, managed to maintain their recruitment levels. Among the secular clergy, absenteeism remained a serious problem in spite of every effort. It was evident at every level, from bishops to curates: few dioceses were graced like those of Meaux and Rodez by the regular personal presence of their bishop, and many parishes lacked even their Sunday mass. 'Where are you,' stormed the preacher Jean Vitrier, 'you priests of Beauce and Brie who happily hold your benefices and hire mercenaries to tend your sheep?'

Such was the religious fervour of the age that, among both clergy and laity, new movements sprang up in reponse to the unquenchable spiritual thirst. Europe saw the foundation of new religious orders, better suited to the times. The Capuchin Friars, an offshoot of the Observant Franciscans founded in Italy in 1526, inspired a wider renewal of the mendicant spirit. Absolutely poor, barefoot and unshaven, they attracted flocks of recruits, and soon expanded beyond the Alps. Genuinely close to the people, they were to be found in plague-stricken towns when even the civic leaders had fled. Later they were to spearhead missionary activity in Protestant areas. The origin of the Jesuits can be traced to France itself, where Ignatius Loyola and his band of friends took their famous vow at Montmartre on 15 August 1534. The date was not without significance. Not only was the day the Feast of the Assumption of the Blessed Virgin Mary, one of the major feasts of the calendar, but the year was one of religious turmoil. The previous November, the rector of the university, Nicolas Cop, had preached an evangelical sermon drawing a sharp distinction between the Law which condemned and the Gospel which saved. And in October 1534 the notorious Placards were posted at Amboise and elsewhere. This was the year that John Calvin, having prudently fled Paris, drafted the first pages of his epoch-making *Institutes of the Christian Religion.* This convergence of events was more than coincidence. It signalled a turning-point in religious history, with the two camps, Catholic and Protestant, squaring up to each other. The Jesuits, who were formally constituted by Pope Paul III in 1540, were to be the Catholic Church's most effective fighting force in the approaching spiritual combat. It was not without significance that Loyola and his first companions had spent the crucial years from 1530 to 1537 in Paris. For there they could see at first hand the radicalisation of critical attitudes towards Roman Catholicism. Alarmed no doubt by the growing revolt, they sought at first not so much confrontation as conservation. Their spirituality focused on the person of Christ and sought to steep itself in the evangelical sources of Christianity. Theirs was a Christian humanism which readily took up and exploited the culture of pagan antiquity. Loyola's followers were schooled to write and speak with elegance in the idiom of Cicero. For Loyola himself realised that in order to consolidate the position of Catholicism among contemporary elites, it was imperative to speak their language, the language of humanism. Nevertheless, Loyola and his companions were unshakeable in their loyalty to the traditions of the Church, to her hierarchy, and to the supremacy of the Pope. Their vow at Montmartre specifically enjoined obedience to the Pope, and they put themselves entirely at the disposal of the successors of St Peter for the good of the universal Church.

The Jesuits devoted themselves above all to the apostolate of the word. They sought, by preaching, teaching, and reaching out, to win the souls of the new world, and to win back the souls of the old. Their personal education was provided partly in the ancient universities and increasingly in their own houses of study, the 'seedbeds and hothouses of the Society'. Gradually, these institutions evolved. The single establishment for both lay students and clerical novices split into the seminary for the latter and the college for the former.[11] The early 1550s saw the emergence of the typical Jesuit college, a model to be replicated across Europe for decades and centuries to come. Its curricular structure owed much to the schools of the Brethren of the Common Life. Pupils were recruited from among the social elites, and from a tender age were imbued with humanist scholarship and Catholic doctrine. They were encouraged to see themselves as soldiers of the Church, whether they pursued ecclesiastical or secular careers. The Jesuits thus applied in their age Gerson's principle of seeking reform through the rising generation. But their educational agenda was also a part of their struggle against Protestantism. For the new doctrines had penetrated the educational system, thanks to civic schoolmasters whose religious allegiances might gradually cross the spectrum from Renaissance spirituality through evangelism to Lutheranism or Calvinism. By providing their own schools, the Jesuits hoped to cut off this insidious influence at its root.

The distribution of Jesuit colleges across France tended to reflect the impact of Protestantism, as civic authorities or anxious bishops called them in to safeguard the religious integrity of a threatened area. In Paris itself the Jesuits were given the site of the Hôtel de Clermont by Guillaume Duprat (son of the famous Chancellor) in 1550, for use as a seminary. At Billom (1556) and Mauriac (1560) they established colleges for lay students as the Auvergne experienced Reforming impulses. They set up another in Tournon in 1561 to oppose the rapid spread of Calvinism along the Rhône valley, and further colleges followed for similar reasons at Toulouse in 1562, and at Lyon and Paris in 1564. For the rest of the century, the foundations of Protestant and Jesuit colleges followed thick and fast across the kingdom.

But despite support from clergy and laity alike, the Society of Jesus did not flourish unopposed. Strongly Gallican institutions like the Sorbonne and the Parlement resisted them at every turn, even though the monarchy itself gave the Jesuits official recognition in 1561 at the Colloquy of Poissy.

The Protestant Reformation

The Protestant Reformation, a logical consequence of social change and of the new and more interiorised forms of piety which accompanied that change, is powerful evidence of the spiritual thirst of the age. It was not so much a sudden break as the culmination of lengthy developments. It took over the evangelical agenda of trust in Christ and passionate concern for scripture. It took onto a new plane the lay involvement in ecclesiastical affairs which had previously been expressed in confraternities and third orders, and in the administration of hospitals and of colleges, means by which the laity had encroached on the sacred monopoly of the clergy. And it reformulated and thus gave effect to the age-old criticisms and complaints about the worldliness, and especially the avarice, of the Catholic hierarchy. For the modern observer, the Protestant Reformation falls into place naturally amid the spiritual searchings of both higher and lower social groups, integrating changes in society and *mentalités* much as, at the same time, were pioneers of the Catholic Reformation like the Jesuits. In itself, the Protestant Reformation was no revolution. But it became one when politics interfered, as new Christians and their new churches had to fight to make space for themselves in society. The Catholic authorities were swift to classify its adherents as heretics.

At what moment in the first twenty years of the sixteenth century would it be fair to describe any particular man or woman as a 'Protestant', that is, as having broken decisively with the Catholic Church? Would not Olivier Maillard and such other preachers of the late fifteenth century have found themselves, a few years later, reckoned heretics for their denunciations of clerical misbehaviour and avarice? Lefèvre d'Étaples was still free to publish in 1516. Yet by 1521 he was being harassed because of his writings. Where then was the point of no-return beyond which the Christian humanist or evangelical became a heretic? As ever, it was the opinions of others which effected the transformation. And it was the schockwave which Luther's ideas sent throughout Europe which hardened the Catholic establishment against the supporters of a 'reformatio' which had been for a century or more the dream of the Catholic elites.

It was from the theological researches and spiritual struggles of Martin Luther that the two fundamental themes of the Protestant Reformation emerged. Reading Paul's Epistles, the German friar was struck by an explosive phrase in the first chapter of Romans: 'For I am not ashamed of the gospel of Christ: for it is the power of God unto salvation to every one that believeth; to the Jew first, and also to the Greek. For therein is the justice of God revealed from faith to faith: as it is written, "The just man liveth by faith".' Commenting on this revelation, Luther wrote: 'God be praised when I understood and knew that the "justice of God" was nothing other than the "justice with which God justifies us by the grace offered in Jesus Christ".' Salvation was offered to those men to whom God, by the sacrifice of Christ the Redeemer, gave the gift of faith. When, a little later, the Augustinian friar found in the Gospel of John the following text: 'You are all a universal priesthood', he was able to formulate the second basic principle of the Reformation. And thus, between 1510 and 1515, the theological foundations of Protestantism were laid in the frantic researches of a man who was passionately concerned for the afterlife but was becoming gradually convinced that the Church had distorted for gain the evangelical message of eternal hope. This man was unable to remain silent. He proclaimed to Christendom that he had reestablished the Gospel: he spoke, he wrote, he preached.

Henceforth, every human being could discover from reading the Gospels how to follow Christ. Henceforth, faith alone sufficed to win the eternal life promised to all by Christ's redeeming sacrifice upon the Cross. This teaching swept away a host of doctrines and practices elaborated over centuries by a Church anxious not only to rule but to reassure the faithful. Our Lady and the saints, hitherto mediators between God and man, were taken down from the pedestals to which the spiritual yearnings of the faithful had raised them. Purgatory, Masses for the dead, and indulgences were redundant at a stroke, along with the prayers offered by monks and nuns for the living and the dead. Moreover, the text with which Luther burst onto the world, the *95 Theses*, if it contained only in germ the theology of justification by faith alone, was harsh in its condemnation of the power by which the Church claimed to remit through indulgences temporal penalties by which the sinner made satisfaction according to the sacrament of penance. On the other hand, Luther emphasised that penance was not an occasional matter, administered by a priest or a prelate, but was rather the very stuff of the Christian life, an unceasing renewal of the inner self according to the teaching of Christ. As well as attacking the excessive and mercenary exploitation of indulgences, Luther stressed their irrelevance: 'Each and every truly repentant Christian has plenary remission from both guilt and penalty even without letters of indulgence' (thesis 36), because 'every true Christian, living or dead, shares fully in all the goods of Christ and the Church' (thesis 37). The Church had made a serious mistake in failing to preach the Word of God to the people, since the Church only existed in so far as the Word was preached. Thus did Luther call the entire Catholic establishment into question. But the seeds of doubt had been sown before his time by a succession of theologians. The Luther affair inflamed tempers. The case against him began at Rome in 1518. He refused to submit, and was excommunicated in January 1521, to be outlawed by the Empire later that year. But his thought resounded louder and louder throughout Germany, igniting social and political disorder. This was schism: after a difficult labour, a new Christian religion had come to birth.

Whole sections of the Empire and northern Europe detached themselves from papal obedience and adopted Lutheranism. The transition was often accomplished on the instructions of the political authorities. The wealthy cities of Strasbourg, Zurich, Berne, Basle, Neufchâtel, Mulhouse, Hamburg and Nuremberg rejected both the temporal and the spiritual supremacy of Rome, and equipped themselves with a new church order, a new catechism, and a new liturgy. So too did the Scandinavian kingdoms between 1526 and 1537. In England, Henry VIII broke with Rome in 1534. Schismatic religious movements disturbed Bohemia and the Netherlands. In Charles V's Flanders, Lutheranism won a following at Tournai and Antwerp. Increasingly draconian edicts were issued against heretics there from 1520, and in 1523 Antwerp witnessed the execution of the first two martyrs of the Protestant Reformation.

France, like the rest of Europe, was receptive to any new ideas on religious or ecclesiastical matters. In 1519 the German printer Johann Froben sent 600 copies of Luther's works to France, and from 1520 the kingdom provided a ready market for the *Appeal to the German Nobility*, the *Babylonian Captivity of the Church*, and later for the *Little Catechism* and the *Commentary on the Ten Commandments*. The French were fascinated and astonished by this sudden storm. In 1519 Lefèvre, Farel, and Roussel made their way variously to Strasbourg and Basle to see the impact of Lutheranism on the ground. The printer–publishers, ensconced in the border-towns of the Empire, worked round the clock to pour out not only Luther's own works but also books and pamphlets espousing the most diverse and extreme religious positions. All sorts of variations emerged in the profusion of speculation, and many found a temporary place on the political map; some only for a time, like the Anabaptists at Münster; and some permanently, like the Zwinglians at Zurich or the Calvinists at Geneva.

Those Frenchmen who read Lutheran books, and were attracted by the Reformed havens on the borders of the kingdom, no longer dreamed of an internal renewal of the Church. They were ready to take the plunge into more radical reform. But if there were many issues on which they were all agreed, there were also myriad differences. The dissidents were at one in rejecting the cult of Our Lady and the saints, together with pilgrimages and the veneration of relics. They agreed likewise in rejecting clerical celibacy, monastic vows, the doctrine of Purgatory, several of the Catholic sacraments, papal primacy, and the concept of a sacerdotal priesthood. And they shared many positive beliefs: justification by faith alone, the freedom of individuals to read the Bible for themselves, and the concept of the pastor as enlightened guide. But differences arose on such matters as, among others, the real presence of Christ in the sacramental species of bread and wine, the sacrament of baptism, and the appointment of pastors. The complexity of the reforming movement in France is such that the historian can find no single thread to give it essential unity. Sometimes only the brutal fact of persecution, which was swiftly unleashed, seems to lend the movement any unity at all.

Though it is obvious that Lutheran ideas entered the kingdom along the great trading routes from the north and the east, it is less clear how those ideas were diffused through the rest of France. Often, as at Poitiers, Bordeaux, Agen, and Lyon, it was through the influence of some powerful personality or fashionable group. In later years, Calvinist teachings were to spread in much the same manner, following trade routes like the Rhône valley and the Garonne. The intellectuals – clerics or teachers – usually led the way, dragging in their wake their congregations, students, or friends: personal connections played a major role in the rapid early progress of the new ideas. The less educated sections of the population became involved in their turn. The early transition from words to deeds testifies to this. Converts who lacked the ability to write or teach could bear witness to their beliefs through acts of ritual sacrilege. Statues of the Virgin were desecrated at Paris and Meaux as early as 1523 in actions which anticipated the great wave of iconoclasm which swept the country in 1561–2.

The famous Placards of October 1534 constituted just such an act, one of unparalleled audacity. The religious campaigners trespassed on royal ground in fixing their posters within the very château of Amboise itself. And the content of the Placards, which were also posted in Paris, Tours, Orléans and Blois, was still more provocative, surpassing all previous polemics, even Luther's, in its venom. Drawn up in French and printed in black letter, anonymous and with no imprint, the Placards were in fact the work of a group of French refugees at Neuchâtel led by Guillaume Farel and Antoine Marcourt (the text itself is generally ascribed to the latter). These gifted enthusiasts sought to bear witness to their convictions, and they made this clear in the striking title which headed their poster:

True articles concerning the gross, repellent and intolerable abuses contained in the Mass devised by the papacy in direct contravention of the Supper of Jesus Christ.

The first article gives the flavour of the rest in its violent rhythm and its vocabulary of anger and frustration:

I call on heaven and earth to bear witness to the truth against this pompous and vainglorious papal Mass, by means of which (if God sends no remedy soon) the world will have been utterly lost, ruined, overwhelmed, and devastated. For in it Our Lord is outrageously blasphemed and the people are defrauded and bamboozled to an insupportable degree. But in order to make the facts of the matter clear and distinct, let us take them one by one.

There then follow four pithy articles which condemn the sacrifice of the Mass and the doctrine of the real presence in the consecrated elements, and define the Supper as a memorial rather than a sacrifice. Marcourt gives vent throughout the tract to his virulent anticatholicism, accusing the Catholic clergy of having betrayed the Gospel in order to fleece the poor by saying Masses for money, and of occupying their benefices like 'ravening wolves'. Devoid of any scriptural, patristic or historical learning, they impose on the people with their 'bells and blethering', anaesthetising, or rather mesmerising, them. And while other believers set out their beliefs and practices for debate and discussion, the Catholic establishment resorts to 'killing, burning, destroying, and murdering' (a plain allusion to the earliest Protestant martyrs).

The Placards had an enormous political impact because, over and above their traditional anticlerical invective, they aimed a mortal blow at a central Catholic doctrine, attacking the sacrifice of the Mass, which lay at the heart of the Catholic religion and' was the foundation for the system of clerical privilege. And with that came crashing down the Roman hierarchy on which, especially since 1516, the monarchy depended so heavily. The Placards, as we shall see, led the hitherto temporising and characteristically politique François I to take harsh and repressive measures. At another level, they showed the diversity of Reformist views now current in France, for their doctrinal position on the eucharist was redolent of Zwingli (for whom the communion was a mere commemoration of the Last Supper), and militated just as strongly against Lutheran consubstantiation as against Catholic transubstantiation.

However, around 1536 there appeared a doctrinal system capable of binding the various threads of French reformism into a single strand. For in that year the clergy and literate laity were exposed to the *Institutes of the Christian Religion* of John Calvin. This French scholar, who had taken refuge in Basle after the sermon of Nicholas Cop and the posting of the Placards, composed his slim volume in a form which has caused some to describe it as 'a kind of sophisticated catechism'. Pocket-sized and easy to use, it comprised six chapters which recapitulated the main themes of Luther's teaching. Oddly enough, Calvin dedicated the book to François I, although there was method in his madness: driven by his sense of justice and clarity, he hoped that his treatise would show the king and his people that the Reformers were neither traitors nor revolutionaries, but simply true Christians faithful to the Gospel. For the king's representatives in Germany, anxious to conciliate his allies in the Lutheran Schmalkaldic League, put it about that the harsh measures taken in response to the Placards were directed solely against fanatics and rebels. Calvin sought partly to clear the exiles, the imprisoned, and those condemned to death, of these charges; and partly to show that their sad fates were not wasted because they bore witness to the religion of the Gospel.

> But our doctrine must stand, high and unconquerable above all the glory and power of the world. For it is not our doctrine, but that of the living God and of his Christ, whom the Father has appointed king, to bear rule from sea to sea and from the rivers to the ends of the earth; to rule in such a way that, striking the earth with the rod of his mouth, he will break it like a potter's vessel with his power and glory, in accordance with what the prophets have said about the greatness of his reign, that he will lay low kingdoms as strong as iron and bronze and as dazzling as gold and silver.

It was not long before other works penned by the reformer, now based in Geneva, were circulating in France. For the most part simple and practical treatises, they were written for the people of both Geneva and France. They included his *Treatise on the Sup-*

per (1540), the *Ecclesiastical Ordinances* (1541), which sketched the plan for the Church on earth, a *Confession of Faith*, and two catechisms, one for adults and the other for children, both employing the question-and-answer format which was to be so often imitated thereafter (even by the Catholics). The *Forms of Prayer and Church Chants* (1542) set out the reformed liturgy drafted by Calvin when he was at Strasbourg with Bucer. Alongside these works we must set the numerous new editions of the *Institutes* – 25, to be precise – between 1536 and 1560, the date of the final version. The work gradually assumed the proportions of a *Summa*, the distillation of a lifetime's spiritual experience and of his pastoral endeavours in Geneva and France. It has two principal objectives: to set out doctrine clearly; and to produce Christians capable of living and applying that doctrine in daily life. Calvin was not simply a lawyer and a theologian but a man of action. He created not so much an original body of doctrine – for Luther had already outlined the main principles of reformed theology – as a new ecclesiastical structure and a new ethical system which played a major part in shaping modern man.

Booksellers and pedlars carried the works of Calvin and his Genevan colleagues throughout the realm. Their readership was on the increase, as can be seen from the decision of the Sorbonne in 1542 to burn a copy of the *Institutes*. Clandestine groups gathered, often at night, in private suburban houses. They prayed in French, sang psalms, and took communion in both kinds in the 'Genevan fashion'. But nothing is more conspicuous than secrecy, and such gatherings soon became suspect, giving rise to those rumours of outlandish goings-on which arise from the fear of the unknown: sexual excess and perversion, satanism, etc. The usual kind of denunciations opened the way for official interventions, arrests and imprisonments. An examination of the proceedings against heretics in the Parlements of Paris, Toulouse, Bordeaux and Aix between 1540 and 1560 already yields an accurate outline of the social composition of subsequent French Protestantism: scholars and teachers, monks and nuns, nobles, merchants and craftsmen were all among those condemned for 'false doctrine'. The geography of French Calvinism also emerges, albeit less clearly: Meaux, Lyon, Paris, Tours and Orléans; and also Bordeaux, Toulouse, Agen, Gaillac, Albi, Nîmes and Montpellier. Towards the end of François's reign, and even more during that of Henri II, who intimated to his parliamentary officials his intention of extirpating heresy from his domains, the registers of the Parlements abound in decrees against those whom they still persist in calling 'Lutherans'.

These conventicles, over which local notables exercised an understandable influence, looked towards Geneva as the spiritual capital from which they could expect ministers, religious advice and leadership. They engaged in tireless correspondence with Calvin and the Genevan Company of Pastors and, from the 1550s, increasingly clamoured for ministers versed in pure doctrine and approved by the Genevan authorities. For its part, Geneva already boasted a number of Frenchmen forced to flee the realm in the aftermath of the Placards or after the clampdown by the tribunals, above all the *Chambre Ardente*, in 1547. This influx strengthened the position of Calvin in Geneva, while internal opposition was weakening, and thus freed him to devote more time to matters beyond the city walls.

Before the opening in 1559 of the famous Genevan Academy, the seminary of Calvinist France and Europe, Calvin and his colleagues personally instructed those Frenchmen who wished to take up a pastoral calling, commenting on every word of every book of the Bible for months on end. The Protestant theology faculty of Lausanne also trained many future pastors, giving them, in addition to theology, courses in practical exegesis according to Calvin's method, as well as in Hebrew and Greek. Thus, beyond the frontiers of the kingdom, there was an entire system for producing ministers, who would gradually take in hand the infant churches and bring them up, administering the sacraments and, with the elders (who were often the leaders of the original secret gatherings), forming the Consistory. These ministers began to arrive from Geneva in 1555 and 1556, reaching first the congregations at Poitiers and Bourges. Between 1557 and 1559 they founded about 60 churches, and the process speeded up still more between 1559 and 1562.

The traditional civil and ecclesiastical authorities felt threatened by the establishment of a new church, and by the manifest enthusiasm for the new beliefs of many men and women, among them individuals close to the centres of power, close even to the king and his government. In April 1559 Henri II even abandoned foreign war – temporarily, he thought – in order to restore religious unity to his realm. He thought he both could and should break the resistance of the Calvinists. But, as we shall see, it was already too late. The Reformers undoubtedly numbered at least 2 million already, at all levels of society, even at the Court itself. They formed a coherent geographical bloc extending across several provinces, from Normandy through Touraine, Angoumois, and Saintonge, to Gascony, Languedoc and the Dauphiné. Even Paris, the royal capital, was home to a powerful group of Protestants, witnessed by the notorious affairs of the rue Saint-Jacques in 1557 and the Pré-aux-Clercs in 1558. The Calvinists felt so secure there that, in May 1559, they made it the venue for the first national synod of the French Reformed churches.

4   Charles VIII and Louis XII

Charles VIII and his Entourage

It was not easy being the son of Louis XI. When Charles VIII succeeded his father, on 30 August 1483, he was aged only 13, and could not show his mettle until much later. His elder sister Anne de France, wife of Pierre de Beaujeu-Bourbon, ruled as Regent in his name not only according to the law but also by the express wish of their dying father.

The Beaujeu regime, like most regencies in French history, had to face an endless series of baronial rebellions – despite its attempt to forge a consensus by convening the Estates General at Tours in early 1484. The representatives who gathered there painted a grim picture of a France bled dry by Louis's exactions. But this was almost a cliché for such assemblies. The two great feudal houses, Orléans and Bourbon, fenced civilly enough in this arena. The Bourbons, in the person of Pierre de Beaujeu, were in control. But the house of Orléans, led by François, Count of Dunois, and his nephew Louis, showed their discontent by raising a revolt in the south-west in 1487; and Duke François II of Brittany was quick to throw his weight behind them in the 'Guerre Folle' ('mad war'). The Battle of Saint-Aubin-du-Cormier (28 July 1488) saw the defeat of the insurgents and the consequent triumph of the king and the Beaujeu faction, and was followed a few days later by the death of the Duke of Brittany.

In 1491, Charles himself took shrewd advantage of the prevailing peace to send home the 'little queen' Margaret (daughter of the Emperor Maximilian), to whom he had been betrothed at his father's instigation in 1482. A month later, he married instead Anne of Brittany, heiress to that troublesome duchy. This act in a sense marked the beginning of his personal rule. His overbearing sister was marginalised by the newly assertive 22-year-old sovereign. Though far from handsome, to judge by the surviving portraits and the comments of contemporaries, he was of a cheerful disposition, and was known to posterity as 'Charles the Charming'. It is said that Louis XI forbade him to learn Latin: instead he mastered Italian. A voracious reader, he pored eagerly over the tales of chivalry given him by his father, and even written for him, such as *Les trois cages*. He also enjoyed the *Grandes chroniques de France*, *Le rosier des suerres*, and the *Livre de la vie du roy Saint Louis*. The heroic and holy feats of Charlemagne's champions made a deep impression on him – the disgust of his Court, he named his son Charles-Orland (after Charles and Roland) – as did the crusading exploits of Saint Louis. Does his literary taste provide the key to his obsession with Italy? Did he see the reconquest of Naples as the first step of a great crusade?

Except for his sister (whose political acumen escaped nobody), the young king's entourage was composed primarily of his childhood friends. Étienne de Vesc, for example, who had been like a big brother or perhaps even a father to him, was thought by some commentators (including Commynes) to be the inspiration behind the Neapolitan campaigns. This impoverished nobleman from the Dauphiné was trusted by Louis XI, and watched over Charles's adolescence, and never lost his affection. Another political heavyweight on the King's Council was Guillaume Briçonnet, the *général des finances* for Languedoc, Dauphiné, Provence and Roussillon who, after losing his wife, took holy orders to become, in 1493, Bishop of Saint-Malo. Briçonnet is an astonishing figure. Born of merchant stock, he was related to the financial dynasty of Morelet de Museau which, in the next generation, was to provide so many notaries and secretaries for the royal service. His proximity to the king brought him a constant stream of offices and benefices. With what looks to modern eyes like exquisite cynicism, he joined the see of Nîmes to that of Toulon, and then added the archdiocese of Reims to the abbey of Saint-Germain-des-Prés (held in commendam). He subsequently resigned Reims in favour of his brother Robert, and exchanged Saint-Germain with his son (Bishop of Lodève) for the abbeys of Grammont and Saint-Nicolas-d'Angers. He divested himself of Reims and Grammont in order to take up the archdiocese of Narbonne. And after the occupation of Italy, he handed Nîmes to his son Michel in order to take the see of Palestrina. These ecclesiastical manoeuvres testify to the naked greed of a man who was at once the Crown's leading servant and the generous patron of his family and clientele. Even the young king stood in awe of him, and from 1493 he was head of the Council:

> The *général*. . . was perhaps the weightiest and liveliest figure at the Court. He had the king's ear and his full confidence, and even M. de Beaucaire [Étienne de Vesc] rarely took a decision without consulting him. These two were unrivalled in their influence over the king.[1]

It was said that Briçonnet egged Charles on to the invasion of Italy because Ludovico Sforza had held out to him the prospect of a cardinal's hat and then, when the Borgia Pope Alexander VI countered with more enticing offers, held back the pay of the troops who were waiting at Lyon for orders to advance, so that the whole expedition was delayed. The cardinal – as he indeed became in 1495 – was thus in both character and avarice much like François I's Chancellor, Antoine Duprat. But while Duprat, of a later generation, at least had some conception of the centralised unitary State, Briçonnet's singleminded pursuit of personal and family profit was unredeemed by any such ideal.

The Marshal Pierre de Rohan, sire de Gié, a faithful though crafty servant, was also among Charles's closest advisers. A friend of Louis XI, he served on the Council, and took a full share of the spoils when Saint-Pol and Nemours were brought down on a charge of conspiracy. He was opposed to the Italian adventure, but accompanied Charles on it nevertheless.

In fact, Charles's closest advisers were mostly Louis XI's men, like Louis Malet, sire de Graville, or Philippe de Commynes, who left a detailed record of the Italian expedition. There was marked continuity in personnel between the two regimes, as there was again between those of Charles and of his successor, Louis XII. The only 'new man' was Briçonnet, a commoner whose shrewd handling of benefices raised him to the highest ranks of the nobility, and who heralded the growing importance of financiers in affairs of State.

In 1498 – if Commynes is to be believed – Charles decided upon a wholehearted reform of his personal life, of his church, and of his government. François de Paule, his spiritual director, had long urged him to put his life in order and set about the reform of the Church. The king busied himself with plans for better justice and fairer taxes, but nevertheless prepared for a return to Italy. Although concerned at his lack of a male heir, he was not seriously worried. Anne, who had just given birth to a still-born girl, was only 22, and he himself was but 27. He scarcely gave a thought to death, which was to come through a brain haemorrhage as a result of a banal accident – banging his head on a low doorway leading to a gallery in the château d'Amboise.

Louis XII and his Entourage

Louis II of Orléans, cousin to the dead king, first prince of the blood royal, and son-in-law of Louis XI (whose second daughter, Jeanne, he had married), succeeded Charles VIII without any trouble. At 36, the new king had the usual background of those long close to the throne. He had been deeply implicated in the noble con-spiracies whose leaders Louis XI had executed. He had claimed the leading places on the *Conseil étroit* for himself and his sup-porters on the accession of Charles VIII, but, rebuffed by the Beaujeu faction, had thrown in his lot with the Duke of Brittany. Defeated, he narrowly escaped execution, but spent at least two years in prison. The man who was crowned as Louis XII was no longer the handsome youth with an eye for the girls. Undersized, ugly and of weak health, he was frequently ill, a fact which caught the attention of foreign observers: 'the slightest accident is dis-turbing for one of such a sickly disposition,' wrote one ambassa-dor, 'and his feeble constitution is going constantly downhill'. Nevertheless, he survived his frequent crises remarkably well, reach-ing what was for the time the respectable age of 52.[2]

Bernard Quilliet, Louis's recent biographer, sees tenacity verg-ing on pigheadedness as the key to his character. He notes that on two issues Louis never wavered for an instant: his determina-tion to rid himself of his ugly wife Jeanne; and his desire to con-solidate and pursue his claim to Milan. The first matter did not take long, for in August 1498 the divorce proceedings were com-mitted to a tribunal of French churchmen assisted by two papal representatives. Four grounds were alleged for the annulment: two concerned marriage within forbidden degrees of kinship;

another was that the marriage had been contracted under duress; and the last, that it had never been consummated. The pope lent all possible assistance because he needed the king's political support, and the marriage which Louis XI had forced upon him was duly dissolved. Even before the case was closed, Louis was arranging his second marriage with Anne of Brittany. The contract of January 1499 echoed the earlier one between Anne and Charles VIII. The province retained its autonomy, and Anne was responsible for governing it and protecting its liberties. Brittany was to devolve upon the couple's second son, or, if they only had one, to his second son. And if Anne predeceased Louis, the king was to assume the government of the duchy, reserving the rights of the legitimate heir. The second issue, that of Milan, was at the top of Louis's agenda from July 1498, but more of that later.

Some of Charles VIII's councillors were retained under the new regime, including the Marshal de Gié, La Trémoille, and even Étienne de Vesc (albeit with diminished powers, and entrusted chiefly with diplomatic missions). But there were two important new arrivals: the Cardinal Georges d'Amboise and Florimond Robertet. A fight to the death swiftly broke out between Gié and Amboise. As later in similar situations under François I, the ramifications of the conflict extended into the Court and even the royal family. There was no love lost between Queen Anne and Pierre de Rohan, and so he betook himself to the Valois house of Angoulême, notably to Louise of Savoy and her son François. While Georges d'Amboise was at Rome in 1503, angling for the papacy, Gié made himself supreme in French domestic politics. In the absence of a male heir to the royal couple, the Marshal promoted a marriage between François of Angoulême and the king's daughter Claude (born 1499), and was negotiating on the matter with Louise of Savoy as early as 1501. He was quite as aware as Anne that, if Louis predeceased her, Brittany would revert to her and her heirs, and could become hostile territory if Claude then married a foreign prince.

Anne of Brittany favoured an alternative matrimonial alliance for the young princess. The prospective husband was Charles of Luxembourg, the heir presumptive to one of the world's greatest empires, the man who was to become Charles V. This plan enjoyed the support of both Georges d'Amboise and the king himself, even though the latter had signed a solemn declaration at Lyon on 30 April 1501 to the effect that Claude would not be betrothed to anyone other than François Valois of Angoulême. Louis's biographer, Bernard Quilliet, maintains that the king's indecisive policy was not Machiavellian dissimulation or even a waiting-game with respect to Charles's grandfathers, the Emperor Maximilian and Ferdinand of Aragon, but simply the manifestation of a character wholly devoid of breadth of view or firmness of purpose. For Quilliet, the king was essentially feudal in outlook, more concerned for the future of his daughter than for the integrity of the realm, which he was prepared to sacrifice for her sake – her dowry would have included Milan, Naples, Burgundy, Brittany, and the county of Blois. In fact, however, his policy does look like a waiting-game: betrothals were easy to break off, and the prospective bride was as yet only two years old.

In 1504 the Marshal de Gié tasted the bitter cup of royal displeasure. The Cardinal of Amboise, Queen Anne, and even Louise of Savoy, whose interests he had tried to serve, all sought to get him out of the way. Gié's position was the more threatening in that he was planning to remodel the French army as a more national force, which would incidentally increase his own importance in it. An unnamed double agent was induced to state that Gié, taking advantage of a moment when the king's life was threatened by illness, had made military plans to prevent the queen and her daughter returning to Brittany and to secure the person of the young Duke of Angoulême. Louis XII instituted criminal proceedings against the Marshal in June 1504, first before a special commission, and then before the *Grand Conseil* itself, reinforced for the purpose with four Councillors from the Parlement de Paris. The latter tribunal could not agree on the charge of high treason which Anne had hoped would stick, and provisionally released the Marshal. Louis, refusing to accept the tribunal's verdict, transferred the case to the Parlement of Toulouse. But there too, despite all the pressure, the charge of treason could not be made to stick. However, the Toulouse Parlement removed him from various posts, including that of governor to François of Angoulême, and temporarily suspended him from his duties as Marshal.

This lenient sentence, which infuriated Queen Anne, shows that the full weight of royal authority did not yet bear down upon the courts of justice as it was to do under François I. And it may also show that Louis did not entirely share his wife's bitter hatred of Gié. For even as the case was proceeding, he was swinging back towards the matrimonial alliance preferred by the Marshal. But the sentence was not so lenient as to leave Pierre de Rohan de Gié any vestige of his former influence at Court, where the Cardinal of Amboise now reigned supreme.

This prelate, who had long since hitched his wagon to Louis's star, was rewarded when the prince ascended the throne. But nobody has ever been able to pin down the precise role he played. He remained the king's closest friend and confidant until his death in 1510. But if his political influence is difficult to make out, it is easy to trace the rewards it brought him. In 1498 he received his cardinal's hat, and later, having hoped in vain for the papacy itself, he at least became legate of France. His family also benefited from his ecclesiastical eminence. A contemporary noted that he had 'showered ecclesiastical and other preferments upon his relatives'. His nephew Claude Chaumont d'Amboise performed rather indifferently as a general during Louis's Italian expedition. But his brothers Louis, Pierre and Jacques gained advancement in the Church, becoming respectively bishops of Albi, Poitiers, and Clermont.

The Cardinal's favour introduced into the ranks of the political elite one commoner of outstanding promise: Florimond Robertet, of an obscure family from Montbrison. True, the previous reign had also seen the spectacular rise of a commoner in the person of Briçonnet, but his ecclesiastical preferments had brought him the prestige of nobility. Robertet had first taken service with Pierre de Bourbon-Beaujeu, and had then gone on to become notary and secretary to Charles VIII. Possessed of an extraordinary capacity for work, and fluent in four foreign languages (Italian, German, Spanish and English – a rare accomplishment in those days), he stood out from his colleagues.[3] Louis XII kept him on as a financial secretary and made him *Trésorier de France* for Normandy. Florimond's marriage to the daughter of Michel Gaillard secured him a place in the powerful coterie of royal financiers. As the Gaillard family were financial agents for the house of Angoulême, Robertet thus had a foot in both camps. He became Louis's private secretary, 'the closest man to his master', and, with the cardinal himself, was one of the most influential figures in the kingdom – a position he retained even under François I. His avarice was legendary, and foreign diplomats were well aware that with 'some token' they could get a lot out of him. Competent, experienced in domestic and foreign affairs, and content to identify private interest with the public good, Florimond Robertet has his place in that long line of rapacious Crown servants who were setting about the construction of the monarchical State.

The Italian Wars

In France, every schoolboy knows that the Italian Wars began under Charles VIII and Louis XII. But let us briefly recapitulate their origin. Back in 1264, Charles of Anjou and Maine, Count of Provence and brother to Saint Louis, was invested by the papacy with the kingdom of Naples. The pope hoped by this coup to dislodge the Hohenstaufen dynasty which had ruled the area since the Norman conquest in the previous century. The Angevin dynasty was established in Naples, but its brief history was a series of bloody tragedies of which the Sicilian Vespers (1282) is the best known. The Angevins were replaced by a branch of the royal house of Aragon. But in 1481 the last representative of the Angevin line, Charles of Maine, made his will in favour of Louis XI, bequeathing him not only his French possessions (Anjou and Provence) but also his claim to Naples.

Charles VIII

Under the influence of Étienne de Vesc, Charles VIII had the charters enshrining his claim to Naples brought from Aix-en-Provence for validation before the Parlement de Paris. Perhaps his dream was to secure southern Italy as a springboard for a crusade. But his real motives remain a matter for debate among modern authorities. Over and above the sheer lust for conquest and the more or less explicit policy of exporting to Italy the youthful nobility that might otherwise have reduced France to a battlefield, there must have been other, more solid reasons for the expedition which Charles prepared with such care.

There was more. The French were literally invited into the peninsula by the Italians themselves. Pope Innocent VIII, an enemy of the house of Aragon, favoured Charles VIII's ambitions on Naples. Florence was divided between the Medici faction, which supported the Aragonese claims, and a pro-French faction. This was the time when, under the spell of Savonarola, the Florentines rushed to hear preachers calling upon 'the chosen one of the

Lord' (i.e. the Valois king) to come and cleanse the peninsula, the cradle of all vice, which had seen the elevation to the papal throne of Alexander VI, the Borgia pope. From Naples itself a group of rebel barons had called upon French aid in 1485, while at the French Court itself there was a group of exiled Italian nobles who peddled hopes of an easy victory. And from Milan, Ludovico Sforza sought French assistance to confirm his hold over the duchy, which he ruled in the place of his own nephew.

The expedition was prepared with the utmost care. The prospect of a subsequent crusade assuaged international concern, even that of the Emperor Maximilian, who in 1492 had occupied Arras and Franche-Comté in revenge for the French rejection of his daughter. The Treaty of Senlis (June 1493) compensated him for the humiliation of his daughter and recognised his right to the Charolais, Artois, Franche-Comté, Auxerre, Mâcon and Barsur-Seine. Charles 'dropped the quarry to chase a shadow', as Henri Lemonnier observed.[4] Spanish acquiescence was secured by the Treaty of Barcelona (January 1493), which returned Louis XI's recent conquests of Roussillon and the Cerdagne, added 200 000 golden *écus* for good measure, and recognised Castilian suzerainty over French Navarre. Henry VII of England, who had sent troops to Calais in October 1492 in response to an appeal from a Breton conspiracy, was bought off with more than 700 000 golden *écus*.

Europe, then, was content to let France leap into the cauldron of Italian politics. Charles concluded a defensive treaty with Ludovico Sforza in 1492, while the other Italian states hesitated between France, Spain, Austria, and even the Ottoman Empire. On 25 January 1494 Ferdinand of Naples died. But the new Pope Alexander VI, in one of those sudden shifts characteristic of Roman and indeed Italian politics, recognised Alfonso as his successor. Ferdinand's death was the signal for preparations in France to commence in earnest. The Neapolitan ambassadors were dismissed from the French Court, and in June the Florentine bankers – allies of the Medici – were expelled from Lyon. As the ambassador Robert Gaguin explained to the English: 'The king is taking up arms to repossess his kingdom of Naples in order to use it as a base for a crusade in Greece. He will use his troops to overthrow the Ottoman Empire.'[5]

The expedition was financed by a sharp increase of the *taille* for 1494 (worth 800 000 *livres* alone), together with a levy on *taille* free towns, a deduction from the salaries of councillors in the sovereign courts, and a 10 per cent tax on ecclesiastical benefices. These measures raised some 2 million *livres*, which put into the field an army of 30 000 men equipped with arquebuses (hand-guns, hitherto little used in war) and canons. The troops assembled at Grenoble and crossed the Alps by the Mont Genèvre to descend into Italy by way of Asti. An advance-guard under the Duke of Orléans (later Louis XII) beat off the Neapolitans near Genoa before defeating them in September at Rapallo. From Pavia by way of Florence and Rome to Naples, the French invasion was more of a triumphal march. Each entry into a city was marked with spectacular pageantry. The Italians offered only token resistance. Naples was entered in February 1495. A popular revolt under the slogan of 'France, France' had swept the city clean of the Aragonese dynasty, and the French wildly set about sharing out the spoils. Commynes, who accompanied the expedition, recorded with some exaggeration: 'Not a single Neapolitan was left in power, as all offices and posts were given to Frenchmen.' Ivan Cloulas tells us that this judgement is too harsh. Even if the council and Court of the new King of Naples were filled with Frenchmen (who also took many major fiefs), the personnel of the lower administration was left largely undisturbed. In the city itself, Charles endeavoured to broaden the civic government, which had formerly been dominated by the nobility, introducing a bourgeois element. A representative of the people was set alongside five nobles to share in civic administration, with a special responsibility for levying taxes on his constituents. The king was also solicitous for the poor, establishing a charitable confraternity, remedying injustices committed at the expense of his Neapolitan supporters, and even touching for the king's evil during Holy Week.

The rose of Naples was not without its thorns. The town quickly tired of the French invaders, who, in their turn, soon grew homesick. Money was running short, despite the policy of levying taxes in advance (thanks to Charles's generosity, at a reduced rate). The dream of a crusade had been abandoned, and Charles's enemies were regrouping to the north. March 1495 saw Venice, Milan, Spain, the Empire and the papacy combine in a hostile alliance.

On 20 May 1495, after the conclusion of the solemn festivities at Naples, the French commenced their withdrawal. Leaving the Duke of Montpensier as his viceroy, Charles marched rapidly northwards via Rome and Siena, to reach Pisa on 23 June. The allied forces under Gonzalo de Córdoba were waiting in the Apennines and gave battle at Fornovo. This indecisive engagement nevertheless left the French free to continue their withdrawal, and they reached Asti, near Turin, on 15 July. Negotiations then opened under disadvantageous circumstances: Maximilian was approaching with a powerful force, and news came from the Pyrenees of Spanish forces massing near the border. French councils were divided, with Commynes and Gié urging peace against the advice of Briçonnet and Trivulzio. On 9 October an agreement was reached with Sforza by which he regained Novara from the Duke of Orléans. Meanwhile, Naples was once more becoming Aragonese. Ferdinand's grandson and heir, Ferrantino, returned to the city amid popular rejoicing, and the French were massacred. One by one the garrisons up the peninsula were forced to surrender, and a treaty signed on 25 February 1497 brought an end to hostilities.

Not that Charles or his interventionist councillors were in the least discouraged by this turn of events. With the French gone, Italian politics once more disintegrated. And in November 1497 France and Spain made an agreement to carve up the peninsula. The death of Charles in April 1498 did nothing to halt preparations for the second expedition, which Louis XII made his own.

Louis XII

The new king was the more enthusiastic to follow in his predecessor's footsteps because he could add to the Angevin claim to Naples his own dynastic claim to the duchy of Milan. When his grandfather, Louis of Orléans, had married Valentina Visconti, daughter of Giangaleazzo I of Milan, it had been agreed that the duchy should revert to their descendants should the Visconti dynasty fail in the male line. This eventuality had come to pass, and the vicissitudes of condottiere politics had combined with the imperial claim to suzerainty over Milan to put the duchy in the hands of Sforza. Louis refused to recognise Sforza, and his primary objective in Italy was to vindicate his own claim.

Before leaving France, he did his best to secure international acquiescence in his project. Agreements were reached with Spain, England, Denmark, and even the Emperor, whose son Philip the Fair agreed to do homage to Louis for his territories in Artois,

Flanders, and the Charolais. In addition, Louis made an agreement with the Swiss, whose infantry were at that time the terror of Europe, by which he could count on their support (although this did nothing to impede the designs which the Swiss themselves had on Milan). A suitable fee for the Duke of Savoy secured free use of the Alpine passes in his domain. And by the Treaty of Blois (1499), Venice offered cavalry and infantry support for the duration of the campaign in exchange for Cremona in the event of victory. Thus, by masterly diplomacy, Louis managed to unite almost the whole of Europe against Milan and Naples.

The French army, which assembled again at Grenoble, was commanded by the Milanese Gian-Giacomo Trivulzio. In the words of Henri Lemonnier, a nationalist historian of the old school, Trivulzio was 'a competent enough general', well able to handle Italians, who were all condottieri at heart, because he himself was 'Italian, a mercenary, and a faction leader'. Lombardy was swiftly captured in October 1499, and equally swiftly retaken by Ludovico Sforza the following February.

Another round began in April 1500. Overall command was now entrusted to Louis de la Trémoille, who sought a decisive confrontation with Sforza so that providence might pass judgement. Louis XII, lying sick at Lyon, devoutly assisted at Masses, prayers, and public processions, waiting upon a sign from heaven. Battle was joined near Novara on 8 April 1500. Sforza, betrayed by the Swiss, was taken prisoner amidst almost comic confusion. Carried off to France, he died there after ten years' captivity – five of them in the Château de Loches. The Cardinal of Amboise, Louis XII's viceroy in Italy, implemented the administrative scheme sketched out the previous year. A senate of 16 men brought together French and Italians under two governors, one civil, the other military. The wealth of the conquered province provided pensions to many French gentlemen; and the cardinal himself became Count of Lomellina (near Alessandria).

In the year 1500, France was easily the most powerful nation in Europe. The cities and principalities accepted the French seizure of Milan. The Emperor Maximilian signed a truce. And eastern Europe sought Louis's aid against the advancing Turks. The time seemed ripe for a crusade, and in 1501 a French fleet even tried to make a landing on Mételin, an island not far from Rhodes. Was this to be the start of a great Christian offensive?

It was not, because France was preparing to resume operations against Naples. A partition of that kingdom was agreed between Louis XII and Ferdinand of Aragon at Granada in 1500. The French army marched south from Milan and once again took possession of Naples while its new king, Federico, fled. Meanwhile, Spanish troops took possession of Apulia.

It was not long before the two invading partners, initially hesitant in their new territories, came to blows and then to outright war. Historians have picked out the battle of Garigliano (autumn 1503) as an engagement of particular importance, for there, although Bayard distinguished himself in traditional style, it was artillery which won the day. The continual confrontations between the troops of France and Spain, where the respective nobilities sized each other up and indulged in chivalric displays reminiscent of medieval romances, were brought to an end after three years by a truce in 1504. Thus France decisively lost the kingdom of Naples, which was to remain in Spanish hands for the next two centuries.

It was time for Louis to give fresh consideration to the political situation outside Italy. The stakes were getting high, for Philip the Fair, Maximilian's son, already in possession of the Burgundian heritage (Franche-Comté and the Netherlands) by right of his mother Marie, had in 1496 married Joanna, second daughter of Isabella of Castile and Ferdinand of Aragon. So Louis in his turn joined the game of matrimonial diplomacy. His objective was to secure for his daughters not only France, but also his conquests in Milan and his putative conquests in Naples. To this end he was quite prepared to consider a marriage which would leave his Orléanais inheritance in the hands of a separate dynasty. For his daughter Claude he planned a marriage to Charles of Luxembourg, son of Philip and Joanna, using her rights to Brittany (through her mother) and to Milan, Naples and Burgundy as the lure. The Cardinal of Amboise conducted the negotiations, which fulfilled Louis's hopes by bringing him imperial investiture with the Duchy of Milan in April 1505.

In 1505 Louis, still without a male heir, fell dangerously ill. He had scarcely recovered when his Council started urging him to make a will. He therefore decided on a marriage between François d'Angoulême and Claude, to whom he promised the family inheritance of the House of Orléans. In order to lend the decision extra weight, a display of national consensus was arranged. In May 1506 an assembly was convened at Tours to witness the cardinal-legate himself solemnly declare the betrothal of François (aged 12) and Claude (aged 7). The people obediently expressed their joy in a series of feasts, pageants and tournaments, while Queen Anne and the ambassadors of Philip and Maximilian looked on in dismay.

In the meantime, Italy was making fresh demands upon French attention: a serious revolt at Genoa (1506–7) threw the future of the peninsula into the balance once more. Venice now found itself the centre of international attention. And under Louis's aegis the League of Cambrai (1508) united Maximilian, Ferdinand and Pope Julius II against the Serene Republic.

Yet another French army crossed the Alps in April 1509, marked out from its predecessors by its deployment of a French national infantry. An ordinance of January 1509 had called for the levy of infantry across the kingdom on the model developed in the fifteenth century for the cavalry. The Marshal de Gié's innovation paved the way for the national legions recruited by François I in his wars against Charles V. But it was already clear that, as Henri Lemonnier observed, Frenchmen now outnumbered foreigners in the royal armies.

The battle of Agnadello, on the Adda, saw the French defeat the Venetians in May 1509. The French now awaited Maximilian's arrival in order to press home their advantage. But Maximilian did not come – for lack of funds, some said. The French took possession of such strongholds as Treviso, Padua and Verona, while the Venetians played a waiting-game. They released their mainland subjects from their oaths of allegiance, confident in the invulnerability of their islands and lagoons. Not that they were wholly inactive: they were busy negotiating with the papacy and the kingdom of Naples, offering various towns in return for support. Their policy culminated in the Holy League of 1511, which brought together the Empire, Spain, England, Venice and the Swiss cantons under papal auspices. Julius II was the life and soul of the alliance, eager to kick the French barbarians out of Italy. Dumbfounded by the pope's hostility, Louis convened the French clergy, and they obliged by affirming the king's supremacy in temporal affairs, assuring him of their support, voting him 240 000 *livres* and appealing for yet another general council.

It was against Julius II, in his new role as warlord, that the French armies fought in 1512, gaining victories at Bologna, Brescia and Ravenna thanks to the generalship of Gaston de Foix, the king's nephew. He, however, lost his life at Ravenna just as circumstances were conspiring against the French. The Swiss descended into Lombardy in May, the Venetians were approaching from the east, and the Spanish were marching up from Naples. The French high command, divided and demoralised after Gaston's death, was short of funds, and its forces melted away. Louis's army slunk back over the Alps in June having lost even Lombardy: Milan itself was retaken by Maximilian Sforza in December 1512. Louis tried to regain lost ground the following year, but his forces were trounced by the Swiss infantry at Novara. Meanwhile, the plans of the Holy League had also resulted in fighting to the north, in the vulnerable areas of Artois and Picardy. The Emperor Maximilian and Henry VIII joined forces and routed the French cavalry. The encounter at Guinegatte (August 1513) became famous among historians as the 'Day of Spurs' because the retreating French horsemen found more use for their spurs than their lances.

The only option left was negotiation, and at some considerable disadvantage. The situation worsened still further as the Swiss infantry combined with German *landsknechts* to invade Burgundy, penetrating as far as Dijon. Louis had to abandon his claims to the duchy of Milan and the county of Asti as well as return various strongholds to the pope and the emperor. In addition, he had to pay dearly to buy off the Swiss. But the treaty was signed only by Louis de La Trémoille, who had tried to resist the Swiss invasion of Burgundy. Louis himself never ratified it, and sought instead, despite the indignant protests of all Europe at his patent lack of good faith, to prise apart the Holy League by negotiation.

The new pope, Leo X, did not share his predecessor's unremitting hatred of France, and allowed himself to be won over in return for French concessions in religious matters. In December 1513 he promulgated a bull calling for peace among the Christian princes. A rapprochement with England was sealed in summer 1514 by a marriage between the recently widowed Louis and Henry VIII's sister Mary. Finally, a new truce was arranged with the ageing Ferdinand of Aragon. Thus the political turmoil unleashed by the French descent upon Italy was temporarily quieted.

Modern historians find two points particularly puzzling when they look back on these twenty years of hectic diplomatic and military manoeuvres. The making and breaking of alliances, the sudden shifts and hasty reversals of policy, leave them baffled. Merely to provide a narrative is a challenge, demanding a high degree of simplification. It remains to seek some broad picture of general tendencies to permit us to make sense of it all. Some tendencies do stand out, but they are not simply lines that one can trace from end to end with regard to the policies of each State. Just as in a diagram, the lines must often be replaced by dots for want of a continuous connection.

Papal policy varied with the character and situation of successive popes. Did Alexander VI (Rodrigo Borgia) support the French descent on Italy because he really believed that Charles VIII would deliver the crusade he promised? Or was he simply scheming to bolster his temporal authority? Julius II (Giulio della Rovere) was inflexible in his hostility to the 'barbarians' as long as they were on the peninsula, and would not sheathe his sword until Italy was once more secured for the Italians. Leo X (Giovanni de Medici), in contrast, disentangled himself from the Holy League dexterously enough once the French Church, at Louis's behest, cut off all fees to the Holy See – his pontificate was always hard pressed for cash.

Spain, under first Ferdinand and Isabella and then Ferdinand alone, was fully occupied with the fulfilment of her peninsular ambitions and with the commencement of colonial expansion; 1492 saw not only Colombus's discovery of America but also the conquest of Granada, the last Moorish stronghold in Spain. Philip the Fair, son-in-law to the Catholic Kings, was a major piece on the diplomatic chessboard. As the son and heir of Mary of Burgundy he looked wistfully back to the days of Charles the Bold's Burgundian State, which he hoped to rebuild for himself or his son Charles. But Ferdinand's relationship with the Aragonese ruling dynasty of Naples ensured that Ferdinand (King first of Aragon, and then of all Spain) could never be entirely uninterested in the fate of the Italian peninsula, even if he once agreed with Louis XII to carve up the Neapolitan kingdom.

The Emperor Maximilian was also mindful of the Burgundian legacy. While his son Philip the Fair laid claim to it outright, Maximilian sought to sweep up the crumbs through the marriage contract between his grandson Charles and Claude of France. Nor did he forget his imperial claim to sovereignty in Italy, especially in Milan. Almost invariably hostile to France, he was drawn irresistibly into an alliance with Spain, an alliance which was ordained in the very territories he acquired or aspired to.

Under the first Tudors, English intervention in the wars was motivated entirely by the traditional enmity with France. The Hundred Years War, when Guyenne had been in English hands, was still, after all, recent history. And so England pursued dynastic ambitions with a policy based on securing bridgeheads on the continental coast.

The Swiss cantons, a reservoir of infantry for the armies of Europe, came only late into the Italian campaigns, seeking to expand from the mountains down the valley of the Ticino. Still notionally part of the Empire, the Swiss Confederation was generally hostile to France in her conflict with Maximilian. But French silver broke the bonds of traditional loyalty, and Louis XII did not have much trouble hiring Swiss mercenaries.

Italy itself was bedevilled by internal problems. Venetian policy looked to expand the 'Terra Firma' westwards. But bordering Milan to the west and the Empire to the north (Maximilian held Trieste, Fiume, and the Trentino) led her to vacillate between a Valois and a Habsburg alliance. Florence was ultimately of little weight in the equation of Italian politics. Generally favourable to the Aragonese dynasty in Naples on account of problems in north–south trade, she was beset by internal turmoil, as the Medici hold on Tuscany was far from secure. Similar problems beset Milan, where Ludovico Sforza called upon France to help defend his duchy against his nephew Giangaleazzo, whose claims were promoted by King Ferdinand of Naples (his wife's grandfather).

There was one constant in the kaleidoscopic diplomacy of this Europe of nascent nationalism and blatant dynastic ambition: the rivalry between France and the Empire. Despite the efforts of Anne of Brittany, whose total indifference to the future of the kingdom was matched by her commitment to a Habsburg match for her daughter (whether to Charles or Ferdinand), the hostility between the two nations and their two dynasties exploded. From time to time, convergent interests brought them together in temporary alliances – as against Venice in 1508 – but competition was the norm. In Italy the issue was the imperial right of investiture over Milan; in Switzerland they bid against each other for mercenaries; in Flanders the issue was whether or not the Emperor would pay homage to the French king as overlord of the Flemish fiefs. Their rivalry extended even to England, with Margaret of Austria (Maximilian's daughter) straining every nerve to prevent the marriage between Louis XII and Henry VIII's sister Mary. And of course it was played out on the battlefield, though perhaps less there than elsewhere: for the Habsburgs found it hard to match the Valois in mobilising military resources. But the roots of the century-long confrontation between France and the Habsburg bloc were spreading at the end of the fifteenth century.

And what are we to make of the Italian Wars in terms of France itself? In considering their rationale, we can dismiss at once the notion that conquering Naples was meant to provide the springboard for a crusade. Although the Turkish advance would have been ample justification, the crusading theme was an archaic ideological cloak to cover grimmer political realities. These realities were the dynastic ambitions of Charles VIII and Louis XII, which entailed a commitment to vindicate hereditary rights and build up family domains in the manner of any good feudal lord. And there were other considerations: a teeming nobility, imbued with youthful high spirits, who were drawn to the Italian campaign as their Castilian counterparts were drawn to the New World, by a sense of adventure. By leading the fighting classes into the Italian peninsula, the Valois certainly earned their own kingdom a respite from baronial belligerence and disorder. By throwing Naples and Milan to the wolves, they satisfied the bloodlust that France would otherwise have been at some costs to quench.

There remains of course the textbook cliché that by their exposure to Italian culture, the French elite was awoken to a sense of beauty and initiated into the arts of refined and luxurious living. And indeed, from the king downwards the French were bowled over by Italian painting and sculpture. But it must not be forgotten that the artistic achievement of Italy was already well-known, and that even before the invasions, transalpine contacts had been established for decades in both intellectual and commercial fields. If in this crucial period the Court, the nobility and the upper bourgeoisie of France were affected more profoundly by the artistic depiction of reality and by a yearning for an elegant lifestyle, then the most important causes of this were economic growth and political and social developments within the kingdom itself.

The Domestic Policy of Charles VIII and Louis XII

Both Charles and Louis ruled the kingdom through a small group of noblemen or commoners whose general tendency was to strengthen the machinery of State which they themselves to a large extent controlled. A few dozen men held the key posts on the King's Council and in the financial, military, judicial and ecclesiastical administrations. Royal policy was shaped by their manoeuvres and ambitions, and sometimes by their concern for administrative reform and rationalisation. But the mixture was thoroughly traditional, and the period from 1483 to 1515 saw no revolution in government.

The Problem of Offices

There was, however, a gradual evolution, accelerating under Louis, towards the 'officeholders' State'.[6] The public service was recruited by the sale to individuals of portions of public authority. At this point such venality, practised by pressure of circumstance, remained discreet to the point of secrecy, disturbed only by occasional bouts of conscience on the part of the chief culprits – the monarchs themselves. Charles VIII, if he did indulge habitually in favouritism, advising Parlement to choose one or another of his friends, did at least combat the sale of offices.[7] Article 68 of his ordinance on justice of July 1493 read: 'We ordain that henceforth nobody shall purchase the office of President, Councillor or any other office within our court [i.e. Parlement], nor likewise any office in the judiciary of our kingdom, nor for any such office pay, or promise to pay, or cause to be paid any sum of gold or silver or any equivalent in kind. . .'

Another measure on the same subject, promulgated by Louis XII's council in 1499, forbade in the strictest terms the sale or purchase of offices of justice. But such edicts were empty threats. The practice of resigning an office to a specified individual for a consideration became prevalent, and members of the King's Council and Court themselves had to pay to take up their offices. Others leased out their offices for rent. Venality of office was not officially avowed by the regime but, as Roland Mousnier has observed, Louis XII, in recognising that he and his predecessors had authorised the transfer of offices for cash, came close to so doing. It is well known that Louis sold offices to raise cash to pay his predecessor's debts. And in 1499 Louis admitted that he was conferring the post of *Conseiller Général des Aides* on Jean Le Coq 'notwithstanding his promise to pay a certain sum'. Mousnier regards this case as 'perhaps the first official sale of office by the king'. Before long, the practice was to become a habitual, indeed an indispensable, business for the monarchy.[8]

The *Grand Conseil*, originally adumbrated in 1460, and put on a firmer basis by Charles VIII, attained its definitive composition and competence under Louis XII in July 1498. Comprising 20 councillors and 2 secretaries (all major officeholders and resident at Court), it handled 'the highest affairs of the kingdom, dynastic or otherwise'. It functioned as the special organ of the king's justice when he revoked cases from the ordinary courts. The Parlement de Paris protested so vehemently against this that the king could only pacify it by openly confirming the preeminence of the Parlement over the *Grand Conseil*, which had to accept the presence of magistrates from the sovereign court in its proceedings. But the foundations of a judicial system entirely at the service of the State were laid in this period.

There was no danger of Charles VIII or Louis XII forgetting that the administration of justice was one of the most fundamental aspects of royal power. To extend the influence of the royal judges was to make the monarchy itself a force throughout the land. So new Parlements were established, for example at Dijon in Burgundy and Aix in Provence. The Exchequer of Normandy was made a sovereign court in 1499. And these new sovereign courts were not slow to intervene in the fiefs, overriding the traditional seigneurial courts and settling disputes between them in the manner of superior jurisdictions.

In order to demonstrate their love of justice, both Charles (in 1493) and Louis (in 1499 and 1510) issued important ordinances on the subject. These measures voiced a paternalistic concern to provide honest, competent and assiduous judges. As they sought to introduce some uniformity to the procedures and methods employed by magistrates, advocates and procurators throughout the kingdom, they laid down in these documents a minutely detailed system of regulations for establishing the facts and claims in cases. Like so many others, these ordinances did not achieve instant success. Indeed, their repeated promulgation (three times in seventeen years) in almost identical words shows that establishing a tradition of public service was going to take a long time.

The codification of customary law – that Utopian dream of French kings and jurists – which had been initiated under Charles VII reached a crucial phase under Charles VIII and his successor. But why was there such a commitment to fixing in writing the various oral traditions of provincial justice? To see in it a desire to look after what Henri Lemonnier called the 'petites gens' seems a little simplistic, even if such a paternal sentiment matches the self-image of the two kings. Perhaps one can also see the love of classification and rational organisation which characterised so many of the leading spirits of the age, and expressed an underlying desire to master the fluid complexities of reality. Moreover, by thus transcribing, revising, and promulgating custom, the monarchy was making good its claim to be the sole fount of law. The numerous ordinances which Charles and Louis issued on the subject showed their close interest in the task adumbrated by Charles VII's Edict of Montis-lès-Tours (1454). The need for the task is brought out by the fact that there were some 370 local legal systems in that part of the country which lay under customary law – among them the major regional blocks of Paris, the Vermandois, Picardy, Champagne, the Orléanais and the Auvergne. Within the jurisdictions of the provincial Parlements the diversity was less dramatic as each sovereign court applied a single customary system within its jurisdiction: Dijon enforced the custom of Burgundy, Rennes that of Brittany, and Rouen that of Normandy. The process of codification was conducted within each bailiwick by an assembly of the three estates (and, from Louis XII's time, representatives of rural communities sat alongside the magistrates of the main towns).[9] A royal commissioner (usually a councillor of the Parlement de Paris) presided over these local assemblies. The basis for discussion was a draft prepared beforehand by the bailiff with the assistance of local nobles and lawyers. The commissioner went through the draft article by article, inviting comments and discussion. Thus revised and corrected, the resultant publication was a veritable law-code. It usually owed much to the royal commissioner, whose dominant role in the proceedings was reflected to a greater or lesser extent in the 'romanisation' or systematisation of the local customs. The bulk of this enormous task was accomplished throughout northern France (for southern France was under Roman law) in the period from 1498 to 1530. But in some places it dragged on longer, as certain hastily compiled codes attracted criticism from jurists and became the subject of new exercises called 'reformations'.[10]

The task of recording, revising, and reforming customary law was enormous. But once custom had been reduced to writing, it was frozen. Although it appeared as the participation of the estates in the legislative organisation of the kingdom, once fixed it could not accommodate innovation except by means of royal ordinances. At the same time, codification prevented the further diffusion of Roman law in the kingdom, even though that law played an important part in the process of codification itself, which allowed jurists to bring to customary law the same sort of approaches as to Roman or Canon law. In 1576 Charles Dumoulin published his *Commentaire* on the customs of Paris (codified in 1515), and the lacunae and inadequacies he showed up led to the 'reformation' of the code in 1580. Bernard d'Argentré did much the same for the Breton code of 1539, which was likewise revised in 1580. The commentators and other scholars attained a view of the underlying unity of customary law – only a relative unity, of course, as that law comprised 60 regional systems and 200 local systems. Charles Dumoulin even attempted to construct a concordance of customary law. Other jurists held up the Parisian code as a model for the rest, even though it later came in for reform itself. But the political results of codification were the most important: customary law was fixed; the northward march of Roman law was halted; and the king had emerged as the sole fount of law, alone able to create or modify it.

The Financial Problem

The financial problem was particularly acute between 1483 and 1515, and again in the 1540s and 1550s. There were constant judicial attempts to purge corruption in the tax-collecting system. This was the subject of ordinances under Charles VIII in 1494 and Louis XII in 1508. Charles threatened countless penalties for officials who persistently failed to submit accounts, or who held back sums due to the king for their own private use. But, as Yvonne Labande-Mailfert has shown, the solidarity of the financial mafia led by Briçonnet was such that royal pronouncements in this area were a dead letter. Louis XII tried to stamp out the abuses of 'élus, receveurs, greffiers, grenetiers, contrôleurs et mesureurs de sel'. He sought to end absenteeism among officials, which led to the employment of 'the pig ignorant' as their deputies; and to reduce the rapacity of *élus* who demanded 'more money from the poorer people than their orders and commissions stipulate'.

Needless to say, no fiscal reform of any moment was achieved. In 1493 Charles VIII considered a new assessment of hearths (the basis for the levy of the *taille*), but the obstructiveness of his general treasurers put paid to that. Committed by now to the Italian expedition, the king's financial expedients were entirely traditional: an increase in the *taille* to 2.8 million *livres* barely covered the cost of the ordinance companies. Its yield fell in times of truce, to about 2.2 million *livres* in 1491 *and* 2.1 million in 1498. The traditional *crues* were replaced by demands for payment in advance, which aroused widespread grievance. But the sums gathered remained far short of the incredible 5.4 million squeezed out by Louis XI in 1482, which Pierre Chaunu has called 'a kind of peak scaled for the first time by the financial State'. They fell short also of the sums raised in later years by François I and Henri II. Under Louis XII the *taille* was lowered to around 1.8 million *livres*, but this was augmented by *crues* in 1503, 1508, 1509, and from 1511 to 1514. And from 1507 to 1511 it fell to the levels of Charles VII's reign, about 1.2 million *livres*. But towards the end of Louis's reign it returned to 3 million livres or more, because the loss of Lombardy and its resources, together with the pressure of the Holy League on all his borders, compelled a king who was normally frugal of his subjects' resources to dig deeper into their pockets. Yet it did not matter, for posterity retained a rosy memory of this monarch – and this despite the fact that, as Pierre Chaunu has observed, the lower *taille* figures were deceptive in what was actually a period of monetary deflation. As the same historian concludes, 'Louis XII's *taille* legitimised the levy, clothing what had traditionally been an extraordinary source of revenue with the comforting garb of immemorial custom.

Relations with the Church

As 'Most Christian Kings', both Charles and Louis took a close interest in the religious condition of their realm. The ideal of ecclesiastical reform was, as we have seen, high on the agenda throughout Christian Europe *and* France was no exception. The issue was raised at the Estates General of Tours (1484), although the disputes between the ultramontane bishops and those who supported the Pragmatic Sanction reached such a pitch that reform was soon forgotten. It was raised again in 1493 when, under the influence of St François de Paule (Charles VIII's spiritual director), a committee met at Tours and called for the restoration of free episcopal and abbatial elections, and an end to the practices of 'commending' and 'reserving' clerical benefices. A provincial synod which convened at Sens at the king's instigation reminded bishops of their obligation to reside in their dioceses. But such efforts were as straws in the wind. Nevertheless, the Pragmatic Sanction issued by Charles VII in 1438 gave the French kings a certain freedom of action within the national church. This lay primarily in the power to appoint bishops. For although the Pragmatic Sanction theoretically vested the power of election in the cathedral chapters or the communities of monks and nuns, 'it was not thought unacceptable for the king or the higher nobility to make benevolent recommendations where they thought certain candidates particularly deserving or dedicated to the common good – provided that they stopped short of force and threats'.[11]

Blessed with a church that was openly Gallican, Charles VII, Louis XI, and Charles VIII availed themselves to the full of their power to make 'benevolent recommendations'. Charles VIII (who, according to his chronicler, was of the opinion that each bishop should be content with a single see) intervened as bluntly as his father before him, proposing royal candidates for election. He pressed Jean de Rely on the chapter of Angers, and allowed Briçonnet to succeed his father Robert in the see of Rheims, thus preventing the election of the more suitable Jean Standonck. Charles also deliberately prolonged vacancies in benefices whose revenues reverted to the Crown. In 1493, several bishoprics were left unfilled because 'on the death of the bishop, the king succeeds him'. As we have seen, the most notorious ecclesiastical abuses were in fact the work of the self-same 'Most Christian King', who in theory could and should have been striving for a Church more conscious and worthy of her proper calling. Curiously enough, to the extent that Charles VIII and Louis XII did concern themselves with clerical standards, they concentrated on the regular clergy, which might be thought to have been a matter of secondary importance. Charles VIII intervened consistently on behalf of Observant Dominicans under attack from their 'conventual' brethren, who were quite happy with a more relaxed interpretation of their order's rule and customs. For example, in 1497 Charles installed 30 Observant Dominicans at Troyes 'in order to teach reformation by example'. The same king 'took the side of the nuns of the Hôtel-Dieu in Paris when they were harassed by their sisters on account of their holy life'. On the other hand, it was for the sake of public order that Cardinal of Amboise intervened in the Parisian houses of Dominicans and Franciscans. The former institution housed a number of brothers who called themselves students but were little more than louts. And when in 1498 the king himself took an interest in the University of Paris, that preeminently clerical stronghold, it was again to guarantee the safety of the citizens. For the scholars, like all tonsured clerks, enjoyed the 'benefit of the clergy' and could thus slip through the fingers of the king's judges when they behaved like hooligans. Order had to be restored, and it had to be made clear that not just anyone could claim to be a student. Under a new ordinance, the privileges of scholarly status were restricted to students affiliated to a particular faculty, and did not apply in the first six months following matriculation. The ordinance also limited the possible duration of studies: four years for the arts course, eight for medicine, and 14 for divinity. This, it was hoped, would weed out the troublemakers who lived as perpetual students. The measure made such an impact that the students went on strike, along with many university preachers. Abusive placards were posted around the city, and the provost had to put patrols on the streets. Protected by a heavily armed escort, Louis XII entered the city and held a *lit de justice*, which concluded with the University backing down. Louis took advantage of the moment to dismiss the austere principal of the Collège de Montaigu, Jean Standonck, who had dared to criticise his recent divorce from Queen Jeanne. A few years later, in 1501, the king showed the Bishop of Embrun just how much more merciful royal justice was than that of the Church. He despatched two commissioners to investigate the proceedings which the bishop was pursuing against the Waldensians with the assistance of the local secular authorities. The affair dragged on for years, until in 1509 the Parlement overturned the rulings made by the local courts in the Dauphiné. Once a number of priests had withdrawn the accusations of heresy levelled against the Waldensian communities, the king's justice ceased to harry the bishop and his followers. Forty years later, François I was to intervene more tactfully to save the Waldensians of Mérindol and Cabrières from the clutches of the Cardinal de Tournon and the magistrates of Aix.

But the kings of France were quite capable of using their church for other than strictly religious objectives. This is seen at its clearest in the Council of Pisa. The context of this affair was the diplomatic situation of 1511, when Pope Julius II was coordinating opposition to Louis in Italy. Louis revived the idea of calling a General Council of the Church to set about reform, an idea as traditional as that of the crusade. The Emperor Maximilian was sympathetic because he hoped to win greater independence from Rome for his church hierarchy, along Gallican lines. But Julius II refused to sanction the assembly which Louis and the Emperor convened at Pisa. Few prelates turned up, most of them French. They moved to Milan in November 1511, but were as unwelcome there as they had been at Pisa. In April 1512, at its final session, the council proclaimed: 'the pope has incurred the penalties laid down by the holy decrees of the Councils of Constance and Basle; we therefore declare that he is suspended from his papal office and that his authority lawfully devolves onto this present assembly'.[12] Louis was imposing a thankless task upon his clergy, as he lacked the means to vindicate these pretentious pronouncements. His army had to evacuate Milan at short notice, dragging in its wake the prelates, who meandered back amid the rabble of soldiers via Asti to Lyon, 'where the council simply faded away'. A few days later, on 3 May 1512, Julius II opened a rival council in the Lateran Basilica. The whole sorry episode achieved nothing beyond showing the complete dominance of the Most Christian King over the French church. François I and Henri II had as much power as Louis in this sphere, but they used it more circumspectly.

The Popularity of Charles VIII and Louis XII

Even more than Charles VIII, Louis XII worked at projecting a positive image of his kingship. Charles had by no means ignored this aspect of politics, expressing his love for his people in perfectly paternalist terms, speaking of 'our concern for the poor' and promising 'relief' for them from the royal bounty. These and similarly conventional utterances are no longer found, or at least not so often, in the official pronouncements of François I and Henri II. It was Charles who came up with the congenial idea of dispensing justice in person. Anyone could put a petition to the king at any time, for his *maîtres de requêtes de l'Hôtel* to handle. Even Louis XIV permitted as much during his walkabouts. But St

Louis's manner of dispensing justice was entirely outdated, even if the Estates General had called on the new king in 1484 to preside at a public audience once a week. Attracted by this rather archaic model, Charles enquired in 1497 about the 'manner in which our royal predecessors, especially St Louis, gave audience to the poor people': he followed St Louis's example at least twice, in January and March 1498, perhaps dreaming also of emulating that king's crusading record.

Louis XII did not resort to these traditional means of advancing his reputation. He used more modern methods, anticipating those of François I, Louis XIII, and even Louis XIV. He was perhaps the first king to concern himself with public opinion. His addresses to Parliament expatiated upon his frugality with the economic resources of his 'poor people', his political skill in forming his Council, and the particular virtues of various articles enshrined in the justice ordinance of March 1499.[13] The 'Father of the People' gave an official pension to the poet Pierre Gringoire, who from 1505 defended and supported Louis's policy towards Julius II. When in 1512 Julius excommunicated the king for convoking the Council of Pisa, Gringoire produced a play for the amusement of the Paris crowd: *Le Jeu du Prince des sots et de la mère Sotte* (*The Prince of Fools and Mother Folly* – staged on Shrove Tuesday at Les Halles). In it the pope was portrayed, complete with tiara, in the role of the Stubborn Man while two persons wearing the emblems of Italy and France complained bitterly of the sufferings they endured at his hands. On a more scholarly level, Jean Lemaire de Belges (a *valet de chambre* to Louis XII), drew up a treatise *De la différence des schismes et des conciles de l'Église universelle et de la prééminence et utilité des conciles de l'Église gallicane* (1511) – a tract which made no attempt to conceal its contempt for the papacy. Other royal propagandists such as Jean de Saint-Gelais and Claude de Seyssel competed to leave posterity the most flattering portrait of their Valois patron.

Both Charles and Louis (who was acclaimed as Father of the People by the assembly at Tours in 1506) enjoyed great popularity. Opposition and resistance to their rule were practically nonexistent. A Breton revolt, a popular rising at Agen, student riots in Paris (1498–99) and a few disputes between Louis XII and the Parlement de Paris make up the list. In short, their combined 32 years saw little to match the disorders of François I's or Louis XIII's reigns. And they were not only obeyed and respected, but

loved by their subjects. It can be argued that the spectacular reduction in the *taille* from the inordinate levels it reached under
Louis XI (and to which it returned under François I) largely accounts for this. The French have never liked paying taxes. But it
takes more than this to explain the mutual harmony of king and
people at the very time when the foundations of the subsequent
authoritarian monarchy were being laid (albeit without fuss).
Domestic peace, interrupted only briefly by the 'Guerre Folle',
brought the country demographic and economic recovery. And
the Italian campaigns freed it from the scourge of an underem-
ployed nobility. France enjoyed the fruits of peace and growth
for a brief time before a swelling population put new pressure
on resources and employment.

The nation was not yet cut off or separated from its rulers, as
they still lived in a relatively modest style. Although Louis XII
doubled the personnel of the Court, the new establishment still
comprised a mere 400. Royal dwellings as yet barely exceeded
generous bourgeois proportions. If Charles VIII's Amboise or Louis
XII's Blois were grandiose, they nevertheless pale into insignificance beside the extravagances of François I's Chambord.

Whether consciously or not, Charles and Louis made the most
of tradition. In the newly acquired provinces (Burgundy, Guyenne
and Provence) they respected time-honoured liberties and preserved the provincial Estates. And even when they introduced
Parlements, the new sovereign courts stood in direct continuity
with the ducal or comital courts they superseded. Brittany remained
the duchy it had always been. Anne, twice queen, watched over it
jealously. And the kingdom as a whole, secure in its provincial
liberties, assumed a growing role in national affairs. The Estates
General of 1484 saw an alliance between the third estate and the
Beaujeu regime to the disadvantage of a section of the nobility,
as Philippe Pot complained. Did he not dare to speak of a time
when the people elected their kings? Cottages buzzed with the
news of his audacious remarks for long enough, for anyone could
imagine themselves in his place as the lowly but bold deputy freely
speaking his mind before the great ones of the land. Opportunities
for leading commoners to negotiate with the political elite multiplied under Charles and Louis: the local assemblies which codifed
customary law, the estates which met in 1498 before the great
justice ordinance, the assembly of notables at Tours in 1506, and
the consultations held in Normandy and Provence with a view to

transforming their feudal courts into Parlements. Plenty of ordinances spoke of 'nobles, barons, and commoners', and these last, thus given a mention in respect of domestic policy, in turn felt themselves to be a part of the political machinery which governed them. We can see here the reality behind the concept of a monarchy moderated by a balance of powers, which Claude de Seyssel outlined in his treatise *La Grande Monarchie de France*. Better still, a king like Louis XII displayed many of the qualities Machiavelli expected of his *Prince*; indeed, Machiavelli, who visited France around this time, made clear on several occasions his high opinion of the French king.

5 Foreign Policy under François I and Henri II

François I, Henri II, and their Entourages

Louis XII, as we have seen, provided for the succession by marrying off his daughter Claude to François d'Angoulême, the son of Charles and Louise of Savoy. Not that he felt any great warmth for François: 'That fat brat will mess up everything', he is said to have predicted. But François was, like Louis himself, descended from Charles V and was thus, according to the Salic Law, the heir presumptive.[1] He was accorded all the privileges of a prince of the blood, and, despite the relatively straitened circumstances of his family (the Valois of Angoulême had little good land), his chances of reaching the throne had never been underestimated. Louis XII, then, explicitly recognised him as his heir. And from the assembly at Tours in 1506 he sought support for breaking the promise he had made to marry Claude to Charles Habsburg (son of the Emperor Maximilian) and for marrying her instead to a pure-born French prince.

When Louis died in January 1515, the 20-year-old François succeeded to what the Venetian ambassadors reckoned the finest kingdom in the world. Despite his relative youth, many of his characteristics were already obvious. Newly raised to the throne, he was fully conscious of the gulf separating him from his subjects, but he shared the tastes of many Renaissance noblemen for high living, fine clothes, and ostentation. Filled with the love of life typical of the age which produced Rabelais and Erasmus, he exuded an egoism fuelled by the unbounded adoration bestowed upon him by his mother Louise and his sister Marguerite (later Queen of Navarre).[2] Louise of Savoy, besotted with her son, enjoyed through him a vicarious sense of power. She lived for the moments when, with him absent in battle, or even imprisoned in Madrid, she could play the Regent. She was obsessed with their dynastic interests, and was not without a certain naked greed – as in the proceedings against the Constable Bourbon.

François I inherited from his uncle, and even more from his great-uncle, the poet Charles of Orléans, a taste for letters and the arts which made him a generous patron. Yet this large man (over six feet tall), strongly built, with a prominent nose and sensual lips, was a complex character. A cavalier of a king, who loved war and riding, he spent long periods on campaign. Addicted to jousting when deprived of real combat, he prized heroic deeds and chivalrous performances. One recalls the ceremony in which Bayard knighted the young king at the Battle of Marignano, an anachronistic gesture at a moment when warfare was becoming increasingly a matter of artillery, and François I's own forces were handsomely equipped with cannons and arquebuses. Yet the ceremony was by no means empty. In kneeling before Bayard, François was paying homage to that nobility which, full of a sense of its own importance, set out to maintain tradition. Nor should we forget the other side of the coin. Already a knight by virtue of his royal anointing, François now received the honour once more, in a different manner, in a place and from a man of his own choosing. Thus he manifested his independence and his royal prerogative in the face of the monarchical legacy of the past.

François remained loyal for years to the friends of his youth. When raised to the throne, he showered favours upon his intimates. 'No previous succession', in Lemonnier's words, 'had seen such a lavish distribution of the spoils of power.' To his mother Louise he made over the county of Angoulême, elevating it to a duchy, and adding the duchy of Anjou and the counties of Maine and Beaufort. The Duke of Alençon, his sister Marguerite's first husband, was made a prince of the blood. Charles Bourbon, his childhood companion, was made Grand Constable and received in addition the governorships of some of France's richest cities and provinces. Artus Gouffier de Boisy, his one-time governor, was made Grand Master of France – in effect, head of the royal household. Artus's brother, Guillaume Gouffier de Bonnivet, became Grand Admiral. Bestowing his royal patrimony and the great offices of State among his cronies, François acted as though the kingdom were his personal property. But amid this largesse of political office and honorific appointments, a new kind of man was also emerging on the scene, exemplified in Antoine Duprat, of whom more later.

The death of the Dauphin François in 1536 paved the way for the succession of his younger brother, Henri.[3] Henri was addicted, like most men of the Renaissance and indeed most French kings, to sport. Tall and well-built, though not as much as his father, he dedicated himself to exercise and physical fitness to a degree which his early death cannot belie. He was avid not only for the hunt but also for jousting and tennis, but unlike his father he took little pleasure in life on campaign. The inevitable comparison with his father is hardly to Henri's advantage. The personality of the father overshadowed that of the son, much as Henri IV later eclipsed Louis XIII. Henri II, though like his father, was always less so: less the Renaissance prince, less charismatic, less appreciative of art and literature. He was introverted, cold, and prone to melancholy, perhaps because deprived of affection in childhood. His 17 years as second-fiddle to the Dauphin had left him withdrawn and mistrustful of himself and others – traits which his father's dominance did little to remedy. His reputedly loveless marriage to Catherine de Medici in 1533 did nothing to heal his psychological wounds. So he turned instead to people older than himself for comfort and affection.

No woman has ever been so renowned for her beauty among both contemporaries and posterity as Diane de Poitiers. Not simply pretty, but stunning, a woman who enjoyed life to the full, Diane was for the painters and poets of her day the embodiment of the Renaissance woman. The wife of one De Brézé (Grand Seneschal of Normandy), she had been at Court since the early years of François I's reign. There she had mastered the courtly virtues so perfectly that François entrusted her with the social education of his sullen son Henri, who rapidly conceived for her a burning passion to which she responded warmly, having been opportunely widowed in 1531. The difference in age meant nothing to their relationship, which ended only with Henri's death. Henri showered lands and titles on her: she received first the château of Chenonceaux, then that of Anet (where Jean Goujon's sculpture of her as Diana the huntress decorated the park). A firm Catholic steeped in aristocratic tradition, she urged on Henri the merits of Montmorency (who had fallen from François's favour in 1541), and later promoted the house of Guise, champions of the old faith and the old nobility.

If Duprat typifies the regime of François, Montmorency gave the tone to Henri's. Scion of an ancient noble family, and possessed of great lands and revenues, he took a rightful place on the King's Council. At first an intimate of François, he became chief *Valet de chambre* in 1520, a Marshal of France and Governor of Languedoc in 1522, and finally Grand Constable in 1538. He was for a while all-powerful, patron of a huge clientage network bound to him by gratitude for offices obtained or by traditional feudal ties. He was a man of simple and unwavering faith, of limited imagination, and of typically aristocratic attitudes: acknowledging and performing his own duties to his family (or clan) and to his king, he expected his due from others. In him the narrow horizons of a mind closed to all innovation matched the limitations of his intellect (it was only with difficulty that he learned to write).

Did François have good reason for overthrowing and almost exiling him? Certainly not. But towards the end of his life the ailing and splenetic victor of Marignano grew increasingly touchy. Montmorency's fall, due partly to his own political misjudgements, partly to the aversion which the king's mistress, Mme d'Étampes, felt for him, and partly to his accumulation of enemies at Court over a long political career, was mitigated by the new warmth which Diane and the Dauphin showed towards him. No sooner did Henri come to the throne than he recalled the Constable, riding out to Saint-Germain to meet him. Montmorency returned to the Council and was elevated to the rank of Duke-Peer of France. He directed Henri's anti-Habsburg foreign policy, but shifted its focus from Italy to the Rhineland, an important change in French priorities.

The political predominance of Montmorency's family network, which included such major noble houses as d'Humières, Cossé-Brissac, and Châtillon, led to the formation of a rival faction under the aegis of the house of Guise.[4] Like the Constable, Duke Claude of Guise and his brother Jean, the Cardinal of Lorraine, were trying under the new king to make up political ground they had lost in François I's declining years. When they died in 1550, their places were taken by Claude's sons, François, the new duke, and Charles, who succeeded his uncle as Cardinal of Lorraine. These gifted and ambitious brothers stood at the centre of a vast network of supporters and clients which extended throughout the nobility and higher clergy. The king was wise enough to hold the two factions in balance and thus make their rivalry work in his favour. It was only after his death that the balance broke down disastrously. During Henri's reign, Montmorency and Guise alike served their master loyally in peace and war.

The Italian Wars

Few periods in French history have been as fraught with diplomatic manoeuvring and military campaigning as the years 1515–59. Under François I and his son the kingdom was engaged in almost incessant combat with a variety of enemies – behind all of whom loomed at more or less remove the powerful Habsburg dynasty. Of the 44 years of their combined reigns, 22 saw France at war.

Like all the nobles of his generation, François I yearned for Italy. The French had been rudely awakened from their Italian dream by Louis XII's defeats at the hands of the Swiss at Novara and the English at Tournai in 1513, which had forced the king to renounce his claims to Naples and Milan. The new king felt that it was up to him to recover Milan and revive the dream. As ever, diplomacy paved the way for aggression. First François bought off Henry VIII for a million *écus*. The Habsburgs were not quite so easily disposed of. Charles, who had come of age at 15 a few days before François I's accession, was already staking a claim to the Burgundian inheritance, which had never been renounced by Maximilian or Mary of Burgundy. But relations improved sufficiently for the two princes to agree an alliance on 24 March 1515: Charles was to marry Renée, François I's second daughter, whose dowry was to consist of the duchy of Berry and 200 000 *écus*. The French then backed out and paid the stipulated forfeit, handing over Ponthieu, Péronne, Amiens, Montdidier, and Abbeville. On the Italian front, agreements with Venice were renewed, and the Doge of Genoa was persuaded to acknowledge French suzerainty.

May 1515 saw military preparations begin in earnest, 8000 Gascons and Basques were levied, along with 23 000 German *landsknechts*, including the notorious 'Black Band'. There were 500 archers

from the royal guard, and the cavalry of the ordinance companies numbered over 2500 lances, together with the 200 gentlemen and another 200 mounted crossbowmen from the king's
household guard. The field commanders were Claude de Lorraine, Charles de Bourbon, Boisy, and the Duke of Alençon, with
Jacques Galiot in charge of the artillery (which comprised some
60 pieces of various calibres). This huge force assembled at
Grenoble but then split up to cross the Alps, avoiding the usual
Mont Cenis and Mont Genèvre passes because their exits into
Italy at Susa and Pinerolo were controlled by a force of 15 000 or
20 000 Swiss mercenaries. The French therefore headed for the
valley of the Durance and then for St-Paul, Larche, Argentera,
and Demonte. Pedro Navarro, the Spanish captain of the Gascon
and Basque troops, scouted and marked out the route. On 9 or
10 August, the advance guard under Bourbon led the way, followed by the main force, which took three days to march out.
The king and his companions brought up the rear, leaving Embrun
on 13 August. The route was arduous, and the men had to proceed on foot one by one, leading their horses by the bridle. There
were no supplies to be found along the way other than water, for
the mountain folk panicked at this unprecedented invasion and
took to the higher ground with all their belongings.

The king's enemies – the pope, the Swiss, and the Spanish Viceroy
of Naples – had put together a force of some 30 000, especially
strong in the renowned Swiss infantry. Hearing that the French
Hannibal was descending by way of Demonte, the Swiss fell back,
leaving open the way to Turin. Following close behind them,
François reoccupied Novara, allowing them to take up position
in Milan. He then headed for Marignano to await developments.
For although both armies were in the field, negotiations between
the four combatant parties were still going on. François was only
a whisker from a bloodless victory, as plans for a treaty with the
Swiss were under way by 8 September, and Leo X was making
peace overtures. But it was no easy thing to disband an army in
the field, and the Swiss, holed up in Milan, were champing at
the bit, dreaming of the plunder within their grasp. They were
egged on by Matthias Schiner, Cardinal of Sion, apostolic legate
and the pope's commander-general in Lombardy. Louis XII's old
enemy exhorted the officers and men to take the fight to the
French. So, on 13 September, the cardinal, resplendent in his
vestments and preceded by his ceremonial cross, marched out of

Milan at the head of his troops. The French were taken somewhat by surprise, but not disastrously so. The Venetians, based a few miles away at Lodi, were ready to come to their aid. The alarm was given by look-outs who saw the dust raised by the advancing Swiss, and the French took the field. Bourbon led the advance guard, and François himself the main force, with Alençon bringing up the rear. The Swiss advanced, undeterred by the artillery that rained down on them, and once battle was joined formations dissolved in confusion amid a cloud of dust so thick that little could be seen until the moon rose. The combatants warily regrouped during the night. François sat tight, sending a messenger to urge the Venetians to make haste. The Venetian infantry arrived at about 11 o'clock the next morning, opportunely coming up behind the Swiss, who were threatening to break through Alençon's troops on the left wing. This decisive intervention justified the Venetians in claiming credit for the victory. But the French claimed the credit equally insistently: 'ours were the men of arms who did the job', wrote one chronicler. By midday it was all over. The defeated Swiss were harried to the walls of Milan.

The importance of Marignano can hardly be overemphasised. It was a victory not only for the king but for the whole realm. News of the battle resounded around the kingdom, celebrated by poets, musicians and balladeers. Towns, villages and cottages resounded with the joy of a nation's triumph and a prince's glory. Even today the words of the anonymous poet which Clément Janequin famously set to music as 'La Bataille' are known throughout France. The victory was skilfully exploited and bore abundant fruit. François was right to trust his commanders and ambassadors, as they served him expertly. In military terms it led to Maximilian Sforza's withdrawal from Milan. He renounced all claim to the province in return for 94 000 *écus* down and a further 36 000 *écus* a year for life. Thus generously provided for, he ended his days in France as the king's pensioner, staying even after Milan was irretrievably lost to the French in 1521. In the meantime, the French reinstalled their provincial administration.

Meanwhile, the negotations with the Swiss that had begun even before Marignano were coming to fruition. A treaty of perpetual peace was duly signed at Fribourg on 29 November 1516. All the cantons were party to it, and they were well rewarded with 1.7 million *écus* in cash and an annual pension of 2000 *livres*. The alliance was dearly bought, but worth it. Henceforth the Swiss 'would neither encourage nor allow their troops to serve any prince, or any lords in the service of any prince, or any other lords, or any communities, that claimed to have any grievance against the King of France relating to his own realm or to his duchy of Milan or to any of its appurtenances'. Strategically this guaranteed the security of a large portion of France's eastern frontier; and militarily it meant that the Swiss mercenaries, no longer free to serve elsewhere, were now at the disposal of the French king.

Of all the treaties signed in the aftermath of Marignano, the Concordat of Bologna agreed between Leo X and François I in 1516 had the most impact on the future of French domestic politics. It followed the pattern of several previous agreements between the papacy and the French monarchy in confirming effective royal control over the commanding heights of the French Church. Drafted by the French Chancellor, Duprat, it took the royal prerogative to new heights.

The treaties of Noyon (1516) and Cambrai (1517) between François and Charles V, after their respective ambassadors had agreed to the carving up of Greece, Switzerland, and England to their mutual advantage, abandoned Naples to the Spaniards and confirmed the French in possession of Milan. As a result, the years 1516 and 1517 saw peace reign throughout Europe. In the words of a chronicler, 'French, English, Spaniards, Germans, indeed all Christian peoples, traded peacefully together, which was a great blessing from God to his people.' But the truce proved to be the calm before a storm which was already brewing.

The Rivalry between François I and Charles V

European politics between 1519 and 1558 revolved around a single axis: the diplomatic and military struggle of France against Spain and the Empire.

Flushed with victory, François now set himself a new aim: nothing less than election to the crown of the Empire. Maximilian was not far short of 60, and everywhere sights were being set on the imperial succession. François I's rival was of course Charles V, four years his junior and the heir of innumerable lands, who considered the Empire virtually part of his patrimony. But the king's hopes rose even higher when, towards the end of 1516, Franz von Sickingen arrived at his Court, offering – for a price –

to further his imperial ambitions. The real powers attached to the title were, truth to tell, meagre enough, for the Empire was a motley conglomerate of cities, states, and episcopal principalities. But sovereignty over the Holy Roman Empire of the German Nation represented in theory the succession to Charlemagne and beyond him to the Caesars of ancient Rome, and thus conferred incomparable esteem. François went to work on the seven imperial Electors, and managed to gain the support of four, as well as of a host of imperial knights besides von Sickingen. But Maximilian was keen to protect the interests of his grandson Charles. At enormous expense he bought off four electors: the Archbishops of Mainz, Cologne and Trier, and the Duke of Brandenburg. When he died suddenly, on 12 January 1519, the intrigue rose to a new pitch of intensity. The French 'went in open-handed', as a chronicler puts it, showering gold and promises on all sides. Some electors, notably the Count Palatine of the Rhine, frankly offered their vote to the highest bidder. With the assistance of his aunt Margaret (Regent of the Netherlands), Charles V raised a huge loan from the Fuggers of Augsburg. Jean Jacquart estimated the price of Charles's successful campaign at 851 000 florins (about two tonnes of gold) – two thirds of it advanced by Jacob Fugger. François could dispose of only 400 000 *écus*, about 1.5 tonnes. But propaganda also played a part. François's Chancellor, Duprat, urged upon the Archbishop of Mainz (brother to another elector, the Duke of Brandenburg) the health, talents and fortune of his royal master, arguing that he was the only man in Europe capable of pushing back the Turks and holding the frontiers of Christendom. Charles made much of his Austrian ancestry and his desire to conserve Christian unity and advance its reform and expansion. The outcome was in doubt until the last moment. The electoral Diet convened at Frankfurt towards the end of June 1519, and the city then found itself blockaded by von Sickingen and a sizeable force of imperial knights. This show of force dispelled the scruples of those electors bought by François, and on 28 June, in the evening, the young King Charles I of Spain became Emperor Charles V. François heard the news on 3 July. He hardly flinched, but withdrew immediately to Fontainebleau and worked off his feelings in several days of furious hunting.

Although François had no choice but to swallow his humiliation at Frankfurt, he was not prepared to accept the hegemony of the Habsburg dynasty which Charles headed. Charles was of course heir to two of Europe's most powerful sovereigns. From his paternal grandfather Maximilian he obtained the Netherlands, Flanders, Artois, Franche-Comté, Austria and the Tyrol, a block of land of which much had come to the family as the dowry of his grandmother Mary of Burgundy, daughter of Duke Charles the Bold. On his mother's side, Charles received from his grand-father Ferdinand the kingdoms of Aragon, Castile, Sardinia, Sicily and Naples, together with the burgeoning transatlantic empire being carved out by Hernán Cortez and Francisco Pizarro in Mexico and Peru. Gold from the Americas was already beginning to pour into Spain along the sea-routes. One can easily understand the fears of encirclement which this vast Habsburg conglomerate aroused in French hearts. And one can almost say that for the next 40 years (for Henri II merely continued his father's policy), the struggle of France against the Habsburg block *was* the his-tory of Europe. This conflict between France and the Habsburgs sucked in England, Italy, Germany, and even the Turk. Its course determined the fate of the Italian states, of the Catholic Church, and of all Christendom with respect to the Turks.

This endemic rivalry erupted into open war five times between Charles's imperial election in 1519 and his abdication in 1556. Before the first broke out, both sides sought to win English sup-port. A personal meeting was arranged between François I and Henry VIII at the legendary Field of Cloth of Gold, just outside Calais, in June 1520. There, in a field beside the village of Guines, Henry VIII constructed a sort of instant city dominated by four huge and gaudy pavilions hung with rich tapestries. Feasting and jousting set the scene for the diplomatic encounters between the two monarchs and their chief ministers, Admiral Bonnivet and Cardinal Wolsey. Legend has it that Henry was nettled at being outshone by the flamboyance of his French counterpart, and was even more discomfited when, in an impromptu wrestling match one morning, the younger and fitter François threw him to the ground. But Jean Jacquart remarks quite correctly that, 'We should not see in these trivialities the roots of future conflict. Henry and Wolsey had made their choice before they even came to Guines – and it was for the battlefield, not the Field of Cloth of Gold.' A matter of days after the extravagant encounter at Guines, Henry proceeded to a meeting with Charles V at Gravelines. The old Anglo-Imperial entente came into play again, and they agreed to meet again to discuss their common interests. But the English king, even in leaning towards Charles, was cautious not to go too far too soon.

The First War against Charles V

Hostilities broke out in March 1521 in the form of skirmishes between feudal barons who, though still powerful, were being left behind by the march of history. Henri d'Albret marched south into Spanish Navarre, hoping to regain that lost portion of his scanty lands. To the north, Robert de La Marck, François I's childhood friend, offered his help against Charles (Robert held the principality of Bouillon, an imperial fief). François urged him to invade Luxembourg and lay siege to imperial strongholds there. But the Habsburgs easily brushed off these pinpricks. Spanish Navarre remained Spanish, and Habsburg forces counterattacked Bouillon, threatening Mézières. Bayard was pinned down there, and his small band of troops worked day and night to strengthen the fortifications, Bayard himself carrying sandbags.[5] Anne de Montmorency brought him valuable reinforcements. The siege began on 30 August, and the Habsburg army bombarded the city for four days without breaching the walls. They raised the siege on 26 September. The threat to French communications in Champagne was thus averted, and Bayard, the 'Loyal Servant', stood higher than ever in the ranks of French heroes. The real achievement of Bayard and Montmorency, however, was to win François time to gather an army in Champagne with which to move against Charles, who was based with his troops at Valenciennes. The two monarchs faced each other across the narrow channel of the Escaut, but as neither was willing to attack, the expected battle never took place. François did manage to take one or two strongholds in Artois, but in his turn was unable to prevent Charles taking Tournai.

This phoney war lasted almost a year, during which the background to the conflict changed. Charles, having extricated himself from some serious domestic problems in both Spain and Germany, set about reorganising the Empire. The Imperial Chamber was reestablished, and a Council of Regency was set up with his brother Ferdinand at its head. The alliance with England was sealed, and papal support was guaranteed by the election of Charles's former tutor as Pope Adrian VI. The Netherlands were entrusted to the capable hands of Charles's aunt, Margaret. François, in contrast, faced growing difficulties: not only the financial burden of recruiting and paying more and more soldiers, but also Constable Bourbon's drift into revenge and treachery. The picture was blackened still further by setbacks in Italy. Wearied of the demands of the French garrison, Milan rose in revolt, and the new governor, Lautrec, was driven out despite having with him the flower of the French army. Under pressure from his Swiss mercenaries, who were aggravated by the irregularity of their pay, Lautrec, an indifferent administrator though a competent general, moved against the Imperial forces based in the region of La Bicocca, a few miles north of Milan.[6] But this almost impregnable position was defended by Charles V's Italian commander-in-chief, the veteran mercenary Prospero Colonna. The Swiss hurled themselves against it on 27 April 1522, but were mown down by Colonna's artillery. They left the field with over 3000 dead. Lautrec, whose French and Venetian troops were as yet unscathed, hoped to mount another attack the next day. But the Swiss headed for home, and Lautrec was consequently forced to abandon Lodi and Cremona and thus most of Lombardy. When Genoa too fell to the Habsburgs, France was left with practically nothing in Italy.

Both sides remained in arms, and sought to undermine the other by various and devious means. Charles negotiated with the disaffected Constable, who announced his readiness to abandon François I's 'disordered and sensual regime'. For his part, François was making overtures to the dukes of Bouillon, Cleves, and Wurttemberg, as well as to some of the Electors and even to Suleiman the Magnificent away in the East.[7]

But François failed to seize the chances which, despite the defeat at La Bicocca, the European situation presented to him. He was obsessed with regaining lost ground in Italy. A fresh army was entrusted to the command of Admiral Bonnivet, who proved a terrible leader, preferring delay to attack. The badly paid Swiss were predictably uncooperative, the Venetians were turning against France, and worst of all, Charles de Bourbon had defected to the Imperial camp. After a series of minor defeats, Bonnivet retreated back across the Alps. It was during this withdrawal that Bayard was fatally wounded, on 30 April 1524, crossing the Sesia near Romagnano. The remnants of the French force limped back to the Dauphiné via the Mont Cenis pass. Milan was lost once again, and in the meantime France itself had been invaded.

Under the terms of a new alliance between Charles V and

Henry VIII, the latter was to invade France by way of Picardy while the 'traitor' Bourbon made himself master of the south-east. Charles himself, whose obsession with his Burgundian inheritance rivalled that of François with Italy, commissioned his brother Ferdinand to raise an army to invade Burgundy. The allies were well aware of François I's financial problems, and had agreed on how to carve up his kingdom. Henry was to receive the royal title, Charles was to have the duchy of Burgundy and its appurtenances, and a principality was to be carved out for Bourbon in Provence. Bourbon's invasion of the south-east went smoothly enough. He crossed the Var on 7 July 1524, and took Antibes, Grasse, Fréjus and Aix in quick succession. By August, he was at the gates of Marseille. But the citizens decided on resistance, and a siege commenced on 20 August. A force of some 3000 or 4000 men held off the besiegers while François marched his troops down the Rhône to Avignon. But the king did not yet dare come to their aid. The citizens repaired the damage to their walls as fast as Bourbon's artillery could inflict it until, on 22–3 September, a breach was opened. But Bourbon failed to deliver the dreaded assault, and instead withdrew with bags and baggage on 26 September. A great storm had supposedly damaged the morale of the besiegers . . . but the troops of François, camped not far away, doubtless had more to do with the withdrawal.

This was not the end of the affair for the French. The king did not look for a showdown with Bourbon because he wanted to keep his army fresh for the conquest of Lombardy on which his heart was still set. He crossed the Alps in October and went straight for Milan, from which the Imperialists scarcely had time to withdraw. But François then hung back, allowing his opponents to dig in at Pavia, whose citizens were bitter enemies of the French. A little way from Milan and not far from Lodi (the centre of the province), Pavia was a strategically placed city with excellently maintained walls and an almost impregnable citadel at its heart. A moat fed from the Ticino ran around the walls, and the Ticino itself, swollen with autumn rains, posed a formidable obstacle. Undoubtedly François ought to have followed the advice of Montmorency and La Trémoille and attacked Lodi, but instead he listened to Bonnivet and Alençon, and, on 27 October, laid siege to Pavia. His army settled down outside the city and imposed a blockade, but then 'wasted December and January in remarkable inactivity'. The force of nearly 30 000 infantry and cavalry, around which hovered the inevitable camp-followers: traders, victuallers, inn-keepers, prostitutes, and stragglers, endured the cold and the rain. Inside the city, food shortages and the pressures of the siege began to take their toll, while outside, the besiegers were suffering from boredom, erratic pay, and rampant disease, and the nobility were grumbling about the discomfort of their position. In short, morale was sinking.

Meanwhile, the imperial generals, Bourbon among them, were gathering a powerful force near Lodi, although its morale was also weakened by irregular pay: Charles V, like François, was running out of funds. But François, confident of superior numbers of men and guns, was not expecting a decisive confrontation, and in fact sent 3000 Swiss mercenaries home to the Grisons in order to save money (according to Blaise de Monluc, an eye-witness).[8] However, on 24 January the imperial force set out from Lodi, clashing with French scouts on 3 February. The two sides remained in uncomfortable proximity for almost a fortnight, engaged in frequent skirmishing. The imperial aim was to encircle the French with a flanking movement.

The great battle took place over 24–5 February, as the imperial forces went onto the attack. Abandoning his entrenched positions, François disposed his troops as if for a tournament, and himself stood at their head with his men-at-arms. Behind him stood the troops of Alençon and, a little further back, of La Palice. In his haste to give battle, François got between his own artillery and the enemy, and then advanced so fast that he lost touch with his infantry. He was cut off, his cavalry were cut down, and his infantry were thrown into disarray. The Swiss broke, and Alençon, it is said, fled the field. It was hand-to-hand fighting, and François, surrounded by his friends and his household guard, held out valiantly. He was almost trampled to death by the mob of soldiers competing for the privilege of capturing him. Completely isolated, he surrendered to Lannoy, the imperial commander – it is said that he would never have handed his sword to Bourbon. The battle was over by midday on 25 February. Between 6000 and 8000 French lay dead, as the imperialists had given no quarter. Rather than burden themselves with prisoners, they simply killed those unable to offer a good ransom. The list of fallen gentlemen was sensational, the list of the captured little less so. Nicolas Versoris, a citizen of Paris whose journal covers the period 1519–30, drew up his account sorrowfully: 'In short, all the flower of the chivalry of France was captured or slain, and if God in his grace, mercy, and goodness gives no remedy, it will mean the ruin and devastation of the realm.'[9] Defeat was a great shock, and the news was rapidly circulated by vicars, peddlars, traders and constables, spreading despair and panic in cottages and workshops across the land.

François himself, at first held in Pavia at the monastery of San Paolo, was taken to the fortress of Pizzighetonne, from which he wrote to his mother Louise a letter well-known for its sad words, 'of all things, nothing is left to me but honour and my life, which is safe'. In May 1525 he was moved again, to Madrid. Shut up in a high tower, he clung to the hope that Charles would agree to a chivalric combat, man to man. He refused categorically to purchase liberty at the cost of a province of France. Worn out by confinement, inactivity, and uncertainty, he fell seriously ill, so much so that Charles V came from Toledo to visit him and promised to bring his sister Marguerite to his bedside. François was the more anxious to go home in that events in France, as we shall see, had taken an unhappy turn. According to a secret report sent to Charles, 'the princes of France are divided, and the Parlement is at loggerheads with the Regent'.

For his part, Charles V could no longer rely on his allies. The plan to invade France came to nothing, and he was facing grave financial and social problems. Germany was convulsed with disorders consequent upon the spread of Lutheranism. So negotiations were opened with France. Burgundy rapidly became the chief bone of contention. According to the Habsburgs, its territory was 'the rightful patrimony of the house and line of the Emperor and head of the Order of the Golden Fleece'. But the idea of ceding a French province stuck in the throats of the French negotiators, the more so as they knew that the sovereign courts would never ratify such a treaty. Yet each side desperately needed a way out of the impasse. And so, on 14 January 1526 a treaty was signed by Jean de Selve (First President of the Parlement de Paris) on behalf of the French and by Gattinara on behalf of the Empire. Under its terms, François ceded Burgundy, renounced his claims in Italy, promised to marry Eleanor, the Emperor's sister, and undertook to restore Charles de Bourbon to his offices and lands. In addition, he was to break off his alliances with the papacy, Venice, and sundry small fry such as the Duke of Guelders and the houses of La Marck and d'Albret. Finally, he was to supply an army and a fleet for an imperial crusade against the Turks.

François knew perfectly well that he would not keep his promises, as indeed did Charles. But Charles sought to encourage compliance by exacting from him not only his word of honour but also his two sons as hostages. After the king's release, the treaty was to be ratified by François himself, the Estates General, the Estates of Burgundy, and the sovereign courts. If the provisions of the treaty had not been met within four months, François was honour bound to return to Madrid and captivity.

The Second War against Charles, 1527–9

Freed on 17 March 1526, François had absolutely no intention of ratifying this disastrous treaty. After a joyous reunion with his family and friends at Bayonne, he sat back to think things over. Lannoy, Charles V's observer at the French Court, reported to his master that the French king 'puts off fulfilling his obligations'.

François took comfort from the offers of alliances pouring in from all over Europe. The Emperor's power made everyone uneasy, and ambassadors spoke of his 'tyranny' and 'pride'. Almost despite itself, the French government was swiftly entangled in an anti-imperial alliance. May 1526 saw the conclusion of the League of Cognac, 'to put an end to the wars which are ravaging Christendom'. Its signatories included Pope Clement VII, Venice, and several Italian states, and Henry VIII was named as its patron. The representatives of Burgundy also came to Cognac, to protest their desire to remain French and to declare François I's undertaking at Madrid null and void – on the grounds that his coronation oath forbade him to alienate any part of his domain. Thus the minor and middling powers in effect pushed the two European superpowers back onto the battlefield.

Hostilities quickly resumed in Italy – too quickly for Henry VIII, who was still hanging back, and for François, who was slow to intervene. The Italian forces advanced slowly up the peninsula towards Milan, but were then obliged to withdraw in the face of Charles de Bourbon. At the head of a badly paid army of Lutheran mercenaries, he marched on Rome. The panic-stricken pope negotiated desperately with both his peninsular allies and the Emperor. But on 5 May 1527 Bourbon gave the order to attack. He himself received a fatal bullet-wound during the assault, but it was successful, and his troops subjected the city to an eight-day orgy of rape and pillage. While the city lay in ruins, Clement VII took refuge in the impregnable Castel Sant'Angelo, where he remained a virtual prisoner until December.

Meanwhile François and Charles were exchanging messages of mutual defiance. Charles called on François to fulfil his treaty obligations, while François replied that only one clause remained to be fulfilled – the payment of a ransom for his sons – as he could not be required to keep promises exacted under duress. Envoys shuttled back and forth between the two Courts as suggestions were even raised of settling matters by recourse to a duel or else to international arbitration. In the meantime, both sides pressed on with war preparations. François shrewdly invited an assembly of notables to give him counsel. It met at Paris in December 1527, and included representatives of all three estates, although it was dominated by princes, prelates and nobles. They responded positively to the king's calculatedly poignant appeals, offering finance for either paying the ransom or levying troops.

In fact, the war had already begun for France. Lautrec, the French commander-in-chief, had already returned to Italy and retaken Lombardy and, having reduced Genoa to obedience, was moving down the Adriatic coast via Rimini, Ancona and Pesaro, with a view to taking Naples, one of the few Italian cities still under imperial control. His army, enfeebled by disease, reached the city on 1 May 1528, but was too weak to seek victory through an immediate assault. Instead, it settled down to a siege – and was weakened still further as disease took an ever stronger hold. When Lautrec himself succumbed, the Marquis of Saluzzo took command and had little choice but to abandon the siege. Driven to take refuge in the fortress of Aversa, a few miles from Naples, he soon had to surrender to the Prince of Orange, commander of the imperial forces. Disaster followed disaster as, to the north, a relief force under the Count of Saint-Pol was intercepted and defeated at Landriano, and its leader taken prisoner. Martin du Bellay recorded in his *Mémoires* that 'of 25 000 infantry barely 4000 remained capable of bearing arms, and of 800 cavalry, barely 100'. When Lautrec's force had left France, it had numbered some 29 000 men; and the relief force under Saint-Pol another 10 000, not to mention those who crossed the Bay of Naples by ship only to perish from combat or disease on disembarking.

French failure made peace inevitable. And François was now facing serious domestic problems. The spread of Lutheranism was manifested in ugly incidents; poor harvests were leading to food shortages and inflated prices; and the fiscal burden was fomenting discontent among both nobility and commons. Charles, the victor, was hardly any better off. Besides similar religious problems, which he attempted to solve at the Diet of Speyer in 1529, he was threatened from the rear by Suleiman and the Turks. In 1526 Suleiman had overwhelmed Hungary at the battle of Mohacz, in which King Louis had lost his life. His death had led to rivalry for the succession to the crowns of Bohemia and Hungary, with Charles V's brother Ferdinand foremost in pursuit. But although the Turks were almost at the gates of Vienna, Ferdinand received little support from the German princes.

Negotiations for a new peace agreement were under way from late 1528, and the representatives of the two sovereigns – François I's mother, Louise of Savoy, and Charles V's aunt, Margaret of Savoy – met at Cambrai on 5 July 1529 to seal it. Henry VIII and the Italian states were unhappy with the outcome, but the treaty was duly signed on 3 August. The King of France was confirmed in possession of Burgundy and of various strongholds in the north (Péronne, Montdidier, the towns along the Somme, and the counties of Boulogne, Ponthieu, and Guines). But in return he gave up other border towns (Tournai, Hesdin, Lille, and Douai) and renounced his sovereignty over Charles V's counties of Flanders and Artois. In addition he handed over all his remaining strongholds in Lombardy and Naples, effectively abandoning his Italian dreams and deserting the League of Cognac. He undertook to restore the deceased Constable Charles of Bourbon in blood, and admit his heirs to their possessions. He promised to refrain from further attacks on Charles V and even provided men, money, and munitions for the Emperor's next peninsular campaign. And France was left to pick up both Charles V's and Henry VIII's debts, a sum estimated at 500 000 *écus* by Jean Jacquart, but more modestly at 290 000 by Henri Lemonnier. The ransom for François and his two sons was set at 2 million *écus* (some 7 tonnes of gold), of which 1.2 million was to be handed over in exchange for the freedom of the princes. Finally, François was to marry Eleanor, the Emperor's sister.

The Treaty of Cambrai (also known as the Ladies' Peace) marked a turning-point in French foreign policy. The kingdom had survived intact, barring the temporary loss of the county of Charolais, ceded to Charles for life, but the French pocket had a shock in the 1530s as the ransom was put together. Italy was no longer a focus for the dreams and hopes of rulers and nobles; and priority was henceforth given to the defence or consolidation of the vague and vulnerable northern frontier.

Ambassadors and Alliances, Warriors and Weapons

From 1530 to 1536 France enjoyed a period of peace. The first priority was to raise the famous ransom. This was done through levies of a tenth upon noble revenues and of four-tenths on clerical revenues (imposed with papal consent), besides further levies on towns and cities. Montmorency masterminded the operation, and in March 1530, accompanied by numerous State dignitaries, he brought the cash to Bayonne, where the Spaniards carefully counted it out. The actual exchange took place on a pontoon-bridge over the Bidassoa, between Hendaye and Fuenterrabía: 50 massive iron-bound wooden chests for 'Messieurs les Enfants', François and Henri. While the princes made their crossing, Eleanor crossed over in another boat in order to join her betrothed, whom she married a few days later near Mont-de-Marsan.

The early 1530s were the years of Montmorency's ascendancy. Honours were heaped upon him by the king and the king's mother, who had relied heavily on 'the first baron of France' in the negotiations at Cambrai. As Grand Master of the royal household and Governor of Languedoc, he was at the head of an aristocratic government which contrasted strongly with the councils of preceding years, dominated as they had been by commoners. However, neither François nor the peace-loving Montmorency could long keep out of the cauldron of European politics, which was now boiling over with religious passion. Germany was falling apart. In March 1531 the Lutheran states (including Electoral Saxony, Hesse, and Brunswick as well as 11 imperial cities) had combined at Schmalkalden to form a defensive league. Although not seeking a complete break with the Emperor, they opposed the religious policy he had pursued at the Diet of Augsburg, and they looked abroad, especially to France, for allies. The princes and electors had shown themselves distinctly unenthusiastic when Charles V had had his brother Ferdinand crowned King of the Romans, and thus designated as his successor, an act which went beyond the powers of the Imperial Diet. Moreover, the Turks were threatening both Austria and the western Mediterranean. Suleiman was advancing by both sea and land, and was deaf to all approaches, whether from the Emperor himself or from his brother, now King of Bohemia.

The French, meanwhile, were engaged in tireless diplomacy. Their agents were busy in Germany, England, Turkey, Italy, and even Switzerland. François employed bishops like Jean du Bellay (Bishop of Paris), cardinals, gentlemen, humanists like Lazare de Baïf, and members of the Parlement. From 1525 his ambassador to Charles V was Jean de Selve, initially First President of the Rouen Parlement, then of Bordeaux, and finally of Paris itself. Five of his sons followed in his diplomatic footsteps, serving the king in Switzerland, Turkey, Rome, Italy, Germany, and Spain. There were veritable ambassadorial dynasties: men were born to diplomacy. But the diplomats of the day faced enormous difficulties, greatest among them that of keeping in contact with their own governments. Travelling by road was slow, travelling by sea perilous. So they often had to take decisions in complete ignorance of political changes in the Courts and councils back home. They were paid poorly and irregularly, for such duties were generally entrusted to men who possessed some lucrative administrative office or ecclesiastical benefice. And they were usually minor cogs in the machinery of State. Their fate was often little better then that of the spies who were despatched in huge numbers to foreign countries – if taken, certainly disowned by their masters and probably executed by their captors, only the fortunate few returning home.

In the years 1534–5, French diplomacy took on for the first time a distinctive and innovative character. Admittedly, policy towards Germany remained indecisive and relatively fluid, as the king sought to undermine the Emperor by cultivating both the Schmalkaldic League and such Catholic princes as were jealous of Habsburg supremacy. But France broke new ground when the French ambassador to Constantinople, La Forest, concluded with Suleiman the famous treaty over which so much ink has subsequently been spilt. All that was committed to writing was a trading agreement, but there was also a verbal agreement on political and military cooperation, an implicit recognition of their shared hostility to Charles V. The Turkish alliance in effect made the French masters of western contact with the Near East.

War was once more looming between François and Charles.

Despite their talk of peace (Charles asked François to suspend his understanding with the Turks to allow him to attack Barbarossa's stronghold of Tunis in June 1535), 'events were nevertheless tending inexorably towards a resumption of hostilities'. At the French Court there was clear evidence for this in Montmorency's gradual fall from power. The Constable's generally pacific inclinations and particular desire for a lasting peace with the Empire were well known. Under the leadership of Admiral Chabot, a party was active around the king in promoting intervention in Germany. Chabot was a close friend (too close, some said) of the Duchesse d'Étampes, herself a companion of the king's youth. In 1535 he emerged at Court as a major player, displacing Montmorency in control of relations with Germany and Italy, while Marguerite de Navarre and the Du Bellay clan, easy-going in matters of religion, were heart and soul in the campaign for an open break with Charles V. The Constable, in contrast, was suspected of imperialist sympathies (or so the rumour ran), and in mid-1535 he withdrew from Court, though without losing the king's affection.

The exigencies of protracted war had combined with a stream of royal legislation and a number of technical innovations to produce considerable changes in France's armed forces in the early sixteenth century. The old feudal levy ('ban-et-arrière-ban') was henceforth used only to provide a reserve force within the kingdom. Regular soldiers, whether recruited from nobles or commons, at home or abroad, now served for a wage from the royal treasury. The introduction of significant bodies of infantry into the royal army was a major innovation. Over a number of campaigns it became as important as the cavalry, acquiring noble status as royal ordinances, edicts, and mandates treated it on the same terms as the cavalry. In time even the nobility lost their disdain for service in such a lowly capacity. Even under Louis XII, the great Bayard accepted command of a company of foot. And by 1536 Monluc was expressing his preference for the infantry: 'Having given careful consideration to both infantry and cavalry, I concluded that I would go further in the infantry.' But by no means all gentlemen shared his views, even though military developments – above all the increasing use of artillery – were rapidly superannuating their chivalric notions.

The French infantry continued to use the pike just as their Swiss and German counterparts still used the halberd. But the preferred weapon was above all the firearm. The arauebus or 'hackbut' was still, at the end of the fifteenth century, regarded as a diabolical instrument whose ability to slay unseen and at a distance was repugnant to military honour. Even so, it remained the principal firearm until the Wars of Religion, which saw the emergence of the musket. The arquebus was a cumbersome weapon, over a yard long, with a range of 200 yards at best. Useless in the rain, and risky to use at any time, it was nevertheless the latest thing in infantry armament. And at this time infantry did not generally wear the colours or insignia used by the men-at-arms of the ordinance companies.

The ordinance companies, or 'men-at-arms of our ordinances', who numbered several thousand men during the Italian Wars and the campaigns against the Empire, were the backbone of the army. The effective strength of these companies, originally established by Charles VII, was set at 100 'lances'. A 'lance' was in fact a small unit of six horsemen whose chief (the 'gendarme' or 'man-at-arms') was further assisted by three archers, a valet, and a page. Under François the three archers were reduced to two, and the company strength itself was cut to about 50 lances – only the highest noblemen were set at the head of 100 lances. The man-at-arms, like his horse, was encased in a steel shell which tended to get heavier as time went on and firearms improved. He tottered under the weight of helmet, breastplate, cuisses, greaves, gauntlets, and other assorted ironmongery. His main weapon was the lance, although in the later sixteenth century companies came to include arquebusiers and pistoleers. The archers were more lightly armed, wearing a corselet of chainmail, a helmet or even a morion without a visor, and fighting by turns with bow, crossbow, or lance.

The light cavalry set up by Louis XII in 1498 were intended for raiding or scouting operations. Under François I some of them used arquebuses, and these mounted gunmen, known as 'argoulets' (as in the time of Charles VI), used to dismount for combat. From the Italian Wars to the mid-sixteenth century, each ordinance company included 50 mounted arquebusiers. But under Henri II the light horse were reorganised by Marshal Brissac as a separate arm, the dragoons – a concept with a great future.

Each member of the ordinance companies was obliged under the regulations of 1515, 1533 and 1549 to wear a tunic or coat in his captain's colours with the captain's emblem or device on the back. The 200 Gentlemen of the King's Household, the Scots

Guard, the French archers and the 100 Swiss formed the king's personal troop. They all carried halberd and side-swords, and had different summer and winter uniforms in colours which changed with each new reign.

A new kind of military body was established by an edict of 24 July 1534, which provided for the recruitment on a provincial basis of seven infantry 'legions' of 6000 men each. Of the 42 000 troops, 12 000 were to be arquebusiers, a sign of the growing importance of firearms. In order to foster an *esprit de corps*, the officers, from the captains down to the sergeants, were to be natives of the legion's home province. The King's Council attached great importance to this, prescribing the death penalty for any soldier who transferred from one unit to another. Each legionary was to take an oath to 'serve the king loyally and well against all foes'. These new model soldiers – veteran infantry, arquebusiers, halberdiers and pikemen – were loaded with privileges. 'Officers and ranks will be wholly exempt from the *taille* and other taxes' up to 20 *sous*. They received a wage, graded by rank, which was doubled on active service. Moreover, any soldier might through valour rise from the ranks as far as the level of lieutenant 'as posts fall vacant'. Bravery in action was to be rewarded, in the Roman style, with a gold ring.

For their part, these elite troops were to set an example to the rest of the soldiery. Their conduct towards civilians, towns and churches was to be above reproach. This was clearly a response to the myriad complaints arising out of the misdemeanours of soldiers, the bane of city and country dwellers alike. The Protestant commanders of the next generation, Condé, Coligny, and La Noue, were equally concerned about the behaviour of their troops. Each legion therefore had a provost and four sergeants to execute justice and inflict due punishment, up to and including death by hanging, on those guilty of robbery, rape, pillage, blasphemy, brawling, mutiny, gambling etc. The whole enterprise was in effect a national army built up on the basis of the province – the widest horizon of most sixteenth-century Frenchmen – with the uniforms varying according to the provinces from which the legions were drawn. This project, inspired partly by classical Roman models and partly by the contemporary Spanish *tercios*, was indeed implemented: by 1535, six legions were on a war footing.

Jean Jacquart maintains that the establishment of the legions, with their automatic ennoblement for any common soldier who rose through the ranks, aroused an aristocratic hostility which soon halted this first move in the direction of a national standing army. And one must concede that the legions did not have a glittering future: they did not survive beyond Henri II's death. But many gentlemen served in the légions as colonels and captains. Antoine de Rochechouart was given command of the Languedoc legion in 1534, while in 1542 Montgomery, sire des Lorges, was colonel of the legions throughout the fourth war against Charles V. And in 1559 Symphorien de Durfort sire de Duras, was in command of the Guyenne legion.

But not even all these troops were enough. The kings had in addition to call upon foreign mercenaries, be they German, Italian or Swiss. The numbers involved are difficult to estimate, because they tended to be recruited from jurisdictions prone to political disorder. According to Ferdinand Lot, the armies which were put into the field during the 20 or so years of conflict rarely exceeded 50 000 men, and this peak was reached only when it was a case of defending the homeland, as in 1536–7, 1544 and 1558. French and foreign infantry together always made up the vast bulk of these forces, with cavalry amounting to at best 10 per cent of the total.

During the reigns of François I and Henri II, salaried troops were numerous, and weighed heavily on the royal budget. We shall return to this point, but for now we will concentrate on the main aspects of military administration – command, supply, and pay. Supreme command lay with the king himself, and after him with the Constable. The Constableship, vacant from 1488 to 1515, was filled upon François I's accession by Charles de Bourbon, who, however, lost it because of his treason in 1523. It was not until 1538 that the office was once more filled, this time by Anne de Montmorency, who retained it until his death in 1567. In practice, the king and the Constable shared command with the Marshals of France, who usually numbered two or three. The post of Marshal was a Crown office, and the baton of rank was granted by royal favour as a reward for outstanding service. The Marshals enjoyed a status comparable to that of the Duke-Peers of France, and, like them, were addressed by the king as 'cousin'. Their formal responsibility was the maintenance of military discipline in war and peace alike, which involved making regular tours of inspection to the area entrusted to them. They were assisted by the Provost-Marshals, but the latter in fact took over their police duties during the sixteenth century, forming the separate institution of the marshalcy.

Commanders in the field bore the title of Lieutenant-General, and were assisted by permanent Field-Marshals assigned to each army for the duration of a campaign. It was the Field-Marshals who constituted the real general staff, for it was their job to pitch or strike camp and to draw up a plan of battle, tasks which required military expertise. These officers gave the orders to the Captains, who in turn exercised direct and complete power over the companies of troops. It was the Captains who, by royal warrant, actually recruited troops. A Captain-General or, more frequently, a Colonel-General on the German model, was a Captain picked out from his colleagues to preside over a group of companies or a special unit (the French companies, a legion, the Picard companies, etc.). Captains and Colonels disposed at pleasure of all subordinate commands within their units, appointing lieutenants, ensigns, 'guidons' (standard-bearers) among the cavalry, sergeants, squadron leaders, etc. From the beginning of François I's reign, officer training was carried out at Court by a body called the *petite écurie* ('little stable'), which comprised a number of pages intent upon a military career. Under Henri II the school of Tournelles, with the Grand Squire of the Court at its head, numbered almost 100 pages ambitious for military preferment.

The Captains were the crucial links in the pay chain, for it was to them that the wages due to their men were handed over every quarter. First, commissioners-of-war or *contrôleurs* reviewed the assembled company, counted its strength, and calculated the amount due. Then the cash was handed over by agents either of the *Trésorier de l'Ordinaire des guerres* (for the ordinance companies and Household troops) or of the *Trésorier de l'Extraordinaire des guerres* (for the commisariat, infantry, and light horse). From 1534 these agents became accredited officials, responsible for paying the cavalry, the light horse, and the infantry. Henri II created 100 of these posts in 1553.

Garrison troops were drawn from the ordinance companies, and so the numerous laws which sought to moderate the excesses inflicted upon the civil population encompassed only these men-at-arms, who came mostly from the gentry. When billeted with householders, these troops were in theory forbidden to demand anything without payment. In fact, as a series of ordinances and edicts testifies, soldiers treated their hosts so badly that harbouring troops seemed to most townsfolk the ultimate calamity. By an ordinance of November 1549, Henri II introduced a new permanent levy on towns (a supplement to the *taille*, later named the *taillon*), intended to supplement soldiers' pay and limit their exactions in kind. In fact this measure, typical of a regime in desperate financial straits, curbed neither civilian resentment nor the demands of the soldiers. Civilian grievances about soldiers flooded in to bailiffs, provincial estates, ministers, and the king himself until the reign of Louis XIV.

As a result of the belligerent policies of François I and his son, the army occupied an enormous place in national and governmental concerns. Indeed one could say that domestic policy was driven largely by the need to raise, equip and finance troops. And thus the roots of administrative centralisation were laid down between 1515 and 1559.

The Third War against Charles V, 1536–8

The European tension which underlay the tension between France and the Empire increased throughout 1535, to such an extent that the hawks on the Council, led by Chabot, managed to squeeze out Montmorency. There were plenty of incidents likely to ignite the latent hostility. A secret agent in the king's service, Maraviglia by name, had been captured in Milan by Duke Francesco Sforza and executed for spying in July 1533. François still yearned to reconquer Italy, which, quite apart from his hopes and dreams, also seemed to him the best ground on which to challenge the Emperor. His agents in Italy were busy once more, renewing links with Venice, approaching leading mercenaries like Fregoso and Orsini, supporting the claims of the petty Marquis of Saluzzo, and protecting the equally insignificant Marquis of Monaco. Charles V, in an effort to draw back from war, sent a special envoy to François in 1534. The Count of Nassau was commissioned to forge a compromise. But François demanded Genoa, Asti and Milan, his only concession a readiness to wait until Sforza's death before taking possession of the duchy. As François was well aware, this was completely unacceptable, and became even more so when Sforza indeed died the following year.

As a prelude to the long-awaited confrontation, the French launched a surprise attack on Savoy and Piedmont in February

1536. Although these were not imperial territories, their sovereign, Duke Charles II, looked to the Habsburgs for protection. Charles V was enraged as he saw the collapse of his own hopes for concerted European action against the Turk, and he declared war on 2 June 1536. The situation soon became extremely serious for France. Imperial forces crossed the Somme in July, to threaten Paris, while Piedmont and Provence were also invaded. A Spanish army crossed the Pyrenees and came as far as Narbonne, attempting to rendezvous with the troops that had invaded from Italy or landed in Provence. As invasion threats mounted from the north, south, and south-east in the summer months, Montmorency was recalled (on 14 July) as Lieutenant-General. He took command in Provence and the Alps while Cardinal du Bellay organised resistance along the Somme. With few enough troops to defend such a large area, Montmorency based himself at Avignon and, in an attempt to starve out the invaders, adopted a scorched-earth policy, burning the crops and the villages. Only the orchards and vineyards were spared, in the hope that a surfeit of fruit would spread dysentery among the invaders![10] The Emperor abandoned the camp he had pitched before Aix and led the remnant of his army, starving and riddled with disease, back to Italy. In the north, imperial forces under the Count of Nassau were driven back at the cost of enormous efforts and of heavy taxation in Paris.

Hostilities were resumed in 1537 after François I, almost incoherent with rage, solemnly stripped the Emperor of his French fiefs (Flanders, Artois, and the Charolais) at a *Chambre des pairs* held in January. Fresh troops were levied, including about 17 000 *landsknechts*. But time was running out. Thérouanne, the key to the northern front, was soon under siege, although the French retook a number of minor strongholds, such as Saint-Pol and Villers. A truce signed on 31 July restored the uneasy *status quo* along the Somme frontier.

The French high command, swayed by the king, was now free to turn its attention to a new campaign in Italy. Command in the field was entrusted to the Grand Master, Montmorency, who, in October 1537, accompanied by the Dauphin, assembled his forces near Briançon. Piedmont was soon retaken and occupied by a substantial French army, as many as 40 000 infantry with 1400 lances (about 4200 cavalry), further light cavalry led by Fregoso, and 40 cannon. This force might have achieved great things, but the negotiations between king and Emperor which had opened the previous year were now coming to fruition. As Henri Lemonnier shrewdly remarks, 'Once again we see – not for the last time – that the two sovereigns who were unable to coexist peacefully were equally unable to bring matters to a decisive confrontation.'

After the usual round of to-ing and fro-ing, shilly-shallying and hesitation, the truce, negotiated at Nice under papal auspices, was signed on 14 July 1538. The two sovereigns met and embraced with every outward sign of friendship, even sharing the same bedchamber. But they were each fudging certain issues, notably that of Lombardy. The Emperor, it is true, was boxed in by problems – the religious situation of Germany, divided between Protestant and Catholic princes, the sheer extent of his domains, the ever-present Turkish threat, and a certain personal weariness with life. François, for his part, heart-broken by the death of his elder son on 10 August 1536, prey to insoluble financial problems caused chiefly by the need to pay troops, and concerned about the spread of brigandage in the heart of his realm and the devastation of the invaded territories in the north and the south, had no choice but to make peace with Charles. But the rapprochement went down badly with his allies, especially the English, who nearly broke off diplomatic relations. The German Lutherans felt let down, as did the Sultan, for whom François was henceforth untrustworthy.

So the two adversaries made up, and their entente was sealed by Charles V's journey through France. He was welcomed at Paris in January 1539 by extravagant festivities in which the two monarchs themselves were prevented by ill-health from taking a prominent part. Nobody mentioned Milan; indeed, nothing at all was discussed. The Emperor was crossing France in order to get to the Netherlands without risk at the very moment when the people of Ghent, in rebellion against the excessive fiscal demands and high-handed policies of Charles's regime, made a desperate appeal to François I. He had laid claim to the sovereignty of Flanders in a *lit de justice* on 15 January 1537 (when he had stripped Charles of his French fiefs), but now made no reply to the rebels. Jean Jacquart observes that 'in the eyes of the king, a man obsessed with his own authority, the people of Ghent were nothing but subjects who had rebelled against their lawful sovereign... commoners who could and should be brought to their knees'. Undoubtedly one should add in the king's defence that, weakened by illness, he was focusing his available energies on Milan. Consequently, every effort was taken to keep Charles sweet. After his sightseeing

tour through France, Charles went straight on to Ghent to preside over the execution of justice.

The Fourth War against Charles V

At the French Court, intrigue and faction were rampant. Every
person of royal blood or high rank stood at the heart of a little
knot of followers. François was ever more debilitated, perhaps by
the syphilis whose symptoms figure in the chronicles, perhaps by
abcesses, or else by a form of tuberculosis which ran in his family. He was clearly losing his grip. The Court was thick with political alternatives. The faction around the Duchesse d'Étampes
was of considerable political weight. She herself, born Anne de
Pisseleu, was the wife of Jean de Brosse, Count of Penthièvre, but
remained the king's official mistress until the end. She, her husband, and her family were showered with bishoprics, state offices,
church benefices, and Court pensions. A bitter enemy of
Montmorency, she turned her royal lover's mind against him.

Henri, aged 22 in 1540, had been Dauphin since the death of
his elder brother in 1536, and was a magnet to the ambitious
and the discontented. Married to Catherine de Medici since 1533,
he was a stubborn and wholly conventional type. His hardline
Catholic following included Montmorency (who had been made
Constable in 1538 after his successful defence of Provence), the
Chancellor Poyet, and Diane de Poitiers. Montmorency had been
in effect chief minister until 1541, with none to act as counterweight to his power. But his star fell as the European situation
deteriorated. The Constable remained unenthusiastic about war
with Germany. He was willing to make war when necessary, but
was always ready to negotiate with the Emperor, who for him was
still the defender of Christendom and Catholicism, even if his
troops had sacked Rome. In order to persuade Charles V to ratify
the agreement made at Nice and Aigues-Mortes, he avoided pressing
the issues of the restoration of Milan to France and its promised
cession to Charles d'Orléans, François I's third son. When in 1540
Charles made over the duchy to his own eldest son, Philip, the
Constable's fate was sealed. He languished in disgrace until Henri's
accession. There existed, then, at the heart of government a split
between proponents of a relative religious tolerance at home
combined with an aggressive policy towards the Emperor, and a

Catholic party which preferred a rapprochement with the Emperor as a bulwark against heresy.

But war was inevitable, for the recovery of Milan continued to obsess the ailing François. The assassination in 1541 of two French agents at Casale Monferrato near Milan provided a suitable *casus belli*, although it was not clear whether the hand behind it was Charles V's or that of his friend the governor. Hostilities commenced in 1541 and 1542 around Perpignan, but with lamentable results. There was some success, however, in the north-east as Landrecies and Luxembourg fell into French hands.

The campaign of 1544 took place in part in Italy, under the command of François de Bourbon, Count of Enghien. A confused and indecisive battle at Ceresole on 13 July 1544 was greeted as a victory by a kingdom starved of military glory since the distant days of Marignano. It did open the way to Milan, but Enghien was unable to press home his advantage. François I, 'despite his obsession with Milan', could not provide him with the reinforcements and money he required, as France was being invaded from the north by Charles V and Henry VIII. Moreover, the Italian commander Piero Strozzi, who was in French service, had suffered a serious defeat shortly before, in June, not far from Novi. The order went out for Strozzi's Italians and Enghien's French troops to return to the defence of France. With heavy hearts the troops and staff withdrew, bitterly lamenting their missed opportunity.

The great invasion, meticulously planned by Charles V and Mary of Hungary (his Regent in the Netherlands) was under way. Their huge army, comprising some 40 000 foot and 10 000 horse, assembled near Metz and advanced through Lorraine towards Paris, intending to rendezvous with the forces of Henry VIII coming from Calais. Commercy and Ligny soon fell, though Saint-Dizier offered some resistance. On 24 July Charles took Vitry-en-Perthois, and, if the chronicle is to be believed, razed it to the ground. He then occupied Épernay and Château-Thierry, close to Paris. In the meantime, a French force of 30 000 infantry and 8000 cavalry was being put together. François I, exhausted and bed-ridden, entrusted its command to the Dauphin Henri, assisted by his friends Brissac and Saint-André and by the newly returned Enghien. But Henri was denied the decisive battle he sought because the Emperor shied away from it. His army was breaking up for lack of pay, and the imperial soldiery, complaining of hunger in land so devastated that it could not support them, were on the verge of mutiny. Moreover, his English ally was dragging his feet, lingering over the siege of Boulogne. On the French side, the government had to take account of the prevailing panic in Paris (now less than 20 leagues from the German army), the weakness of the country, and the political pressure from the peace party led by the Duchesse d'Étampes. So, thanks to the good offices of the king's wife Eleanor (the Emperor's sister), negotiations commenced. Admiral d'Annebaut met Charles V at Soissons, and a treaty was signed on 18 September at Crépy-en-Artois, near Laon. Once again a diplomatic rapprochement was sealed by a marriage agreement, this time between Charles d'Orléans and a daughter of either the Emperor himself or his brother Ferdinand – either way with a handsome dowry. As usual, François was liberal in promises of duchies to his son. The heart of the treaty, though, was a mutual renunciation of territorial claims, François abandoning Piedmont and Savoy, and the Emperor, Burgundy. There was also the usual agreement to fight the Turk.

That still left England in possession of Calais and Boulogne, and 1545 saw a campaign on three fronts, with a raid on Dover, military intervention in Scotland to support Mary Queen of Scots, and an assault on Boulogne. All three operations came to nothing, and in 1546 France agreed to the equally disastrous peace of Ardres. The greedy Henry VIII demanded nearly 2 million *livres* over eight years, and would not hand over Boulogne until it was all paid. But for once there was a stroke of luck. Henry died in 1547, leaving the young Edward VI under the protection of his uncle, the Duke of Somerset. Henri II, now King of France, struck a new deal and regained Boulogne for 400 000 *écus* (little more than 1 million *livres*). And in 1558 François de Guise recaptured Calais, the last English outpost in France.

From 1544 to 1547 peace prevailed between the rival powers, though not without tensions and underhand blows. Charles V had still not resolved the delicate question of whether to give the hand of a daughter or a niece to Charles d'Orléans, when that youth died of the plague in September 1545. For his part, François, ever more haggard and diseased, delayed handing over Savoy. Taking advantage of the emerging confrontation between the Emperor and the Lutheran Schmalkaldic League, François held talks with the Protestant princes and cities, offering military aid against Charles. He mended fences with the papacy and Venice, and, by means of the ambassador Odet de Selve, offered a new defensive alliance to the Council of Edward VI. The stage was apparently set for yet another episode of the unending saga of the Habsburg–Valois conflict, with war on everyone's lips, when François I died, aged 53, on 31 March 1547.

Henri II and the Final Struggle

For a while Henri II kept the armed peace established by his father. His reign had opened to the accompaniment of a huge rising in the south-west over increases in the *gabelle*. French intervention in Scotland during 1547–8 was watched closely by the Emperor from his ringside seat in Brussels. The issue was the young Queen of Scots, in whose name her mother, Mary of Guise, ruled as Regent. Under pressure from the threat of England abroad and the rise of Protestantism at home, she looked to Henri for assistance. Her Guise relatives (she was the sister of Duke François) were vocal in her support. François d'Aumale (another brother) landed in Scotland with 6000 men in June 1548. The rumour was that he would take the young Mary to safety in France. With the Emperor remaining strictly neutral, Protector Somerset, short of money and men, agreed terms, and in March 1550 signed a treaty which surrendered Boulogne and saved France some 400 000 *écus* (about 1 million *livres*).

Although the kingdom enjoyed a brief respite from war, tension between France and the Habsburgs remained high. Following precedent, Henri sought foreign allies. But the 1550 settlement with England was soon to be overturned by the accession in 1553 of Henry VIII's passionately Catholic daughter Mary, who married Charles V's son Philip in 1554. In effect, England was a Habsburg territory until her death. Moreover, François I's bold alliance with the Sultan was unravelling. The Turks had lost confidence in the French, and concentrated their efforts on the southern frontiers of the Empire. Relations with the Protestant princes of Germany were kept up, but not without vicissitudes. In January 1552 the representatives of Mecklenburg, Saxony, Strasbourg and Nuremberg allied with France in the Treaty of Chambord. In part it was to combat 'the beastly servitude to which the Emperor strives to reduce their fatherland', but there were also secret clauses about Henri's candidacy for the imperial succession. For his part, Henri undertook to provide 240 000 *écus* and prompt military assistance to defend 'German liberties'. However, this axis was first disturbed by the annulment of the Augsburg Interim at Passau in October 1552, and then destroyed by the Peace of Augsburg in 1555.

But in compensation a new ally came on the scene in the shape of the new pope, Paul IV, a scion of the Neapolitan house of Caraffa and, like many Neapolitans, bitterly hostile to Spain. No sooner was he upon the See of Peter than, in June 1556, he despatched his nephew (newly made cardinal) to the French Court. He dangled before Henri the prospect of the duchy of Milan for his second son, Charles, and won to the cause of French intervention on the peninsula not only the king himself but also the Guises, the none the less peace-loving Constable Montmorency, and even the almost Protestant Gaspard de Coligny.

But despite a momentary consensus over French intervention in support of a papacy fearful of an imperial threat, Henri's government was factionally divided. As Lucien Romier has shown, there was a schism at the heart of the royal council between the dove Montmorency and the Guise hawks. The wars which dominated Henri's reign, a period crucial for the internal balance of the kingdom, left the frequently victorious Guises on top, while the often defeated Montmorency sank down. But it was not just for reasons of personal prestige that Henri II's favourite urged peace. He undoubtedly set the public interest much higher than was usual at that time.

Despite Montmorency's misgivings, hostilities were resumed in spring 1552, as both Henri and the Emperor intended. French strategy was once more to advance on two fronts, towards the north-east and towards Italy. The Rhineland campaign was under the overall command of Montmorency, with François de Guise given special responsibility for operations in Lorraine. Some rapid advances led to the easy conquest of the three bishoprics (Metz, Toul and Verdun). But this was followed by a fruitless thrust into Germany which became a withdrawal after 15 May, when France found herself isolated as the Protestant princes opened negotiations with Charles V. The German venture brought no further gain to Henri, although the three imperial cities he acquired have been accorded great importance in traditional French historiography. The Emperor refused to accept this setback, and sent a huge army under the Duke of Alba to retake Metz. But Guise led heroic resistance for nearly three months, and on 26 December the imperial forces, worn down by hardship, disease, rain and cold, raised the siege. Unlike Guise, the Constable came out of the campaign badly, though it is not clear whether this was because he was poorly motivated to lead an enterprise of which he disapproved, because he was simply not up to it, or because he was too frightened to expose the king's huge army to risk. In May 1553, when campaigning was resumed, he betook himself to the north-west, where Charles V was advancing on Thérouanne, a French thorn in the flesh of the Habsburg Netherlands. Yet despite its excellent fortifications and the spirited resistance of its garrison, it capitulated on 20 June, to be followed on 17 July by the castle of Hesdin. Both were promptly razed to the ground.

In spring 1554 a new French offensive was aimed at Brussels, where Charles V was residing. An army of 40 000 foot and 12 000 horse set about capturing Dinant. But, when the town had fallen and been looted, an imperial counter-force took the field under the command of the brilliant Emmanuel Philibert of Savoy. Montmorency, indecisive as ever, withdrew towards the north-west and the Calais region, finally settling to lay siege to Renty. Charles V's troops failed to relieve the town and incurred heavy losses, but Montmorency failed to press home his advantage, and instead relaxed his grip on the town and led his forces off towards Compiègne. If he had any strategy at all, it was certainly not appreciated by the French, who saw him as a craven coward.

On the Italian front, operations were entrusted to an ally of the Guises, Charles de Cossé, Count of Brissac. He sought to consolidate the French hold on Turin by taking Vercelli in 1553 and Ivrea and Casale in 1554. But the main action unfolded in Tuscany, where the political exiles from Florence and other Italian cities, the 'fuorisciti', supporters of French intervention in central Italy, had their eyes on Siena. The Sienese had driven out the Spanish garrison in 1552 at the instigation of Henri II's agents. When Piero Strozzi, the mastermind of the liberation, called upon France for aid, Blaise de Monluc undertook the welcome task of returning to the peninsula. An imperial force under the Marquis of Marignano besieged the rebel city, but Monluc defended it vigorously (as he tells us at length in his *Commentaires*). The siege dragged on for over a year, from January 1554 to April 1555, and in the end it was sheer hunger that overcame Sienese resistance. On 17 April the French troops were allowed to leave with military honours.

All this while, the driving force had been the personality of Charles V. But he, worn out and ill, and disturbed by the divisions in Germany, agreed in October 1555 to the Peace of Augsburg, which brought the wars between German Lutherans and Catholics to a provisional conclusion. A few days later he abdicated, making over the Netherlands and Spain (with its overseas possessions) to his son Philip II, and leaving the Habsburg patrimony in the Empire to his brother Ferdinand. Peace between the Valois and the Habsburgs soon followed. Under the five-year truce of Vaucelles (15 February 1556), France retained her gains in Piedmont, the three bishoprics, and Corsica, without having to break off any alliances.

But it was not long before Henri, egged on by Pope Paul IV, renounced the truce. The Papal States were promptly invaded by the Duke of Alba (Viceroy of Naples), and France was once more drawn into the Italian arena. The campaign was led by François de Guise, who effected a rendezvous with Brissac in Piedmont and then marched south in May 1557 with the aim of conquering Naples for the king's second son (or, if Lucien Romier is right, for himself). But the operation miscarried as, in August, Guise was recalled by the king to save the realm after the disaster of Saint-Quentin.

Aware of Guise's departure, Philip II had decided to force the pace. First he persuaded his wife, Mary Tudor, to declare war on France, which she did on 7 June 1557. Then he put Emmanuel Philibert at the head of 'the most powerful army of the century' – a force of some 10–12 000 horse and 35–40 000 infantry, which appeared suddenly before the walls of Saint-Quentin on 2 August 1557. This town of some 7–8000 inhabitants was the key to northern France. It received some limited assistance from Coligny, who succeeded in sneaking a small force inside the walls before the siege began in earnest. He set about organising the defence in anticipation of the arrival of the royal army under the Constable. Montmorency took up position to the south of the town while the Spanish concentrated their attack on the north and east. On 10 August he tried to get reinforcements inside, but the operation was so ineptly executed that the enemy were able to trap the advancing French with a flanking movement and slaughter them almost methodically. It was an even greater disaster than Pavia: 3000 dead, 4–5000 wounded and 6000 prisoners. Panic seized government and kingdom alike, and the damage to morale compounded the material impact of defeat. 'I reckoned the kingdom lost', wrote Blaise de Monluc. The French army was virtually leaderless, for among the prisoners were the Constable himself, his four sons, the Count of La Rochefoucauld, Charles de Bourbon, and the Marshal Saint-André. Coligny kept up his heroic resistance inside Saint-Quentin until 27 August, when the Spaniards finally broke through to wreak indescribable carnage. But Philip II's army, which on any sensible plan would have marched on Paris, hung around to pick off minor strongholds like Ham and Le Catelet. And it soon hit severe problems with both supplies and money, which obliged Emmanuel Philibert to disband his forces in November.

Thus it was that when François de Guise reached France at the beginning of October he found the kingdom still free and the enemy less than aggressive, despite the captivity of the leading French generals. The kingdom was taxed heavily in order to levy Swiss and German mercenaries, and Guise, appointed Lieutenant-General, prepared his brilliant counter-stroke to the disaster of Saint-Quentin. In the depth of winter he first occupied Guines and then, on 8 January 1558, took Calais. In the flush of victory he led his forces on to Thionville in the spring, and the town surrendered on 22 June. But the Spanish, under Count Egmont, broke through on the Somme to defeat Marshal de Termes at Gravelines in July and thus threaten Paris anew. Guise at once proceeded to neutralise this threat by establishing a base at Pierrepoint where, from 28 July, he concentrated a force of nearly 50 000 men. This huge effort was an adequate deterrent, as both sides were exhausted. Talks commenced in September through Montmorency and Saint-André (both still prisoners). In early October considerable progress was made at Cercamp, and a truce was signed on 17 September. When the English arrived a few days later, all sides were represented at the negotiation table.

The final treaty of 2–3 April 1559 bears the name of Cateau-Cambrésis because the crowd of diplomats preferred that place to Cercamp. Five months of hectic negotiations with Montmorency, Saint-André and the Cardinal of Lorraine on one side, and Alba, William of Nassau and Cardinal Granvelle on the other, came down to two main points:

(i) Marriages. As usual, dynastic marriages were a crucial element in international diplomacy. The recent death of Mary Tudor, Philip II's second wife, left him free to marry

Elizabeth, Henri II's daughter, while Henri's sister Marguerite was betrothed to Emmanuel Philibert of Savoy.

(ii) Territorial deals. France abandoned her claims to Savoy, Piedmont, Bresse, Bugey, Corsica and Lombardy in the south; and in the north, to the strongholds of Marienbourg, Thionville, Damvillers and Montmédy. But she retained Turin, Chieri, Pinerolo, Chivasso and Villanova d'Asti, and regained Saint-Quentin, Thérouanne, Ham and Le Catelet. France was to retain Calais for eight years, and the three bishoprics were not even on the table as the Emperor Ferdinand was not represented in the negotiations.

As one might imagine, this settlement provoked controversy in France. Contemporaries already embroiled in the developing civil wars – Protestants like Coligny, moderates like Brantôme, and hardline Catholics like Monluc and Brissac – all alike bewailed this bitter end to a 20-year struggle. They regretted the cessation of operations which in 1558 had not been going too badly for the French, and which simply demobilised thousands of gentlemen whose next battlefield would be the kingdom itself. But whatever the controversy, one thing remains clear: the Treaty of Cateau-Cambrésis was a turning-point in French history. As Fernand Braudel remarked in October 1972, one can properly speak of a 'before' and an 'after' Cateau-Cambrésis. The year 1559, like 1815 and 1940, was a channel which engulfed 'French passions'.

6 Domestic Politics under François I and Henri II

The causes of the process of centralisation that took place under François I and Henri II are found in the earlier history of the French monarchy. The emergence of lay elites, which we have already observed, lent it strong support. These men, brought up of necessity on Roman Law, were infused from an early age with the sense of royal prerogative enshrined in the dictum 'rex in regno suo est imperator' ('a king is an emperor in his kingdom'). It was no coincidence that in 1461 Louis XI founded a law school at Bourges, which was to produce some of the greatest jurists of the following century, such as Cujas, Hotman and Doneau; nor that François I took such an interest in the law school at Poitiers. Oddly enough, in this age of secularisation of royal government, the teaching of canon law in the schools and universities (especially that of Paris) harmonised with that of the civilians in the writings of the theoreticians of monarchical authority. In his *Insignia peculiaria Christianissimi Francorum regni* (1520), Jean Ferrault derived his absolutist theory from that of the papal theocracy, enumerating twenty royal prerogatives. Charles de Grassaille took a similar approach in his *Regalium Franciae libri duo* (1538). Guillaume Budé, whose education at Paris had included studying canon law at the Sorbonne, composed a treatise for François I (perhaps in 1518) entitled *L'Institution du Prince*, in which he expounded the merits of a monarchy exempt from any accountability to clergy, aristocracy, or people. As the king held his power from God alone, God alone could call him to account.[1]

True, the age of François I and his son also saw the appearance in 1519 of Claude de Seyssel's great work, *La Grande Monarchie de France*. Towards the end of his life this bishop, a veteran diplomat and administrator of Louis XII's days, described on paper the workings of the 'Royal State' under the 'Father of the People'. Seyssel's model was a monarchy restrained by three 'bridles': the king's Christian conscience, the existing corpus of legislation, which the king could neither 'contravene nor annul', and the moderating influence of the Parlement. Although he made only occasional mention of the Estates General, he saw the sovereign court of justice as an effective barrier against princely despotism. In addition, he advocated the maintenance of the rights and privileges of social orders and groups as the guarantee of a stable social system in which everyone knew their place. In similar fashion the jurist Charles Dumoulin (the famous commentator on the customary law of Paris) emphasised that royal power was 'more limited than absolute'. But his 1561 masterpiece, *Traité de l'origine, progrès et excellence du Royaume et Monarchie des Français*, was in effect a rearguard action, although it received a new lease of life in the propaganda produced by the religious and political factions during the Wars of Religion.

Although Seyssel and Dumoulin accurately reflected moderate French opinion of the time, a higher view of royal authority was taking shape. It is difficult to assess the impact Machiavelli had in France, but his words provide the background to the royal policies of François I and Henri II. Irrespective of right and wrong, the 'Royal State' exerted its influence over its subjects. And the fact is that many of the key figures in the Valois regime were steeped in this concept of the 'Royal State'. Men as different as the Chancellors Duprat and Poyet and the Constable Montmorency played a major part in the increasingly authoritarian orientation of the monarchy. In addition, the primacy of an aggressive foreign policy under François I and Henri II led inevitably to a concentration of power at the centre amid the hectic mobilisation of men and money for war. The enormous and unflagging efforts this entailed were manifested in the torrent of legislation from the King's Council. Edicts, declarations, ordinances, decrees, often issued in response to immediate needs, made the regime's attitudes clear. If their determination was rooted in an authoritarian view of monarchy, the pressures of necessity dictated by the belligerent policy they were pursuing tended to bring decision-making closer to the king in person.

The Characteristics of Centralisation

Central Power

Though one cannot properly speak of a 'revolution in government' in the Valois period, there was nevertheless a remarkable degree of evolution, manifested primarily in the subdivision and specialisation of the royal councils and in the new importance they enjoyed. However, change was piecemeal and pragmatic rather than spectacular and systematic. Public affairs remained very much a conciliar or collegial business, even if a single individual – monarch, Regent (like Louise of Savoy), or favourite (like Anne de Montmorency) – could still exercise disproportionate influence.

Two councils derived from the medieval Curia Regis emerged with increasingly specialised roles in the early sixteenth century. As under Charles VIII and Louis XII, the King's Council comprised the princes of the blood, the peers of the realm, and the major Crown officers – namely the Constable, the Grand Master, the Admiral of France, and above all the Chancellor, the effective head of the civil administration.[2] This Council was a flexible instrument, to which the king might invite members of the Parlement, churchmen, or military men to help with particularly pressing or specialised matters. The number of councillors of state created by brevet or letters patent, whose appointments thus remained dependent on the king's pleasure, varied between and even within reigns. Under François I it fluctuated between 10 and 20, while Henri II's Council numbered 21 on 2 April 1547, and as many as 31 in 1551.

The King's Council became increasingly specialised in the first half of the century. Despite problems of both demarcation and nomenclature, one can safely distinguish a judicial section, known as the *Grand Conseil* or *Conseil des parties*; an occasional *Conseil des finances*; and the omnicompetent *Conseil des affaires*, also known as the *Conseil étroit* or *Conseil secret*. These were in effect different manifestations of one single institution, comprising the same pool of councillors, but dealing with separate categories of business. The newest of these specialised councils was the *Grand Conseil*, already in evidence in the reign of Louis XI, and meeting regularly under Charles VIII, whose ordinance of 1497 (confirmed by that of Louis XII in 1498) defined its position as an instrument of immediate royal justice. The system of appeals, by which cases were removed from ordinary judges to be brought before the *Grand Conseil*, was implemented and refined under the first Valois in a series of edicts in 1522, 1527, 1529, 1533, 1539, 1547, and 1552. The *Grand Conseil* also dealt with conflicts between rival jurisdictions, petitions against royal officers, disputes involving fiefs and ecclesiastical benefices, and criminal matters involving benefices, as well as tithes and the management of hospitals and charitable foundations. The *Grand Conseil* thus revoked to the central administration some of the jurisdiction previously delegated to the sovereign courts and other bodies. This inevitably aroused the hostility of the Parlements, and in 1527 François I had to hold a *lit de justice* to compel the Parlement de Paris to recognise its jurisdiction in matters relating to benefices. The *Grand Conseil* fulfilled two main roles. First it was a court of justice, staffed by men entirely loyal to the king in their capacity as Councillors of State or Masters of Requests. Secondly, it brought about a degree of harmony between the various branches of jurisprudence which covered benefices, civil administration and conflicting jurisdictions. This unity was limited, but it represented the aspirations of the regime.

The increasing division of labour between branches of the council made especial progress under François I. The *Conseil des affaires* was a small group of men, five or six, all members of the King's Council, but picked out by the king to meet with him first thing every morning. This inner ring lay at the heart of policy-making. In 1535 it comprised Chancellor Duprat, Poyet (President of the Parlement de Paris), Mathieu de Longuejoue (Bishop of Soissons, and later *Maître des requêtes*), Marguerite de Navarre and her husband Henri d'Albret, Anne de Montmorency, the Admiral Chabot, Claude d'Annebaut, Claude de Guise, and the Cardinals of Lorraine and Tournon. In Henri II's reign, Montmorency held pride of place, together with François de Guise and his brother the Cardinal of Lorraine, Marshal Saint-André, Chancellor Olivier, and on occasion Marshals La Marck and Brissac. The council's daily sessions resolved immediate problems and laid down fundamental policies and aims. It had competence over every aspect of political life. Its discussions and deliberations were shrouded in secrecy: no minutes were taken. Everyone of national political consequence figured at one time or another on the *Conseil étroit* under François and his son. And Henri IV was later to resume the practice introduced by his great-uncle. The system was perfect for a monarch whose intention was to concentrate power on a small group of trusted colleagues: and from one day to the next, access to this prestigious company depended solely on the written or spoken word of the king.

*The *Conseil d'état* and the *Conseil secret* exercised legislative powers in the form of instruments variously described as ordinances, declarations, edicts, and *arrêts* (or decrees). These documents, drawn up by the Chancery, were written out by the 119 King's notaries or secretaries. The 120th was the king himself, whose signature authenticated personal correspondence.[3] The monarchy had, from at least the reign of Charles V, established among them a new category of officials, whose task was to draw up in correct form documents regarding matters of finance or dealing with delicate affairs of State. These 'secret clerks' soon rose above the run of ordinary scribes, and came to be known as *Secrétaires des finances* or *des commandements*. They were kept in attendance on the *Conseil d'état* and even the *Conseil des affaires*, and some actually attained the status of royal councillors.[4] Certain families held onto such positions as part of their inheritance, as it was unclear whether it was a public office or a special commission. By the end of the fifteenth century the secretaries were almost all related, composing veritable dynasties such as the Robertet, Gedoyn, Bohier, Neufville, and Bochetel. Although they were not among his closest advisers, François I employed them regularly on financial or diplomatic business. A decisive transition occurred when in 1547 Henri II picked out four secretaries (who held posts held by their fathers before them) 'to attend upon his person'. Their responsibilities were divided geographically, each in charge of expediting State business and official despatches for a particular quarter of the kingdom.[5] The title 'Secretaries of State' was first applied to them in 1559, when they were described as 'Secrétaires d'état de nos finances', and 'Secrétaires d'état de nos finances et commandements'. These men, who did not belong to the great aristocratic families, were henceforth indispensable cogs in the machinery of monarchy, and in the following century fulfilled an effectively ministerial function (a remark which applies not only to the four principal secretaries picked out by Henri II, but also to some other *secrétaires des finances* who rose high through royal favour).

The rise of the *maîtres de requêtes* was driven by a similar dynamic. It was a question of the slow infiltration of government by experts – in this case, of the most intimate networks of royal decision-making by magistrates. The administrative position of these jurists is rather clearer than that of the *secrétaires d'état* or *des finances*. Usually members of the Parlement de Paris, these men had bought their offices dear.[6] Since the thirteenth century, two clerks, known as 'royal pursuivants', had assisted the king in dispensing justice. Their jurisdiction was soon termed that of 'Requêtes de l'Hôtel'. As the number of cases directly involving the king's justice multiplied, so did the number of clerks: 8 by 1500, and 20 by 1553. As with other offices, each reign saw further posts created, either through necessity or as a financial expedient. Like the Chancery secretariat, these offices were hereditary, passed from father to son, uncle to nephew, or father-in-law to son-in-law. Their role, as was often the case in a central administration whose contours were so vague, was not closely defined, but it gave them certain judicial prerogatives. They dealt with cases involving offices or relating to the Chancery; they had powers to investigate and reform the Parlements and secondary tribunals; and they were often entrusted with tours of inspection in the provinces. If this body of lawyers and administrators had an ill-defined function, it was flexible enough to meet the needs of the Crown. The 1553 edict suggests that the group had a range of functions. It provided for 20 *maîtres des requêtes*, divided as follows: 3 to attend on the king; 2 on the Grand Council; 2 on the Parlement de Paris; 3 in the chamber of *Requêtes de l'Hôtel*; 6 on tour around the provinces (forerunners of the 'commissioners'); and 4 at the disposal of the king or the Chancellor.

Three of the great officers of the Crown – the Constable, the Admiral, and the Chancellor, all of them descendants of the great household servants of the medieval monarchy – played an active part in central government. Except for the Chancellor, their role was defined in effect at the king's pleasure. Under François I, the Admirals Bonnivet, Chabot and d'Annebaut had only a nominal connection with the sea. In fact they operated on land in command of armies. Bonnivet, a close friend of the king and the brother of Boisy, was said to be responsible for the disaster of Pavia; Philippe de Chabot campaigned in Italy; and d'Annebaut, a commander-in-chief, also served on the *Conseil des finances* and, more influentially still, upon the *Conseil secret*. Under Henri II, Admiral Coligny shut himself up in Saint-Quentin, with disastrous consequences. And, except for his seven years of disgrace (1541–7), the Constable Montmorency was one of the foremost members of the *Conseil secret*.

Notwithstanding the mistrust with which François I regarded them, the Chancellors remained the dominant figures in home policy. The office was held under François by two great names, Duprat and Poyet, and under Henri II by a rather lesser figure, Olivier.

Antoine Duprat was born in 1463 at Issoire in the Auvergne, to a family long prominent in commerce and civic affairs, and already linked to the Auvergne dynasty of Bohier, a nursery of royal notaries, secretaries, and *généraux des finances*.[7] So the common idea that he rose from a shop to the Chancery ignores the slow but steady rise of his family throughout the fifteenth century. Suitably enough for a future Chancellor, he studied law (whether at Pavia, Padua, Ferrara, or more prosaically at Orléans no one knows), attaining a doctorate in Roman Law. He was a strange fellow: a workaholic with limitless ambition and insatiable avarice. He married well, like his forefathers: Françoise Veiny d'Arbousse was the daughter of a bourgeois financier who rose to the nobility. And Duprat built up his public career in virtuoso fashion. Endowed with the office of lieutenant in the bailiwick of Montferrand, he became an advocate-general in the Toulouse Parlement in 1495, and a *maître des requêtes* in 1503. Within two years he had become a councillor in the Parlement de Paris. He was at first badly received by his new colleagues, who accused him, doubtless correctly, of having paid 4500 *livres* for his position. But they were fighting a losing battle, as venality was already at the heart of the administrative system. At the express request of Louis XII, he secretly compiled a dossier on the activities of Marshal de Gié. Anne of Brittany, bent on destroying de Gié, owed the decisive blow to Duprat, and from this time he was accepted at the very highest levels. In 1508 he became First President of the Parlement de Paris, and at the same time Louis XII entrusted him with the codification of the customs of the Auvergne. He became Chancellor in January 1515 upon François I's accession, and accompanied the king to Italy. It was he who led the negotiations leading to the famous Concordat of Bologna, which delivered the Gallican Church into the king's hands: a fitting triumph for a jurist imbued with the values and principles of Roman Law. Duprat was subsequently more active in diplomatic than administrative business. In 1517 he masterminded François I's campaign for the imperial election, and in 1518 he met the ambitious young Cardinal Wolsey at Calais for somewhat tentative discussions about an alliance. After the king's capture at Pavia, Duprat was once more the wily lawyer, negotiating with imperial representatives first for the release of the king, and subsequently for the release of the princes who had taken his place. He strained every nerve to amass the huge ransom demanded by the victorious Charles V. And in order to bring the Habsburg–Valois conflict to a temporary conclusion he negotiated the treaty of Cambrai, which he then did his best not to implement.

Rather like the Grand Master and future Constable Montmorency, Duprat was a peaceloving man, a trait perhaps confirmed when, after the death of his wife, he entered upon a further career in the Church. He soon acquired the abbeys of Fleury and Saint-Benoît-sur-Loire, together with five bishoprics. By 1525 he was Archbishop of Sens, by 1527 a cardinal, and by 1530 the papal legate, promotions which helped him amass enormous wealth. His commitment to the State and to imperial kingship led him to open a dossier on the financier Semblançay. With icy determination he gathered damning evidence of malpractice, and secured a conviction by means of a special tribunal of the kind which became customary under François I and was subsequently used extensively by Louis XIII and Richelieu. It was a show trial, with the added bonus of bringing some 300 000 *livres* into the royal coffers (not to mention considerable sums for Duprat himself). The Chancellor swept a number of other dodgy financiers into the bag, including some of his own relatives, and thus enhanced the king's image as a hammer of corruption. This avid exponent of the royal prerogative was equally hard on Lutherans, whom he saw less as heretics than as traitors, for abandoning the king's religion. The Council of Sens, over which he presided in 1528, trenchantly condemned 'the false prophets with Luther at their head', but also inaugurated reforms within the embattled Church. In his reaction to the reformist challenge to Catholicism and its institutions, Duprat was running ahead of his royal master who, at least until the affair of the Placards, took a more tolerant or hesitant line. But that scandal threw the king into the arms of the hardline conservatives who in fact best served the Crown's interests. Duprat himself was tireless in his struggle against those whom he saw as infringing the royal prerogative. He drew up lists of suspects, and had them imprisoned or executed. And it was he who, in January 1535, led through the streets of Paris a macabre expiatory procession which included the king, foreign ambassadors, and councillors of the Parlement. It made six halts for recollection, and at each there was a platform from which the king could witness the burning of one of those condemned for real or supposed involvement in the posting of the Placards.

Antoine Duprat died at Paris on 9 July 1535, and was hardly cold before the royal hands which had showered such prodigious patronage upon him began to retrieve the vast fortune he had built up through public office. Gifts, opulent rewards for services rendered to the king and his mother, ill-gotten gains, made up a substantial fortune. Sully, Richelieu and Mazarin were to do the same. François was prompt to seal off Duprat's château at Nantouillet, the Maison d'Hercule near the Austin Friars in Paris, and the episcopal palace in Sens. President Poyet organised the pillage, impounding the State papers at Nantouillet, taking 100 000 *écus soleil* to the royal coffers in the Louvre (as a loan!), and confiscating all the Chancellor's gold and silver plate. Strange recognition for the unflagging – though far from self-sacrificing – devotion to the Crown of the man from the Auvergne.

Poyet, who supervised the seizure of the spoils, was quick to step into the dead man's shoes. This was reasonable enough, as most Chancellors before and since were former First Presidents of the Parlement de Paris. Poyet himself had started as an advocate at the Paris bar, and had been appointed by Louise of Savoy to look after her interests during the proceedings against Charles de Bourbon. He became advocate-general in 1531, and then life President of the Parlement. Once again royal favour had come to a major dignitary through the patronage of the Queen Mother. The new Chancellor, who took office in 1538, was a wholehearted royalist. He was behind the famous ordinance of Villers-Cotterêts (1539), with its authoritarian and centralist tendencies. But Pierre Poyet soon found out how short a walk it was from the Capitol to the Tarpeian rock. Arrested in 1542 for corruption and convicted in 1545, he was stripped of all offices, fined 100 000 *livres*, and sent to prison, where he died in 1548.

The rise and fall of these two great Crown servants, annihilated by royal suspicion, one after and the other before his death, show that in effect the monarch could not bear the existence of any power beside his own.

The Administrative Machinery of the Realm

The king's agents were appointed to administrative, judicial, or financial office. It is worth dwelling on this group, the distinctive feature of the Ancien Régime.

In the Middle Ages men obtained office without paying. But gradually the custom arose of selling positions in the public service. This was not done lightly. The kings were not so politically blind as to be unaware that this was an alienation of their sovereignty. A series of ordinances from the fourteenth to the sixteenth centuries testify to the misgivings of the central authorities by forbidding 'private venality', that is, the resignation of a public office to a specific person in return for money. At the time when the sale of offices was in fact becoming a State business, the authorities could not carry it out with a clear conscience, because marketing the power conceded to the king by God looked like simony. When Louise of Savoy fell seriously ill in 1522 she interpreted her affliction as a divine punishment for the trade in offices so enthusiastically pursued by her son. She forced him to swear that he would desist, and promptly recovered. In 1535, at the time of the promulgation of the lengthy ordinance of justice, the entirely ineffectual prohibition of the trade in judicial offices was renewed. But the jurist Charles Loyseau laid the responsibility for the market in public offices squarely at the king's door, stating:

> King François, Louis XII's successor, carried on the trade in public offices openly and without restraint, turning it into a new source of ordinary revenue in place of the royal domain, which was already largely alienated. In 1522 he established the *Bureau des parties casuelles* to serve as a clearing house for this new market.[8]

Under François I and his son the number of offices swelled immeasurably. Seeing that statistical analysis is in fashion, we can turn to the findings of Roland Mousnier and Pierre Chaunu to play the numbers game.[9] In attempting to evaluate the 'burden of the State' in 1515, Chaunu reckons that for a kingdom of some 460 000 km^2 there were 4041 officials, rising to about 8000 if you include their assistants and clerks. This represented an 'administrative infrastructure' of one official per 115 km^2 or, 'including the petty bureaucracy', 1 per 60 km^2. Assuming a total population of about 16 million, this meant that there was one royal official for every 3950 people, and a representative of the king for every 2000.

From the point of view of the centre, it was a matter of the utmost importance to control this immense country, which was certainly under-administered if the deficiencies of its means of communications are taken into account. The proliferation of royal officials was a response to this problem. However, historians are quick to emphasise that the fragmentation of public authority through the increasing sale of offices was more of a response to the financial needs of a monarchy at war.[10] Offices were sold dear and yielded immediate revenue to the Crown, even if, second time round, it was necessary to give guarantees to the occupants of these posts. It is true that the release of tranches of offices onto the market coincided with the outbreak of each of the wars of the Valois against Charles V or Philip II. But it also remains true that the 'Royal State' first assumed its true form in this period, and that officials were its backbone. Offices could be acquired in two ways: by direct purchase from the *Bureau des casuels*, or by resignation of the incumbent in favour of a relative or a purchaser. Once named in letters of appointment, the official became the owner of his post, removable only by forfeiture or judicial sentence. Judicial offices were valued especially highly. They could be obtained only with sureties of good behaviour and suitable age and education. Candidates for the best position of all, that of a councillor in Parlement, were subject to an examination by their future colleagues.

The stampede for office on the part of the French elite is further explained by the tax privileges office conferred. Incumbents were exempt from the *taille* (except in the *pays d'oc* where the *taille* was levied on taxable land). They could buy salt at cost price, the privilege of 'franc-salé'. And they did not have to billet royal troops. But the greatest attraction of all was the noble status conferred by certain offices: presidents and councillors in the sovereign courts, the *trésoriers de France*, notaries and *maîtres des requêtes*, procurators-general, etc., were ennobled in the first generation.[11] This privilege, together with the various tax exemptions, made royal officials, above all the judicial officers, a distinct social group between the *haute bourgeoisie* and the nobility. The monarchy was creating a dependent 'class' which owed its existence to royal service. Throughout the century these men strove to promote royal centralisation. Even at the height of the League they propped up the legitimate authority of Henri III and Henri IV. However, from as early as the reign of François I they displayed a resolute corporate opposition to any enlargement of their own number through the creation of new offices which would inevitably devalue those already established. Here lay the roots of the tension between Crown and officials which culminated in the Fronde.

Between 1515 and 1559 officials protested constantly as the Crown, ever short of money, multiplied new offices. They were particularly vocal between 1521 and 1523, when François I introduced a phalanx of new financial, judicial and administrative personnel; and again in 1552, when Henri II introduced his new tribunals, the *présidiaux*. *Lettres de jussion* and even *lits de justice* were needed to compel the magistrates of the Parlement de Paris, in effect the focus of opposition, to register the relevant edicts so that they became part of the law of the land. This conflict masked a deeper misunderstanding, for the officials, especially those of the Parlements, believed that they were the descendants of the royal councillors who had directly advised the king in the medieval *Curia Regis*. They therefore claimed the right to supervise the royal legislative power: hence the chorus of protest whenever a pronouncement of the Council touched on their personal interests, or even occasionally on higher interests. In 1518, for example, François I had to compel the Grenoble Parlement to register the Concordat of Bologna, which that court thought excessively ultramontane.

Nevertheless, royal power could not function without the cooperation of the administrative and judicial officers, who transmitted throughout the towns and provinces the ordinances, edicts, and *arrêts* issued by the central councils. Already in the age of Charles VIII and Louis XII, and even more under François I and Henri II, the king's law had a long arm, reaching into the darkest corners of the land. The law was for the most part applicable throughout the whole kingdom, a step towards legislative uniformity. Of course this statement is subject to qualification: much of the output of the royal chancery was concerned only with particular provinces and thus reinforced localism. Brittany was handled with care, especially in the steps towards integration taken by the justice ordinances of 1536 and 1539, and the forest laws of 1544. But Provence was treated more firmly. The Edict of Joinville (1535) reorganised the Aix Parlement along Parisian lines and curtailed the traditional powers of the governor. One can see in the different treatment accorded to the provinces recently reunited to the kingdom the way in which François I and Henri II pursued centralisation: generally cautious but occasionally brutal.

Justice

Besides the *Grand Conseil* described above, royal justice was also dispensed by the councillors of the Parisian and provincial Parlements. The Parlement de Paris, whose jurisdiction covered nearly half the kingdom, was by far the most prestigious. It was followed by those of Toulouse, Rouen and Bordeaux. The Aix Parlement took a long time to be established. Louis XII confirmed as early as 1501 that it replaced the High Council of the Counts of Provence, but it did not really operate as an instrument of royal justice until after 1535.

The Crown acted in the same cautious way in Brittany, notoriously jealous of its local privileges. In 1492 Charles VIII reorganised ducal justice in the form of the 'Grand Jours' (or Parlement), composed both of Breton magistrates and of officials from the Parlement de Paris. This body sat intermittently, but continuity was provided by a council of judges drawn from the province. A power struggle broke out between this council (backed by the provincial estates) and the Parlement (backed by the Crown). Louis XII confirmed the supremacy of the latter, determining that the 'men of the council are subordinate and accountable to the Parlement'. François I did not relish a dispute with the Bretons, and in 1526, at the petition of the provincial estates, he increased the staff of the organisation, where two chambers dispensed justice. Finally, in 1554, a permanent Parlement was established under Henri II. It was composed partly of Bretons and partly of others, but the president was never a native of the duchy. It divided its sessions between Nantes and Rennes until it finally settled at Rennes in 1569.

The Parlements were of particular concern to the Crown because in matters of justice they were vigorous defenders of the royal prerogative, even if in other matters relations could be confrontational. The *Grande chambre* – the original court – was supplemented, thanks to the creation of new offices, by first a criminal chamber, the *Tournelle*, and then in 1531, at Paris, a *chambre des vacations*, followed by one or two *chambres des enquêtes* in 1515 and 1534, and also the *chambres des requêtes*.

In the field of justice, the regimes of François I and Henri II set about reorganising the old tribunals of Capetian origin. The *prévotés* introduced by Philip Augustus became in this period the tribunals of first instance.[12] These offices, which were as a rule venal, were in practice often leased out, despite the ordinances of 1493 and 1499 which decreed that provosts would henceforth be 'literate men or learned in customary law, of good repute, appointed by the judges of the locality'. The *prévoté* became the seat of better organised justice, and the provost was henceforth assisted in his administrative and judicial functions by various colleagues, all of them royal officials. In 1536 the Edict of Crémieu tried to demarcate more clearly between the jurisdiction of the provosts and that of the bailiffs. The provosts were to be the judges of first instance in all civil and criminal matters (except in the towns, where the municipality exercised high justice), which might however be taken on appeal to higher tribunals. The staff of the *prévotés* also exercised police functions and supervised trades.

These ordinary jurisdictions, useful to the Crown on account of the relentlessness with which they nibbled away at seigneurial and municipal jurisdictions, were nevertheless, from the first half of the sixteenth century, condemned to redundancy or even impotence by the reorganisation of the *bailliages* (bailiwicks) and the establishment of the *présidiaux*. The bailiwicks (or *sénéchaussées* as they were termed in the *pays d'oc*) corresponded to the judicial and administrative districts first established on the royal domain in the feudal period, and then extended later to the newly acquired provinces. Bailiffs or seneschals appointed by the king from among his noble entourage, and for this reason known as officials '*de robe courte*', had long since delegated their functions to lowly subordinates, their 'lieutenants'. In the sixteenth century, bailiffs and seneschals hardly ever visited their districts except in times of unrest, and even this military role was being taken over by the governors. The lieutenants (at first 'lieutenants-general', then also 'particular lieutenants', and finally, from 1523, 'criminal lieutenants' too), graduates in law of bourgeois origin, were imposed upon each district, a decision renewed by Henri II in 1554. There was a market in such offices, known as '*de robe longue*', from the late fifteenth century, and it boomed in the sixteenth century, when the king nominated to all posts within the *prévotés* and bailiwicks, seeing that it was he who chose the recipients of the offices he put on sale. The size of these tribunals gradually increased. From 1515 each one had two inquisitors and examiners. Then, from 1522, a royal proctor and various other accredited councillors took the numbers to between twelve and fifteen. And the institutions were also equipped with a large auxiliary personnel of notaries, clerks and sergeants.

The role of the bailiwicks was a complicated, not to say confused, matter, as was the case with all institutions of the time, royal or not. Royal ordinances had to be registered by them in order to come into force, though they might be modified by local ordinances valid only within the district. A further legislative function was the codification of local customary law, which was done on a district basis. But their main function was judicial, whether in civil or criminal matters. These tribunals were the courts of the first instance in all civil matters concerning nobles or royal officials, ecclesiastical benefices, or the royal domain. They also took cognisance of a number of criminal matters reserved to royal justice and therefore *ultra vires* for seigneurial courts. Finally, they dealt with appeals from seigneurial courts and *prévotés*. Their officers had in addition a wide-ranging brief to keep the peace and maintain public order. Together with the municipal *élus* they dealt with the collection of tolls, the regulation of trades, fairs and markets, and indirect taxation. It was the Seneschal of Lyon who, in 1541, stepped in to resolve a strike by the journeymen printers.

In the interests of establishing firmer control of towns, the Crown backed its own agents in conflicts between bailiwick and civic officials. The ordinance of Crémieu stipulated that assemblies of townsfolk had to be presided over by bailiffs or seneschals, who should exact an oath from municipal *élus* and assist at the auditing of public accounts. By the end of the fifteenth century, France had about 86 bailiwicks, but their geography remained fluid throughout the sixteenth century, as the original districts were frequently subdivided for the benefit of 'particular lieutenants'.

In 1552, Henri II's regime introduced new tribunals, the *présidiaux* – a radical administrative measure for a dynasty which on the whole preferred reorganising, transforming, or even wiping out institutions rather than establishing new ones. The avowed aim, according to the original ordinance, was to relieve the Parlements of an excessive burden of petty business while delivering justice more directly to plaintiffs. And the Parlements of Paris and Toulouse were indeed so snowed under that too much scope remained for seigneurial, ecclesiastical, municipal, and other local providers of justice not subject to the direct control of the Crown or its agents. But the real motive was fiscal. The sale of 500 new offices was a valuable bonus to the treasury at a time when the king was planning an offensive against Charles V. However, not all the offices were entirely new, as 61 bailiwick jurisdictions were transformed into *présidiaux* by an expansion of their personnel. These particular bodies thus exercised a two-fold competence, combining the new role with that of the existing bailiwick. They heard appeals from provosts' and bailiffs' courts in civil cases (sometimes as the court of final appeal), and were the court of first instance for cases in which the sums at issue did not exceed amounts ranging from 250 to 500 *livres* according to the case (raised in 1557 to 1000–1200 *livres*).

The Parlements bitterly resented the introduction of these rival tribunals, and that of Paris refused to register the edict until the third *lettre de jussion*, extracting two concessions: that the judgements of the *présidiaux* should be known as sentences rather than *arrêts*; and that their seals should bear only a single fleur de lys, rather than the three traditionally borne by the sovereign courts. Nor did their opposition stop there. The Parlements went so far as to hear appeals in cases which the *présidiaux* had heard as courts of final appeal. In short, the new tribunals provoked dissension for the rest of the century, with numerous appeals made to the *Grand Conseil* by their own officers or by those of the Parlements. It was as though royal justice was going round in circles, feeding on itself. Nevertheless, the new officials were in place, forming a further link in the chains binding the outlying provinces to the centre of power, and diffusing a uniform system of justice in the various localities in which they were established. François I and Henri II, all too aware of the patchwork of judicial procedures and techniques which covered their kingdom, sought – not always with success – to impose a degree of harmony on it. In the wake of those of Charles VIII and Louis XII they promulgated their own 'great ordinances' of justice in 1527, 1538, 1539, 1543, 1546 and beyond, instructing officials to reside within their jurisdictions, and defining the role of the advocate-general, the form of pleas, the conduct of cases (1528), and the methods of investigation (1540). In addition, procedures for appeals to the Parlements and the *Grand Conseil* were defined more strictly and brought into line.

A large tranche of the legislative output of François I and his son was devoted to the organisation of the judicial and administrative apparatus. Under François, 65 acts of one kind or another (ordinances, edicts, arrêts and declarations) concerned such matters, and as many as 42 in the far shorter reign of Henri II. Louis XII, in contrast, had produced only 10 acts on such questions, and Charles VIII only 5. And this is without taking account of the many other laws and regulations which sought to raise the moral standards of public officials, a matter to which we shall return later.

Finance

The reorganisation of finances necessitated by the exigencies of war itself further encouraged the centralisation of power. Royal revenues were derived from a variety of sources: the 'ordinary' revenues from the Crown lands, and the 'extraordinary' from direct and indirect taxation. Feudal revenues (quit-rents, ground-rents, rights and profits of justice, sales of wood, etc.) accrued to the king in his capacity as seigneur. Their importance in the overall picture was little more than symbolic, for the traditional view that the king should 'live of his own' (that is, from his own domain) had not been lost, and tended to be voiced whenever the burden of taxation weighed too heavily.

Taxes were the backbone of the State budget. The oldest tax was the *taille*, first levied in 1349 to pay for mercenaries. In theory it was levied upon non-combatant commoners, and its name acquired over the years undesirable connotations as a synonym for non-noble status. It was also known as the 'octroi' or 'deniers du roi' in Normandy, the 'fouage' in Brittany, and the 'aides' in Languedoc. Around 1500 this widely resented tax was like a mirror of the nation: various, unpredictable, and unjust. North of a line running roughly from La Rochelle to Geneva, the *taille* was a personal levy on the income of the liable taxpayer, arbitrarily assessed by the collector. In the south it was a property tax, levied on taxable land irrespective of the status of its owner and assessed by means of surveys, the *compoix*, which were regularly revised.

The target sum for the *taille* was fixed by the King's Council each year and then allocated among the various provinces, where it was assessed and levied on a parochial level. Certain provinces, such as Languedoc and Burgundy, equipped in the fifteenth century with Estates by a monarchy keen to establish chains of command or to protect institutions established before integration, had their own virtually autonomous fiscal administration. Elsewhere, in rather smaller geographical units, there were Estates operating at the district level (as in Agenais, Quercy, Périgord, and the Auvergne) which had similar powers. But alongside the Estates, which 'consented' to direct taxation (that is, had the power to negotiate the sum with the king's representative), there was a purely monarchical administration whose sphere of operations was the *élection* (an area roughly coterminous with a diocese), run by an *élu* who was responsible for allocating the *taille* among the parishes entrusted to him, and for collecting the receipts. At the grass-roots level, these local communities themselves appointed an assessor to allocate the tax-charge among the parishioners and collect it.

The financial crisis induced by the preparations for war against Charles V, the need to find silver, and the extreme distrust with which François regarded the *trésoriers de France* and the *généraux des finances* combined to produce the carefully considered reform of 1523.[13] François had already broken the mould: in 1521 he increased duties; and in 1522 he put a huge number of offices on the market. At the same time he introduced the '*rentes sur l'Hôtel de ville*'. These expedients were not enough to cover the deficit run up through military expenditure. A thorough reform of the financial machine was planned in 1523, but, as with many enterprises of this kind, it was not fully implemented until the reign of Henri II. The *Trésor de l'Épargne* was established by letters patent in 1523. Based in the tower of the Louvre, this central royal treasury gathered in all the ordinary and extraordinary Crown revenues. All expenditures were henceforth to be sanctioned by the King's Council, which kept a general account of income and outgoings, a very basic kind of budget. Under Henri II, Montmorency took personal control of financial affairs, and he was succeeded by Claude de Saint-Marcé and then, in 1559, by the Cardinal of Lorraine. The Cardinal was succeeded in 1561 by Artus de Cossé, the first official to bear the title *Surintendant des finances*. The council, or its deputy, was assisted in drawing up the budget by the *maîtres des requêtes* known as the *commissaires au Louvre*. In 1554 they were renamed *intendants des finances*. Commissioned on a temporary basis, holding office at royal pleasure, and thus entirely under royal control, they represented an institution with a great future.

Warrants authorising the disbursement of public funds had to be signed by the *Trésorier de l'Épargne* and his colleague, the *Trésorier des parties casuelles*, and then by the *receveurs généraux* of the particular account in question. A warrant was 'nothing more than an invitation to go to this or that receiver's office and be paid from this or that particular account',[14] a procedure which avoided the onerous and dangerous business of transporting large sums of money. But the creditor who arrived with his warrant often found that the cupboard was bare because the tax had not yet come in. If he needed cash badly, he could sell on his warrant (later known as 'Épargne paper') to another creditor less pressed than himself, or else better placed to secure rapid payment.

Under Henri II, in 1547, two auditors were established in central government to countersign all discharges and to register all the financial transactions of the *Trésor de l'Épargne*. One was based at Court, the other at the Louvre. But the ordinances of 1534 and 1556 allowed for only one *Contrôleur général*, who had sole power to oversee Treasury income and outgoings, and who kept records which enabled the *Chambre des comptes* to keep track of State liquidity. From this point the central coffers were indeed those of the nation: they were no longer the king's piggy-bank. From now on the *Contrôleur général* was, together with the *Surintendant des finances*, the principal official in the central financial administration.

In the provinces there were various administrative divisions. The *généralités*, whose number was increased to 16 in 1542, were run by *receveurs généraux* with the assistance of treasurers – the former acting as collectors and accountants, the latter handling outgoings. The *receveurs généraux*, all-powerful until the reform of 1523, were henceforth obliged to reside in the district. As they now held office by turns, they increased in number, forming within each *généralité* the '*Bureau des trésoriers des finances*', or '*Bureau des finances*' for short. The *généralités* were themselves divided into *élections* under the authority of officials called *élus*. *Généralités* tended to coincide roughly with groups of districts, *élections* with dioceses. But the latter constantly proliferated, reaching 87 under François I and passing 150 under Henri II.

The power of the *élus* was overshadowed by that of the new officials in the *généralités* – the *contrôleurs*, and the *trésoriers* and *généraux des finances* – even though these were no more than delegates of the man at the top. The basic task of the *élus* was, as in the past, to allocate the *taille* among the parishes and to supervise the assessment of individual taxpayers. This entailed frequent tours of inspection (*chevauchées*) in order to visit local communities, remedy injustices, and protect the tax-collectors against the violence of receivers and sergeants. They settled all matters relating to the assessment or collection of the tax. These officials, of more than dubious integrity, took advantage of their position to exempt themselves from the *taille*, a first step towards noble status. Boasting the title – now as vague as it was widespread – of royal councillor, they flocked to purchase their nobility under François I, as did the *greffiers* (the district receivers). The injustice and dishonesty of the *élus* made them scapegoats for fiscal grievances. Universally hated, they were symbols of the accumulated burdens of the taxpayers, and they often paid with their lives during popular risings. The officials who managed the salt warehouses, generally known as *gabelleurs*, shared with the *élus* the disagreeable and often dangerous role of political lightning conductor.

The fiscal administration, thoroughly reorganised along centralising lines, set about rationalising the levying of taxes in order to secure the effective collection of the spiralling fiscal burden. The annual *brevet* which levied the *taille* fixed it at around 2.4 million *livres*, which was supplemented each year by the *crue* (or surtax), usually between 400 000 and 600 000 *livres*, occasionally as much as a million (as in 1519, when François I's candidature for the imperial crown wrought havoc with the finances of the king and his subjects). From 1522 the *taille* settled definitively at about 3 million *livres*, with occasional exceptions. In 1524 the fortunes of war took it up to 5 761 000 *livres*, a level it approached again in 1529 when the conflict with Charles V was resumed. However, such increases remained sporadic, and the average levy between 1524 and 1541 was 4 269 000 *livres*. It remained at around 4.4 million *livres* until 1547, but the swingeing double levy of 1524 was never repeated, under François at least.[15] Henri II's wars made equally crushing financial demands upon the people. The *brevet* for the *taille* in 1552 fixed it at 5 million *livres*, and the *taillon* levied from 1549 onwards was worth about a million *livres* a year. On top of these direct levies came a staggering increase in *aides* and *gabelles* as well as the extension in 1555 of taxes on walled towns (*villes closes*) to the countryside; the taxing of wealthy citizens (a way of clawing back some of the tax exemptions enjoyed by the swelling ranks of royal officials); 'gifts' from the clergy;

and loans from bankers and financiers, without which the monarchy could hardly survive. In 1552 Henri II borrowed 400 000 *livres* from Italian bankers and 50 000 from French.

Thus the first steps in the real centralisation of French government took place in the field of financial administration, which was hardly surprising seeing that the kingdom was in an almost constant state of war.

Economic Policy

The legislation of François I and Henri II provides ample evidence of the new attention being devoted to economic policy. After Louis XI, Charles VIII was content to restore the Lyon fairs, and Louis XII took a certain interest in trades (2 measures), and in the export of grain and the price of victuals in inns (4 measures). But François I and Henri II issued a huge number of regulations and even edicts – nigh on 100. Their first priority was the coin of the realm. Only the king had the right to strike coin, and coins stamped with the royal likeness were minted at various workshops across the country. Gold coins were rare, except for the *écu de soleil* (or 'sun crown'). Silver was more common, and in 1513 Louis XII had had a *teston* struck with his image on it. But most coin was of 'billon' (an alloy of copper and silver): *deniers, douzains, liards, sous* etc. Foreign coin circulated alongside that of the realm: German florins, Spanish ducats and pistoles, and English rose nobles. For this reason, the royal right to mint money found its main expression in the periodical fixing of the values of all these coins in terms of the currency of account, the *livre tournois*. Ordinances laid down what weight of metal should be deemed equivalent to this abstract pound, which was divided into twenty *sous*, with each *sou* further divided into twelve *deniers*. In the first half of the sixteenth century the *écu de soleil* was fixed at 3 *livres*, the *teston* at 12 *sous*, and the *liard* at 4 *sous*. The monarchy could exploit this power to manipulate the monetary system. There were considerable short-term gains in raising the accounting value of coins or reducing the real value of the *livre*. The public, often irritated and even harmed by such manoeuvres, had a relatively simple remedy: trade was conducted according to the market value of coins, namely their weight. This precaution was doubly necessary, not only because of royal manipulation but also because coiners shaved and clipped precious metal from coins. The government threatened the direst punishments, similar to those for counterfeiters, against these criminals in 1532, 1536, 1542, 1543, 1545 etc., but the very repetition of the laws testifies to their inefficacy. With the same objective of ensuring that sound money circulated in the kingdom, the King's Council frequently took measures against certain kinds of coin in order to discredit them with the people. In 1538, for example, coins from Béarn called *vaches* and *liards* from Lausanne, were both forbidden to circulate. But the Béarn coin was re-authorised in 1541. The following year, before the influx of foreign gold and silver coins, royal authorisation was sought for their use. François I and Henri II aspired, like Louis XI before them, to standardise weights and measures. The Estates General petitioned for this whenever they convened. Louis XII had tried to bring some uniformity to the measures of the Auvergne in 1510, and his failure did not discourage his successor, who decreed that the *aune du roi* (or 'king's ell') should be the standard measure of length for the whole kingdom. But in 1543 François had to concede to the drapers the right to use whatever measure of length they chose. Henri II returned to the fray and renewed Louis XII's edict, first for Paris in 1557, and then for the entire realm in 1558. But it proved impossible to enforce, and real reform had to await the Revolution.

The economic policy of François I and his son has been called 'interventionist', but the term is too strong, even if their interventions were frequent. Besides the matters we have already considered, they legislated to regulate trades and crafts, to fix prices, to control imports and exports, to license fairs, and to encourage industry and commerce.

· The guild system of craft production had early emerged as the means by which local and central authorities could exercise powers of supervision over the world of manual labour, and it was particularly effective in the towns. The Crown displayed firm and consistent support for the system of sworn guilds and *jurandes*, and encouraged their extension, all the more so because every stage of the guild career (notably advancement to the status of master craftsman), as well as the grant or confirmation of guild statutes, meant fees for the Treasury. Indeed, at high points in their personal lives, such as marriage or the birth of a child, kings were happy to sell patents of mastership which exempted their beneficiaries from the usual tests. Thus, in 1528, François I created a new master craftsman in every sworn guild in order to celebrate the birth of his niece Jeanne d'Albret, and put on the market as many patents as it took.

However, some trades, such as goldsmiths and jewellers, were closely supervised in order to protect the public from the risk of fraud. Thus in 1543 an ordinance stipulated that accurate marks should indicate the grade of gold or silver in precious goods. And craftsmen producing goods destined for export were strictly controlled by royal officials, as in the village of Darnétal. Elsewhere the King's Council encouraged the manufacture of luxury goods for export or for the domestic market. Privileges and monopolies were granted to the drapers of Tours, and their interests were protected by a prohibition on the import of Spanish cloth.

Under François I and Henri II, concern with commercial matters even extended to the creation of a more favourable infrastructure, with intervention in the field of communications. The maintenance of roads and bridges was not the responsibility of the Crown except within the royal domain – and thus the great highway from Paris to Orléans was suitably maintained. Elsewhere, towns were responsible for the upkeep of their approach roads. But the highways between towns and cities were frequently in a state of terrible disrepair which was made worse – if that was possible – during the Wars of Religion. The tolls levied by seigneurs, whether personal or corporate, on the rivers and navigable waterways, paths and roads were in theory meant to finance the repair of bridges, the maintenance of banks, and the upkeep of thoroughfares. In towns, the tolls granted by the king and levied on merchandise were meant to pay for the paving of the streets which continued the main roads within the city walls. In Paris, each gate meant a further levy. In practice, tolls and fees were ways of exploiting trade rather than improving traffic.

The Crown did strive to reduce the number of tolls in order to encourage trade. For example, on the Loire and its tributaries there were 200 tolls levied at 120 points. The Crown encouraged the carriers to form associations under State protection and privilege in the face of the myriad levies. The merchants of the Loire were the oldest association of this kind. In 1498 Louis XII promulgated an ordinance urging merchants using other waterways to form similar associations. Thus the Three Rivers association (covering the Tarn, Garonne and Aveyron) was formed in 1499, and held its general meeting (the *états de rivière*) every three years.

François I and Henri II continued the struggle against seigneurial tolls. In 1532 any toll which could not be shown to have been collected for at least a century was annulled. And in 1535 seigneurs were reminded that toll revenues were meant for the maintenance of highways and waterways. In 1547, all usurped tolls on the Isère, the Rhône and the Seine were declared null, but to little avail. For all the instructions sent to bailiffs, *trésoriers-généraux*, *élus*, and wardens of rivers and forests, there was to be no improvement until the days of Henri IV and Sully – and little enough even then. Nevertheless, the fact remains that François I and Henri II appreciated, albeit for political rather than commercial reasons, the importance of a good communications network.

To return to the strictly commercial policy of the Valois kings, there was an attempt to encourage businessmen by establishing stock exchanges in Lyon, Toulouse, Paris and Rouen. There was also a close interest in trade fairs, although these were already a somewhat dated way of doing business. The privileges of the Lyon fair were regularly confirmed, although the toll levied on goods entering the precincts of the fair was not firmly settled. Restored by Charles VIII and then suppressed by François I and Henri II, it was a sword of Damocles hanging over the merchants. Privileges were also granted to the old fairs of Brie and Champagne and to that of Lendit, but it was something of a rearguard action.

The legislation of François I and his son was marked, above, all by a determination to control prices. Did this reflect a concern to equalise the prices of commodities in their patchwork kingdom, or a rather medieval paternalist desire to protect the consumer? The two goals were clearly linked in their minds, even if the second was highlighted in the preambles of their edicts. The power to fix prices had been spread widely among municipal authorities, feudal lords and royal judges, but henceforth it was increasingly taken over by the King's Council. In 1499 and 1508, Louis XII began the process by inveighing against the dishonesty of innkeepers and taverners who fleeced innocent travellers. François I and Henri II went further, laying down limits for taverners and fixing maximum prices for certain goods. In 1519, 1522, 1540, 1546, 1549, 1551 and 1557, edicts fixed prices chargeable for 'bed and bedding', 'tablecloths and napkins', and victuals – with little success, to judge by the frequency of the edicts.

The great innovation of the early sixteenth century was in customs duties. Until this time the frontiers of the realm had been open to all merchants and goods except cloth of gold or silver. But now, for the first time in French history, import duties were systematically imposed as a further means of filling the Treasury. The King's Council was particularly concerned about the import of spices, a commodity as valuable as gold, which had become even more important in European markets in the Age of Discovery. Laws of 1539 and 1541 attempted to provide a strict definition of spices, and import duties were imposed on them in 1541, 1544, 1549 and 1555. The duties were to be paid to the *maître des ports*, and luxury goods were to enter the kingdom only at a certain number of places, and were not to circulate without a certificate of duty paid.

The State also kept a close eye on the import and export of grain, although its concern here was not so much with revenue as with public order. Profiteering merchants could not be allowed to sell corn abroad at the risk of destabilising domestic markets and unleashing riots. Thus corn exports were forbidden in 1531, 1535, 1536 and 1544, but were permitted in 1539 and 1540. An edict of 1555 set down the principle governing these shifts of policy: exports were to be allowed in times of plenty once domestic markets had been adequately supplied.

Internal trade continued to labour under the burden of innumerable tolls. These internal tariffs were the subject of frequent negotiations between the King's Council and the provinces where they operated. And it seems that during the reign of Henri II their number fell as toll rights were bought up by interested parties – modest progress towards the introductions of a single internal market. But the tariff levied on goods entering the walls of Lyon survived and prospered. It is worth noting that the word '*douane*' (from the Turkish term '*divan*' via the Italian '*dogana*') first appeared in French around this time, and the first actual customs house was set up in 1544. Closed down in 1545, it was reopened in 1552 during Henri II's offensive against the Habsburgs, and was definitively incorporated into the royal resources in 1564.

Public Order

In the sixteenth century the Crown gave itself the chance to have a real coercive force within the realm – the marshalcy. It was headed by the two or three Marshals of France, the great officers of the Crown responsible for maintaining discipline among troops in the field or in garrisons. Beneath their command, in the provinces or in the field, were the Provost-Marshals, who also played their part in general police duties at times when (as in 1493 and 1513) bands of brigands were pillaging a region. From 1500 the Provost-Marshals purchased their offices, and their wages were paid by a supplement to the *taille*, an expedient which drew forth bitter protests from the provincial Estates. The powers of the Provost-Marshals were first properly defined by François I in 1537, as covering cases of theft, treason, vagabondage, offences by soldiers, mendicancy and brigandage. Their jurisdiction was extended in 1538 and 1539 to hunting offences, sacrilege and counterfeiting. They dispensed swift justice in the form of capital punishment for flagrant offences, or else instigated proceedings leading to a more considered judgement.

One can appreciate how the refined sensitivities of ordinary judges recoiled from the crude proceedings of these officers. 'The heart abhors the butcheries of the Provost-Marshals', wrote one; and a flood of protests reached the King's Council in the name of humanity, although they were really motivated by jealousy of what was seen as unfair competition. In 1554, Henri II, anxious to conciliate magistrates already annoyed by the creation of the *présidiaux*, agreed to the suppression of the Provost-Marshals, replacing them in each bailiwick by a '*lieutenant criminel de robe courte*'. The powers of the lieutenants were much the same as those of the provosts, and covered the same kinds of cases. Like most of the laws and regulations of François I and Henri II, this one was not uniformly applied: Languedoc was happy with its provosts and retained them at its own charge, but they were supplemented by lieutenants in each of the dioceses under the aegis of the provincial Estates. Indeed, in 1555, a year after the suppression of the provosts, it was decided to restore thirteen of them, so that lieutenants, vice-lieutenants and Provost-Marshals rubbed shoulders in merry confusion – but all still powerless to stem the rising tide of crime (real or imagined) in the later sixteenth century.

The fact remains, however, that, at least in intention, there was a domestic police force acting on a national scale, superior to the urban militias and seigneurial forces. At the same time measures were taken to confront the disorders of the age, or such of them as the Valois regime could not tolerate.

The State intervened on a national level for the first time in three major areas. Measures against illegal assemblies, like those forbidding civilians to carry firearms, were aimed primarily against the armed bands which pillaged the countryside and the outskirts of towns. Consisting often enough of soldiers left unemployed during brief outbreaks of peace, they terrorised town and country alike. But the 'assemblies' with which Provost-Marshals, bailiffs, or municipal magistrates concerned themselves were not confined to gangs: they also included assemblies of Lutherans, Zwinglians and Calvinists, the advocates of religious change. The repeated prohibitions of 'illicit' or clandestine assemblies even extended to the meetings of craft guilds. The protests of the journeymen printers of Lyon in 1539 against the conditions imposed by their masters led to a royal prohibition on confraternities and other secret gatherings. The label of 'enemy of the peace' thus included those who assembled 'on the pretext of war'; bands of hooligans wearing 'masks'; journeymen 'creating monopolies'; and the adherents of new beliefs. The motley crew of those henceforth labelled enemies of the king's peace was further extended to the traditional vagabonds as well as to drunkards, idlers, and gipsies. The connection between these groups is clear enough to modern eyes: criminals or not, none of them adhered to the virtues of hard work and stability upheld by and embodied in the apostles of a stricter and more authoritarian social order.

Likewise, in order to keep people in their allotted roles and stations, to avoid the blurring of social distinctions, and to establish social codes compatible with an authoritarian monarchy, there was a sustained attempt to stop people pretending to a status to which they were not entitled. Measures were introduced against hunting offences, dressing above one's station, and clandestine marriages which risked the dilution of noble blood.

Finally, the monarchy strove to raise moral standards among public officials. Charles VIII and Louis XII had already taken measures against fraudulent bankrupts. Their successors went further. François I acted against the wilful prolongation of legal actions and the malpractices of financial officials and war commissioners (in 1524, 1530, 1532 and 1546). Henri II followed this up by calling for the shortening of legal proceedings, in 1550, and requiring accounting officers to deposit taxpayers' money in the *Trésor de l'Épargne* (1556 and 1557). Like his father, he took strong measures against dishonest notaries and proctors who exploited simple and illiterate clients.

The Crown and Religion

The Catholic Church

The relations of Catholic France and its Most Christian King with the papacy were put on a new footing in 1516 thanks to François I. He was completing a process begun by his distant predecessors and signally advanced by Charles VII, whose Pragmatic Sanction of 1538 had been badly received in Rome. The rapprochement with Rome commenced towards the end of Louis XII's reign when Giovanni de'Medici became Pope Leo X in 1513. Conciliatory by nature, and frightened of Spanish expansion, Leo looked to France as a friend and ally, the more so as he hoped to enrich his kinsmen with French benefices. But the friendly truce broke down over François I's Italian ambitions. Leo made no secret of his desire to put the question of the intolerable Pragmatic Sanction before a general council, gave financial assistance to the Swiss and sent troops to Milan. But the 'cannon of Marignano upset his calculations':[16] there was nothing for it but to negotiate. On the territorial side, Parma and Piacenza were handed over to Milan – and thus to France (13 October 1515) – and then the talks turned to the ecclesiastical organisation of France.

Leo and François met at Bologna amid festivities whose splendour is recorded by the chroniclers. The Chancellor Duprat and the Cardinals Pucci and Accolti settled down to hammer out an agreement. The broad terms, agreed in a brief interview between the king and the pope, had already been discussed by the King's Council in October. But the negotiations, though limited to practical details, dragged on until August 1516 – although this was perhaps quick work for an agreement which remained the basis of the French Church until the Revolution.

The main point was the abolition of the free elections of abbots and bishops, which had been reinstated by the Pragmatic Sanction. Henceforth, bishops and abbots were to be nominated by the king and invested with their spiritual office by the pope. The king could in fact present anyone he liked, and could not be gainsaid, despite the canonical conditions for appointment which were written into the Concordat (which reiterated that a bishop should be a bachelor or doctor of theology or canon law, and at least 27 years old, and that an abbot should be at least 23 and of sound morals – Rome retained the right to refuse spiritual investiture where these conditions were not met). The Concordat eliminated not only the Gallican custom of elections but also the papal practice of reservations when benefices became vacant – except where the incumbent died 'at the Roman curia'. Without spelling it out clearly, the Concordat also preserved the papacy's right to levy annates (a sum equivalent to one year's revenue) on newly appointed incumbents. But the king was now able to claim a tenth of that sum.

Although the Concordat abolished elections for major benefices, it retained them, at least in theory, for minor ones. But the kings of France had for so long been accustomed to install their own candidates that the papacy turned a blind eye when the king intervened. At first, François nominated a fair number of Italian prelates, and then he formally decided in 1531 to nominate to minor benefices.

The Concordat was a crucial document in aligning the Church of France and its enormous landed wealth behind the Crown. From now on, bishops and abbots were the king's men. He dispensed benefices to the sons of noble courtiers and expected unquestioning loyalty in return. He gave out benefices as rewards or tokens of friendship, and the French clergy became the monarchy's closest ally.

This is clear from the 182 nominations of François I's reign: 38 went to foreigners, mostly Italians, in order to oil the wheels of diplomacy; 15 or so went to eminent humanists like Gérard Roussel, the friend of Marguerite de Navarre, who became Bishop of Oloron. Other sees went to trusted men in the upper echelons of royal administration, members of such families as Briçonnet, Semblançay and Du Bourg. But the lion's share went to the nobility: the princes of the blood, the Guises, and the provincial gentlemen whose loyalty required constant cultivation. Like Crown offices, bishoprics gradually became almost hereditary, so that when one incumbent died, his family strove to persuade the king to replace him with a nephew or a cousin. From that time the often denounced abuses could hardly be reformed: when Jean de Guise, brother of Duke Claude, held nine bishoprics and six abbeys, how could he avoid non-residence or curtail pluralism?

The French clergy thus became the king's trump card. What need was there now to follow Henry VIII into schism, or to emulate the German princes in raising the banner of Reformation in order to secularise church lands?

The Parlement was deeply hostile to the Concordat and refused to register it, harking back to the Gallican perfection of the Pragmatic Sanction. It took particular exception to the power which the Concordat gave the papacy over the French Church by providing that certain cases (involving, for example, cardinals or curial officials) be heard at Rome, and by recognising the pope's power to value French benefices for the levying of annates. Parlement even inveighed against the papacy's power of spiritual investiture, arguing that the secret papal aim was the power of nomination. The Concordat was not incorporated into French law until 1518, and then only by means of a *lit de justice*. Parlement also dragged its feet over implementing the Concordat, the more easily because it applied only to the kingdom as it had stood in 1438, at the time of the Pragmatic Sanction: Brittany and Provence were not included. The Crown patiently secured the extension of the Concordat to those provinces by means of a papal indult granted in 1516, and renewed for the benefit of Henri II in 1549. Weary of delay, and finding that the system of elections survived with parliamentary connivance, François I issued an edict in 1528 which transferred jurisdiction over cases involving benefices to the *Grand Conseil*. The Sorbonne, and to a lesser extent the clergy, also objected to the Concordat. A document drafted in the name of the whole university in 1518 denounced the agreement between Crown and papacy, while preachers thundered from the pulpit against the infringement of Gallican liberties. But a royal edict required the university to confine itself to education, and some professors were gaoled and preachers silenced. However, even the people as a whole, or at least the elite, were less than enthusiastic. At the Estates-General of 1560, all three estates called for the restoration of elections – that is, for a return to the Pragmatic Sanction. And at Blois in 1588 this call was renewed, although nobody was under any illusion as to its practicality.

François I and Henri II, already in control of the higher clergy, did not scruple to encroach upon papal or even simply ecclesiastical prerogatives. The Concordat acknowledged, it is true, that in ecclesiastical cases, before appealing to the supreme tribunal of the papacy, a cleric ought to appear before royal judges according to the formula 'No one can be summoned to judgement outside the kingdom.' If for some special reason, such as an outbreak of heresy, the Holy See wished to exercise immediate jurisdiction, it had to nominate French 'judges delegate'. This was the title used to describe the commissioners appointed by the Parlement and the Sorbonne to prosecute Lutherans in 1525. But their powers were short-lived, ending in 1529. On the other hand, the King's Council continually encroached upon ecclesiastical jurisdiction. The ordinance of Villers-Cotterêts in 1539 is of particular importance in this context because it forbade the summoning of laymen before ecclesiastical courts except in cases regarding the sacraments or other purely spiritual matters. The king's courts, in contrast, exercised full jurisdiction over clergy and laity alike. This fatally enfeebled diocesan tribunals, to such an extent that in 1540 Parlements were for a while given jurisdiction even over cases of heresy.

There were various other encroachments, notably in the affairs of hospitals and almshouses. François appointed royal commissioners to verify their accounts and deeds of foundation. An edict of 19 December 1543 ordered an investigation into lazar houses, providing for the replacement of incompetent administrators with able men nominated by civic authorities. In 1546 another edict empowered the Parlements to reorganise charitable foundations and royal judges to audit their accounts. Finally, in 1561, a further edict set the seal on this process of laicisation by establishing in each town two officials, one appointed by the municipality and the other by those responsible for the hospital.[17] The clergy made no protest at this invasion, retaining a right of inspection in that one of the two officials prescribed by the edict was often a churchman. And within such establishments the clergy continued to manage religious worship and sometimes the education of poor children.

But if the monarchy was intervening in areas once reserved strictly for the clergy, it was also more and more taking on the protection of the traditional Church. The Crown legislated for the levying of the tithe, which guaranteed the clergy a good part of their revenues. Later, during the Wars of Religion, when the tithe became a bone of contention between Catholics and Protestants, the King's Council, the Parlements and the provincial authorities intervened to ensure that the clergy received their dues.

The King of France sought with good reason to improve his hierarchy and make it truer to Christian ideals and more hospitable to the faithful. The king and his Council, at least at first, looked favourably on the Church's efforts at internal reform. François I made no secret of his sympathy for the work of the Christian humanists in translating and restoring sacred texts. Some of these men found preferment in the Collège de France. François was certainly influenced by his sister, Marguerite de Navarre, who was thoroughly abreast of new religious ideas and movements. He supported Briçonnet's experiment at Meaux, and intervened to save Berquin, among others, from the stake. In 1522 he took steps to have provincial synods convoked throughout the realm 'in order to reform the Church, stamp out abuses, and ensure that benefices within his kingdom no longer lay vacant'.[18]

Nevertheless, the progress of Lutheranism in France was such that the priority changed from making the Church more evangelical to keeping it Catholic. Thus in 1528 François supported Chancellor Duprat when he, having been made Archbishop of Sens, suggested that a national council be held to define the Catholic position with respect to the new doctrines. In the same year the king encouraged the holding of provincial synods at Bordeaux, Toulouse, Lyon and Bourges. The fact that the national council was presided over by such a fierce defender of royal prerogatives shows how deeply François, like his son after him, was involved in the defence and maintenance of Catholicism. The attending bishops (of Meaux, Chartres, Paris, Troyes and Auxerre), together with theologians from the Sorbonne, condemned once more the teachings of Luther and his followers: 'these nauseating men', as they termed the disciples of the German Reformer, 'have thrown up such repulsive and foetid outrages that they seem to have no other aim than to sully and stain the hitherto immaculate face of the Church'. Invoking the metaphor, already a cliché, of heresy as a plague, they produced a 16-point summary of the Catholic faith to which every true Christian was obliged to adhere. This affirmed as truths of the faith the doctrines of the eucharist, purgatory, the seven sacraments, and the necessity of both faith and good works for salvation. It also affirmed the necessity of clerical celibacy, the validity of the cult of the saints and of monastic vows, the infallibility of the Church, and the authority of councils. Alongside these clearly explained articles of faith were 40 'decreta morum', disciplinary provisions intended to remedy notorious ecclesiastical abuses. We will spare the reader a tedious enumeration, instead simply picking out a few salient points which show that internal Church reform was under way in France long before the Council of Trent. The text concentrated on four main areas: the duties of parish priests; the conduct of the clergy in general, and in particular of priests and vicars; the reform of male and female religious orders; and the rights of bishops. The authority of the royally nominated bishops within their dioceses was reinforced. They were given powers of investigation and censorship, and collaborated with secular authorities in keeping public order, by curbing the excesses of preachers and the supposed intrigues of the confraternities. Catholic Reform was, if not directed, then at least underwritten by the French monarchy.

One can well understand the Crown's attitude to the Council of Trent: at the first phase, in 1545, the French delegation consisted of one bishop and one archbishop. François himself was opposed to the Council because he feared the healing of the religious divisions in Germany which suited him so well. And the Gallican Church was more than somewhat suspicious of Paul III's ultramontane aims. When the second phase of the Council opened, in 1551, Henri II was at loggerheads with the new pope, Julius III. Against Henri's wishes the pope had reconvened the council at Trent, in imperial territory, although he had previously promised not to choose that city. When the papal nuncio arrived in July 1550 to advise him of the council's summons, Henri replied in fury that he had no need of a council to deal with the religious problems of his kingdom. Moreover, relations between the king and the Emperor were on the brink of collapse, and Henri had no wish to look as though he was on the Emperor's side when his negotiations for an alliance with the Lutheran princes of Germany were drawing to a conclusion in January 1552. So no French bishops attended, and public opinion encouraged the king in his hostility to pope and council. Gallican and openly antipapal treatises appeared, such as Dumoulin's *Les petites dates* and, in 1552, Rabelais's *Quart livre*, in which Frère Jean and Pantagruel ridiculed the 'Kingdom of Chitterlings' and the 'land of King Lent'. The third and last phase of the council saw French bishops arrive, albeit late, duly commissioned by Catherine de Medici. But more of that later. At the Council of Trent the French delegation complied more with the wishes of their temporal than those of their spiritual head.

Religious Dissidents

At first neither François nor his regime were particularly disturbed by the progress of the Reformation. While there were sporadic outbreaks of iconoclasm on the part of the devotees of the new doctrines, it was the Parlement and the Sorbonne which reacted violently, not the king, who indeed often held them back. Moreover, the ruling classes were divided over the best course of action. Under the influence of his sister, Marguerite of Navarre, François was on the whole tolerant. But his Chancellor, Duprat, wished to stamp out the sparks of heresy and clamp down on public scandals, and the Parlements and the Sorbonne shared his opinion.

The progression from words to deeds on the part of Reformers was spectacular. They were proposing reforms far more radical than anything undertaken at Meaux or envisaged by the Christian humanists. They extolled their beliefs as the truths of a purer religion, and attacked the visible symbols peddled by the Church as palliatives for existential anguish. Their symbolic discourse took the form of profaning holy water stoups, smashing statues of Our Lady and the saints, mocking Blessed Sacrament processions, provocatively cooking savoury meats during Lent or on fast days, and insulting priests during the celebration of Mass. In 1523, at Paris and Meaux, pictures of the Virgin Mary were vandalised; later, in 1528, a Parisian statue of Mary was beheaded; and in 1530, at Toulouse, a listener stopped a preacher in full flow and accused him of lying. The early history of the French Reformation is a catalogue of such iconoclastic incidents.

Under both François I and Henri II, royal legislation showed little enough interest in 'Lutherans' and 'heretical vermin', with their reigns producing only 20 and 11 acts respectively. Henri's measures ratified the 25 articles of faith proclaimed by the Sorbonne and enshrined them in the law of the land, to mark the boundary between Catholic orthodoxy on the one hand and heresy or even just Christian humanism on the other. Other measures (in 1535, 1536, 1540, 1542 and 1543) dealt with the pursuit of heretics, which was entrusted to both secular and ecclesiastical judges. Penalties for those who concealed heretics were laid down during François I's reign, while informers were to receive a quarter of the goods confiscated from those convicted (1535). Tighter censorship was introduced for printers (who were not to work without a privilege granted under the Great Seal) and booksellers, who were not to sell religious books without a licence from the Sorbonne (1537, 1542, 1547, 1551 and 1557). The frequent reiteration of such legislation testifies to both the profusion of subversive literature and the ready market it attracted.

Repressive measures came thick and fast in the wake of the affair of the Placards, which almost compelled the Crown to take some sort of action. The affair was reported in the following terms by the 'Citizen of Paris':

> On the night of the 17th–18th October 1534, leaflets impugning the honour and truth of the Blessed Sacrament and the saints were dropped or posted in streets and public places throughout Paris and the provinces, and even at the door of the king's bedchamber in the Château of Amboise, in the very locker where he leaves his handkerchief. . . . The pope and all his rabble of cardinals, bishops, priests and monks were decried as liars and blasphemers.

The initial reactions were of course collective. The clergy knew how to mobilise the faithful. Processions were organised, or took place spontaneously, on all sides. On 21 January 1535 François himself took to the streets of Paris at the head of an enormous procession. All the relics and sacred things were brought out for the occasion, all the signs of God's presence among men and all the objects on which the hopes (or despair) of believers focused. Last of all came the Blessed Sacrament itself, held aloft by the Bishop of Paris beneath a canopy carried by four princes of the blood. The king, who, as we have seen, marched at the head of the column 'alone, with a candle of pure wax in his hand and his head uncovered' dined that same day with the bishop and some leading citizens. In their presence he voiced his anger at 'the stunts that a few wicked blasphemers, men of little standing and less learning, have contrived against the honour of the Blessed Sacrament, using words unheard of among any other nation'.[19]

A period of fierce repression was inaugurated by an edict of 13 January 1535 which, somewhat neurotically, forbade 'the printing of anything, under penalty of the gallows', and ordered the closure of all bookshops. This extreme aberration was revoked ten days later, when the book trade was placed under the supervision of a commission of Parlement. On 29 January a new edict expressed a more chilling purpose, announcing the king's intention to exterminate 'the Lutheran sect and the other heresies which, to our bitter regret and displeasure, have broken out and fester within our realm'. The traditional penalties for heretical beliefs and practices were imposed, but they were also threatened against those who actively concealed or simply failed to report heretics. Those good subjects, in contrast, who informed on 'sectaries' were now entitled to a share of the goods confiscated or fines exacted from offenders.

For over a year a kind of terror gripped Paris and the major cities. Several malcontents fled the country: 75, including John Calvin, from the jurisdiction of the Parlement de Paris. Others who had, in the words of the Genevan Reformer, 'tasted the Gospel', took fright and retreated into conformity. In December 1535 Rabelais petitioned the pope for absolution from his 'apostasy'. Clément Marot immediately took to his heels on the kind of peripatetic journey characteristic of the gospellers, from Nérac, via Ferrara, to Venice, before finally returning to France in 1537 at the cost of a public abjuration. Those two escaped the stake: 'I am dry enough by nature without being heated any more', as Pantagruel declared. But not everyone managed to manoeuvre so adeptly. From October 1534 until the promulgation of the royal edict of 29 January 1535, two heralds walked the streets of Paris announcing that the Parlement would pay 200 *écus* to anyone who informed against the 'Lutheran supporters of the placards and leaflets'. The reward was tempting (about 660 *livres*) at a time when a summoner (a lowly court official responsible for serving court papers) earned about 30 *livres* a year. Denunciations flooded in. On 7 November, 7 death sentences were pronounced, the first in a long line of people 'converted to ash', in Marot's bitter words; 35 'Lutherans' were burned in Paris during January 1535.

For diplomatic reasons this clampdown could not long continue at such a ferocious level. The pope called on François to moderate his anger, explaining sensibly enough that 'it is a cruel death for a man to be burned alive'. And whatever care one should exercise in reading this document, it is clear that at this point Paul III was engaged in tortuous negotiations to bring Catholics and Lutherans back together. For his part, François had to consider the Reformed party in Germany. His explanations to them sought to put a velvet glove on the iron hand: 'The enemy of all truth and peace', he explained, 'has stirred up certain men, more criminal than insane, to encompass the overthrow of the established order.' This kind of talk made sense to the princes and urban patriciates who within a matter of years had faced the Knights' War, the Peasants' Revolt, and finally the Anabaptist crisis at Münster. On 1 February 1535 the ambassador Du Bellay took the same line in a widely distributed pamphlet.

The terror ended in July 1535, when the Edict of Coucy offered an amnesty to all adherents of reformed doctrines, and allowed refugees to return to France on condition of formal abjuration. But the respite was brief indeed. In June 1538 the diplomatic wheel of fortune turned once more. Paul III, Charles V and François I combined in a league against the Protestants, and repression was once more given its head. The Sorbonne, the Parlements and the Crown stood shoulder to shoulder against the heretics, be they Lutheran or Calvinist. Henceforth, those who hoped for a new faith and a new Church were not only 'heretics', an almost comfortingly traditional term, but also 'disturbers of the public peace' and, above all, 'practisers of treason'. To deny Catholicism was to deny the religion of the king, and thus in effect to deny the king himself. François, like his son, equipped himself with the judicial and administrative machinery necessary to combat a religious movement tantamount in his eyes to sedition. Secular tribunals, like their ecclesiastical counterparts, could now take cognisance of religious cases. Edict followed on edict, each further tightening the screw of repression: the Edict of Fontainebleau in 1539, and others in 1540, 1542 and 1547, set 'blasphemers' in their sights. The Edict of Châteaubriand (1551) sought to make the tribunals more effective in pursuit of those who were still being called 'Lutherans'. In 1559 the Edict of Écouen envisaged no other penalty than death for those convicted of heresy. Henri II, the instigator of this measure, had already, in 1547, established the *Chambre ardente*, a tribunal whose sole function was to track down and prosecute Protestants within the jurisdiction of the Parlement de Paris (which covered about half the kingdom). In little more than two years it passed sentence on more than 500 heretics. In southern France the Parlements of Bordeaux, Toulouse and Aix poured forth threatening decrees and death sentences. The Parlement of Aix enjoys the dubious distinction of having set in motion a punitive expedition against the Waldensians of Provence, who had been ensconced around Mérindol and Cabrières for 200 years. They had supported 'the holy reformation' and collected the sum of 500 *écus* to finance the printing of a French Bible at Geneva. Translated by Pierre-Robert Olivier, or 'Olivetanus' (probably a relative of Calvin's, who had taken refuge at Geneva), it was printed by Pierre de Vingle at Neuchâtel, and appeared in 1535. Hearing of this, the Parlement of Aix condemned 17 Waldensians to the stake in 1540, and decreed that Mérindol be razed to the ground. Despite an attempt by François I to suspend execution of the decree, the Waldensians, accused of heresy and sedition, were tracked into their mountains and slaughtered in their hundreds. Twenty-two townships, including Lourmarin, Mérindol, and Cabrières, were looted and burned. Some survivors hid, hoping to return to their ruined homes. Others fled to Switzerland.[20]

At the same time, a further regulation was issued by the King's Council and, with sundry modifications, registered by the provincial Parlements. It introduced censorship, with strict surveillance for bookshops and printing houses, together with control of schoolteaching. If they wished to take up public posts, teachers had to swear adherence to orthodoxy. Discussion of religious issues was strictly forbidden to all except the clergy. The Sorbonne, allying itself closely with the Crown, set about sifting through the books then in circulation, alert to the slightest hint of heresy. From 1523 onwards hosts of books were worked through and then forbidden: the works of Luther and Melanchthon, the Gospels of Lefèvre, and any translation of the Bible. The Sorbonne found more than enough on its plate as dissident books proliferated. It was in order to facilitate the task of censorship that it defined the 25 articles of the faith in 1543. A good Catholic was to believe in the necessity of baptism and confession, in free will and good works, in transubstantiation, the intercession of the saints, and purgatory, etc. The following year, the feverish theology faculty issued a new Index forbidding 65 books on account of their heretical positions. The royal courts used the 25 articles in their own investigations, and promulgated lists of forbidden books and pamphlets within their various jurisdictions. Repression assumed many forms. For some it led to the stake for involvement in acts of public opposition to the established religion, such as iconoclastic vandalism, mocking religious processions, heckling preachers, or profaning altars or holy water stoups. For others, it meant intolerable petty harrassment, with searches, investigations, arrests and fines. For others still it meant flight abroad, to towns or cities where their form of religion was already established, above all to Strasbourg and Geneva. In Geneva, the long influx of French immigrants began around 1542. It speeded up when persecution became especially severe, as at the start of Henri II's reign, between 1547 and 1549. Two thirds of the 5000 foreigners who sought asylum in Geneva between 1549 and 1560 were from France. They came mainly from Languedoc and Normandy, which sent nearly a thousand refugees between them, but the Ile-de-France, Guyenne, and Gascony also sent significant numbers. These figures testify to the harshness of both ecclesiastical and secular authorities, above all the Parlements, in those regions. But all the exiles, martyrdoms, systematic massacres (like that of the Waldensians), and daily vexations served only to swell the numbers of adherents to the new faith.

7 The Monarchy and its Image

The Court

The Court was the mirror or stage of the monarchy. As such it was the creation of François I and Henri II, and as such it survived down to the Revolution. Of course, the origins of the Court lie far back in history, with the origins of power itself. Every chief, however uncouth, had his entourage of comrades and priests. But under François I and Henri II the Court was formally organised. This development was common to the other monarchies heading for authoritarian rule, such as England and above all Spain, but the model came from Italy, where, in the princely cities of Florence, Urbino and Modena, those complex institutions, with their combination of social, political, cultural and symbolic roles, had first come into existence. From this time on women took a full part in daily life at the hub of politics, making the medieval assembly of barons a thing of the past.

The French Court was a peripatetic institution. When based at the Louvre or Tournelles palaces in Paris, it formed a town within a town. But more often it was to be found at some château in the Loire valley or the Ile-de-France. It was almost like Merovingian times, when the kings came and went from one domain to another, 'living of their own'. The king and his Court spent the year going from Blois to Chenonceaux, from Vincennes to Fontainebleau, or from Chambord to Saint-Germain, driven by the need for provisions, the desire for a change of scene, or the pursuit of seasonal pleasures like the hunt. Along the roads snaked columns of horsemen, of carriages bearing the ladies, and of carts loaded with tableware, silver, furniture and tapestries. Ahead of them rode the purveyors who were responsible, on journeys of more than a day, for arranging food and shelter for this little world. Not that it was that small. In peacetime, when the men were not away on campaign, it numbered some 18 000 persons in the days of Charles IX, and not much less in those of his father and grandfather.

The Court was organised like a private household, with various departments concerned with the different aspects of its life. Six departments were clearly demarcated: the pantry, the buttery, the kitchen, the grocery, the stable, and the purveyors. Other departments did not correspond to trades: the King's Chamber, the chapel, the household guard, and the sub-households of the queen and of the royal children (which alone accounted for 240 persons in 1523). The King's Household, the Court properly so called, was presided over by the Grand Master of the Household. This post, the exclusive preserve of the nobility, was much sought after because it brought with it the closest degree of personal familiarity with the king. Here, at the very highest level of domestic affairs, was found that indefinable combination of political and private life characteristic of the king's Court from Saint Louis to Louis XIV. Henri Lemonnier has said of the office of Grand Master that it was 'the culmination or epitome of every political role'.[1] The post conferred enormous power, and its holder was an intimate adviser of the king (enjoying, in the words of Jean Jacquart, 'access to the royal person at all times and places'[2]), who together with the king assigned offices and responsibilities at Court. The first recipient of this high office under François I was Artus Gouffier, sire de Boisy, whom Louise of Savoy had appointed governor to her son. He was succeeded by the king's uncle René, the 'Bastard of Savoy'. And finally, from 1526, the office was held by Anne de Montmorency. Excluded from the centre of power by royal disfavour later in the reign, Montmorency recovered his influence on the accession of Henri II in 1547, serving simultaneously as Constable, Governor of Languedoc, and most importantly, head of the Council.[3]

Among the other household offices which conferred political power upon its incumbent was that of the *Grand écuyer* (or Master of the Horse). In charge of both the greater and the lesser stables, and in particular of the corps of 120 couriers who carried royal missives throughout the realm, the Master of the Horse was also among the closest associates of the king. In the reign of François this office was held by Galiot de Génouillac, who also served as

Master of the Artillery. The other major post was that of Constable, the commander in chief of the French army. This office was originally conferred at first upon Charles de Bourbon. After his sudden fall, it went to the already all-powerful Montmorency, who in turn lost the exercise and fruits of the office through his fall from grace, to recover them only under the new king in 1547.

Service in the King's Chamber was highly prized by noblemen – and purchased at great expense – because it brought with it personal contact with the monarch. The office of *Grand chambrier* was replaced in 1545 by the almost identical office of Grand Chamberlain, assisted by ordinary Chamberlains and *Valets de chambre*. Together they saw to the needs of the king within his private apartments, managing the routines and ceremonies of rising and going to bed. In the reign of François I, ever concerned for the status of his Court, the Gentlemen of the Chamber, Chamberlains, and Valets assumed a greater importance than in the past, and could attain high political office. Thus Guillaume du Bellay, appointed First Gentleman of the Chamber in 1533, became Viceroy of Piedmont four years later. Subsequently, Jacques d'Albon de Saint-André took over the post. He retained it under Henri II, and served at the same time on the King's Council. Among the *Valets de chambre*, a number of commoners broke the predominant pattern of noble birth, men like Clément Marot, whose artistic talent had earned them the patronage of a State pension. The Chamber also employed the services of sundry pages, boys from prominent noble families who from their infancy were brought up by the king and were thus close to him.

Two great officers of State who owed their appointment to royal favour combined courtly and adminstrative functions. The more important was the Chancellor, an officer with whom, as we shall see, the monarch sometimes had rather strained relations. He obviously played a central role. The Grand Admiral, who might also be a provincial governor, field commander, and royal councillor, was a figure of no less importance. At his accession, François conferred the admiralty upon his childhood friend Guillaume Gouffier, sire de Bonnivet, the brother of his governor Artus Gouffier. Bonnivet, something of an adventurer, fought alongside the king at Marignano, conducted the preliminary negotiations for the Concordat, attempted to seduce the king's sister Marguerite, and served as ambassador to Henry VIII. He finally sought and found death amid the disaster at Pavia, a defeat for which he must probably take much of the blame. He was succeeded by Chabot, who was soon disgraced. Later on, Henri II was to please his friend Constable Montmorency by appointing to the admiralty his nephew Gaspard de Châtillon, seigneur de Coligny, a man whose personality and profound convictions were to weigh heavily in the early years of the civil wars. He too sat upon the King's Council.

Another figure about Court was the Grand Almoner, who performed royal baptisms and marriages. He was assisted by ordinary almoners, among whom were men such as Philibert Delorme, Pierre Lescot and Pierre Ronsard, who drew their pensions more for their talents than for any particular duties. Such was not the case with the king's physician and surgeon. They were in constant attendance, ever on the alert, and were assisted by teams of physicians and apothecaries.

It was Anne of Brittany, Louis XII's second wife, who introduced the practice of surrounding herself with matrons and maids of honour drawn from the foremost families in the kingdom. Anne's nine matrons and 40 maids added a distinctly feminine dimension to Court life, along the lines of the Italian Courts where conventions of courtly love were much in vogue. Kings looked to these women for favourites, and noblemen found among them some relaxation from their warlike pursuits. Catherine de Medici increased the number of her female attendants to around a hundred, including not only matrons and maids of honour but also governesses, maids of the chamber, and *courtisanes*. This body made up her 'flying squad', employed for underhand political purposes.

The policing of this populous and varied society was supervised by the *prévôt de l'Hôtel* (or 'Provost of the Household'), assisted by lieutenants, archers and scribes. As the Court steadily expanded, so the Provost's role grew in importance. He had sovereign jurisdiction over all crimes and offences committed within royal residences or within a radius of five miles of the royal person.[4] When the Court was on the road, he also had civil responsibilities, making sure that prices were not excessively inflated by the presence of the Court, and securing or even requisitioning daily supplies.

The Royal Household, or the Court proper, also included a military force, as much for protection as display. 200 gentlemen, divided into two companies under two captains, were armed with a halberd and a sword. There were also 100 Scottish guards in a household otherwise dominated by Frenchmen, and from their number were chosen the 25 men who day and night formed the king's bodyguard. From Charles VIII's reign this force was augmented by 100 Swiss guards with a largely ceremonial role, specialising in providing guards of honour. And finally there were three companies of French archers. The soldiers of the royal guard were equipped with fine uniforms whose colours changed with each reign. Under François I it was a tunic of blue, scarlet and beige, embroidered with silver and gold. Under Henri II the basic colours were white, silver and black; under Charles IX, white, blue and pink; and under Henri III, green and yellow. But for all their splendour these troops were genuine fighting units which served on the battlefield. After all, their members were mostly noblemen, for whom warfare was a way of life.

The Court was a complex and fascinating organisation whose many roles made it the constant centre of attention for the kingdom's political elite. Its purely domestic role was far from insignificant. The Court provided for the day-to-day existence of the royal family, catering for their physical and spiritual needs, their personal safety, and the upbringing and education of the royal children. In this sense the name 'household' remained strictly accurate. But the Court also had a political role. The members of the *Conseil secret* and *Conseil d'état*, the secretaries and the notaries had to attend upon the king and therefore, as the Court was always on the move, had to live at Court: the royal administration remained at work, legislating and making decisions, whether at Chambord or at Blois. All those who moved in the upper echelons of power attended at Court and took part in the comings and goings of its public existence, whether they were commoners, new nobility, or nobles of ancient lineage. The Court had a symbolic function as the showcase of royal power and majesty, providing the scenery and cast for the continuing drama that was Valois sovereignty. Receptions for ambassadors or for prominent figures, whether French or foreign, celebrations or ceremonies for happy or sad events in the life of the royal family, all alike were occasions for more or less ritualised performances designed to make an impact on both participants and spectators. The kind of courtier in attendance varied subtly with the predilections of the sovereign and his inclination towards this or that method of affirming his omnipotence. Artists and writers predominated under François I; nobles, dukes and peers under Henri II and Catherine de Medici. But such matters affected only the nuances, not the general tone.

Equipping nobles from powerful families with important positions which kept them close to the king enabled him to keep a watchful eye on them. When a great noble withdrew from Court, whether in disgrace, dudgeon, or just on impulse, there was everything to fear from what he might do back in his province, where he could foment grievances and agitations. The regime could only breathe easily when it could welcome and harbour such men, be they princes of the blood or magnates.

The Court, in the form developed by François I and Henri II, was the arena in which the monarchy exerted its power over the magnates of the land. Through the subtle manipulation of favour – now offered, now moderated, sometimes even withdrawn – the king kept a grip on his nobility and gentry. Each of them could appreciate the power of his good will, or for that matter his ill will, and realise that their political existence depended on it. That same power which toppled the disgraced Montmorency in 1541 raised him up again on Henri II's accession, heaping him anew with offices, grants and pensions. We have seen how that power worked first for and then against Admiral Chabot, how it helped bring Chancellor Poyet to gaol, and how it rewarded or penalised other courtiers. The Court was the universe in which the king, like some petty deity, worked his will upon his subjects.

One can easily see how the life of men and women of the Court differed from that of ordinary folk. Spontaneous and natural behaviour was forgotten, or else confined to life back in their provincial châteaux. Set apart by royal favour, courtiers had a different outlook on life, dominated by a sense of mutability. Attendance on the king necessitated a vigorous restraint of natural impulses, a re-education of body and soul, a polished impassivity and a long training in the physical and mental pursuits of the Court. The self-restraint of courtiers helped make the Court a wholly elitist institution, sharply distinct from the country. We might add that in this crowded world, where people were forced into each other's company day and night, and where humiliation, confrontation and misfortune were endemic, it was impossible to express anger, coarseness, or even candour without the significance of the act being amplified by the number of witnesses. Wearing the mask was an existential necessity for the courtier.[5]

The first half of the sixteenth century saw the emergence of a genre of courtly literature, and, almost inevitably, also of a counter-genre which allowed opponents of the courtly ethic to lament or decry it. Both genres served to delineate the character and emphasise the importance of the institution. The authors of these works (we need look at only a few examples) were interested less in the political and symbolic functions of the Court than in the new models of behaviour which they necessitated and promoted. Baldassarre Castiglione's *Book of the Courtier* (Venice, 1528) inaugurated this almost moralistic genre. François I's copy of the first edition, decorated with his royal arms, is preserved in the Bibliothèque Nationale. Castiglione provided the Courts of Europe with an idealised self-image, and his book was an immediate success. It was translated into French in 1537 by Jacques Colin, the king's secretary, and a new translation followed in 1538. A third version, by Gabriel Chappuis, appeared in 1585 and was reprinted three times before the end of the century.

Castiglione's story inspired later writers on the subject in what were often pretty shameless imitations. The castle of Urbino around 1500 had housed a brilliant circle of lords, ladies, and intellectuals. A haven of peace and civility in an Italy torn apart by the rivalry of great powers, it gave itself over to the delights of conversation. To prevent aimlessness, a theme was laid down: the delineation of the ideal courtier. On the third day of the proceedings, they turned to sketch the perfect lady of the Court. On the fourth, they dealt with the relations between a courtier and his prince. Finally, at dawn on the fifth day, they discussed love as it should be conceived by true gentlemen. In the course of the discussions they not only outlined an entire code of worldly conduct and courtly ritual, but also, and more profoundly, an entire and coherent system of courtly ethics and mores – a model no sooner proposed than adopted by the aristocracy.

Was Marguerite de Navarre's *Heptaméron* perhaps inspired more by Castiglione's *Courtier* than Boccaccio's *Decameron*? It seems that this question has never in fact been addressed, not even by Lucien Febvre in his famous study of the work.[6] At any rate, Marguerite's work was for the most part written after the appearance of the *Courtier*, and even of its French translations, sketched out as it was from about 1542. Following the lighthearted but none the less meaningful diversions of a group of nobles trapped by some natural disaster at Cauterets in the Pyrenees, the *Heptaméron* describes a courtly society which was probably closer to reality than the more formal and didactic creation of Castiglione.

Other works took as their theme the Court and its often

dangerous relationships. The *De civilitate morum puerilium* of Erasmus, first published in 1530, offered itself as a handbook for the young nobleman born into the ruling elite. Advising on how to dress, eat, drink, blow one's nose, speak and carry oneself, it proposed basic rules of tact and good manners, if not princely, then at least courtly and certainly elitist. The *De civilitate* was frequently reprinted, widely plagiarised by obscure imitators, and soon found its way onto the reading lists of the Jesuit and Protestant colleges which educated the servants of the State. Henceforth students learned how to restrain their impulses, rule their bodies and control their tempers. It was, in short, the triumph of culture over nature. The role of courtly literature and the success of the courtly ethic lay in this, the transformation of aristocratic men and women. Formed in a single mould, they were set apart from the common run of humanity, and were represented to society at large as embodying the only possible model of conduct.

Royal Progresses

In the age of François I and Henri II, royal display grew ever more ostentatious and sophisticated, attaining unprecedented peaks. Royal progresses, during which the king paraded before his dazzled subjects, had an important part to play. It was not so much what today the French would call a 'bain de foule' (or 'walkabout') as a manifestation of divinity. Planned in minute detail, progresses allowed the common people to see their sovereign in the flesh, and gave the towns, through their duly constituted authorities, a chance to participate in the cult of monarchy. Such events were often organised when fervour was waning and the regime wished to rekindle it. Accompanied by Queen Eleanor and the Dauphin François, François I undertook an extensive tour of his kingdom between 1531 and spring 1534. Never before had a French king left the centres of power for so long. Around the same time, and in the most difficult of conditions, Charles V was engaged in a tour of his diffuse European empire. François I's itinerary took him from Picardy to Normandy, through Brittany to the Loire valley, then across Champagne to the Bourbonnais, down the Rhône to Lyon and Marseille, on to Puy and Toulouse, thence to Avignon via Nîmes, back to Marseille for the wedding of his second son Henri to Catherine de Medici, and finally by way of Dijon, Langres,

Bar-le-Duc and Troyes, to Paris, which he entered on 9 February 1534. Only the progress of Catherine de Medici with her son Charles IX, thirty years later, proved as long and as varied. Like a true Renaissance prince, François displayed a voracious curiosity in his visitation of the realm. Fascinated by the Roman remains at Nîmes, he ordered the arenas to be cleared of their overlay of cottages. But political priorities were never forgotten. Even if François indulged the pleasures of tourism to the full, he took care to meet the local notables, the district and provincial authorities, and the personages who never came to Court. In Brittany, he had the Dauphin proclaimed the legal heir of his mother Claude – but reserved the usufruct of the duchy to himself. It was a delicate balancing act. The Bretons were jealous of their autonomy, so in exchange they received confirmation of their privileges. The progress of the royal train through the Bourbonnais in 1533 was no idle tour. It was necessary to reinforce the loyalty of a province only recently acquired through the fall of the Constable. The journey through the Auvergne to Marseille was likewise designed to manifest the royal presence in a fief only recently confiscated from Charles de Bourbon. At Toulouse, the capital of Languedoc and the seat of the kingdom's second most senior Parlement, François visited the abbey and shrine of Saint-Sernin, paying due respect to the relics, before going to an agreeable dinner with Bernuy, the wealthy woad-dealer. By these contacts, meetings and official displays, the king strengthened (or forged) links of loyalty between the provincial elites and the Crown.

For their part, the towns which were privileged with a royal entry expressed their gratitude and fidelity by arranging superb festivities. At Rouen on 3 February 1532, and at Rennes on 13 August, the cities greeted their sovereign by laying out gardens and erecting scenery replete with symbolism based on the scriptural text 'I have found my heart's desire'.[7] In Brittany, to be sure, the fervent acclamation was addressed more to the Dauphin, their duke, than to the king, but so what? The cult of kingship was served all the same. Amid rather insipid pastoral motifs, the towns offered themselves like immaculate virgins to their amorous conqueror. In 1533, Lyon organised two entries, one for the Dauphin and the other for Queen Eleanor. Triumphal arches were decked with suitable imagery, and greenery lined the royal route. Writers and artists collaborated in the symbolic exaltation of the ruling dynasty. Classical mythology was invoked in the form of the Graces, and classical antiquity in the programmatic identification of François I with Alexander the Great.

Henri II, preoccupied with war, did not have the time for such an extensive progress. But he did not fail to make entries in his major towns. The authorities of Paris were advised in 1547 to spare no expense in welcoming the new king and queen. On 12 April letters patent instructed the aldermen to 'do their duty and set an example to other towns'. Trembling with deference, they replied that they would 'arrange the greatest triumph possible'. The plan was not accomplished for another two years, once the civic authorities had raised the wherewithal through a loan from the merchants and a municipal levy on wine and grazing cattle. Philibert Delorme, the commissioner for royal buildings, played his part in laying out the city's streets and squares, as did the painters Jean Cousin and Charles Dorigny, and the sculptor Jean Goujon. In short, no stone was left unturned, and the total cost was in excess of 100 000 *livres*. Commencing on 16 June 1549, the festivities lasted for several days, during which the corporation paraded in all its finery before not only the king but also the queen, who had just been crowned at Saint-Denis. There was a tournament in the rue Saint-Antoine and a naval battle on the Seine. Triumphal arches were set up before the portals of Saint-Denis, and an extraordinary construction in the form of a 'three-sided needle' was put up on the Pont Notre-Dame in front of the church of the Holy Sepulchre. A costly gift of finely wrought gold was presented to the king. There was a midsummer bonfire with fireworks in the square before the Hôtel-de-Ville to celebrate the king and his wife, and the whole thing was rounded off by a living fire, whose flames were fed by heretics, in the cemetery of Saint-Jean and the Place Maubert. The celebrations lasted for more than a fortnight. Demanded by the king and organised by the city, these festivities sealed the union between Henri II and his capital. The symbols and images set out by the designers left no room for doubt. The king, the 'Gallic Hercules' and son of François, was represented by the mythical figure of Tiphys, the pilot of the Argonauts. The commentary spelled out its significance:

> Just as, in ancient days, Tiphys steered Argo
> To gain the conquest of the golden fleece;
> So our great ship, wise king, shall find increase
> Beneath your guidance, and an equal cargo.

The Parisian elites agreed with the policy of their sovereign for steering the 'great ship'. His foreign policy met with approval: the obelisk set up before the church of the Holy Sepulchre showed France clothed in a toga on which heraldic beasts were depicted placing triumphant paws on an imperial crown. But Henri was doubtless even more pleased by the 250 000 *livres* offered by the city towards his forthcoming campaign against England. This sum was raised by issuing bonds which yielded a penny in every shilling (or 8.33 per cent) on the security of the two levies conceded on wine and 'cloven hooves'. The king's religious policy received equally frank endorsement. The burnings of 4 July emphasised the vigour of the repressive policy by presenting it to the city as a part of the celebration of the dynasty. The response by the Mayor conformed to expectations:

> Sire, the motto which your good city of Paris, the capital of your kingdom, has long borne and bears to this day, namely 'One God, one king, one faith, one law', is ample testimony to the Catholic faith and life of its inhabitants.

The recapture of Boulogne from the English was marked by a triumphal entry at Rouen on 1 October 1550, a few months after the victory. Planning had begun in August, and the spectacle was designed to demonstrate Henri's military success and French mastery of the sea, achievements brought about by the consensus of all those around the king. On this occasion the royal propaganda was put into print for the benefit of the literate. Three lavishly illustrated booklets described the king's route through the city and explained the significance of the decorations and ceremonies. They were a success, and were reprinted a year later. As usual, the processions of guildsmen were headed by the Admiral's archers and by the secular and regular clergy. These were followed by the crossbowmen and the sergeants of the city, and then the aldermen on horseback accompanying the citizens and merchants. Finally came the king's men: councillors of the Parlement, officers of the Admiralty, and of the Rivers and Forests, officials of the courts, and advocates. After a slight gap came the military: arquebusiers, footsoldiers, and captains. Then came the long-awaited marchpast of allegorical representations: chariots bearing Renown, Religion, Victory, and Good Fortune constituted a panegyric to a royal family accorded divine honours. Henri II

then left the platform from which he had surveyed the impressive procession in order to take part in other ceremonies laid on
by the civic authorities. There was a portrayal of daily life among
the Tupinambas of Brazil, well known to the traders of Rouen,
who had established an outpost near Pernambuco and sought to
hold it despite Portuguese hostility. The actors included not only
a number of Normans in make-up and costume, but also 'fifty
native savages, freshly transported from that land'. No detail was
omitted from the reconstruction, which even included a mock
battle between the real and pretend Tupinambas and a hostile
tribe. This ethnological showpiece enjoyed enormous success not
only in Rouen but throughout the kingdom. It was matter for
fireside gossip and for bookish comment: Montaigne devoted one
of his essays to 'Cannibals', but he did not see any Indians until
much later, in the reign of Charles IX. Other scenes were played
out as Henri moved step by step towards the centre of the town,
all of them vaunting his military triumphs and his mental and
spiritual virtues. A final allegory summed up the whole proceedings: Orpheus and the Muses were depicted in contented conversation with the victorious Hercules.

Lits de Justice and Causes Célèbres

There were other, equally spectacular ways in which the monarch
could impress upon his people, and above all on the elite, the
image and reality of his power. François I made more use of them
than did his son, to the point that he abused them, jealous as he
was of an authority which was more often put to the test. The lit
de justice, employed to extort parliamentary registration of disputed laws, was a frequent feature of his reign, used more by
François than by any other Capetian king, Valois or Bourbon.
His relations with his sovereign courts were in general far from
harmonious, punctuated by lettres de jussion and registrations 'at
the king's express command'. But we shall come back to that.
The lit de justice was a piece of royal theatre, magnificently staged,
and crushing for those it was designed to coerce. This can be
seen from the minutes of the lit de justice held on 24 July 1527 in
order to compel the Parlement de Paris to register a measure
concerning appeals to the Grand Council:

The king was seated on his throne in full court in the Parlement de Paris, holding his *lit de justice.*

To the king's right, on the high benches of the court, were: the King of Navarre, Knight of the Order of St Michael, Peer of France; the Duke of Vendôme, Peer of France, Lieutenant-General and Governor of Picardy; the Count of Saint-Pol, Lieutenant-General and Governor of the Dauphiné; the Count of Guise, Lieutenant-General and Governor of Brie and Champagne; Monsieur Anne de Montmorency, Grand Master and Marshal of France, Governor of Languedoc, and of Upper and Lower Alsace; Monsieur Gilles de Genouilac, Grand Master of the Artillery of France and Seneschal of Armagnac; and Monsieur Robert Stuart, seigneur d'Aubigny, Captain of the Hundred Lances of the Ordinances and of the Scots Guard of the King's Body.

To his left, similarly seated, were: the Cardinal of Bourbon, Bishop and Duke of Lyon, Peer of France; the Bishop and Count of Noyon, Peer of France; the Archbishop of Bourges, Primate of Aquitaine and Primate of the Gauls; and the Bishop of Lisieux.

At the king's feet: the Duke of Longueville, Grand Chamberlain of France, right next to the king on the right-hand side, seated on the floor in the highest place; Monsieur Louis de Brézé, Governor and Grand Seneschal of Normandy, First Chamberlain, a little lower, on the king's left, also seated on the floor; Messire Jean de Labarre, Provost of Paris, below and to the right of the king's feet, bearing a white staff in his hand, also seated on the ground, in the lowest place.

On their knees before the king were two Ushers of the Chamber, each holding a staff.

On the low benches of the court, where the Presidents usually sit during sessions of Parlement, were: Messire Antoine Duprat, Archbishop of Sens, Chancellor of France, and three Presidents. On the low benches to the right: seven Masters of Ordinary Requests of the King's Household, with two Masters of the recent creation. And on the low benches to the left: various churchmen and 36 Councillors, with three clerks and two notaries of the court.

Behind the benches were several Gentlemen of the King's Chamber, together with the Provost of the Household. And within the court on the little benches sat Messire François Robertet, Chancellor, seigneur d'Allaye, Clerk of the Order of St Michael, and Bailiff of Paris; and Messire G. de la Châtre, Provost of the Order of St Michael, one of the Captains of the King's French Bodyguard. The Lieutenants of the Captains of the Guard were on guard at the doors of the Parlement.

Before the king's arrival, the Bishop and Count of Noyon, Peer of France, administered to the court the ordinary oath to the Peers of France.

Once the king was seated upon his throne, the Chancellor of France, the Archbishop of Sens, told the court that if they had any comments to offer the king, then they could offer them. The Presidents and Councillors sank to their knees, and once the king had bidden them to arise, M. Claude Guillard, President, delivered to the king a lengthy oration packed with citations from Homer, Cicero, the Bible, etc.[8]

The spectacular performances which each king put on for the benefit of his leading subjects were designed to show that he was master over the powers within the land, and that their leading position in the State was contingent upon royal favour: an intention highly characteristic of François I's jealous and suspicious nature. Certain lawsuits were handled in highly public fashion in order to provide food for thought. The charges of misappropriation brought against the financier Jacques de Beaune de Semblançay and others of his kind (Gilles Berthelot, Jean Poncher and Thomas Bohier) were handled in this way. The custom was of course an ancient one. Accusations of embezzlement levelled against the financial managers close to the king provided a smokescreen for a monarchy short of money and obliged to make ever-increasing demands. The Semblançay case was typical in more ways than one.[9] Semblançay himself, born to a merchant's family in Tours, had had a sensational career. He served as treasurer to first Anne of Brittany and then Louise of Savoy, the latter making him a baron. Under Louis XII he became *général des finances*, and in 1518 François I made him superintendent over all ordinary and extraordinary revenues, a delicate commission at a time when war was devouring private and public fortunes. State responsibilities notwithstanding, Semblançay remained what he had always been – a money-lender like his father (albeit on a smaller scale) before him. He lent to cities (like Tours), to private individuals, to princes (even to François as Duke of Angoulême), and to sovereigns (like Federico of Naples). And he had friends in the highest circles of the nobility and the Court, men like the Grand Master Artus Gouffier.

Semblançay was linked in varying degrees of friendship or relationship to the aristocracy of secretaries and treasurers which had administered the kingdom for several decades and would do so for many more. He was a cousin of Pierre Le Gendre (*général des aides* and *trésorier de l'extraordinaire*); and father-in-law to Raoul de Hurault, sire de Cheverny. He was a pillar of the establishment. But despite his lofty public responsibilities, he continued to operate as a private financier and manager, administering the properties of, among others, Louise of Savoy. It was to him that François turned in 1522 when his financial problems became overwhelming, and 'extraordinary innovations' proliferated. In the wake of the disaster at Pavia, it was on him, after Lautrec, that François turned, announcing that 'I give my servants fair warning that I do not want to be tricked any more.' The threat soon proved far from idle. While the new financial machinery was being put in place, Semblançay continued to carry out his supervisory functions, but the dark shadow of disgrace was already looming over him. In 1524 François appointed four commissioners from the *Chambre de comptes* to investigate his administration. Semblançay at first refused to hand over the books, but, when he finally produced them, the legal proceedings showed how the royal accounts had been confused with those of Louise of Savoy. He was accused of spending 600 000 *livres* of her money on the war effort. But the judges found in his favour, accepting that he had acted under the king's orders. However, they declared him in debt to Louise, and the king likewise to him. Semblançay offered to reimburse her immediately, and to write off the royal debt to himself.

After his return from captivity in Spain, François and his mother returned to the offensive. From their point of view it was partly a matter of refilling the Treasury by forcing those with money to cough up, and partly of parading the virtues of the new financial regime by condemning the malpractices of the old guard as personified by Semblançay – who was imprisoned with several of his colleagues on 27 January 1527. A new commission of inquiry, called the *Commission de la Tour carrée*, was convened, staffed by magistrates from the Parlement de Paris, Masters of Requests, and men from the *Chambre des comptes* and the *Grand Conseil*. It pursued criminal proceedings against Semblançay, and continued to prosecute financiers until 1536. Its exceptional powers enabled it to show up Semblançay's malpractices quite easily. Like most of his colleagues, he was not a man of scrupulous honesty. The king needed a scapegoat, and he was the man for the job. He was the victim of the blurring of private and public spheres, of the inextricable confusion amidst which the monarchy took the first steps towards absolutism; the victim of the pressure which the king put upon him to raise money for war; the victim, in short, of a monarchy which fought beyond its means. On 9 August 1527 he was sentenced to death for malpractice and misappropriation. And on 12 August he made his last journey along the Rue Saint-Antoine and the Rue Saint-Denis, from the Bastille to Montfaucon. The chronicler Versoris never missed such occasions. Having witnessed the old man's execution, he remarked:

> Do not be surprised if I described Semblançay's fate at some length, for in my time I saw him reckoned almost as a king in France, with none prepared to gainsay anything he said or did, any more than they would withstand the king. May Our Lord God in his mercy and grace have mercy upon his soul. His passing was much regretted and lamented by the people, who would have been happy if it had pleased the king to pardon him. From his story we may appreciate the mutability and instability of fortune, and learn that the service of a lord is neither inheritance nor eternal grace.

Only Semblançay received the death penalty, but the funeral rites of the old financial and political establishment went on. Gilles Bohier had to face the music in place of his father, Thomas, who had died four years previously. He paid a fine of 190 000 *livres* and surrendered to the king his château of Chenonceaux. Gilles Berthelot escaped by flight, as did Semblançay's son Guillaume (a *général des finances*). But the Crown bled them for compensation of some 300 000 *livres*. Semblançay's daughter Marie, the wife of Raoul Hurault, was fined 100 000 *livres*. Jean Poncher, the first to flee, had a brief respite and resumed his work as *général des finances* in Languedoc. But in 1535 the *Commission de la Tour carrée* returned to the attack, condemning him to death and compelling his family to refund 300 000 *livres*. There were many other victims, such as Jean Ruzé, Gaillard Spifame, Lambert Maigret and Jean Lallemand. The 'Bourgeois of Paris' gave a detailed account of their names and circumstances. Rumour put the total fines at about 2 million *livres*, but the defendants managed to reduce their obligations by negotiation. Nevertheless, François squeezed them for all he could get. This process of administrative purgation and fiscal recuperation made a big impression on the informed public. The chroniclers reflect this, not without pity for Semblançay. The '*Complainte du riche fortuné messire Jacques de Beaune*' was sold and sung through the streets of Paris. And Clément Marot, himself scarcely out of prison, wrote a bitter epigram on the death of 'the sturdy old man'.

More sensational by far, and equally illustrative of the Crown's all-powerful sway, was the case brought against the Constable of France, Charles de Bourbon. The Constable was to François what Charles the Bold had been to Louis XI. The same ingredients spiced the tale of conflict between a great feudal magnate and his king, with the same tragic end in battle, albeit under different circumstances.

The clash between François and his Constable arose ultimately from the demands of Louise of Savoy, whose heart was set on Bourbon's lands in the centre of France. He held a clutch of major fiefs there – the duchy of Auvergne, the county of Montpensier, and the duchies of Châtellerault and the Bourbonnais – as well as the county of Clermont-en-Beauvaisis to the north of Paris. The bulk of these lands had come to him by virtue of his wife, Suzanne de Bourbon. So when she died in 1521, Louise of Savoy, her next of kin, laid claim to lands which, having once constituted an appanage, would have reverted to the Crown if special agreements and shrewd will-making had not kept them for the Bourbons. The Constable refused to hand them over, and in 1524 legal proceedings, which were to drag on until 1527, were commenced before the Parlement de Paris. As early as 1524 François, preparing for the invasion of Italy, held a *lit de justice* to compel the Parlement to issue a decree of sequestration on Bourbon's goods. Notwithstanding his high office and his status as a prince of the blood, Charles had endured a succession of insults at the hands of his king. Now that he reckoned his honour touched, he put himself at the disposal of Charles V. The traitor (if that is the right term for the humiliated feudatory) was to die stupidly in 1527 while Rome was being pillaged by troops under his command.

The Bourbon fiefs thus reverted first to Louise and, after her death, to the royal domain. The gain was considerable: the

Bourbonnais, the Beaujolais, the Auvergne, Châtellerault, Forez, Marche, Montpensier and many other estates and towns of lesser importance. Although the affair had been managed to a large extent in order to make a point, it also yielded a rich territorial harvest.

The proceedings against a childhood friend of the king's, Philippe Chabot de Brion, were of a similar stamp. This prominent states-man, who helped negotiate the Treaty of Madrid, was Governor of Burgundy, Grand Admiral of France, and a member of the Privy Council. He was suddenly charged with treason in 1539, and arraigned before one of those special tribunals beloved of the Valois, with Duprat's successor as Chancellor, Pierre Poyet, presiding. Yesterday's man received a harsh prison sentence and heavy fines, though in 1541 they were equally suddenly remitted by the king's grace.

Even the highest officer of State, the Chancellor, whom royal ritual made second only to the king – the Chancellor was re-quired neither to bare his head in the king's presence nor to wear mourning when the king died – was not immune from sud-den disgrace. Although Duprat, despite his double helping of civil and ecclesiastical authority, never knew what it was to suffer the king's pleasure, he was scarcely dead before the king's hand de-scended upon his inheritance. His château of Nantouillet, his Parisian mansion beside the Austin Friars, and his archiepiscopal palace at Sens were put under lock and key, and his vast fortune was sequestered, together with all his gold and silver plate. The king behaved as though he were the Chancellor's principal ben-eficiary, and, as the 'Bourgeois of Paris' rightly observed, the Chan-cellor 'had acquired stupendous wealth in his time'. Duprat's less fortunate successor, Poyet, lived to meet his fall. Montmorency's withdrawal from Court had left him in effect chief minister, yet in 1542 he suddenly found himself in the Bastille. Once again a special tribunal was convened to investigate 'offences, abuses, mal-practices, crimes, and misdemeanours'. The king testified in per-son that Poyet had forged the royal seal in order to misappropriate funds. Other witnesses stated that he had created and sold offices, that he had misappropriated the goods of convicts, that he had been granted the archbishopric of Narbonne by the pope, and much else besides. The charges were by no means all unfounded. Poyet was fined 100 000 *livres*, sentenced to five years' house arrest, and, of course, deprived of his office.[10]

François I's style of government was indeed peculiar. He looked upon his immediate entourage with the suspicion of an oriental despot, and toyed with favour and grace to make or break the highest officers of State in a moment. Was such suspicion the accompaniment of absolutism? Or was it simply a concomitant of his freely given favour? At any rate, the royal theatre was playing throughout the reign, with each scenario following the same basic plot: first favour and power were heaped on a man, then came sudden disgrace, the restitution of gains (ill-gotten or not) to the Treasury, a harsh sentence, and occasionally, as a final act – as in the drama which starred Chabot – the restoration of favour and the remission of punishments.

The years of Henri II do not present the modern historian with such a picture of royal capriciousness. The king was more concerned with foreign war than domestic domination. The notorious duel between Jarnac and La Châtaigneraie – a judicial combat between two courtiers – can stand as a symbol of the change. It was a confrontation between the old and the new, the old regime of François, lax, hedonistic and disorderly, and the new regime of Henri, strict, upright, and Catholic. It resulted in the death of La Châtaigneraie, the royal champion, followed by an invasion of the lists by the crowd of what were supposed to be spectators. It signified the passing of an outdated form of royal justice, one which sought in the manner of St Louis to invoke divine judgement in purely human quarrels. The bloody *Chambre ardente* was a better stage for Henri than one which made him a passive spectator of divine intervention.

The *Collège de France*

It may seem strange to include in an account of royal 'display' the establishment and maintenance of the royal professorships of the *Collège de France*, an institution which, on the margins of the University of Paris, brought together scholars to pursue teaching and learning. It was also known as a 'collegium trilingue' (a college of three languages), for its members specialised in Latin, Greek and Hebrew (but also mathematics). Of these subjects, the Sorbonne taught only Latin. When François installed the first professors in 1530, humanist scholarship, imbued with philology and the restoration of antiquity, had already long preoccupied the cultural elite of France. The king, a man of an open and inquiring mind, was personally interested in humanism. To sanction it by means of the college was perhaps to control it, but was it not also a new feather in the Valois cap? But it was not done in a hurry. The king took some time to furnish his college with statutes, and it was hard to find the first master. Erasmus was approached in 1511, but politely declined. Guillaume Budé pressed the king to keep his former promises: 'you promised me, my Lord . . . that you would found a college, a kind of nursery for clerks and scholars'. In 1531 funds were set aside for the wages of the professors appointed the previous year, but Budé's dream of a 'magnificent monument' to house scholars and students never materialised.

But the professorships themselves survived, and among their first incumbents were some of the greatest scholars of the age. Some of them were French, such as Pierre Danès, Jacques Toussain, François Vatable and Pierre Chérame, scholars of Greek more interested in teaching, it seems, than publishing. Toussain had a Greek and Latin dictionary published in 1552, and Vatable translated Aristotle, but such efforts were scarcely far removed from teaching. Other professors came from Italy. Agathio Guidacerio, from Calabria, had taught Hebrew at Rome before coming to the king's college. Paul Paradis, a Venetian Jew, also taught Hebrew, and both men were anxious to pass on their learning. Guidacerio compiled a Hebrew grammar, and Paradis composed a *Dialogue sur la manière de lire l'hébreu*. Oratory received, as it were, a patent of nobility through being taught in the college, where it seems to have been regarded as an indispensable accomplishment of any self-respecting Renaissance man. The first professor of oratory was Barthélemy Latomus of Luxembourg, who not only composed quantities of Latin verse, but also drew up a textbook of dialectic and published several works of controversy. He was succeeded in 1545 by Pierre Galland, who put his theories into practice by delivering a funeral eulogy for François I himself in 1547, and a eulogy for François de Guise in 1558.

Mathematics, a discipline largely neglected in medieval education, was accorded full weight in the college thanks to Oronce Fine, born at Briançon in 1494, a productive scholar and inventor who published more than 30 books, and found time to make a chiming clock for the Cardinal of Lorraine. Anatomy was taught by a Florentine, Guido Vidius, François I's chief physician. But the most brilliant star in the galaxy of these first professors was Guillaume Postel (1510–81), who held chairs in mathematics and oriental languages. He was well-known to François I, and went on the first French embassy to Constantinople, whence he brought back a number of scientific manuscripts in Arabic. His extraordinary life, filled with physical and philosophical voyages and wanderings, took full advantage of the garden of delights which the Renaissance opened up to those of a bold spirit. It would take an entire book to do him justice.

All of these 'professors' or 'readers', or simply 'lecturers in the University' were men of a single generation. Born around the turn of the century, they belonged to the European republic of letters, taught subjects which hardly figured at all in the traditional university curriculum, and, whatever the nuances of their particular positions, were in the main stream of humanism. Many were clerics. Pierre Danès was Bishop of Lavaur, Pierre Galland was a canon of Notre-Dame, and François Vatable was abbot of Bellozane. Most of them were the personal protégés of François himself or his sister, like Vatable, Postel and Vidius. Some of them, like Danès and Postel, played a part in public affairs as ambassadors or commissioners. A fairly homogeneous group of teachers and scholars in the new vein, chosen by merit, they all owed much to Guillaume Budé. For since 1517 he had persistently urged the king to establish the college. After many delays and difficulties François had done so, and the fact is greatly to his credit, even if he derived a not inconsiderable personal satisfaction from it. His son Henri appreciated the advantage he could derive from continuing his father's work, and doubled the number of royal professorships in the college, thus fully deserving the title of patron of learning which the panegyrists accorded the 'Gallic Hercules'.

The conditions of employment of the first professors meant that their posts were far from sinecures. Notices posted in the Latin quarter gave the times and places of lectures for students and informed amateurs: 'Agathio Guidacerio, royal professor, will continue his lectures for students on the Psalms tomorrow at 7 o'clock in the *Collège de Cambrai*, with Psalm 20. . . . Paul Paradis, royal interpreter of Hebrew, will resume his course on Monday at 10 o'clock, beginning with the rudiments of grammar by Sanctus Pagninus, which he has already covered in the previous lessons. At the same time he will begin a commentary on the Proverbs of Solomon in the *Collège des Trois-Évêques*.' The professors were conscientious enough to tell their students which booksellers stocked copies of the grammars, treatises or scriptural texts on which they proposed to 'read' (i.e. lecture). 'This text, printed with the utmost care, can be bought from Antoine Angereau at the sign of Saint-Jacques in the rue Saint-Jacques', was the advice about a work of Aristotle's on which Pierre Danès was lecturing.

With the times, methods and subjects of their lectures entirely at their own discretion, the royal professors were privileged in comparison with their counterparts in the University of Paris. This was so because François protected them. In 1534 the old Sorbonne tried to forbid them to engage in unauthorised teaching, calling on the Parlement for support. But in reply François gave his professors the privilege of *committimus*. For all that, the Treasury was far from regular in paying the salaries of these prestigious intellectuals, and became less so as the number of posts was increased in view of the success of the public lectures. In 1546 the *Collège de France* had three chairs each in Hebrew and Greek, two in mathematics, and one each in Latin, medicine and philosophy. Henri II increased the number further. The nominal stipends of 400 *livres* a year were so far in the realms of fantasy that in fact the kings supplemented the incomes of the professors (many of whom were their close friends) with a prebend, a benefice, or a deanery.

Royal Patronage: Fontainebleau

In literature as in art, both François I and Henri II (the son no less than the father, appearances notwithstanding) gave a great impetus to the projection of the image of kingship. Their personal taste, itself borne up on a wave of new ideas, genres and aspirations, was in complete harmony with the artistic and literary endeavours of their age – though it might easily have been otherwise. But this personal sympathy must not blind us to the political advantages which a sovereign could derive from the direct or indirect propaganda which artists could provide.

We have already seen that a Court appointment, especially as a *valet de chambre*, was a way of giving a living to sculptors and poets (Clément Marot held such a post from time to time). The title 'king's painter' enjoyed by Jean Clouet conferred upon him a certain social status as well as a pension. Leonardo da Vinci came in his last years to Amboise, secure in provision for his old age. It is not known precisely what tasks the ageing master carried out for his patron François (did he perhaps conceive the spiral staircase of Chambord?), but at his death in 1519 he left a number of major works which found their way into the royal collections. It seems, however, that the Louvre's famous *Virgin of the Rocks* had already been brought from Milan by Louis XII, and had then become part of the collection assembled by François at Fontainebleau.

Henri II employed Philibert Delorme, François I's architect, and made him superintendent over all royal buildings except for the Louvre, which was in the charge of Pierre Lescot. Philibert in turn gave work to a team of sculptors, among them Pierre Bontemps, creator of the famous bas-relief cycle depicting the Battle of Marignano.

Artists, intellectuals and writers, protected and supported by the Crown, played a full part in the cult of monarchy. When the king desired, according to the canons of Renaissance taste, to be Hercules, Mercury, or an emperor (besides being an image the God of the Christians), it had to be inscribed on paper, cloth or stone. The royal patrons François and Henri were fully conscious of the political importance of their image, and they surrounded themselves with artists who were recruited, wittingly or not, into the production-team of the sacred royal theatre.

Two examples of royal patronage will suffice here, for the subject has been amply and minutely handled by Anne-Marie Lecoq: the château of Fontainebleau, to pick just one of many; and the poets of the Pléiade, among the many coteries of eulogists.

Among the royal residences constructed or embellished by the first Valois kings, Fontainebleau had such an imposing character that, after François, several generations of monarchs lavished all their attention on it.[11] François I set about the extension of the château in 1528 with all his love and passion. As the engraver Jacques Androuet Du Cerceau wrote in 1580: 'The late King François, who built it, loved it marvellously and spent most of his time there . . . anything of excellence that he could lay his hands on was destined for his Fontainebleau. He delighted in it so much that when he was on his way there, he would say that he was going home.' In 1547, at the king's death, Fontainebleau seemed to visitors 'a sumptuous residence, a truly royal building, decorated with statues from many places, rich in the works of the greatest painters, a residence worthy of such a great king'.

The old château, constructed around a keep in the forest of

Bière, obsessed François after his return from captivity. The forest swarmed with red deer for the hunt, and was not too far from Paris at a time when the Ile-de-France was replacing the Loire valley as the centre of power. The famous first-floor gallery, the *Galerie François I,* has borne until our day the name of the first Valois of Angoulême: 60 metres long and 6 metres wide, it is redolent of courtly existence, the more so as the mural decorations elaborated by Rosso between 1534 and 1536 were wholly given over to the cult of monarchy. François I figures in various allegorical guises along the panelling: as a warrior, he chases ignorance from the temple of Jupiter; as a fatherly dispenser of justice, he sits amidst his people depicted in their various stations and callings; an elephant clothed in a garment covered in the fleur-de-lis and the monogram F symbolises life and goodness. No visitor to the gallery could remain oblivious of its dedication to the cult of monarchy.

A true collector, François filled Fontainebleau with fine paintings and sculptures, and precious ornaments. The paintings were, strangely enough, kept in the *Appartement des Bains* beneath the *Galerie François I:* even if the works were not hung in the bathrooms as such, many of those that were in the first room, known as the *Salle du Conseil,* were to be damaged by damp. Henri IV had a number of them moved to the *Cabinet des Peintures.* François I's italianate tastes were particularly apparent in his choice of paintings. Many came as presents. Lorenzo the Magnificent and Leo X presented pieces by Raphael, the *St Michael* and the *Holy Family* (both now in the Louvre). The donors knew François I's special devotion to St Michael, the insignia of whose chivalric order he wore with pride. The *Holy Family* celebrated the alliance between the pope and the king, sealed by the marriage between the pope's nephew Lorenzo and Madeleine de La Tour d'Auvergne, the king's niece. Other donations with a political significance (both now in the Louvre) included Raphael's *St Margaret,* perhaps commissioned in honour of Marguerite of Navarre, and the *Jeanne d'Aragon* of Giulio Romano given by the papal legate in France.

François I's collection included works inherited from Louis XII, not only the *Virgin of the Rocks* already mentioned, which Louis had probably acquired in Milan, but also other works by Leonardo and other Florentine artists. When Leonardo came to France he brought with him a number of pictures which after his death found their way into the collection at Fontainebleau. The *Mona*

Lisa, the *Virgin and Child with St Anne*, and the *John the Baptist* are among the best known. But François found other ways to enrich his collection. On his return from Madrid in 1526 he engaged buyers who, according to Vasari, would have 'despoiled Florence of untold treasures without a second thought on the orders of the King of France'. He used Pietro Aretino for similar purposes in Venice. Aretino sent a great many pictures, and advised Rosso to offer his services to the Most Christian King. Thus many a work of the Florentine masters, in the style beloved of a king who was said to have little or no time for the Roman school, came to France. Among the wealth of examples, one can think of Andrea del Sarto's *Holy Family*, which earned its painter an invitation to the French Court. He stayed there a year, long enough to create several masterpieces, among them the *Charity* now in the Louvre. Finally, the collection was enriched by paintings produced by the two Italian artists hired for the works at Fontainebleau: Rosso and Primaticcio. These two, the founders of the first school of Fontainebleau painting, produced, besides their decorative pieces, some fine equestrian pictures. Among the other Italians hung in the Fontainebleau gallery were a number of Titians sent from Venice by Aretino (including the famous portrait of François himself), some Fra Bartolommeos, and a Bronzino. But the king was not so addicted to the Italian style that he could not invite to his Court Flemish portrait painters like Jean Clouet, Joos Van Cleeve, and later François Clouet.

At Fontainebleau François installed engravers' workshops where craftsmen like Étienne Delaune, Jacques Androuet du Cerceau, Antoine Caron and Jean Mignon produced their fine works. Between 1543 and 1547 they produced engravings of the paintings presented to the château. Many lost works are known to us only through etched or cut engravings. The engravings were produced in limited numbers at a time when the Parisian workshops of Pierre Milan and René Boyvin were producing far more copies (up to a thousand), but all the same they engraved pictures painted at Fontainebleau itself, the works of Rosso, Primaticcio, and Penni.

The monumental paintings of François I's favourite château inspired not only engravings but also tapestries throughout the sixteenth century. The hangings of the *Galerie François I* reproduced six bays of the south wall of the collection. Manufactured between 1541 and 1555, with the painter Claude Baduin doing the sketches, and the 'high-warp tapestry' worker Jean Le Bris weaving the cloths, this work is 'a sort of manifesto for the school of Fontainebleau, a remarkable synthesis of stylistic and iconographic innovations'. Like the engravings, the tapestries took up exotic or classical decorative themes and played their part in the cult of monarchy. The hangings of the *Story of Diana*, probably commissioned by Henri II for the château of Anet and sketched by Jean Cousin, celebrated the king's mistress. Later on the *Tentures des fêtes de Valois* evoked the ostentation of the Court: nautical shows, tournaments and jousts, a far cry from the allegorical elephant of François I.

François I also had a taste for sculpture. The Florentine agent della Palla sent him, in Vasari's dismissive words, 'all sorts of junk'. In 1529 Michelangelo came close to accepting a royal invitation, though he never did. And in 1540, Primaticcio made his way to Rome, from where he brought back, again according to Vasari, some 125 ancient marble pieces of which we know nothing, and castings which the artist made there (a Laocoon, a Mercury, a Diana, an Ariane). We know that, in Henri II's days, they decorated the *Jardin de la Reine*, the *Cour de la Fontaine*, the Ballroom, and the *Cour du Cheval Blanc*. The collection must have been stunning. Vasari saw Fontainebleau as 'almost a new Rome'.

The king's passion for collecting reached into many spheres: statuettes, jewels and precious vessels adorned his 'Cabinet des curiosités'. Some pieces, like a Rafael perfume-brazier, came as gifts; others were made on site. Benvenuto Cellini lived at the French Court from 1540 to 1545, and was perfectly at home with the Mannerism of Fontainebleau. The salt-cellar which he made at François I's request (now in the museum at Vienna) is a masterpiece of rare virtuosity, more a sculpture than an artefact. For Cellini, who had always wanted to sculpt, found the leisure in his French period to essay his first creations. One of them, the bronze *Nymph* of Fontainebleau, remains to this day at the main entrance of the château.

François threw himself enthusiastically into the construction and decoration of Fontainebleau and into the formation of its collections. They offer a true reflection of the king's artistic policy, his grand plan for a French Renaissance, indeed, a French 'Italy'. Fontainebleau itself, a museum almost since its construction, was mostly open to the public. The king himself offered a personal guided tour to visitors of note, such as the former English ambassador Sir John Wallop in 1543. Humbler callers were shown around by a 'concierge', a sort of proto-curator. Both the collections and the decorations belonging to the fabric of the château were viewed, admired, and taken in – as can be seen from the numerous prints and contemporary copies made of the king's paintings. By these means, the style and content were diffused through and assimilated into French art for the rest of the century. The first school of Fontainebleau, born on the site itself, reflected the Italianate tastes of the sovereigns, of François I above all, but also of Henri II and later of Henri IV. It was displayed to the public not only in painting but also in sculpture, tapestry, precious vessels, and even in bookbindings. It was a question of style. The style, inspired by the king, was essentially decorative, and became henceforth a Court art, an art of the artificial, mannered and elitist world of royal display. The presence of Italian artists, Rosso from 1540, Primaticcio from 1532 to 1570, and Niccolò dell'Abate from 1552, marked that style with the note of Mannerism. There were clear signs of the influence of Michelangelo, Raphael, Giulio Romano, Corregio, Parmigiano, and of course da Vinci. The essence of the school of Fontainebleau lay in the primacy of language, even of ornament; the artists laid stress less on what they had to say than on the way that they said it, an attitude which emerged in the mores of the courtly elite for whom this artistic expression was intended. Specific features of the style included the play of line, the rigour of treatment, and the sharpness of design, which indicated a highly intellectual, sometimes rather cold, representation of the subject: hence the rather blurred borderline that then divided painting from engraving. Many engravers (such as Antonio Fantuzzi and Jean Mignon) were also painters, while several painters (such as Rosso, Primaticcio, and Penni) dabbled in etching with blade or acid. And engraving is as much a medium of line, contour, and volume as sculpture, which became around 1550 the principal medium of expression. Line, the exaltation of line, was so characteristic of the Fontainebleau style that the artists used it as a theme, playing with it and embroidering it far beyond the reality depicted, as in the extreme elongation of the body (in, for example, the nymphs of the Fontainebleau staircase, or the *Eva Prima Pandora* of Jean Cousin the elder) and the sinuous curves used to suggest immediate or imminent movement. The artists of Fontainbleau used line against space, suggesting the multiplicity of space and dethroning its dogmatic and dominating character.

Their subjects were an explosive reworking of tradition. The creative talents of the time, almost all scholars and humanists, grabbed with both hands the opportunities offered by the rediscovery of antiquity. Subjects drawn from mythology (Rosso's *Venus chastising Cupid*, dell'Abate's *Rape of Proserpine*, and François Clouet's *Diana* bathing), or ancient history (Antoine Caron's *Les massacres de Triumvirat*), suggest an almost scholarly familiarity with classical antiquity. Contemporary subjects (*La Salle de Bal*, the *Fêtes des Valois*, *La Bataille*) or metaphorical ones (François I as an elephant, by Rosso) played their part in the celebration of the patron. Monumental allegories (*Charity*, and *Piety*) underlined the intellectualism of an art which nevertheless gave sacred subjects, especially the Virgin, an important place, notably in the works of da Vinci and Rosso. The grotesque and the exotic made occasional appearances, as if to trouble the waters of an excessive refinement.

Whether acquired, created on site, or merely inspired by the Fontainebleau style, all these works, or nearly all, had one thing in common: man (and woman) nourished artistic creativity. Landscape was given but a subordinate role, while the human took centre stage to the point of excluding both space and nature. Nature began to creep back around 1550. The body, often enough naked, expressed the sheer lust for life which characterised the French Renaissance. It dripped eroticism, the art and knowledge of pleasure. Self-conscious and recherché, it was an art of sophistication rather than simplicity. Humanist perspectives and the wretchedness of man, themes of age and death, mediated through the material of mythology or classical antiquity, replied to the theme of triumphant youth: *Lost Youth* and the *Death of Adonis* figured in François I's gallery. To the inevitability of war, the butcher of youth, corresponded the ageing of the recently triumphant nymphs. The poet Ronsard springs to mind.

The Fontainebleau school created a style, a complex iconographical repertoire whose echoes rang around the realm until the end of the century. Artists working apart from the Court were influenced by developments at Fontainebleau, and drew, painted, engraved, or sculpted accordingly. Under Henri II and his successors, Germain Pilon, Philibert Delorme and Jean Goujon scarcely deviated from the laws of the genre. Nor did the French painter Noel Jallier who, between 1546 and 1549, created at Oiron, for the Master of the Horse Claude Gouffier, a series of paintings *a secco* relating the history of Troy and various scenes from the Aeneid. This otherwise completely unknown artist likewise decorated the grand gallery of the château in a style akin to that of Rosso. At his residence in Écouen, Montmorency employed the men who had made Fontainebleau. A group of painters and engravers (the latter, whom we have already met, belonging to the school of Fontainebleau) worked in Paris: Antoine Caron, François Clouet (the portrait artist who succeeded his father as the King's Painter), and both the elder and the younger Jean Cousin. Some of them had worked on the scaffolding at Fontainebleau alongside Rosso and Primaticcio, and their personal creations were stamped with the seal of that school. Much later, during the reign of Henri IV, so many artists fell once more under this influence that people speak readily of a second school of Fontainebleau.

François I occupies a prominent place in French history, but it was in the field of art that his reign enjoyed its most striking and enduring success. François never once deviated from his cultural programme, pursuing it unflaggingly throughout his reign. Fontainebleau encapsulated that programme in a glorious synthesis. There the royal patron narcissistically fashioned for himself a frame in which to display his power. It was indeed 'a mirror for princes in which the reflections were multiplied to infinity'.

Royal Patronage: the Pléiade

Can one say that the writers of the Pléiade were to Henri II's reign what the artists of Fontainebleau were to François I's?[12] In the field of poetry and scholarship the comparison seems apposite. It was 1549 that saw the appearance of the *Défense et illustration de la langue française*, a treatise drawn up by Joachim du Bellay in close collaboration with Pierre Ronsard, and aimed as much against the rhetoricians of the previous reign (especially Mellin de Saint-Gelais) as against those who wrote their verse in Latin. This entirely platonic dispute was brought before Henri II, whose Court resembled henceforth 'the inspired hill of Parnassus', and it was concluded by the 'sentence' which declared Ronsard as a royal poet. But leaving aside this patently literary anecdote, the gathering of the 'Brigade' around the figure of Ronsard was a matter of profound significance.

The group which formally adopted the title of the Pléiade in 1556 was made up of seven poets representing a variety of styles and movements. Constantly supported by royal patronage, it provided in return, in an almost commercial relationship, a constant supply of original compositions. Building on the achievements of the previous two generations, and proposing, in its turn, as an absolute principle the primacy of antiquity, the Pléiade advocated in the field of literary expression the imitation of the great Greek and Latin classics: hence the reference to the Latin poets that they translated, imitated, or plagiarised – but in French. Here is the essence of what literary historians have called the Pléiade's revolution, just like the 1539 Edict of Villers-Cotterêts (article 111) against the 'graecisers and latinisers'. They stood for not only the defence but also the enrichment and aggrandisement of the French language. Du Bellay advocated the adoption of archaisms, neologisms, and technical terms, as well as the coining of new turns of phrase and figures of speech, metaphors, allegories, comparisons and similes. And while he was concerned primarily with poetry, his reflections also went on to encompass prose and drama. At the same time that the Pléiade was striving to promote French itself, the French of deepest provincial France and of 'rude mechanicals', it was establishing a hierarchy of genres which long influenced authors. If the national language was to be made illustrious, it had to manifest itself in elevated and noble genres: out went roundels, ballades, mystery plays, epigrams and eclogues; and in came tragedy, comedy, epic, lyric, and that new form of lyric pioneered in Italy, the sonnet. The manifesto of the Brigade also advanced a number of other proposals which we shall not detail here, but which made the text – tediously familiar though it has become through textbooks of French literary history – both dynamic and innovative.

The *Défense* had in addition a political aspect. For the 'sentence' of Henri II, to which we have already alluded, meant in effect government approval of a national literature: an ironic development, given our knowledge of what the Pléiade could not yet know, namely that France would shatter into fragments in 1559. Yet perhaps the prescience of poets gave them some inkling, for they seemed bent on haste, producing both theoretical texts (like Ronsard's *Abrégé de l'art poétique français* of 1565) and practical literary applications at great speed. Before France tore itself apart and the monarchy dissolved, the Pléiade gathered around the Crown as a veritable court of writers. The idea of the nation may have remained inchoate, but that of the kingdom and the King of France had solid roots and bore plentiful fruit. The Pléiade composed their works in the language of the sovereign as an act of homage to their princely patron. Although, like their manifesto, somewhat provocative at first, the men of the Pléiade, under the guidance of that peerless public relations officer Pierre Ronsard, formed a cohesive literary coterie. The original quarrel between the 'rhetoricians', the established Court poets, on the one hand, and the 'young Turks' of the new wave on the other, was soon resolved by a public and official reconciliation with Mellin de Saint-Gelais. So it is difficult to agree with Robert Muchembled that the Pléiade represented a third voice, a bourgeois middle way between the Court and the people. Rather, as its membership suggests, it was a sort of intelligentsia gathered around the prince. To the seven original members (Ronsard, Jodelle, Des Autels, du Bellay, Baïf, La Péruse and Pontus de Tyard) were added, like a stellar cloud, the poets of the school of Lyon led by Maurice Scève. The group changed as members died. Towards 1555, Ronsard replaced La Péruse with Rémi Belleau, and Des Autels with Jacques Peletier du Mans. The Brigade was self-consciously inclusive of all literary tendencies, whatever they might be. Thus it ended the notorious hostility between the Parisians of the Collège Coqueret and those of the Collège Boncourt. The former, the early nursery of the Pléiade, revolved around poetry, the latter around drama. In 1554, the dramatist Jodelle, together with La Péruse, joined the Pléiade as representatives of Boncourt.

The Pléiade was also catholic with regard to genres: if poetry was its primary concern, virtually its trademark, this was far from its only form of literary expression. They not only toyed with rhyme but also produced many a translation from Greek or Latin, as well as grammatical treatises (e.g. Peletier's *Dialogue de l'orthographie et de la prononciation française*, 1550), and tragedies (e.g. Jodelle's *Cléopâtre captive*, performed at Henri II's Court in 1553). A satellite of the Pléiade, the historian Étienne Pasquier, started publishing his *Recherches sur la France* in 1560, the first in a long line of scholars who, in the latter half of the century, were to devote themselves to forging a national identity for the ravaged kingdom.

Over and above its particular achievements, the Pléiade created in Henri II's France an intellectual consensus. That Ronsard should have received the very highest accolade from the *Académie des Jeux floraux de Toulouse* showed how far that old-fashioned medieval body had aligned itself with the designers of a royal and national French literature. Consensus extended far beyond assent to new literary doctrines, for the members and supporters of the Brigade took up a definite political position. The recently coined slogan 'une loi, un roi, un foi' (one law, one king, one faith), at once memorable and insistent, remained their guiding principle in an increasingly tense situation. More or less all these writers lined up behind the Crown and Catholicism in the political and religious crisis which loomed on the horizon, even if one or two, like Jodelle, briefly flirted with the Reformation. These intellectuals, handsomely rewarded by Henri and his sons, Charles IX and Henri III, never once bit the hand that fed them. Regarding writing as their trade, they plied it on behalf of the Crown. All 'powdered mountebanks . . . tipplers, . . . rakes', according to Ronsard, the Protestants appeared to them as a cancer polluting the realm. The same poet struck a lyrical note in his *Discours des misères de ce temps* (1562), addressed to Catherine de Medici, whom alone, amidst the feudal factions and religious parties, he considered capable of reforging that national unity shattered by the presence of factious Genevan proselytes.

'The great fleet of poets produced by the reign of Henri II', as Pasquier put it, and, one might add, the crowd of intellectuals attracted by royal patronage, sought to bring together the provinces around the figure of the king, to unify literary expression in the language of the Prince, and to project towards France as a whole the image of kingship; in short, to do for Henri II what the school of Fontainebleau had done for François I in the field of the fine arts.

Paris

The concentration at the heart of government of an elite of birth, office, and talent could not long tolerate the multiplicity of centres of power. True, the peripatetic nature of the Court endured well into the reign of Henri IV, but little by little Paris rose to the rank of royal capital. François I, as we know, had recognised the need for a relocation of government after his return from captivity. Although he never loved Paris, he nevertheless paid close attention to it, though never as much as Henri II.

François and Henri took many measures with regard to the administration of Paris. The city was governed by a council, the *Bureau de ville*, composed of the mayor (*prévôt des marchands*), 4 aldermen, and 24 councillors. The mayor was elected for two years, as were the aldermen, who were elected by pairs in alternate years. The electors, a small and select body, were the *quarteniers* (the administrators of each of the city's 16 'quarters'), together with 32 prominent citizens (2 from each quarter) and the outgoing city magistrates. The councillors were appointed by the Provost of Paris, the king's representative, as and when posts fell vacant by death. Finally, the *quarteniers*, together with their subordinates (*cinquanteniers* and *dizainiers*), were chosen from lists of prominent citizens drawn up with the aid of the outgoing officials.

Paris, as has often been said, was the least independent of all the cities of France. The Parlement kept the *Bureau de ville* under strict control, as did the sovereign courts in the provincial cities. When François I was taken prisoner in 1525, the Parlement took advantage of the emergency to establish a new commission to hear municipal lawsuits, with the aldermen in a distinct minority. But, even more than the Parlement, the king too, kept his eye on the city. He took a particularly close interest in the personnel of the *Bureau*. François had no hesitation in suspending aldermen or mayors, and Henri II readily changed the names on the lists of appointments presented to him. Henri IV was to follow their lead with a vengeance.

The king administered justice in the city through the person of the Provost of Paris, but this royal appointee, in effect a mere bailiff, gradually lost his powers to a *lieutenant civil* acting in collaboration with a *lieutenant criminel*. These two officials were assisted by about 30 *conseillers*, as well as by *auditeurs* and *commissaires*. The latter, who combined the roles of police officers and examining magistrates, originally numbered 16, but were increased to 32 in 1521 – 2 for every quarter. The Provost's jurisdiction was based at the Châtelet, whence it derived its name. In 1540 the seigneurial jurisdictions of Paris were amalgamated with that of the royal domain.

The city watch, intended as much for night-time surveillance within the city as for external defence, ceased to be a municipal body in 1540, and instead became an appendage to the royal watch, an appointed body made up of foot and horse sergeants under the command of a royal officer known as the Knight of the Watch. Later, Henri II suppressed the municipal troop, imposing a tax on tradesmen in place of personal service. The urban militia, in effect all fit male Parisians, armed and equipped at their own cost, dwindled away in the first half of the century.

Each quarter provided a company under the command of the *quartenier*, who was replaced in 1562 by a captain (later by a colonel) appointed by the king. This largely untrained force was hardly capable of contributing usefully to military operations, but was aggressive enough to do great harm to the Protestants of Paris on St Bartholomew's day. In fact, under François and Henri, the militia withered away in the face of three companies known as the *Trois Nombres*, composed of crossbowmen, arquebusiers and archers, and of the force of 30 archers under the *prévôt des connétables*.

Although a city under strict control, Paris was nevertheless highly privileged. François I and Henri II respected its 'liberties' even if they did not add to them. The privileges of the university were renewed by Charles VIII, Louis XII, and their two successors, and the powers of the mayor were at least superficially respected. The crafts, notably the cloth trade, were protected from external competition, especially from the bagmen, whose trade was limited in 1540 to certain times and places. At a time when Parisians already faced particularly heavy taxation, the king authorised the mayor to levy taxes on consumption. Thus, 12 *deniers* a head was charged on every cloven-footed beast brought into the city, and in 1543 a levy was imposed on herring. But this generosity was not entirely disinterested: in 1539, the levy paid for 3000 footsoldiers.

Paris, the capital city, and an important arena for monarchical display, was a cause of constant concern to the Valois kings. It had to be kept clean (at all levels), well-lit, tranquil, and beautiful.

Paris had to be kept clean. The city was a tip, the Seine a sewer, and the springs and wells teemed with bacteria. Plague and seasonal epidemics flared up, as elsewhere, in 1520, 1522, 1525, 1531, 1533, etc. Ordinances of 1539 and 1540 called for the paving and maintenance of the roads. The civic administration, for its part, saw to the rebuilding of the arches and conduits of the city fountain, which was finished in 1530. It organised work on the Pré-Saint-Germain aqueduct, which fed the other public fountains from sources in Pantin, Belleville and Romainville; and exerted itself in refurbishing the other basins providing drinking water for the citizens. The famous fountain of the Innocents at the corner of the rue Saint-Denis and the rue aux Fers, carved by Jean Goujon and Pierre Lescot, sums up in its elegance the policy of bringing water to Paris that was pursued under François and Henri. Yet even this effort was not enough to prevent water-shortages in summer and in periods of drought.

To bring light to the city – to open it up and make it easier to keep under surveillance – was to avert the risks which lurked in the shadows. From 1504 the inhabitants were obliged to place lanterns in their windows at night. But the reiteration of this order in 1558 confirms that Paris remained a murky and troubling city. Only in the eighteenth century would there be any real change.[13]

Keeping the city at peace meant ensuring an adequate supply of food and fuel. Feeding 300 000 people in 120 000 households laid a heavy burden on the surrounding region. Provisions were brought in from an area covering more than a dozen modern *départements*. Royal intervention backed up the efforts of the *Bureau de ville* to ensure that Paris received the requisite supplies of grain and wood. But the efforts were not invariably successful. Like other cities, Paris occasionally underwent subsistence crises, with the usual consequences. Poverty, begging, and the expansion of the urban population – the consequence of economic breakdowns – caused the city grave problems which Crown and *Bureau de ville* worked together to solve. In the eyes of both the central and the civic administration, the Church, the medieval manager of almshouses and charitable operations, was no longer able to cope with the pressure of poverty. Welfare had to be laicised. The first municipal relief organisation, the *Aumône-Générale*, already functioning in Paris by 1530, was formally established in 1544 by the Parlement under the name of the *Grand Bureau des Pauvres*. Its management was entrusted to the municipality, but royal officials sat together with churchmen and prominent citizens on its board, as the monarchy had to be represented in this initiative regarding the rationalisation of public welfare.

Neither François I nor Henri II could be content with anything less in order to impose their authority on Paris. The grandiose royal entries, like those for François in 1515 or for his wife Claude in 1517, and above all that of Henri II in April 1547, laid a heavy strain on municipal finances. They amazed the onlookers, but presented no more than a fleeting image of monarchical power. Architecture could make a more lasting impression. When in 1523 François I informed the *Bureau de ville* of his intention 'henceforth to make this fair city my habitual residence', these were no idle words. The king was bent on making Paris a royal city, notwithstanding his consuming passion for Fontainebleau. He was already dreaming of refurbishing the old Louvre, virtually unchanged since Charles V's time, more of a fortress than a palace fit for a Renaissance Prince. In 1528 the city was astonished by the collapse of the great tower of the Louvre, the keep of Philip Augustus. In 1546, the architect Pierre Lescot was appointed to direct the works which, as is well known, lasted into the next century. A great paved quay was begun along the Seine, and the main entrance now opened onto the city of Paris at the rue de l'Autruche. Henri II, retaining the same master of the works, continued his father's plan by replacing the west wing of the château with a group of comfortable modern buildings. After the old stonework was demolished, the new wing went up, sumptuously decorated by Jean Goujon, designed not so much for political uses as for royal festivities. In 1551 Lescot had the southern buildings demolished to make way for the royal pavilion, a building on three floors overlooking the Seine, with the Council chamber on the ground, the royal apartments above, and at the top the 'grand cabinet' which was to house the Crown treasures.

For the duration of the works on the Louvre, the royal family resided at the palace of the Tournelles, near the Bastille, a green and pleasant place, 'a botanical and zoological garden' with good sport. Henri II, we should recall, was addicted to physical exercise. Philibert Delorme added the 'salle de triomphe', and he also finished the palace of Madrid outside Paris, begun under François I by the Italian Girolamo Della Robbia. Other royal building works in Paris included the construction of the Arsenal between 1547 and 1549, and major works on the Bourbon, Rheims, Nesle and d'Étampes hotels. The royal presence in Paris was further emphasised by the construction or improvement of multiple residences where the main power groups – the nobles and leading public officials – rubbed shoulders.

Resistance

The introduction of authoritarian government was a process neither untroubled nor unopposed. We have already seen how the Parlements reacted to the proliferation of public offices. Each new creation constituted in their eyes both an infringement of their prerogatives and a slight on their dignity, and they left no stone unturned in delaying registration of the relevant edicts. Relations between king and Parlement were gravely strained under François I, but improved somewhat under Henri II – although the creation of the *présidiaux* in 1552 unleashed a flood of new protests. But over and above this corporate obstructiveness, over and above even the spread of Protestantism, which the Crown regarded as an affront to its political and religious sovereignty, the French people felt the impact of the State in the increasing burden of direct and indirect taxation. It was the labouring classes that felt the full impact of the demands of a regime lustful for domination at home and abroad; especially when their standard of living fell, as, from about 1530 (it is hard to fix the date precisely), times of plenty became a mere happy memory, the memory of Louis XII, 'the Father of the People'.

Social conflict began to shake the industrious 'good cities' of the kingdom under François I and Henri II. Given its population of artisans and journeymen, it is hardly surprising that Lyon was, within a few years, the focus of two kinds of popular protest. The *Grande Rebeyne* of 1529 was in effect a gigantic hunger riot, more a raid by the poor on the property of the rich than a revolt against authority. The great strike of journeymen printers ten years later called into question the living conditions imposed on the workers by the masters of the trade, and appealed to royal arbitration. Proceedings against the employers were initiated before the Seneschal of Lyon by the journeymen, who had combined in a secret confraternity known as the Tric. He awarded them a derisory pay rise. The aggrieved print workers appealed to the Dijon Parlement, which required the master printers to reduce the numbers of apprentices working alongside the journeymen. The master printers promptly laid the matter before the King's Council, which did not believe in half measures. Regarding the strikers as rebels, it referred the plaintiffs back to the Seneschal of Lyon on that very charge. Penalties followed thick and fast. The journeymen were treated like common criminals: outlawed or sent to the galleys. One was condemned to death. The Crown viewed labour disputes as a threat to peace and the social order, and was determined to nip them in the bud. The Lyon strike was seen as an affront to royal authority, and was mentioned in the Edict of Villers-Cotterêts, which included an article clearly alluding to the Tric and similar workers' organisations: 'We forbid the masters, journeymen and servants of any trade to combine in any congregation or assembly, great or small . . . or to confer with one another about the conditions of their trade.'

Confraternities of journeymen alone had proliferated in the

1530s as social tensions mounted. Such secret organisations sprang up, for example, in Toulouse and Paris. At Poitiers the city authorities banned a fraternity of labouring carpenters in 1538. These organisations have left few traces in the official histories, and remain largely unknown to historians. The powers-that-be regarded them as dangerous because, unlike their properly incorporated counterparts, they evaded surveillance. They could form secret focuses of social or religious dissent rather like the first Reformed congregations. And so, anxious about public order and fearful of secret threats to authority, the Crown sided decisively with the masters of the established trade guilds.

The massive rising of the Pitauds which made Guyenne tremble at the start of Henri II's reign was a movement of an entirely different order. It was a case of open resistance to the monarchy. The revolt is not widely known. Only two chronicles record its obscure events. Drawn up by Jean Bouchet in 1537 and Guillaume Paradin in 1552, they were published together at Bordeaux in 1981. In 1906, Stéphane Gigon published *La révolte de la gabelle en Guyenne, 1548–1549* (Paris, 1906), an invaluable collection of relevant texts and information.

In 1548, France was enjoying a breathing space between wars, but everyone knew that further hostilities between Henri II and Charles V were inevitable. The French king was away in Italy mending fences with the papacy and the Duke of Ferrara, and taking stock of his forces in Piedmont. Since 1542 the *taille*, had been supplemented by the *crues* levied to finance the war. The direct tax, which had been about 2.6 million *livres* in 1526, was hovering around 4.5 million between 1542 and 1547. Yet even this was not enough, and further demands had to be made on the taxpayer. Above all, money was sought right where it was to be found, in the cities and ports. In 1542 a levy upon the wealthier cities, meant to raise 1.6 million *livres* in all, demanded 20 500 *livres* from Bordeaux alone. And in 1543, the levy on walled towns demanded a further 30 000 *livres* from Bordeaux, and the creation of new offices in the Bordeaux Parlement, whose membership rose from 24 in 1515 to 83 in 1559. Unfortunately for the rest of the population, the new magistrates, like the old, were exempt from ordinary taxation, billeting troops, and the *gabelle*. And the rate of the *gabelle* had been increasing constantly since the reign of Louis XII, along with the *aides*, indirect taxes on a region's main product (in this case, of course, wine).

While the *aides* were still payable by the whole population, without privilege of rank, this was not the case with the *gabelle*, which was in any case subject to wide variations across the kingdom. The regions of the *grande gabelle*, namely the ancient royal domain, saw salt sold from *greniers* managed by royal officials at grossly inflated and ever increasing prices. Under Louis XII the *muid* (1850 pounds weight) cost 15 *livres*. By 1530 it was 30 *livres*, and by 1537, 45 *livres*. But in the regions of the *petite gabelle* (Languedoc, the Dauphiné, Provence and Burgundy), salt was far cheaper; while in the regions of *quartage* (Poitou, Guyenne, Périgord and La Marche) the government levied a tax of 25 per cent on the retail price. The price differential between the regions of *grande gabelle* and those of *quartage* led to massive fraud: in 1537, when a *muid* of salt was 45 *livres* in the former, it was only 15 *livres* in the latter.

In the interests of uniformity, François I suppressed the systems of *grande gabelle* and *quartage* in 1541–2, replacing them with a single tax of 44 *livres* a *muid* (reduced to 24 *livres* for salt taken from saltmarshes), allowing salt to circulate and trade freely, but extending the tax to salt destined for export and for preserving fish (hitherto exempt). The salt-producing regions of Aunis and Saintonge, hard hit by this measure, took arms and broke out in revolt. The coastal and island areas of Marennes, Ré, Oléron and Arvert experienced severe disorder which extended to La Rochelle. But the sudden agitation was not so serious that the arrival of troops and of François I in person to threaten the destruction of the city could not suppress it, and on 1 January 1543 the king published an amnesty for crimes of sedition.

But the government pulled back, reluctant to risk a trial of strength at home while the fourth war with Charles V was unfolding in Italy and on the northern front. In 1544, however, a difficult year for the French army, when everyone expected war to last forever, it was necessary once again to find money to continue hostilities. Edicts of 1 July and 6 December 1544 pressed ahead with the *gabelle*. The machinery of *greniers* associated with the *grande gabelle* was extended throughout the realm. Only the provinces of Languedoc, the Dauphiné, Provence and Brittany retained their customary system. 1545 saw *greniers* installed throughout regions which had previously lacked them: in Guyenne, for example, at Ruffec, Châteauneuf, Saintes, Saint-Jean-d'Angély, La Réole, Libourne, Pons, and elsewhere. Households were obliged to purchase a certain amount of salt irrespective of actual needs, and the *receveur du grenier* had to consult the assessment records of the *taille* in order to allocate the level of compulsory purchase according to wealth. Edicts of 1546 introduced severe penalties for fraud. The temptation to defraud the treasury was all the greater because, on top of the tax of 45 *livres* per *muid* of salt, the price varied further according to the distance from the place of production, the difficulty of transportation, the tolls paid on the way, and the expenses of tax collection itself (wages, tools, buildings etc.).

As in 1542, people were quick to voice their discontent. This was quite understandable, as some people were being compelled to pay for a product which was available in abundance. There were riots in Périgord in 1545, and more serious disturbances in Saintonge the following year. But the real trouble erupted when the government decided to lease out the *greniers*. Whether because the returns from the extension of the *grande gabelle* had not fulfilled their expectations, or because it was hoped to extract still more from this expedient, letters patent of 15 March 1546 invited tenders for ten years' leases on the *greniers*. The lessees were to deliver the tax yield to the royal treasury quarterly, and to pay the staff themselves. They were empowered to employ special agents alongside the *gabelle* police already in place in each district in order to improve the monitoring of the system and the detection of fraud. *Gabelle* offences were put within the jurisdiction of the Provost-Marshals, and were generally punishable by a heavy fine (100 *livres*) and the confiscation of the means of transport. The legislation suggested that companies be formed to advance the leaseholders the required cautionary deposits, or the quarterly payments. Nobles and churchmen were urged to join such companies, and were assured that such actions would not be deemed derogatory to their dignity and privileges. But royal officials were excluded.

Once the new leasing regime was installed in Saintonge and Angoumois in 1548, the price of compulsory salt could only rise: for it now had to meet the wages of a private police and provide profits for the lessees and their partners. At the same time, opportunities for evading the tax were drastically reduced by increased surveillance.

Our objective in thus setting out the background at some length is not simply to tell the story of the *gabelle* revolt in Guyenne in the summer of 1548. But it is necessary to understand that massive popular revolt in order to assess, as the throne changed hands,

French opinion of royal policy: François I's policy, in effect, seeing that Henri II, king for barely a year, was merely reaping the bitter harvest of his father's wars.

The revolt began at Châteauneuf in Angoumois, where peasants imprisoned for *gabelle* fraud were set free by friends who threatened the manager of the *grenier* with death. The movement spread quickly, organised almost spontaneously on a parish basis. Parish representatives combined in a general assembly and appointed a supreme commander, Bois-Menier, known as Boullon, a citizen of Blanzac, who took the title of 'Colonel of Angoumois, Périgord, and Saintonge'. Soon, as the revolt gained followers and ground, a local squire named Puymoreau joined him in command. Guyenne was stripped of troops in order to deal with the threat to public order posed by this uprising. The governor, Henri d'Albret, had a company of gendarmes at Pau, and, hearing of developments, he counted on a good response from the local nobility to the summons of the feudal levy. When the revolt broke out, the king himself was in Burgundy, preparing to travel to Savoy and Piedmont (territories returned to France by the Treaty of Nice in 1538). He gave full authority to handle the revolt to Henri d'Albret, who ordered his company of 100 horsemen to advance against the rebels. The forces clashed between Blanzac and Barbezieux around 24 July and, amazingly, the peasants (now calling themselves the Pitauds) routed their knightly opponents.

The revolt then spread south, towards Bordelais. The parish priests and curates received letters signed by the two colonels ordering them to summon their men with the alarm, and to prepare them to march. In August, the towns and villages on the right bank of the Garonne rose in their turn, choosing as their chief a blacksmith named Tallemagne. Bordeaux rose on 18 August, and the Lieutenant-General, Tristan de Moneins, was murdered along with several *gabelle* officials.

Informed of the gravity of the situation, Henri II concluded that neither the local regular forces nor the local nobility were up to the task. So he called down troops from the northern front, while the Constable Montmorency began to march westwards from Piedmont. Saintonge and Angoumois fell under military occupation in October. The colonels and the parish captains were executed in barbaric fashion. The bells which had signalled revolt were taken down and smashed. The peasants were disarmed and subjected to the billeting of troops, who were authorised to behave as though in occupied territory. Bordeaux underwent a particularly terrible fate, occupied for more than three months by the Constable's troops, and witnessing over 120 death sentences from a summary tribunal. The city council was replaced by magistrates appointed by the king, and the Parlement was suspended and replaced by a tribunal of councillors from the Parlement de Paris. And the citizens were not only deprived of their weapons and bells but made to pay a fine of 200 000 *livres*.

The government acted here with exceptional but ephemeral severity, because it did not really have the means to implement its authoritarian leanings in a vast province with traditions of independence, which had only recently (in the case of Bordeaux at least) been integrated into the kingdom. And so in 1549 an amnesty restored the Bordeaux Parlement and the city council; while in 1553 the *gabelle*, having been the subject of lengthy negotiations between the provincial authorities and central government, was entirely suppressed in Guyenne. This privilege was bought at the cost of 1 149 000 *livres* together with full compensation for the purchasers of posts in the now redundant *gabelle* administration. But from this time until the Revolution in 1789, Guyenne remained a 'redeemed' province, exempt from all taxation of salt.

So Henri II's government had backed down. Admittedly it was beset with external problems which meant that it could not risk domestic trouble in an outlying province which had not only a frontier with the Habsburg foe but also traditional ties with England. And this sets the revolt of Guyenne in its proper perspective. Poorly armed peasants with the aid of craftsmen and small townsmen had notified the monarchy of their categorical refusal to accept the Crown's new aims and ambitions. That is why the revolt made such a lasting impact on the collective memory of the province; why it struck fear into the authorities; and why it remains for historians clear evidence of the radical transformation in the nature of power under François I and Henri II.

If further proof were needed, we have a magnificent text, at once perceptive and prophetic, *Les articles des habitants et communes de Guyenne demandés au Roi*. For its authors, its claims were neither revolutionary nor even very extraordinary. Indeed, it was entrusted by the Pitauds to a messenger, Laurent Journault, *Maître des Eaux et Forêts*, to be taken to the king at Turin like any other statement of grievances. Written in an archaic hand, it presented its argument scholastically, in three sections: the first listed the wave

of royal financial demands; the next drew out the harsh consequences of these fiscal 'innovations'; and the third, opening a
dialogue with the king, stated their claims and sought an amnesty
for 'the said rising', under pain of further risings.

The document is a curious mixture of gut conservatism and a
clear awareness of the advance of the State. Its complaints against
the increase of the *taille*, the new taxes, and above all the *gabelle*,
are almost banal, as indeed are those against the proliferation of
offices and the dishonesty of royal officials. But the criticism of
the sale of church benefices is less traditional, as is that of the
State control of the Church, seen as the root of the taxes levied
upon clerical property. Less traditional too are the bitter denunciations of a Crown which rode roughshod over its own legal system; and of the sentences for *gabelle* offences in the *Grand Conseil*,
which 'allowed no ordinary court to take cognisance of them',
and eroded the jurisdiction of the *cour des aides*. And there was a
severe and direct accusation of the king himself for breaking the
promise made at his accession 'to make no demands on his people
beyond the ordinary *taille*'.

The rhythm of the text, as it lists 'novelties' and 'innovations'
paragraph by paragraph, bespeaks its conservatism and its desire
to return to a traditional social order. Yet that order was of the
recent rather than the distant past. The authors of the *Articles*
were content to pay 12.5 *livres* a *muid* for salt. And they were
equally happy to pay the *taille*, and to recognise royal, noble, and
ecclesiastical authority.

However, the Pitauds' refusal was equally clear-cut. They protested with almost tragic foresight against the modern State and
that total penetration of society at every level which brought its
authority home to all. And it was clear that the authority used to
levy taxes was all the more intolerable because those taxes were
imposed more heavily, more ruthlessly, and perhaps more effectively. But let us return to the *Articles*. They clamour against the
invasiveness of the State and take a stand against the tide of government officials whose physical presence is 'intolerable': 'officials
have been created'; 'other officials are raised up'; 'another op-
pression inflicted on the people by the soldiery'. The draughtsmen convey a sense of crowding and suffocation, and of the loss
of that free space which had hitherto remained immune from
authority. The peasants clearly show how the net was closing around
them while the well-off were exploiting the system by exempting

themselves from tax and purchasing office or shares in tax-farms which gave them 'goodly power and authority'. The draughtsmen, if they saw the inevitability of that advance of the State which they portrayed, nevertheless felt themselves free enough to negotiate with the king himself, confident that they had right on their side and that their *Articles*, by exposing the Crown's hidden agenda, could put a brake on the process.

Étienne de La Boétie, it is said, was moved to write his *Discours de la servitude volontaire* by the harsh repression that followed the great *gabelle* revolt. This friend of Montaigne felt, as did the Pitauds, the 'emergence of a new kind of State', and in writing of tyranny he was undoubtedly sniping at the Valois monarchy. The *Discours* did not, of course, denounce the ill effects of authoritarian kingship in the frank style of the *Articles* of the Pitauds. But La Boétie's deconstruction of Leviathan emphasised that the revolt had not settled the question of the subjugation of the people: 'I do not urge you to push or shove', he wrote about the tyrant to the people of his time, and to people of every age, 'but simply no longer to uphold it. For then you shall see how the great colossus, once its foundation is removed, will crash to ruin under its own weight.'

Part III

Faction and Civil War

Introduction to Part III

In the history of any country there are portentous dates – dates heavy with significance for the future. In the history of France, 1559 is one such. April saw the Treaty of Cateau-Cambrésis demobilise the warrior nobility after 40 years of active service abroad. And July saw the death of Henri II, the linchpin of the chariot of State.

A gash was opened in the French body politic through which burst out all the accumulated tensions, conflicts and frustrations which François I and his son, aided by largely favourable circumstances, had just about held in check. The economy of Europe was already in trouble, and as the century wore on it sank into crisis, exacerbating social tensions in town and country alike. A population on whose growth 'mortality' was the only effective check was beset by the calamities of famine, plague and war, which exacerbated each other in a vicious spiral of disaster. In the 1580s, war became the dominant player in the scenario. Men sought both compensation and scapegoats for their misfortunes, called authority itself into question, and strove to exorcise their accursed fate through cathartic violence. The new religion now being professed within the land acted partly as a vehicle for the expression of the complicated underlying discontents, and partly as a catalyst for violent social and political reactions.

8   The People in Power

In a kingdom already tormented by economic crisis, and about to be torn apart by civil war, the personal qualities of the ministers and advisers closest to the king took on a new importance. Amid the storm of ambition which raged around a throne successively occupied by three youths, and amid the white heat of religious fanaticism, the individual character of those in power not only provided role models and scapegoats, but could also give a decisive turn to events.

Catherine de Medici and the Politics of Compromise

It was on 10 July 1559, when Henri II died from the blow inflicted by Montgomery's lance, that Catherine de Medici, the deceived wife but recognised Queen, a woman who had already acted as Regent during her husband's campaigns abroad, stepped to the centre of the historical stage. From then, and perhaps even more from the death of François II in 1560, until her own death in 1589, her image, coloured by the widow's weeds she invariably wore, was stamped upon French politics.[1] Hers is the personality which contemporaries and posterity alike have variously struggled to discover or to decode, to accuse or to acquit, heaping up on her account gossip, scandal, and falsehood – and on occasion (though much less often) admiration and good will. This is hardly the place for an exhaustive account of her character and career. Neither is there space to dispel the fog of criticism and even malice that has clung to her, nor to exculpate her from the charges which history has built up against her. For centuries she has played the scapegoat (and how well the part suited her!), allowing the French to forget the bitter taste left by the Wars of Religion and to discharge their consciences of the burden of guilt.

The daughter of Lorenzo de Medici (whom the nobility of France regarded more as a banker than as a Florentine prince and patron), she was in fact of French blood on her mother's side: Madeleine de La Tour d'Auvergne came from one of the kingdom's most illustrious families. But this was rarely allowed to Catherine's credit, for she was indeed an Italian, and her intimates were drawn mostly from the peninsula. However, Italians had been playing a major role in the politics, economics and culture of France for more than a century. As the great-niece of a pope (Leo X), Catherine might have expected rather more favour among hardline Catholics, but if anything the relationship proved an embarrassment. She found herself accused now of acting in the interests of Rome, and now of sharing in the debauchery of her papal ancestor. She was not a pretty woman, to judge from the surviving portraits, and masculine opinion has therefore been reluctant to forgive in her what it so readily overlooks in a Diane de Poitiers or a Marguerite de Valois. Even her fidelity to her husband's memory through 40 years of widowhood is made suspect, as if her lack of a love life was a moral defect. And even her maternal feelings as the mother of four sons (three of whom reigned) and three daughters (two of whom married kings) have been turned against her on the grounds that she sought to live out her own ambitions for power through her children. A patron of arts and letters, like her father and grandfather before her, she has been depicted as a spendthrift who squandered scarce royal resources on gardens, châteaux, jewellery, feasts, and dances. As superstitious as most of her contemporaries, her taste for divination has been transmuted into a political witchcraft which enabled her to secure the timely elimination of opponents. One can see the roots of the antipathy, understand its growth, and appreciate its durability. It is hard to lift the veil on the real woman beneath. Yet for 30 years this woman was at the centre of French politics. And if religious division and aristocratic faction reduced her to subterfuge, she none the less possessed certain political views to which she clung through thick and thin. Perhaps she was the Machiavellian she was thought to be: but the French elite of the time were too narrowminded to read Machiavelli aright. She certainly had a functioning concept of the State. Did she owe this to her father-in-law François I, with whom she had always enjoyed an excellent understanding, or to her husband Henri, or simply to the spirit of an age which was tending towards authoritarian monarchy? Throughout her life she fought to keep the monarchy above faction, seeking to raise it above the turmoil and prevent it being swallowed up by noble or religious parties. Hence arose a policy meandering in its course but fixed in its aim. Unlike the hardline Catholics, she never aimed to exterminate the Protestant minority, whose strength and tenacity she always acknowledged. She preferred peaceful means to national reconciliation. When, with the death of her son François in 1560, the Guise policy of religious repression (itself a mere continuation of Henri II's policy) fizzled out, Catherine, as Regent for the under-age Charles IX, implemented a *de facto* toleration that came naturally to her. Repressive measures were relaxed, the captive prince of the blood Condé was released, and the new Chancellor, Michel de L'Hôpital, a man of peace, reconvened the Estates General convoked by the late king and then convoked a new conference for 1561: the Colloquy of Poissy, an attempt to find a Gallican *via media* between the two faiths, which met at the behest of the Queen Mother and her Chancellor. And in 1562 the Edict of January extended to Protestants freedom of conscience and a degree of freedom of worship.

It was Catherine's influence also which shaped the Peace of Saint-Germain (1570) which was so favourable to the Protestants despite their recent defeat at the hands of royal forces. For it was not in her nature to drive a defeated opponent to despair and in so doing ally herself with the hardline Catholic party and its Guise leadership. Nor can the Massacre of Saint Bartholomew, the violent outburst of a crown under severe pressure from the Huguenots, be laid entirely at her door, even if, as regards the political crime, she was the principal culprit. This indelible stain is charged to her alone before the bar of history, yet when, a few days before, her daughter Marguerite had married Henri de Navarre, the Protestant leader, she had been buckling down once more to the task of national reconciliation. But as the tragedy unfolded, events rapidly escaped her control. When her son Henri III, inextricably entangled in the toils of the League, sought to break its hold by having the Guise leaders assassinated at Blois, Catherine recalled the attempted coup of August 1572 and was deeply uneasy. 'Ah, the wretch,' she remarked, 'I see him rushing upon his own ruin and I fear he will lose body, soul, and kingdom.'

In a kingdom up for grabs, the ordinary mechanisms of government were useless. Ruling from Paris or the other royal centres in the Ile-de-France and the Loire valley, as Henri IV was to do, was simply impossible when feudatories and factions had carved up the country between them. In her efforts to knit up the ravelled sleeve, Catherine paid with her life. She wrote thousands of letters, forcing herself to believe that mere words could win back for her son the loyalty of men, cities and institutions. Scribbled by her teams of secretaries, letters poured forth in the effort to rebuild the bridges between central and provincial authorities. Collected in the nineteenth century, they filled ten weighty tomes.[2] Catherine herself took to the road, endlessly meeting people, sizing them up, and playing on their affection or their pity. The long, hard voyages became increasingly tiring as the years wore on. Catherine was carried in a litter which doubled as an office: secretaries and writing materials were never far from her side.

In the aftermath of the first conflict and the atrocities of both sides, Catherine looked to the example of François I, who was always prepared to display the majesty of his royal person to his people. She set out with her son Charles IX on a protracted 'tour de France' which lasted from 1564 to 1566, showing off the young king to his fortunate people in order to rekindle the flames of monarchical zeal, which had almost guttered out amid minorities and regencies, baronial rivalries and religious contentions.[3] The vast caravan of close on 20 000 souls (including the entire government) lingered deliberately in areas where Protestantism had struck root. Passing slowly through Lyon, the Rhône valley, Provence and Languedoc, it came to rest at Bayonne, where, in 1565, Catherine met the Duke of Alba for a notorious interview, the subject of extensive historical investigation or speculation, which has, over the years, acquired a sinister reputation. The meeting between Philip II's hard man and the woman held responsible for the Massacre of Saint Bartholomew came to be seen as paving the way for the massacres that lay ahead. In fact, the negotiations between the Spanish ambassador and the Regent dragged on as she angled for Spanish marriages for her children and Alba sought from her a commitment to the elimination of heresy in France, together with the dismissal of the conciliatory Chancellor L'Hôpital. Neither party made any headway.

Leaving at last the feasts, pageants and negotiations of Bayonne, the Court once more set out along the roads of France, visiting Béarn, Saintonge, and Poitou, turning aside into Brittany, and then returning by way of Moulins and the Loire valley to Paris – arriving in summer 1566 after more than two years on the move.

Until the very end of her life, in 1589, Catherine kept on criss-crossing France in her efforts to maintain national unity and royal authority. She returned often to those parts of central and southern France dominated by the Huguenots, and had frequent meetings with her son-in-law Navarre, their patron. One of these took her in 1579 to Nérac to inspect and pacify Provence, which had been pillaged by rival gangs, the 'razés' and the 'carcistes'.[4] In summer she reached the Dauphiné, where she tried without success to soothe passions aroused by fiscal grievances and social tensions. In the following years, ageing and often ill, she ventured forth wherever national unity and royal authority were in jeopardy. A tireless pilgrim on behalf of her royal son, she was borne in her litter to Bourgueil in April 1580, La Fère in 1581, and in 1584 to Château-Thierry in an attempt to restrain her fourth son, the Duke of Alençon, who was always ready to ally with the Protestants against his brother or to seek to gather malcontents around him. In 1585, when the League became an extremist faction bent on risking everything for victory, she hurried to Épernay in Champagne to negotiate with the Guise barons, and then to Châlons, where she arranged the Treaty of Nemours. In 1586, with Henri III's consent, she once more returned to the south-west, meeting Navarre at the Château de Saint-Brice (between Cognac and Jarnac), and urging him without success to return to Court as a counterweight to the League barons. The following year saw her once more in Champagne to cajole Henri de Guise and his brothers. And when, on the 'Day of the Barricades' in May 1588, the king was ignominiously bundled out of his own capital by a mob as much embittered by his government as inflamed by the Catholic extremists, Catherine remained in Paris, a virtual hostage, to see what she might salvage from the wreck. What journeys were made by this woman, who convinced herself that if she could meet her adversaries in person, she could win them over and thus put an end to the troubles! What kind of government was it when the Queen Mother rushed hither and thither throughout France, meeting on their own ground the men who were prepared to tear the country to pieces? And what kind of country, in which predatory princes could, from the security of their provinces, thus trifle with Catherine de Medici?

In a Europe torn by religious division, the main foreign policy objective of Catherine and her sons was to maintain national independence from both Catholic and Protestant States, especially as internal dissensions made France easy prey for greedy neighbours. Spain, which under Philip II became the champion of European Catholicism, took a close interest in French affairs, and was concerned about the rise of the Huguenots. The French Protestants took a similar interest in the affairs of the Netherlands, where in August 1566 the 'Beggars' had unleashed a national and religious revolt against Spanish rule. William of Orange led the Dutch rebels, and his brother Louis of Nassau, a friend of the Huguenot leaders, urged them to intervene. The threat of intervention in the Netherlands, where the Duke of Alba was pursuing a policy of harsh religious repression, in effect precipitated the Massacre of Saint Bartholomew. Catherine had no more stomach than the rest of the Council for war with Spain: her son-in-law Philip II was the most powerful ruler in Christendom. With respect to the papacy, Catherine took a traditionally Gallican line. When the Council of Trent drew to its close in 1563, the Cardinal of Lorraine, head of the French delegation, undertook to have its canons approved by the King's Council in accordance with French law. But in 1564 Catherine and her Chancellor opposed this strenuously. Likewise, when Pope Pius IV summoned seven French bishops to Rome on charges of heresy in 1563, and then in 1564 proclaimed the deposition of Jeanne d'Albret from the throne of Navarre for her conversion to Protestantism, Catherine registered vigorous protests against papal interference in French affairs. On a more personal level, when she desperately wanted to see her daughter married to the Huguenot Henri de Navarre and the requisite papal dispensation was slow in coming, she had the ceremony performed without waiting for the papal bull, concerned more for national unity than papal sanction.

Elizabeth I of England took quite as much pleasure as Philip II of Spain in the troubles of France. She extended to the French Protestants frequent, though rarely generous, assistance in men, money, and material. During the first conflict she signed the Treaty of Hampton Court (1562) with Condé and Coligny, by which they agreed to deliver Le Havre to her in exchange for 6 000 men and 100 000 crowns.[5] Later she assisted La Rochelle when it rebelled in the aftermath of the Saint-Bartholomew. And she helped Navarre with men and money during the sixth and seventh conflicts. The English Queen was adept at stirring the French pot, and Catherine did her utmost to neutralise her, although she had few enough means at her disposal. She tried to win Elizabeth's friendship by offering first her son Henri and then his brother François as potential husbands. Her policy was thus a long way from the big sticks and bold strokes of François I or Henri II, but then her domestic problems were overwhelming.

'Governess' of a France which was at the mercy of predatory barons, Catherine managed affairs, whether as Regent or in partnership with her son Henri III, with the assistance of a team of loyal servants drawn from the commons or the 'noblesse de robe'. Her closest advisers were never recruited from the great barons, of whose overweening ambition and affiliation to religious faction she was instinctively suspicious. Montmorency, Guise, and their kind were never among her intimates, who were mostly the kind of Secretaries of State whose role in the machinery of government had grown so dramatically under François I and Henri II. Catherine used these men in roles unprecedented in those earlier reigns, as ambassadors, envoys and supervisors. They became her jacks of all trades, and accompanied her on her countless journeys. She worked in this way with du Fresne, Nicolas de Neufville, Claude de L'Aubespine and his son Simon Fizes, Brulart, Révol, and Pomponne de Bellièvre. They held themselves aloof from faction (although Neufville, sire de Villeroy, was an ardent Catholic) and for the most part were later to be faithful servants of Henri IV. But in her anxiety to keep the Crown above faction and party, Catherine, although according her ministers enormous political importance, none the less kept them under firm control. She insisted on reading all incoming despatches and on being informed about all outgoing correspondence. But she was also on good terms with these men, and was careful to choose young well-educated men who enjoyed the life of the Court. Claude de L'Aubespine and Nicolas de Neufville were aged scarcely 25 when they became secretaries, and both were patrons of poetry as well as lovers of fine art and architecture.

For nearly 30 years Catherine threw herself wholeheartedly into the business of government; young, old, and even ill, she tramped the roads of the kingdom, for power had to be seen in order to be effective. The lessons of François I and Henri II bore fruit

here, combining with the Queen Mother's temperament and the
cultural tradition of the Medici which she continued in fine style.
The Court, which she and Henri III made especially sumptuous,
symbolised the wealth of the nation and the power of the Crown.
Feasts, balls, and tournaments, as well as luxuriant ritual, displayed
the majesty of kingship and held in close proximity to the royal
family gentlemen who might otherwise have been tempted to return
to the provinces. Catherine, like her husband Henri, had a taste
for poetry, and like him she subsidised the poets of the Pléiade,
such as Ronsard, Baïf, Dorat and Belleau. With her sons she shared
a taste for Italian music, and she helped the career of Orlando
di Lasso. Like her father-in-law and husband before her – and
her son-in-law Henri IV later – she loved building. The extension
and decoration of the Louvre, begun in the previous reign, continued under her watchful eye, which never tired of architects'
plans. When Pierre Lescot died in 1578 he was replaced by Jean
Bullant, who was charged by Catherine de Medici with the construction of the luxurious Tuileries palace, ringed with gardens,
fountains and waterways. For her personal use Catherine built
the Hôtel de la Reine (later known as the Hôtel Soissons) in the
centre of Paris, not far from the Louvre, so that she could work
close to the Court but undisturbed by courtiers.

The Crowned Sons of Catherine de Medici

History and myth alike offer ample testimony to Catherine's love
for her sons. When her husband died, her eldest son, François
II, had reached the 16 years defined under French law as the age
of majority. Married to Mary Queen of Scots, François was a sickly
youth like his brothers, and he wasted away through a year-long
reign which was dominated by his wife's uncles, the Duke of Guise
and his brothers. Charles IX succeeded him in 1560 at the tender
age of ten. On the advice of Antoine de Bourbon, desperate to
oust the Guise from power, the Council made Catherine 'Governess
of the Realm'.[6] History has hardly heaped laurels on the head of
this boy, who at Rouen was declared to have attained his majority
in 1563 at the age of 14. His short reign (which ended in 1574)
was stained with the Massacre of Saint Bartholomew. Some pamphleteers accused him in a transport of fury of having personally
taken pot-shots at fleeing Protestants – hence the nickname

'Chasseur Deloyal' (treacherous hunter) formed from the letters of his name ('Charles de Ualoys') by Agrippa d'Aubigné in his *Les Tragiques*. While Charles gave himself up to the pleasures of the chase, and even drew up a handbook on hunting, his mother ruled in his stead. It is not clear whether we should pay any attention to the rumours peddled by chroniclers, would-be historians, and mere libellers, to the effect that Charles was consumed with jealousy of his brother Henri. Henri was undoubtedly the apple of his mother's eye, which, together with his victories at Jarnac and Moncontour, might well have aroused the king's envy. So when, in 1571, the Protestants were lobbying for French intervention in the Netherlands in support of William of Orange against Philip II, Charles, intent on military glory, was seized with enthusiasm for Coligny's policy. When he died in 1574, eaten up by tuberculosis like all the Valois, the shades of the Saint-Bartholomew victims tormented him in his agony.

Henri III has cut an altogether different figure before posterity.[7] The political crisis came to its peak in his reign, and myth has amplified history. A brilliant commander, who led his forces to victory in the Third War of Religion, he accepted the crown which the Polish Diet, after assiduous lobbying by Catherine's agents, offered him in 1573. But that chilly and cheerless land bored him to tears. Relief came with the news of his brother's death. Except for the illegitimate Charles de Valois (Charles d'Angoulême), Charles IX had left no issue. So Henri succeeded to the crown of France on 30 May 1574. But he was in Poland, and virtually had to flee the country. On his return to France in September 1574, he showed his authoritarian and hard-working character by reducing the size of the Council, insisting on checking the despatches of the Secretaries of State, and distributing Crown offices to trusted favourites.

A fine figure of a man, like his grandfather François, and of undeniable intellectual calibre, Henri III had the misfortune to reign in a time of acute crisis. Something of a neurotic, he underwent a profound depression in 1582–3 which compelled him to remain aloof from the life of the Court. Religious and prone to excess – how could one forget his participation in processions of religious flagellants! – and always alert to the risk of betrayal, he was of all French kings the most reviled in his own day – much like his mother Catherine. However, these two, united in a common purpose, strove to keep the Crown above faction. Steering by dead reckoning and ruling from hand to mouth, they lacked the freedom of action that had characterised Henri II's government. The band of 'mignons', the guard of 45, and the isolation into which Henri himself readily retreated between frantic bouts of sensual indulgence or religious enthusiasm, all testify to his anxiety about his personal safety in an age when assassination had become a routine political exercise. His policy towards the League – seizing the leadership in 1576, standing aside for the Guises in 1585, and finally having them eliminated at Blois in 1588 – shows the clear head he kept in the face of that movement as he sought to dominate or defuse it. He acted similarly with regard to Henri de Navarre, the Protector of the Huguenots, whom he fought in 1574, 1577, 1579, and again in 1587 (when his forces were beaten at Coutras). But during the long years that Navarre spent in Guyenne, Henri III never missed an opportunity to keep in touch with him. His mother was the envoy he sent into the south-western provinces. And his frequent correspondence with Navarre reflected his keen desire for the latter's return to Court and the Church, which would make him an acceptable heir. For Henri III, with no son of his own, was worried about the succession, especially once his brother François d'Alençon died in 1584, leaving as heir presumptive according to the fundamental laws of the realm that very Prince of Navarre rejected by the League.

Perhaps it was in compensation for the insecurity of a monarchy beset by faction and ambition that Henri III and Catherine de Medici strove to make Court life as strictly ordered as possible. On his mother's advice, Henri promulgated between 1582 and 1585 a series of ordinances prescribing the code by which that little world was to conduct itself, exalting royal majesty (which was prone to depreciation in the rough and tumble of daily life), and dictating how courtiers and sovereign alike should spend their time. As in the preceding reigns, Court and government were inextricably intertwined: councils were held in the King's presence each morning between 6.00 and 9.30, and in the afternoon between 1.00 and 4.00. As ever, Court appointments in the various royal and princely households were reserved for the ancient nobility, but the 'noblesse de la robe' – the Councillors and Secretaries of State – also took part in courtly ceremonies and rituals. And the Court tended to reside in Paris itself, a city for which both Henri and his mother had a particular affection.

The Valois Court

The Court was not only a large body – with 3000 people serving in various capacities it amounted to a city within a city – but a complex one. Despite the advice lavished on its members by the authors of courtly manuals, violence often characterised relationships at Court, as witnessed by the bloody duels which Henri III tried with little success to restrain. But the brutality which marks the chronicles of both Court and city life masks relationships which, though not physical, were no less based on violence, for the Court of Charles IX and above all of Henri III held a faithful mirror to contemporary France. The kings tried to keep the great nobles close at hand in order to thwart their secessionist ambitions. For example, it was a great relief to Catherine and Charles IX when Gaspar de Coligny, the leader of the Huguenots since Condé's death, returned to Court in 1571. Likewise, after the Massacre of Saint Bartholomew, they kept their Bourbon relatives, Navarre and the young Condé, under close surveillance in the gilded gaol of the Court, lest they slip away to assume command of the Huguenot party. It was for the same reason that Catherine and Henri III showered Navarre with invitations to Court when, after his flight in 1576, he went to ground in Guyenne. Conversely, the powerful Guise dynasty knew what disquiet they were causing the regime when they withdrew from Court after Alençon's death in 1584.

In these troubled times, the Crown found the Court an indispensable instrument in the task of rebuilding loyalties shattered by civil and religious conflict. The notorious 'mignons' from whom Henri III could scarcely be separated shared the spoils of courtly office and reforged links of solidarity with the Crown which civil wars and dissensions had loosened if not dissolved. Hence the meteoric rise of the Dukes of Épernon and Joyeuse, and also the astonishing tombs erected for Maugiron and Quélus, which reflected their loyalty to the sovereign for whose honour they had died in a duel with the rival favourites of Alençon in 1578.

1578 also saw Henri III found a new order of chivalry, the Order of the Holy Spirit, whose 26 members had to be of impeccable ancestry and orthodoxy, and took an oath of fealty to the Grand Master, the king himself. For Henri III the Order was one more way of securing the loyalty of nobles from the enticements of Navarre and Guise, as was his policy of swelling the ranks of the high nobility (he created 11 *duchés-pairies*, or peer-duchies, in his 15 year reign).[8]

Even if it reflected contemporary confrontations all too well, the Court nevertheless remained a safe haven for arts and letters. Italian fashions had an increasing hold over both courtiers and the events and spectacles of Court life. The *Ballet comique de la Royne*, performed in 1581, a mixture of speech, song, and dance, was a masterpiece. Theatrical spectacles drew inspiration from the *commedia dell'arte*, with whose *dramatis personae* (Pantaloon, Zanni and Harlequin) courtiers became thoroughly familiar. Troupes of Italian performers, the *Gelosi* and the *Confidenti*, appeared at the French Court in 1576–7 and 1584–5. Spectacles which combined masque, dance, and music were lavishly staged, establishing among the courtiers a brief artistic unity which the regime wanted to believe reflected political reality. Poets and writers like Ronsard, Baïf, Yver, Desportes and Belleau were salaried by the royal family or by courtiers, and their works read or sung at Court.

As the locus of power and government, the mirror of the tensions of the age, the engine of social advancement and the nursery of culture, the Court of the last Valois Kings maintained the traditions handed on by François I. But around the 'Governess of France' and her three sons raged ungovernable feudal ambition. And as France had learned before and was to learn again, in periods of minority or regency the throne might as well have been vacant.

The Princes of the Blood: François d'Alençon

François d'Alençon, the last son of Henri II and Catherine, was in every way typical of the ambitious nobles of his day, except that he rarely invoked religion to justify his machinations.[9] This unprepossessing and undoubtedly homosexual youth played the familiar role of royal younger sons, that of the perpetual malcontent ever ready to plunge the realm into confusion for the sake of personal gain or even simply to affirm his own existence. In 1573, in concert with the Huguenots, he took charge of the Politique faction and dabbled in various plots against the crown, if not the life, of Charles IX. His relationship with Henri III was no better: they hated each other, and François sided once more with the Huguenots in the Fifth War of Religion (they were of

course only too happy to have the backing of a prince of the
blood who could promote their cause at the very highest level).
Later, in 1577, he took up the old Huguenot policy of intervening in the Netherlands, and forged links with the friends of William
of Orange. Always energetic in opposition to his royal brothers,
he sought to build up a noble faction, filling the court with tensions, rivalries and confrontations. Duels and murders punctuated the tense years from 1574 to 1579, reaching their climax
with the famous Duel of the Mignons in 1578, when half a dozen
of his and the king's favourites fought to the death. When François
withdrew from court, his mother would take fright at his scheming. And not without reason, seeing that from 1579 he pursued
an essentially sovereign policy on his own account. Emboldened
by the progress of his courtship of Queen Elizabeth, he took up
Coligny's dream of intervention in the Netherlands. If his motives had not been so transparently ambitious, they might have
been thought statesmanlike: to reunite the French nobility against
the old enemy and assist the victims of Philip II and Alba. But
things turned sour, even though Catherine, delighted to see her
son causing trouble outside the kingdom for once, supported him
with men and money. The States General of the Netherlands offered him sovereignty in 1580, by the Treaty of Plessis-les-Tours,
on condition that he secured French aid against Spain. But the
brutality with which Alençon and his troops conducted themselves
at Antwerp alienated the Flemings. They refused him admission
to their towns, and in 1583 he withdrew to Dunkirk and disbanded
his forces. It was stalemate, but Alençon was already suffering
from the tuberculosis that would carry him off the following year.

Besides the disturbances consequent upon the unbridled ambition of Alençon, the throne was beset by a number of especially
powerful and grasping families devoid of any sense of national
interest, and only out to take what they could for themselves from
a kingdom fragmented by religious divisions. These grandees took
seats by right at the royal council tables, and monopolised the
major Crown offices and wealthier dioceses. They led the royal
armies, held the governorships, and drew handsome pensions.
They maintained crowds of clients, and established extensive family
networks through judicious marriages. Their wealth in land, rents,
fees, and royal gifts, albeit unevenly distributed, was enormous
when set against the modest possessions of ordinary people or
even of the lesser nobility. This group of grandees included the

princes of the blood royal, foreign princes (such as those of Lorraine, Rohan, Cleves, and Mantua), the peer-dukes, and the other dukes.[10]

The Princes of the Blood: the Bourbons

Antoine de Bourbon was the foremost prince of the blood outside the immediate royal family. He enjoyed great rank and dignity because, according to the Salic Law, he was next in succession to the throne after the four sons of Catherine de Medici. But his high rank was not matched by his wealth, which was relatively modest. True, he held a scattering of counties and baronies north of the Loire, including Vendôme, Condé-en-Brie, and La Fère. And he had many dynastic connections among the highest nobility of France: the Guises, the Montpensiers, and even the Nevers were related to him in various ways. And he made an advantageous marriage to Jeanne d'Albret, Viscountess of Béarn and Queen of Navarre, heiress to the kingdom's last great feudal house.[11] Its territories included not only the sovereign lands of Béarn and Navarre, but also a range of seigneurial lands throughout the south-west: the viscounty of Limoges, and the counties of Périgord and Foix. The House of Navarre presided over a host of vassals and clients, swollen still further by the governorship of Guyenne which the French kings customarily conferred upon the King of Navarre. From François I onwards, the French monarchy sought to forge closer links with the Albret dynasty. François married off his beloved sister Marguerite (grandmother of the future Henri IV) to Henri d'Albret. And he in turn prevailed upon his daughter Jeanne, after some hesitation, to marry Antoine de Bourbon. Much later, Jeanne d'Albret and Catherine de Medici agreed on the marriage in August 1572 of Jeanne's son Henri to Catherine's daughter Marguerite (known to her Valois brothers as Margot).

When, in 1560, Jeanne was converted to Protestantism, a large number of southern French nobility and gentry followed suit, either from conviction or from feudal loyalty. This made the region particularly redoubtable for the Valois regime.[12] But Jeanne's husband Antoine, having briefly flirted with the new faith, remained Catholic. On the death of François II, he did not claim the regency (as French custom might have encouraged him to do), but left it instead to Catherine, contenting himself with the sonorous title of Lieutenant-General of the Realm. He died not long after, in November 1562, at the siege of Rouen (which Protestant forces were holding against the royal army). His seven-year-old son Henri inherited his rank as first prince of the blood, but his brother Louis became the effective head of the Bourbon dynasty.

Louis de Bourbon-Condé wholeheartedly espoused the Protestant cause, which he used from 1559 to justify his opposition to the Guises, who were jealously guarding the young King François and were continuing the harsh policy of religious repression inaugurated by Henri II.[13] The conspiracy of Amboise, which, if it had succeeded, would have led to the imprisonment and trial of François de Guise and his brother, the Cardinal of Lorraine, was a tragic failure which cost several Protestants their lives.[14] Condé, imprisoned in Orléans, was saved from execution only by the death of the king, which cut short Guise hegemony together with their intolerant religious policy. Before the outbreak of the First War of Religion, when, early in 1562, Catherine, having made too many concessions to the Calvinists, began to seek a rapprochement with the Catholics on the Council, and when conflicts between Catholics and Protestants were already breaking out in the provinces, Condé got ready for the struggle which he regarded as inevitable and which, when all is said and done, he desired. He called upon the nascent Protestant churches to provide soldiers, and then he conceived the tactic of seizing towns which was pursued by the Huguenots throughout the first war. He was in part responsible for the outbreaks of the second and third wars in 1567 and 1568, and he met his death at the Battle of Jarnac in 1569. It was Condé, a nobleman who felt defrauded of his rights during the Guise predominance, who turned French Protestantism into a power-hungry faction. Seeking to justify his rebellion to both national and international audiences, he published trenchant declarations in 1562, accusing the Guises of having the king and the Queen Mother under their thumb, and proclaiming that his only desire was to set them free.[15] He did likewise in 1567, publishing pamphlets which claimed that he had taken up arms to defend not only Protestants but the whole population, 'without respect for persons or for creed'. On these grounds he summoned the Estates General to set about the reform of the realm – in short, a new 'League of the Common Weal'.[16] In fact, all the noble leaders, motivated by the desire for power among other things, sought to justify the resort to arms by appealing to national ideals and the defence of the common good. Montmorency-Damville, Henri de Navarre, and Henri de Guise published many such manifestos, or else had their scribblers write them without bringing their own names into it. As we shall see, the period of the Wars of Religion saw an unprecedented flood of oral and written propaganda.

When Condé died, leaving a son, Henri, who would prove a more intransigent Calvinist than his father, Jeanne d'Albret and her son Henri de Navarre became the princely leaders of the Huguenot movement. Jeanne made Calvinism the official religion of Béarn in 1565, enforcing Calvinist ethics with the apparatus of the State (the Church ordinances). Catholics were no longer tolerated in the principality. She took up the baton from Condé and had her son's authority as a prince of the blood and leader of the Huguenots recognised by the army, thus revealing her consuming ambition to win for herself and her son a prominent position in the kingdom as a whole.

When the Third War of Religion was brought to an end by the Treaty of Saint-Germain in 1570, negotiations resumed for a marriage between Henri de Navarre and Marguerite de Valois. Jeanne d'Albret died in Paris, in the spring of 1572, before the marriage was celebrated (it took place in August). The young King of Navarre now became the prince of the Huguenots and the sworn enemy of the Catholic Guise dynasty, which sought to dominate the King's Council and exploit the royal prerogative to its own political and religious ends.[17]

By 1572 the 19-year-old prince had already changed his religion three times (and would do so again later that year when, after the Massacre of Saint Bartholomew, he was forced to abjure Protestantism together with his cousin Condé), had fought in two great battles, and was soon to see his friends and servants massacred in the court and precincts of the Louvre. A prisoner at Court for four years, perforce a part of all its celebrations and peregrinations, he was watched, guarded, or courted as the times required. During this time he gained a complete self-mastery, a profound mistrust of others, and beyond doubt a certain distaste for violence. He retained also from his time as a hostage a certain sense of his own value and that of the cards he might play. Escaping in 1576, he returned to Calvinism after some reflection, swayed by the political and financial support which the Protestants could offer. Between then and 1589 he never ventured north of the Loire. As protector of the Huguenots, and Governor of Guyenne (an appointment which Catherine de Medici thought made him less dangerous), he remained in south-western and mid-western France fulfilling these rather contradictory roles. He was waiting his moment. His mother had instilled in him a profound sense of his rank and dignity. As the first prince of the blood he might one day be brought by dynastic accident to the throne. It was his sure sense of his own destiny which kept him going through those long years of withdrawal, when he preferred to be number one in Guyenne rather than number two at the Louvre. He manoeuvred between Catherine de Medici, Henri III, and the Protestant churches, and regarded the Guises as his principal foes. When Alençon's death in 1584 left him heir presumptive, he knew well how to display to best advantage his right to the succession, which the League disputed. He despatched lengthy addresses to the Parlement and the Sorbonne, the foremost moral authorities of the realm, presenting himself as the lawful successor to Henri III and holding out the prospect of his conversion. Countering the League, he advanced his credentials as a trueborn Frenchman, in contrast to the foreign background of the Guises in Lorraine and to the Spanish alliance forged by the Catholic leaders and their extremist lackeys. His victory over the royal army led by Joyeuse at Coutras in October 1587 represented not only the victory of a rebel prince over his sovereign, but also the victory of good Frenchmen over the supporters of a foreigner. After Coutras, Navarre remained wary of driving home his advantage by marching north towards Tours, where Henri III had fixed his government. Instead, he stayed in Guyenne. He buried the conquered dead with full military honours, demanded no ransom for prisoners, and instead wrote a celebrated letter to the last Valois: 'I am truly sorry that today I was unable to distinguish trueborn Frenchmen from League partisans. But those who have fallen into my hands may bear witness to the good treatment they have received from me and my servants, their captors.'

When Henri III had the Guise brothers assassinated at Blois in 1588, he found himself facing an irresistible increase in League support, and was forced to ally himself with Navarre to avoid being overwhelmed. Navarre, who had been angling for this alliance ever since his flight from Court in 1576 (despite consistently rejecting all invitations to return to Court), led his army to join the king at Tours on 30 April 1589. At last he had attained the position befitting his rank, the office of first prince of the blood that he had coveted for years. He could not yet know that within three months Henri III's death at the hand of Jacques Clément would leave him King of France.

The Grandees: Montmorency

The role of the Montmorency family in the Wars of Religion, though rather neglected by historians obsessed with the Guises or the Bourbons, still merits close consideration. The Constable Anne de Montmorency, a statesman of the first rank under François I and Henri II, had been eclipsed by the Guises under François II. Ill at ease amid the religious tensions affecting all levels of society, he nevertheless remained by temperament a loyal Catholic. Disgusted and troubled by the Protestant advances at Court, the psalm-singing in the noble households (e.g. those of Coligny, the Princess of Condé, and the Duchess of Ferrara), the Huguenot disturbances in the provinces, and the plots of Condé, he made his peace with the Duke of Guise, his long-time political adversary, in March 1561. Together with that other hardline Catholic, the Marshal de Saint-André, they formed the Triumvirate, dedicated to the defence of France's traditional religious values.[18] Other participants in this early version of the League included the Cardinal of Tournon and the Marshal de Brissac. To underline their repudiation of the tolerant policy espoused by the Regent and her Chancellor Michel de L'Hôpital, Montmorency and Guise withdrew from court a few days later.

The Constable, recalled by the Regent when the first war broke out in the following year, led the royal forces to victory at Dreux. But during the second war he met his death at the Battle of Saint-Denis in 1567. After his death, two of his sons, Marshal François de Montmorency, and Henri Damville, took the role of referees in the political games of the Grandees. Although they remained firm Catholics, they had no truck with the extremism of the Guises. After their father's death they even made overtures towards their Châtillon cousins, the leading Protestant family after the Bourbons. When the Massacre of Saint Bartholomew broke out, François was away from Paris, and Damville was performing his duties as Governor in Languedoc. After the Massacre, François aligned himself with the Duke of Alençon, the Cinderella of the Valois dynasty, to form a faction of the middle ground, known as the

Malcontents or the Politiques. This attracted many gentlemen of high birth, including Thoré (the Constable's fifth son) and Turenne (the future Duke of Bouillon). The Malcontents, who maintained their links with Henri de Condé and Henri de Navarre, had a simple policy: at home, religious toleration; and abroad, intervention in the Netherlands in support of William of Orange against Spain. But when their plottings were reported, François Montmorency was sent to the Bastille on 4 May 1574. His brother Damville then allied himself with the Protestants of the Midi, and published a manifesto calling for an assembly of the Estates General, the rehabilitation of the victims of Saint-Bartholomew, the prosecution of those responsible for the massacre, and the free exercise of Protestant worship.[19] At this stage Damville envisaged carving out for himself a principality in Languedoc, to rule as viceroy. He convened the provincial estates when, for his part, Henri III, returning from Poland, summoned their equivalent at Villeneuve-lès-Avignon, and, by recourse to arms, took possession of a number of towns in Languedoc in the name of a Union of Catholics and Protestants. However, this rebel governor, manoeuvring between Henri de Navarre and central government, immediately recognised Navarre as heir presumptive when Alençon died in 1584. The importance of Damville and his brother François Montmorency remains considerable because, after Alençon, they were the leaders of that Politique faction among the Grandees which supported Henri IV against the League in his bid for the throne.[20]

The Grandees: the Guises

The Guise dynasty was of a different stamp, monolithic in its vigorous defence of Catholicism from generation to generation. A cadet branch of the ducal house of Lorraine, the Guises made their careers in the French army and the French Church. By 1559 the head of the family, Duke François, enjoyed a solid reputation for courage, confirmed by his victories at Metz and Calais, and witnessed by his famous 'scarface', the result of an encounter with a lance at the siege of Boulogne in 1545. His brother Charles, the Cardinal of Lorraine, was well regarded at Rome and headed the French delegation to the final session of the Council of Trent. Like his elder brother, he sat on the King's Council. The two men took complete control of the government when their nephew

by marriage, François II, came to the throne in 1559. The family
never had the vast resources of the Montmorency dynasty in land,
lordships, rents and houses. Their power lay elsewhere, in the
loyalty of the family as a whole to its head, the Duke, first of all
to François and then, after his assassination in 1563, to his eldest
son Henri. The brothers of François – Claude, Duke of Aumale,
Louis, Cardinal of Guise, and René, Marquis of Elboeuf – sought
not to make their own destiny, but to pursue that of their elder
brothers. It was the same in the next generation, when Duke Henri
lived in a perfect harmony of aims and ideals with his siblings –
Charles, Duke of Mayenne, Louis, Cardinal of Guise, and Catherine,
Duchess of Montpensier. This unanimity extended to his cousins,
the Duke of Aumale, and his brother the Chevalier, and the Duke
of Elboeuf. The family stood at the heart of an enormous network of friends, clients, and distant relatives whom they cultivated assiduously. The Guises were tireless in providing this vast
clientele with posts in the army, the Church, the administration,
and the royal and princely households. In addition, they commanded throughout the realm a vast and faithful following which
would support them at every turn.

The care which the Guises lavished on shaping their public
image enabled them to lead by prestige and reputation without
having to dig too deep into their personal resources. Duke François
presented himself as the 'perfect knight', winning the admiration of his contemporaries in much the same way as the Protestant François La Noue. Duke Henri in his turn, like his father,
handsome, facially scarred (a result of the Battle of Dormans in
1575) and a favourite with the ladies (among them Marguerite
de Valois), cultivated a spectacular gallantry which won many hearts.
Henri expanded his clientage, and did not disdain to seek supporters from below the nobility, among mere townsfolk. Paris was
already teeming with Guisards in the time of Duke François. Duke
Henri had even more supporters there, including the Mayor, Claude
de Marcel.

The finest feather in the Guise cap, which they displayed to the
maximum advantage, was their inflexible Catholicism. François
played the true Christian soldier, moderating the brutality of his
troops and making his communion with zeal. He made peace
with his sworn enemy Montmorency for the sake of defending
the faith. His brother the Cardinal of Lorraine, though hardly of
a clerical lifestyle, used his talents to wreck the Colloquy of Poissy.

The cardinal and his nephew, Duke Henri, opposed the Protestant Coligny in 1572, when he was pressing the King's Council to intervene in the Netherlands against Spain, the spearhead of European Catholicism. Later, in 1576, when the League first emerged, Henri III assumed its leadership in order to cut the ground from under the feet of the duke just as the latter was being assiduously courted by the agents of Philip II. But when Alençon died in 1584, the duke reacted with horror to Henri III's plan to achieve the conversion of Navarre in order to make him an acceptable claimant to the throne. He dismissed the possibility in advance as insincere and mere opportunism. But he himself seized the opportunity to put himself at the head of the League. Shortly afterwards, in December 1584, he accepted a Spanish proposal for an alliance. From then until his assassination he took possession by force of a number of towns and provinces, creating for himself, much as Henri de Navarre had already done, a scattered principality but a coherent party.

What were the aims and ambitions of the Guises? The defence of Catholicism of course – their sincerity was beyond doubt, and Duke Henri spent recklessly on its behalf, selling plate, silver and land, and piling up debts in order to pay soldiers, purchase arms, and reward followers. Some historians have credited them with seeking, on the basis of their descent from Charlemagne (a more ancient royal lineage than Capetians or Valois), to replace the impotent and discredited Henri III. But, according to their most recent biographer, Duke Henri was pursuing a feudal ideal.[21] His Christian and baronial ideology entailed a return of the high nobility to the forefront of government, a return to a traditional polity in which the Grandees were the 'natural councillors' of the king, and a reliance on the Estates General to guide the monarch's fundamental policy choices both at home and abroad. It was, in short, a throwback to a model of monarchy which the first Angoulême–Valois kings had rendered obsolete.

Threats to the Powerful

Many men and women paid with their lives as the monarchy struggled to keep its head above the turbulent waters of feudal rebellion decked out in the cloak of religion, Protestant or Catholic. Catherine de Medici, as we have seen, wore herself out traversing discontented provinces in order to negotiate with rebel nobles like Guise, Navarre, or Damville. Henri III sought to rebuild a nobility loyal only to himself. Each in turn summoned the Estates General – in 1560, 1561, 1576 and 1588 – in an effort to find some common ground with the traditional representatives of the kingdom amid the turmoil. Each in their turn fell victim to their own desperate efforts to keep the crown, and the State, out of the hands of factions. They were showered with abuse from all sides as Protestants, Leaguers, and even Politiques poured out pamphlets, leaflets, speeches and manifestos against them. The *Discours merveilleux de la vie, actions et déportements de la Reyne Catherine de Médicis*, doubtless the work of a Huguenot in the wake of the Massacre of Saint Bartholomew, hinted darkly at the 'monstrous vices' of the Queen Mother, but without detailing them, presumably for want of any real information. And Henri III was more vilified than any other French king. The famous diarist Pierre de l'Estoile avidly gathered the daily harvest of hate. Henri was accused of sodomy, hypocrisy, thriftlessness, tyranny, and finally murder. The chorus of execration reached its climax after the king had the Guise brothers murdered at Blois. In January 1589 L'Estoile noted in his *Journal*, 'there is not a mother's son in Paris who has anything but abuse and scurrility to say of the king'.[22]

Thoughts of regicide were nourished by inflammatory preaching against the king, by the Sorbonne's decree releasing Christian subjects from the obedience due to their sovereign, and by the vengeful propaganda of a Guise clan which was far from being finished by the coup at Blois. On 1 August 1589, Jacques Clément turned words into action, assassinating a king who had been desacralised by execration and calumny.[23]

Henri de Navarre, the leader of a faction but also a prince of the blood, went in fear from Alençon's death onwards. This fear grew after the poisoning of his cousin Henri de Condé in 1588, and he lived in dread of a poisoned cup or a sharpened dagger. Having become king – a king, as we shall see, poorly received by hardline Catholics – he narrowly escaped assassination in 1593 and again in 1594. And in the ensuing years his police arrested a succession of would-be assassins until, in 1610, Ravaillac successfully accomplished his foul design. The first Bourbon, like the last Valois, never reached a complete understanding with his kingdom.

The faction leaders had, in the eyes of their opponents, such

physical and symbolic power that their personal elimination became a vital necessity. During the Wars of Religion, spectacular
assassinations were a common feature of royal and noble policy.
François de Guise – dare one say it, scarcely deserving such an
end – was murdered before Orléans by a Protestant gentleman
named Poltrot de Méré. The peerless Catholic general, renowned
warrior, and living symbol of the nascent Catholic party, was such
a charismatic figure that only his death could destroy his prestige. The murder of Condé was of a similar kind. From 1567 the
charismatic Huguenot leader was locked in rivalry with the Duke
of Anjou (the future Henri III) for the position of Lieutenant-
General of the Realm. Some said that this rivalry sparked off the
Third War of Religion. In the course of the battle of Jarnac in
1569, which Anjou won, Condé fell under his horse and broke
his leg. Against all the laws of war, Anjou sent one of his captains
to finish him off with a pistol. Not content with his easy victory,
he pursued his vanquished foe beyond the grave and, to humiliate him further, had his corpse borne on an ass to the square of
Jarnac, where it was hung up on a pillar. This 'ritual of defiance'
performed by Anjou aimed at destroying and humiliating not only
his rival of 1567 but also the prince whose personality and rank
had justified the Protestants in their struggle against their king.

No less spectacular was the assassination of Coligny during the
Massacre of Saint Bartholomew. In deciding to kill the Admiral,
the King's Council hoped to lay to rest with him the anti-Spanish
foreign policy he had advocated. In entrusting the deed to the
Guises, the Council sought to involve them in the proscription of
the Protestant leaders, knowing how keen they were to avenge
the murder of François – which Coligny was said to have ordered.

When in 1588 Henri III decided to rid himself of the Guises,
he was merely following the example set by his mother, his brother,
and the King's Council in 1572. With his back to the wall, and
his royal authority a joke, his decision was not only a political
crime but the personal vengeance of a humiliated prince. That
the corpses were burned on his orders shows how determined he
was to eliminate every trace of the authors of his personal
misfortunes and to prevent their remains from fuelling a cult of
League martyrs.

It was a tragic age, as rich in exotic, powerful, and passionate
personalities as in heroic deeds and dramatic events, and one which
never ceases to suggest parallels and lessons for our own times.

9 The Church and the Protestant Faction

The policy of harsh repression implemented by Henri II and his Parlements was unable to crush the rise of Protestantism. Its converts were now being drawn from among the highest noble families, the magistrates of the sovereign courts, the civic elites of merchants and officeholders, and ordinary townsfolk. Public demonstrations like those in the rue Saint-Jacques in 1557 or the Pré-aux-Clercs in 1558 bore witness to the strength and zeal of the reformed community in the royal city of Paris. Elsewhere small groups were forming, more and more openly, celebrating communion in the Genevan fashion, reading the Gospels, and singing the Psalms. The makeshift pastors who guided them, though clearly Protestants in breach with the Catholic Church, were not always adherents of strict Calvinist orthodoxy. A stream of appeals flowed to Calvin, to whom the French Protestants looked for leadership, asking for pastors trained in the master's pure doctrine. Often enough it was local notables, worried by the risk of doctrinal or even social deviance, who wrote to Geneva, anxious to take the decisive step and belong to a gathered Church.[1]

By 1555 Calvin had at last solved a number of organisational problems in Geneva and was thus free to turn his attention to France. Geneva was sheltering a substantial number of refugees from the persecutions inaugurated by François I and intensified by his son. The city contained more than 3000 French refugees. Over a third were from Languedoc and Normandy, with others from the Ile-de-France, Guyenne, and Gascony. Among them were many candidates for the ministry who yearned to return and 'bring the Gospel' to their compatriots once they themselves had received

279

a thorough grounding in the pure doctrine of Calvin. So Calvin formed the Genevan Company of Pastors, which sent into France duly constituted ministers to take in hand the nascent congregations and make them into gathered churches. Between 1555 and 1562 a hundred or so men returned to their native land, now a missionary territory, and founded the first French congregations along Genevan lines at Poitiers and Paris in 1555, Bourges in 1556, and subsequently at Meaux, Angers, and many other places.[2]

In 1559 Henri II took fright at the spread of Calvinism and, recognising the inadequacy of the repressive measures hitherto employed, hurriedly called off hostilities with the Habsburgs in order to prepare a decisive blow against 'this abominable heresy'. By one of those ironies of history, it was in this hostile climate, in Paris itself, where the Protestants were hated by the majority of the population despite their number and social standing, that the first National Synod of the French Reformed Church was convened. The rue Visconti, in an area already known as 'Little Geneva' because of the strength of the Calvinists there, was the meeting-place for the lay and clerical representatives of a dozen congregations. Three days of discussions resulted in the two founding charters of French Protestantism: the *Confession de foi*, and the *Discipline ecclésiastique*. These laid down the essential articles of the Reformed faith, the basic structures of the new church, and the ethical standards by which the new Christians were required to live.

The Schism: Texts and Deeds

The texts which embodied the schism highlighted the distance between the Reformed faith and Catholicism. In matters of faith, Protestants would accept nothing but the Bible as truth, drawing the knowledge of the divine will from it alone. Convinced of humanity's irremediable loss of grace through original sin, they attributed salvation to faith alone, a gratuitous gift made by God to his elect by virtue of Christ's sacrifice. Works performed by people lost in the mire of sin could not be anything but sinful. The French *Confession de foi* set itself squarely in the Calvinist tradition, laying particular stress on the predestination of those whom God 'in his eternal and immutable wisdom . . . has chosen though his mere favour and mercy in Our Lord Jesus Christ, without

regard for their works, leaving the rest in a state of . . . corruption and damnation, so as to manifest in the latter his justice
and in the former the riches of his mercy'. The dangerous situation in which all the Protestants of the kingdom then found themselves, and the social standing of the mostly noble deputies in
that synod, supply the interpretative context for this particular
article of faith. The persecutions which lay ahead could deprive
the believers of their 'divine predestination', and it conferred on
the synodal aristocracy a further distinction. Relations with the
State, at that moment a crucial issue for the history of the French
Reformation, were dealt with in the final articles (nos 39–40).
These upheld the divine and civil office of the temporal power
together with the respect due to it. However, article 40 introduced a subtle ambiguity with regard to the limits of obedience.
Obedience was to be almost total, for the temporal power was to
be respected 'even when it is irreligious, as long as the sovereignty of the kingdom of God is not infringed'. This was no innocent qualification. The fathers of the synod were well aware of
the royal determination to destroy heresy by force. Were they
thinking of releasing the Protestant conscience in advance with a
view to possible armed resistance and even the formation of a
religious and political party?

The *Discipline ecclésiastique*, issued together with the *Confession*,
established a church order along the lines of Strasbourg and
Geneva. Power belonged at the base, in the local church. There
was no hierarchy, 'because no church can lay claim to any primacy or supremacy over any other' (article 1). However, there
were representative institutions: the colloquies held every other
year and composed of deputies from a 'region' of some 10 to 15
parishes; the provincial synods held each year and composed of
elders and pastors nominated by the colloquies comprising the
province; and at the top, the annual national synod, composed
of two elders and two pastors from each province. But the troubles
of the time inevitably frustrated this scheme: there were no national
synods between that of Vitré in 1583 and that of Montauban in
1594. The functions of the national synod were much the same
as those of the provincial and local bodies, except that it constituted
the court of final appeal in ecclesiastical and secular matters. The
decisions reached by the national synod in response to appeals
from the localities constituted a veritable corpus of jurisprudence,
especially in matrimonial cases (for France had no secular legislation

on marriage, only Catholic canon law). Only the national synod was authorised to amend the *Confession* and the *Discipline*. The latter, originally 40 articles in 1559, was constantly amended, expanded and modified on a case-by-case basis until the final synod at Loudun in 1659.

At the local level, spiritual and temporal authority were vested in the minister (or ministers) and elders of the consistory. The pastor's duties were to preach, to administer the two evangelical sacraments (baptism and the Lord's Supper), and to represent the congregation at assemblies. But he had to be 'elected', that is, accepted by the congregation – which could reject him in certain circumstances. The role given to the elders was one of the great innovations of Calvinist ecclesiology. The elders, in the early stages an emanation of the clandestine nascent congregation, were, according to the *Discipline*, subject to annual appointment in the gathered church. In theory they ought to have reflected the composition of the congregation, but in practice they were drawn for the most part from the social elite (though this did not seriously misrepresent the social tone of French Protestantism as a whole). Their powers far exceeded those accorded by the traditional Church to members of the vestry, for in presenting the minister to the congregation they exercised influence over the final decision. One or two of them would be delegates to colloquies or synods, and they raised and managed money to assist the poor and to pay the pastors. They kept up an often copious correspondence with Geneva and with other parishes. And they kept the books – registers of baptisms and weddings, accounts of charitable income and expenditure, and records of consistory proceedings. As a 'people of the book', the Calvinists felt the imperative of the text so much that a church became 'gathered' as much through the opening of registers as through the appointment of a properly constituted minister. Calvinist discipline, whether Genevan or French, gave a primary role to the elders. They sat by the same right as the ministers on the weekly assembly, forming a moral tribunal which took cognisance of the 'scandals' and offences of the faithful against the moral law (essentially, the Decalogue together with a number of prohibitions peculiar to Calvin, the ethics of the age and the *Discipline*). Those cited before this curious tribunal included blasphemers, swearers, brawlers, fornicators, gamblers, dancers, drinkers, and sabbath-breakers – in short, all men and women who offended against the moral code. The vast majority confessed their misdeed, swore never to repeat it, and left cleansed from their sins. When the offence was serious, the consistory imposed the ecclesiastical penalties of provisional or, in the case of 'heinous crimes' within the cognisance of the public courts, definitive excommunication. Thus a small group of laymen was invested with the power of the keys (to forgive, absolve and excommunicate) in accordance with the great reformed concept of the priesthood of all believers. And so, when incessant conflict cut off towns and cities where the Calvinist system prevailed, and the royal courts were too distant or too hostile, the consistory became in effect the justice of the peace and the tribunal of first instance. Untold numbers of minor disputes were resolved through the arbitration of the elders. The elders, in daily contact with the faithful, yet also on an equal footing with the minister, fulfilled an important function, that of ensuring that the political order established by Calvin prevailed among the congregation. That order was a human institution, of course, but to its adherents it was superior to its Catholic predecessor, bringing people to serve God in obeying the rules laid down by the Commandments, the Gospels . . . and the Genevan Reformers.

This church, built as it was according to the model commonly known by that frightful word 'synodo-presbyterian', was nothing like its rival. The power structure was the reverse of that of the Catholic system, in which everything came from above, from the pope and then the bishop, by way of the parish clergy, to the laity. The doctrinal gulf between the two confessions was even more dramatic. The Protestant exclusion of works from the economy of salvation entailed the rejection of a large part of Catholic beliefs and practices. Purgatory disappeared, along with the millions of masses it had prompted. Pilgrimages, processions, mortifications, offerings to saints and to the Virgin, and the prayers and devotions performed by those professionals of intercession, the monks and nuns – all this now seemed null and void. Gone too was the sexual asceticism of a celibate priesthood: celibacy, tainted as it was by original sin, could no longer be made an offering to God. The interpretation of the Lord's Supper as a spiritual communion was poles apart from the mystery of transubstantiation performed by the priest. And the new model pastor, an educated man 'trained in the humanities', 'endowed with the special grace of preaching', 'of upright life and conduct', was a man like any other, married and with children. At least this ideal minister was nothing like the priests and vicars who had been targets of ridicule and censure throughout the early sixteenth century. Well-equipped through their studies at Geneva or one of the French academies (Orthez, Nîmes, Montauban or Saumur), and thoroughly trained in rhetoric and the exposition of scripture, these leaders of the young Reformed churches, often scions of the nobility or the urban patriciate, made an impressive clergy. Often, as we shall see, politics unfortunately distracted them from their strictly religious duties, and several of them were prey to the delusions of the age. But others paid with their lives for their courage in preaching a new religion.

The Geography and Sociology of Protestantism

From 1555, and even more from 1559, the new churches proliferated with solid institutional support. Converts poured in, and Calvinist congregations multiplied. Expansion continued until about 1565, when contraction set in. The new churches were not distributed evenly throughout the kingdom. Protestantism made a particularly dramatic impact in the Midi and the mid-west. A crescent stretching from Poitou to Lyon, skirting around the high central plateau, held some 700 churches, and there were perhaps 500 more in northern France. The provinces of greatest Calvinist strength were Aunis, Saintonge, and southern Poitou. In the Occitan regions, Calvinism made headway in Guyenne, Gascony, Béarn, lower Languedoc, the Cévennes and the Vivarais, as also in the franco-provençale Dauphiné. The Protestants came close to dominating entire provinces. In the old Capetian lands of the *langue d'oïl*, in contrast, the Calvinist communities were rarely thick on the ground (as in the plain of Caen). More often, they were widely dispersed. There were some flourishing and powerful churches, as at Rouen, Orléans and Paris, but they were bobbing on a Catholic sea. In addition, a number of parishes belonged to lords, and the existence of a Reformed church was often a reflection of the religion of the seigneur.[3]

Open conversion to Protestantism involved a break with the past whose gravity many who took the step failed to appreciate. For the reformed were henceforth on the margins of French society, which was shaped by a traditional religion to which the majority of the people and the State authorities continued to adhere. To belong to another church, to practise another faith, was in effect to found an alternative society with its own social groups and ranks, its own hierarchies of age and sex, and its own power structures. By examining the period of Calvinist expansion between 1559 and 1565 we can attempt to sketch the social matrix of which it was the religious expression.

The Catholic clergy were passionately interested in the idea of ecclesiastical reform, and many clerics did not flinch from schism, even if many more returned to their roots after a brief flirtation with the Reformation. The early ministers of the Reformed churches included many former monks, priests and vicars who, after a visit to Geneva, were sent back to a parish in France. Not even the Catholic hierarchy was immune, and some bishops played a part in the introduction and consolidation of French Protestantism. Thus the Bishop of Valence, while still exercising his episcopal functions, 'made an amalgam of the two religions', denying transubstantiation, supporting communion under both kinds, and even introducing a baptismal service on Calvinist lines. In fact, Jean de Monluc was in favour of a national church which would bring the two faiths together. It is hardly surprising, then, that in the area of Valence an exceptional number of 'gathered' churches sprang up, even though the bishop himself never took the final step of conversion. Jean de Chaumont, Bishop of Aix, was more decisive, authorising the public exercise of Calvinist worship in Catholic churches. And at Christmas 1566, from his episcopal throne in the cathedral, he decried the papacy, threw down his mitre and crook, and left the city to join the Calvinist army. Known now as the Captain Saint-Romain, he led the Huguenots of Languedoc in the Wars of Religion. And another prelate had been deprived of his ecclesiastical appointment by papal bull in March 1563. The extraordinary Odet de Châtillon, Count-Bishop of Beauvais and brother to Admiral Coligny, was in addition a Cardinal. Married, he lived splendidly on his ecclesiastical revenues and organised worship in his episcopal palace on Calvinist lines until scandal obliged him to take refuge in England.

The nobility provided massive support for the new religion. It has been said that, during the Protestant explosion of 1559–65, half the nobility were converted. This is doubtless an exaggeration, for there were considerable regional variations. In Brittany the squires and their peasants remained solidly Catholic. In Burgundy it was much the same. In some southern provinces, on the other hand, and in Normandy, Brie, and Champagne, a Calvinist gentry emerged. Converts came even from the highest families, from those who sat by right on the King's Council and received the lion's share of the great Crown offices and the plum abbeys and dioceses. The famous names included those of Bourbon, Condé, La Rochefoucauld, Crussol-Uzès, Caumont La Force and Châtillon. Such families were of immense importance in the emergence of a Protestant society. Thanks to their political influence, whole tranches of the royal administration came over to the new church. Conversion was not merely self-interest. It involved a complex mixture of motives: loyalty to a patron, religious conviction, and perhaps frustration after the demobilisation consequent upon Cateau-Cambrésis.

There was a similar kind of trickle-down by virtue of the seigneurial powers of the nobles. As lords they owned, in effect, entire villages and sometimes towns. In Normandy, Brie, Champagne and Beauce, Protestantism was often introduced because, quite simply, they replaced the parish priests with pastors in the churches over which they were patrons. The role of the Caumont La Force family in the Midi is typical. In Agenais and Périgord the distribution of the Protestant churches matches that of the family holdings, the more so as a cadet of the family, Charles de Caumont, sent into the Church according to aristocratic custom, became both abbot and lord of Clairac. Monluc loathed him, and accused him – not without reason – of having sustained 'all the sedition in Agenais and Périgord' against which Monluc fought in the years 1562–5. Charles de Caumont did indeed bring Reformed ministers and preachers to Clairac. In 1560 he convoked and presided over a provincial synod there, and by 1562 Catholicism had ceased to exist in the town. However, despite the extreme example of Béarn, where Jeanne d'Albret suppressed Catholicism in 1565 and made Protestantism the State religion, one cannot conclude that the principle 'cuius regio, eius religio' was generally applied in the territories of Protestant nobles. Many of them respected the beliefs of those who remained faithful to Rome; and many Calvinist churches sprang up without any seigneurial support.

Another social group which contributed significantly to the growth of the Calvinist churches, one whose members pursued various professions and often verged on the nobility through holding land or office, was that of the university graduates. Doctors and bachelors of law or medicine helped give French Protestantism that juridical tone foreshadowed in Calvin himself. It would be tiresome to detail the different patterns within this complex and shifting group. A few examples will suffice to illustrate the influence these men wielded within the community and the role they played. The upper levels of royal service, where officials combined judicial and administrative functions in the way typical of the Ancien Régime, were largely staffed by law graduates. In his *Commentaries*, Monluc observed sadly, 'the source from which all these ills derived was the judiciary: officers of Parlements, seneschals, and other judges gave up the old religion, the King's religion, for the new'. The role of Parlementarians is astonishing when one recalls the zeal with which the Parlements had persecuted heretics throughout the realm before the advent of schism. Nevertheless, some did become Protestant, at least for a while. The sovereign courts of Grenoble, Rouen, Toulouse, Bordeaux, and even Paris contained many councillors who followed the new faith. But internal purges eliminated Calvinist converts or sympathisers around 1559–62. In Paris, Anne Du Bourg, a magistrate respected by all except the fanatics, was burned at the stake in December 1559. Between 1562 and 1568, the Parlement of Toulouse proceeded against 30 of its 80 councillors – an eloquent statistic. The proportion was rather lower among the magistrates of Rouen (at least among the higher ranks) and Dijon.

The inferior jurisdictions – bailiwicks and *présidiaux* – also furnished converts to Calvinism. Almost all the presidial judges of Agen, Saintes, Dax, Béziers and Nîmes came over to the new religion during its expansionist phase. The *présidiaux* of Nantes and Vienne were also full of heretics. Philip Benedict has highlighted the impact of the new religion among the holders of lesser offices in Rouen (as was also the case at Dijon and Vienne).

Advocates too, whatever their rank, converted in large numbers. And lower down the social scale there followed a crowd of sergeants, bailiffs, solicitors, ushers, proctors and attorneys. In this legal underworld, where scraps of knowledge were picked up from practice rather than from the University, notaries were especially prominent. By 1566, more than half the notaries practising in Bordeaux and Lyon, and most of those in Nîmes and Béziers, were on the registers of the new church.

As is well known, merchants made up an important part of the new faithful. At Rouen, Nantes, La Rochelle and Bordeaux, businessmen operating on an international scale became Calvinists. At Lyon, where 13 per cent of the Protestants were merchants, half of those merchants belonged to the commercial elite, including some prodigiously wealthy grocers and clothiers. The case of the Toulouse woad industry was equally striking. Surrounded by relatives who had acquired royal offices or lordships, by their partners, and by their agents, the traders formed a milieu in which Calvinism received a warm welcome. But many of the Protestant merchants operated on a humbler scale. Contemporary texts evoke an entire society, with apothecaries, goldsmiths, furriers, and haberdashers. This merchant class, on the borderline between the urban elites and the common people, was strongly represented, above all among the printers and booksellers. At Toulouse, Béziers, Grenoble, Dijon, Paris, Rouen and Vienne, it provided between a fifth and a third of the Calvinist community – an impressive proportion.

Descending on the social scale, we find that craftsmen formed another major group within early Protestantism. 'The basest sort', as Loyseau defined them, provided half the faithful in such cities as Lyon, Dijon, Vienne, Valence, Rouen, Tours, Beaune and Montpellier, though the proportion was lower in cities like Toulouse or Grenoble, or in regions like Guyenne where industry was less developed. Between 1549 and 1560, the majority of French refugees in Geneva were craftsmen. But these figures cannot give a reliable idea of the social reality of Protestantism in France as a whole, because so many of the refugees had little or nothing to lose by flight. Magistrates, advocates, and nobles, tied to their lands or their offices, would abandon them only under duress. Among the manual trades, some welcomed Calvinism more readily than others: the textiles (weavers, dyers, carders – but textiles were of course the largest industry), leather (cobblers above all, but also tanners and saddlers), and hospitality (innkeepers and taverners). If one recalls that Calvinist doctrines reached the people mainly through oral transmission, and that inns and taverns were the privileged space in which to meet people and discuss ideas, one can hardly be surprised that their proprietors took part in the religious debates of the century. In the areas in which they were a majority, the peasants evinced little interest in the new religion. Of course, the figures given so far refer to the towns rather than the country, but in the sixteenth century the suburbs were occupied by peasants who sometimes amounted to as much as half a city's population. These rustics joined the new church only where the seigneurial patron replaced the parish priest or vicar with a minister. Thus rural Calvinists were found in the Cotentin, Brie, Gascony, Provence, and the Dauphiné. But the vast majority of the peasantry (like a large part of the humbler townsfolk) remained loyal to Catholicism. Often they nourished a profound hatred for the Protestants – townsfolk and villagers, iconoclasts and desecrators – enough, on several occasions, to lead to massacres. Even in Béarn, where Calvinism was the State religion, the peasants were never wholly won over.

In the sociology of Protestantism, two important groups stood outside traditional social classification. The first was women, who flocked to the new religion. From great ladies like Jeanne d'Albret and the Duchess of Ferrara to bourgeois and petty bourgeois wives – or often widows – they took an active part in secret assemblies or public gatherings. When figures for congregations can be produced, women usually amount to about 30 per cent – a significant figure for an age in which neither wives nor daughters had much freedom of action. The other group was the young, who, irrespective of their family background or trade, were passionately involved in the Protestant adventure. They were especially prominent when it came to actions rather than words. The iconoclasm for which the Huguenots have so often been blamed was almost always the work of the younger element. It was often the youth who first brought out into the open communities which had hitherto been clandestine. It was the young people too who often secured the first minister from Geneva. And almost always it was youthful voices that struck up the Psalms in French, making the presence of a Calvinist congregation loud and clear. While their elders hesitated and dithered with a caution which Calvin loathed and which merely guaranteed harsh repression, while they endured prison, fines, and all sorts of troubles in silence, the young cast prudence and patience to the winds. Breaking with the past, they came out of the closet. Several lists survive in which local authorities enumerated the names and status of fugitives from a town or a district: young men, or even women, made up over 10 per cent. Many of the young men went to swell the armed bands preparing for war, but most went to Geneva. The *Livre des habitants* records the names and status of those who sought asylum in Geneva in the years 1549–60, 1572–4 and 1585–7.[4] In the first period, they were mostly craftsmen, as we have said, but many were bachelors, and therefore probably young.

Thus, considered collectively, conversions often fall into certain broad patterns. Groups established themselves inside which belonging to Calvinism answered not only to religious needs but also to social and cultural realities. Whole social worlds were constructed around the traditional (and vertical) relationships linking lord to peasant, the king's agent to the local hierarchy over which he presided, the councillor of Parlement to the clerk, or the University to its printers and booksellers. The complex interplay of loyalties, relationships and dependencies could turn these groups into the cores of new churches. In other cases, more homogeneous groups set up other structures of welcome: outside the usual hierarchies, young people and women opted for the Reformation. Elsewhere, literacy, university education, or public office, brought together another type of community in which clerks rubbed shoulders with advocates, and magistrates with notaries. Similarities of age, sex and culture created networks of horizontal relationships. A shared spiritual restlessness, derived from a shared culture or shared existential imperatives, led people to Protestantism.

Protestantism was essentially an urban religion, and in the urban context the local notables assumed particular importance. Even when artisans made up half or more of the Reformed community, they were still under-represented in terms of their position in the city as a whole. The elites were everywhere, or almost everywhere, in absolute or relative terms, far more numerous than the artisans in the Calvinist churches. The elites were literate (though so too were some of the artisans). In the Midi they spoke both French and the *langue d'oc*. They used the king's French to keep the books – baptismal and marriage registers, consistory records, and accounts of alms and of collections for the maintenance of the pastor. Sitting in the synods and consistories they tried to form their co-religionists in the Calvinist mould. In sixteenth-century society, Protestantism was predominantly the religion of a culturally advanced minority. It was an ethically demanding religion of the book that called men and women to a deeper spirituality and a new and austere morality. However, in human terms it was hard to take the decisive step of conversion. For the two million or so French people who crossed over gradually or suddenly to the new religion, leaving the traditional Catholic faith, the further shore seemed steep and forbidding. In a kingdom shaped by Catholicism, Protestantism was a foreign body which had to be expelled by force. The Protestants were marginalised, attacked, and even

killed. Nobles removed from their positions at Court, officials relieved of their responsibilities, and artisans excluded from their
confraternities and convivial feasts, found these restrictions hard
to bear. On the other hand, the Calvinist church was less indulgent than the old Church to the faithful. It demanded regular
attendance at worship, behaviour in accordance with the commandments, and significant financial sacrifices (it lacked the rich
endowments of the Roman Church as well as the system of tithe
for maintaining the clergy). Often, the converts of the 1560s grew
tired of these constraints, fearing for their lives and worn out by
the conflict of loyalties between the Crown and their conscience.
The human capital of French Protestantism was eroded by aggression, persecution, confiscation, and execution during the first
three Wars of Religion, and then by forced conversion after the
Massacre of Saint Bartholomew. Later, in 1593, Henri IV's solemn
abjuration – followed by his strenuous efforts to win over his friends
and relatives – led to a significant drift back to the Church. By
the start of the seventeenth century, the Protestants of France numbered little more than a million.

The Changing Fortunes of the Protestant Party

For forty years Protestants and Protestantism were at the heart of
France's political turmoil, to such an extent that 'church' and
'party' became almost synonymous. Protestantism became a party
as it emerged from the closet, because a king committed by his
coronation oath to protect the Catholic Church could scarcely
tolerate within his realm the open practice of any religion other
than his own. The heretic was thus guilty of treason. Henri II was
inflexible on this point, and, as he signed the Treaty of Cateau-
Cambrésis, was already preparing for the eradication of Protestantism.
    However, French Calvinists, following Calvin and Beza, remained
convinced of the necessity of loyalty to the king, whatever the
consequences for themselves. It put them in a difficult position.
Torn between the rival claims of conscience and the Crown, con-
sistency could be found only in the martyrdom which many underwent. But this is to leave one decisive factor out of the reckoning
– the massive adherence of the nobility to Protestantism. In a
time of weak monarchy, the baronial and federal concepts kept
in check by the firm rule of François I and Henri II resurfaced.

Noblemen would not sacrifice their political position to their religious convictions, especially as this would mean leaving the Guises a free hand to crush dissent. In this situation, a resort to arms was the only practical solution for the Huguenot nobility. The person of the king became the prize, because during royal minorities to be close to the king – to advise him and guide his decisions – was in effect to wield sovereignty. Hence Condé's attempts to seize François II in 1559 and Charles IX in 1567. For their part, the Guises behaved no differently. The ventures of the Protestant nobility, evidence of the political corner into which they were boxed, might be called rebellions. But the nobles had long experience of such affairs and of the requisite rhetoric with which to justify them. The themes and tone of their propaganda remained constant throughout the first three wars of religion: if the Huguenots took up arms, it was not so much to defend themselves and their beliefs as to deliver the king from the pernicious tutelage of the Guise interlopers, and to allow true-born Frenchmen to take their rightful place as the natural protectors of the king and his kingdom.

After the Massacre of Saint Bartholomew, however, the tone changed, becoming more aggressive, more direct, and more innovative. As the Huguenots established their State within a State – the United Provinces of the Midi – a chorus of Protestant voices rose up in a utopian clamour provoked by the horror of the massacre.[5] Repelled by the bloody tyranny of the Crown, they embarked on a searching analysis and fundamental reevaluation of royal power. While before 1572 the Huguenots had not called divine-right monarchy into question, now they assaulted it in a series of trenchant polemics: François Hotman's *Franco-Gallia* (1573), the anonymous *Réveille-matin des Français et de leurs voisins* (1574), Beza's *Droit des magistrats sur leurs sujets* (1757), and the anonymous *Vindiciae contra tyrannos* (1579). Beza advanced the modern concept that because the purpose of the State was the security and welfare of the people, in a sense sovereignty belonged to the people. And history confirmed this, as in former times kings had been elected. A sovereign created by popular consent wielded an authority limited by obedience not only to divine law but also to natural law and the common good. Therefore rebellion against a sovereign who violated the laws of both God and man was authorised by God. And it could be lawfully carried out through the resistance of 'inferior magistrates', officials who enjoyed powers derived from the king. The author of the *Vindiciae* went further: for him, legitimate resistance could be organised on a provincial or urban basis. And all these authors stressed an idea with a long future, namely that a contract bound the people to their sovereign, and that when a sovereign broke this contract through heinous deeds (like the murder of his subjects), he became a tyrant and could therefore be killed, deposed or replaced. Some of the 'monarchomachs' laid emphasis on the need in the State for intermediate bodies such as the Estates General, whose members (according to Beza) could defend the nation and the people against the depradations of a disordered regime.

The principle that monarchy was absolute because of its divine origin was attacked with uncommon violence, and alternative models were proposed. The monarchomachs tended instead towards federal or aristocratic systems, where the 'senior pars' (nobility, officials, urban elites) possessed extensive local powers and rights of consultation and control with respect to the sovereign. These were the theoretical foundations of the independent State which was set up from 1573 by the Protestants and the 'good' Catholics, providing the justification for the transfer of sovereignty from Charles IX to the Estates General of the Union.

But the tides shifted again when the death of Alençon in 1584 left the Protector of the Union as the heir presumptive. It was now necessary to promote arguments which would serve his cause. The central theme was now the unity of the French nation, jeopardised by the alliance between Spain and the 'bad Frenchmen' of the League. National unity could only be founded on the person of the legitimate sovereign according to the fundamental laws. Henri de Navarre was presented as truly French, in stark contrast to the 'hispanicised bastards' of the Guise party. Navarre's victory at Coutras was in fact a sign of his legitimacy, for that battle was a confrontation not between Navarrists and royalists, but between Navarrists and Henri III's League enemies. Two supporters of the Bourbon cause excelled in keen and copious propaganda. With remarkable intellectual agility, François Hotman abandoned his monarchomach postures of the preceding decade to maintain with talent and conviction the indefeasible hereditary right of princes of the blood. And Philippe Duplessis-Mornay, a close adviser of Navarre, bombarded Protestants and moderate Catholics alike with moderate images of the future king – a true patriot devoted to his country and to the welfare of all his subjects. 'I am French, I am your prince, I have your interests at heart' – such were the sentiments which Duplessis-Mornay put in Navarre's mouth in pamphlet after pamphlet.

When in 1593 Navarre became king of a country many of whose inhabitants refused to recognise him, the propaganda slid easily between king and country. Royalism and patriotism were now inseparable categories. To serve the king was to serve France and to be a true Frenchman. And did not the first Bourbon display all the qualities traditionally associated with French princes? An able general, merciful, good-natured and tolerant, an 'all-rounder', well equipped to keep 'the affairs of the realm in good order' – here began the legend of 'Good King Henri' handed down to posterity.

The Resources of the Party

To form a party one needs militants, money, and – if one is proposing a new religion, or even more a new political order – intellectuals capable of providing a convincing account of the motives, sincere or not, of those involved. The Protestant party at war appealed to the faithful by means of the churches. In 1561, and again in 1567–8, Condé secured considerable subsidies from them in order to pay his soldiers. After 1572, the Protestant Union, acting alone or in collaboration with the Politiques, levied heavy taxes. These grew even more burdensome after 1584, when Navarre felt the throne within his grasp. But as early as the first war it was necessary also to call on foreign aid. In 1562 Elizabeth I provided 100 000 *livres* and 6000 men, albeit in exchange for Le Havre until such time as Calais should be restored to her. The notorious Treaty of Hampton Court which sealed this agreement besmirched the Protestant cause with the charge of selling the country to the enemy.[6] But if money was needed, so too were men. Recruitment was abundant in France. In 1562, 2000 volunteers from Béarn, Gascony and Languedoc came to join Condé at Orléans. And in 1567, when arms were being taken up for the second time, a force of 4000 men gathered in the Midi and set off to rendezvous with Condé near Chartres. In the following year, Jeanne d'Albret and her lieutenants recruited 6000 Gascons to send to La Rochelle, while 20 000 men assembled in Languedoc. But populous as France was, the kingdom alone could not provide enough soldiers for the civil wars. Like the king, the Huguenots called on foreign aid. Coligny's brother d'Andelot levied 4000 foot and 3000 horse in the Palatinate, Württemberg and Hesse while the first war unfolded. During the second and third conflicts, 6500 *reiters* and 3000 *landsknechts* arrived from the east under the command of John Casimir, the son of the Elector Palatine. And in 1569, soldiers under Wolfgang of Bavaria, Duke of Zweibrucken, marched through Franche-Comté and Burgundy to join the Huguenot force in Poitou before the battle of Montcontour. During the fifth war John Casimir invaded the realm at the head of 16 000 troops at the instigation of Alençon and Henri de Condé. In return he demanded an enormous pension and the grant of the Three Bishoprics (Toul, Metz and Verdun) for life. And when Henri de Navarre was preparing to face the forces of Henri III at Coutras in 1587, he was relying on the assistance of a substantial force of Swiss and German mercenaries. Nearly 25 000 *reiters* under the command of Baron Dohna passed through Lorraine into Champagne and were preparing to march south to join him when the Duke of Guise cut them to pieces at Auneau on 24 November.[7] In Catholic eyes, this repeated recourse to foreign mercenaries was high treason and helped stoke up hatred for the Huguenots.

Iconoclasm

If the Huguenot faithful gave their money and often their blood for the Protestant cause, there was also another way for them to affirm their beliefs: the spontaneous and violent iconoclasm which sprang from their revulsion at the Roman Church. It was this church that was, in the eyes of Calvinist militants, the real enemy. Certainty of belonging to the 'true religion', a religion faithful to the pristine purity of the Gospel, drove the Huguenots to frenzied attacks on an institution they accused of error and falsehood. Believing that this Church had through the ages misrepresented Christ's message and buried it beneath unscriptural rites, dogmas and institutions, they saw it as a monstrous and mendacious idol, spoiled by a wealth acquired through human credulity. This 'noisome Nineveh', 'Baal', or 'great Babylon' – such were the terms which expressed the almost holy horror which Protestants felt when faced with the papacy's immense machine. An iconoclasm which aimed at destroying the earthly instruments of idolatry appeared in France together with the first 'Lutherans'.[8] But these few and isolated incidents were vigorously pursued and severely punished under François I. It was from about 1560, especially during the first war, that iconoclasm became a more general problem, fuelled by the growth of the Huguenot party. But it was not simply gratuitous violence: it resulted from three potent ideas put into circulation by the Reformation.[9] The first, formulated in Calvin's *Catechism*, was a rejection of the representation of the divine in 'corporal, dead, corruptible and visible matter'. The second was a denial of the worship addressed to the saints, whose familiar presence in the form of statues, paintings and 'images' thronged churches, squares, crossroads and private houses. And the third was the charge that the 'popish' clergy, priests, monks and nuns, had neglected their true mission and deceived the Christian people by substituting their own religion of Purgatory and good works for the doctrine of justification by faith alone. Despite the appeals for calm issued by the Protestant authorities, converts persisted in attacking the paintings, reliefs, engravings, statues, and personnel of Catholic churches, desecrating, humiliating, and killing them.

Thus France saw the emergence not only of a church but of a party, one whose coherence, power and determination were to shake the religious and political foundations of the realm.

10 The Church and the Catholic Faction

The emergence of Protestantism called into question the existing Church, which might have found itself forced onto the defensive had it not already been stirred by a vigorous movement of internal reform which enabled it to draw on new forces and new ideas in the conflict ahead. In fact, during the Wars of Religion, the French Catholic Church showed a surprising resilience. Aggressive and pragmatic by turns, it succeeded in preserving the Catholic culture of the kingdom, and emerged much strengthened from the tribulations of the period 1559–98.

The Council of Trent and the Reforming Bishops

Although by the end of the fifteenth century immense efforts had produced some local improvements in the religious orders, the parish clergy, and the instruction and Christianisation of the faithful, these efforts nevertheless lacked coherence and a sense of direction. It was the Council of Trent which presented a clarified doctrine, a uniform ritual, and a fresh plan of action to a Catholic Europe threatened by Protestantism. But while the orders now tended to come from Rome, at the local level bishops found their authority reinforced, giving them wider powers which often enabled them to take the initiative in reform.

France, of course, took no part in the first two phases of the Council. But in the third phase (1562–3), a number of French prelates, accompanied by lay envoys, came to the Council, commissioned by Catherine de Medici to put the particular demands of France before the assembled fathers.[1] Catherine, anxious to defuse religious conflict in France, wanted the Council to make concessions on clerical marriage and communion under both kinds, and to condemn such abuses as pluralism and the 'commendam' system. But in presenting their 'Articles of Reformation' on 2 January 1562, the French representatives met the opposition of the Italian prelates who dominated the Council. The Italians countered by proposing a 'Reformation of Princes' which would have increased the powers of the papacy and the church courts at the expense of nation-states and secular institutions. This provoked Arnaud Du Ferrier, President of the Parlement de Paris and one of Catherine's three lay representatives, to declare in full council, 'The Reformation of Princes aims at nothing less than the abolition of the ancient liberties of the Gallican Church and the diminution of the majesty and authority of the Most Christian King.'

The ambassadors did not appear at any further sessions, but the French bishops, Gallican though they were, and successful in obstructing some elements of the Reformation of Princes, could hardly oppose a number of others which extended ecclesiastical jurisdiction at the expense of the Parlements and strengthened episcopal power in matters of censorship, the management of hospitals, and matrimonial causes. Between July and December 1563 they joined the other Council fathers in approving the last disciplinary and moral decrees. When, on their return, the bishops petitioned the King's Council through the person of the Cardinal of Lorraine for the Tridentine decrees to be promulgated as the law of the land, the Chancellor, Michel de L'Hôpital, opposed vigorously. But while the Tridentine decrees were not formally received by the governments of Charles IX, Henri III, Henri IV, or even Louis XIII, they nevertheless watered the seeds of a thoroughgoing reform of the French Church.

This reform was the achievement of the French clergy, helped in part by the Crown, in so far as it was a prerequisite of success that the hierarchy should be graced with those Christian virtues that they were responsible for instilling into the people. When the Wars of Religion were at their height, the clergy assembled at Melun in 1579 once more petitioned for the reception of the decrees of Trent and castigated the simony of a Crown which peddled the goods of the Church and conferred bishoprics upon laymen. Henri III, who was anxious to make what concessions he could to the clergy, especially as he had just assumed the leadership of the League, recapitulated a number of the decrees of Trent (those which did not infringe upon the royal prerogative!) in the ordinance of Blois (1579) and then the Edict of Paris (February 1580).[2] Clerical privileges in matters of taxation and military obligations were confirmed, as was their right to levy the tithe. The clergy thus, in principle at least, saw its property protected from the encroachments of noblemen and civic authorities. On the other hand, the episcopal obligations to conduct diocesan visitations, to supervise the maintenance of buildings and the provision of liturgical apparatus, and to safeguard the material welfare of priests, and the duty of residence, were all clearly set forth, as they had been at Trent.

On the ground, it was the hierarchy which implemented the Tridentine decrees. From the 1570s, some reforming bishops and archbishops set to work in their dioceses and provinces – a mere handful of men, drawing their inspiration from the example of Charles Borromeo at Milan. Bishops like Grimaldi, Tarugi and Cheisolm at Avignon, Sacrato at Carpentras, Roechi and Bordini at Cavaillon, Sourdis at Bordeaux, Joyeuse at Toulouse, La Rochefoucauld at Clermont and then Senlis, and Pierre d'Épinac at Lyon, were the forerunners of the troops of reforming prelates of the following century.[3] They resided in their dioceses and conducted visitations as circumstances allowed, inspecting places of worship, making inquiries about the parish priests or vicars, and inquiring after heretics. They convened the clergy under their jurisdiction in diocesan synods and then published the consequent decrees on discipline, on liturgical vestments and clerical garb, on ritual, and on the required minimum of liturgical apparatus. They strove to provide respectable, educated and pious priests at least to those benefices within their gift. And they established seminaries to train the clergy: the first was founded at Reims in 1567, and others followed at Cavaillon and Avignon in 1586, and Toulouse in 1590. These militant Catholic bishops aimed, in rooting out long-criticised abuses, to produce a more evangelical Church and above all to fight Protestantism on its own ground. Henceforth they strove to instil in the faithful the spirit of a renewed Catholicism, to guide religious aspirations in channels unpolluted by the Reformation, and to get to the roots of the problem by forming the soul from the earliest age. So the Tridentine episcopate sought to establish schools where the catechism was at the heart of the curriculum: moreover, the Edict of Paris instructed bishops to provide for schools and colleges out of diocesan revenues. And above all they exploited the formidable machinery for forming Catholics which was provided by the Jesuit colleges. The Cardinal of Armagnac brought them to Toulouse, the Cardinal of Tournon to Tournon, and Bishop Grimaldi to Avignon. Other Jesuit colleges were founded at Carpentras, Aubenas, Orléans, Le Mans, Puy, Dijon, and elsewhere. These prestigious institutions spread not only at the instigation of bishops, but also thanks to civic authorities anxious that the children of the bourgeoisie and sometimes of the gentry should be properly instructed in the elements of learning and the faith.[4] By 1590 there were 20 such colleges in France.

There was still the matter of winning over and looking after the souls of the common people. The Tridentine decrees were far from forgetting the unlettered majority of the faithful. Ceremonies, images, preaching, and the collective devotions of the confraternities were the means of forming and guiding lay piety. The church, as the house of God, was meant to further his glory. But in the course of their diocesan visitations, the bishops discovered the lamentable condition of many churches, and ordered the clergy and churchwardens to provide a confessional, and an altar and tabernacle for the reservation of the Blessed Sacrament. But these orders were not always carried out; and towards the end of the century the troubles frustrated the efforts at building, rebuilding, and adornment. France was hardly in a position to match the achievements of Italian artists in the service of Catholic renewal. But it was possible to restrain the excesses of the faithful by controlling the cult of relics which had been the butt of so many humanists, and latterly Huguenots. Diocesan synods held between 1581 and 1586 at Rouen, Reims, Aix, Bordeaux, Toulouse and elsewhere sought to set reasonable limits to this cult. Instead, bishops favoured the establishment or expansion of confraternities dedicated to Our Lady or the Blessed Sacrament – the Council of Trent had, after all, sought to oppose Protestantism by laying fresh emphasis on Marian devotion and on the real presence in the eucharist. And penitential confraternities also enjoyed renewed vigour.

Catholic reformers had great faith in the spoken word as a means of winning souls, whether literate or not. Famous preachers (Jesuits, often enough) were drafted into the cathedrals for major feasts, and public disputations were arranged between Catholic and Protestant clergy. These disputations became quite the fashion in the 1590s, not only in the provinces, but also at Court: in 1600 Henri IV listened with relish to the verbal duel between Duplessis-Mornay and Cardinal du Perron on the subject of the eucharist.

The seeds of reform sown by the bishops in an unfavourable season of conflict and disorder were not to bear much fruit until the following century, but neither were they the only signs of Catholic renewal. The 'mystical invasion' was conquering hearts and minds from the early years of Henri IV's reign, but its origins lay much further back. The revival of devotion of which the League was the most extreme expression had begun at the start of the century, with the creation of new religious orders and the reform of older ones. The success of the Capuchins in Catholic Europe testifies to the appeal of sacrifice and apostolate to sixteenth-century Christians, as does the success of the Jesuits to that of crusade and proselytism. But the influence of the Jesuits was somewhat curtailed when the Parlement de Paris declared them unwelcome within its jurisdiction. The Jesuits were already implicated in the League, and the Parlement was already suspicious of Jesuit ultramontanism, so when a Jesuit pupil, Jean Châtel, attempted to knife Henri IV in 1594, this gave Parlement the pretext it needed for a ban. But the Parlements of Toulouse and Bordeaux, less inclined to Gallicanism, did not follow the Parisian lead, and thus provided a haven for Jesuits from northern France. In any case, the ban was of short duration. For in 1602 Henri IV, who was anxious to make some concession to the pope in compensation for the Edict of Nantes, readmitted the Jesuits to the Parisian jurisdiction on the advice of Père Coton (a Jesuit).

A similar fervour seized the souls of women. Again, it did not reach the heights of the seventeenth century, but the Ursuline nuns, established in the Comtat Venaissin by 1592, were already spreading into the dioceses of Bordeaux and Toulouse, invited by bishops, who entrusted them with the education of girls. And the mystical and contemplative teaching of St Teresa of Avila was already attracting souls in love with the absolute – the order of Discalced Carmelites would come to France in 1604.

But all the commitment to Catholicism and renewal of devotion could hardly conceal the damage that the Catholic Church suffered during the Wars of Religion. The target of Protestant proselytes zealous to bring down the 'great Babylon', overwhelmed with the taunts (not invariably from Huguenots) at its wealth and luxury, and its pastoral and disciplinary failings, the Church in addition saw a section of its clergy and laity defect to Calvinism. And the monarchy, for all its protestations of commitment to religious renewal, was hardly going to renounce the opportunities the Church provided for rewarding supporters and raising money.

Popular Religion and Anti-protestantism

When, towards the end of the civil wars, assemblies of the clergy (notably that of 1596) drew up a balance-sheet, the bottom line was pretty grim. Men and women, dignitaries, priests, vicars, monks and nuns, had been slaughtered in dozens. But the Protestants, undoubtedly less murderous than their opponents, had also set about the material symbols of Catholicism with a will, attacking churches, images, statues and liturgical apparatus. When Nicolas de Villars visited the 427 churches of his Agen diocese between 1592 and 1608, he found scarcely two dozen in a fit state for worship. And when Joyeuse visited his archdiocese of Toulouse in the same period, 139 out of 337 places of worship were burnt out, wrecked, pillaged, dilapidated, or roofless. Even before the wars, many church buildings had hardly been in the best of states. And the Huguenots were not the only culprits during the wars: League troops did not do much good to the churches and convents where they were billeted. In short, the Church's properties suffered grievous damage. Nor must one overlook the theft of treasures, the destruction of vestments and church goods, and the pillage of statues, pictures, sculptures and reliquaries. The finances and revenues of the Church were equally hard hit. The tithe, a major component of ecclesiastical income, could not be levied regularly. In 1560–61 the peasants of certain areas, notably in the south-west, refused to hand over the tithe of their harvest to canons, bishops, abbots and other priests. Later on, in the provinces governed by the Protestant Union, the tithe was diverted to pay Huguenot ministers and schoolmasters, as well as the permanent officials of the Huguenot State, and even its soldiers. In Béarn, Jeanne d'Albret and her council continued to demand the tithe from the owners and workers of the land, but, managed by an ecclesiastical administration, it was used to finance the Protestant Church. One of the articles of the Edict of Nantes required

Huguenots to submit to the levy of the tithe – evidence of their previous noncompliance or misappropriation.[5]

The Catholic Church, anxious as it was to defend its faith, was put to the test by the Crown. On 21 September 1561 the contract of Poissy, agreed between the Crown and the ecclesiastical representatives who had come to the Estates General at Pontoise, established a financial arrangement between Crown and Church. The Church undertook to fund a certain share of the royal debt, by levying a tithe on incumbents and on some occasions by alienating endowment (thrice each under Charles IX and Henri III). The agreement, made for 16 years, expired in 1579, and the clergy convened anew at Melun at the king's request. Dissatisfaction was voiced at the way the king conferred ecclesiastical benefices, and repeated demands were made for the decrees of Trent to be incorporated into the law of the land, which led Henri III to make some concessions. In return for the Edict of Paris already mentioned, the clergy granted the king further supplies for campaigns against the Huguenots and inaugurated the practice of the 'free gift' which the periodic assemblies of the clergy would continue to offer as a contribution to the public purse until the Revolution.[6]

The French people remained for the most part Catholics, faithful to the teachings and practices of the Roman Church. The Church and its clock guided the lives of men and women from the cradle to the grave, marking the passage of both sacred and profane time. Whether or not to believe was hardly an available option for 'papists' or Huguenots. Setting aside a few rare and bold spirits, everyone from a nobleman to a cobbler believed in God. And most of the time it was a simple faith, a basic gut feeling, branded deep in the heart and the flesh.

Catholic Perceptions of the Protestant Challenge

Religion, faith, and Church were for sixteenth-century Catholics three inseparable concepts which formed a closed world, a closed universe. The Church, unchanging in its hierarchy from the papacy to the parish priest, guaranteed the permanence of religion and formed the faith of the laity. The Church taught them that an inscrutable order prevailed both in heaven above and on the earth below. It taught also that the antiquity of the Roman, Catholic and universal Church was a token of the truth of the doctrines it mediated, and that those truths were of divine origin. Whoever challenged them was challenging the evidence of the kingdom of God, and undermining the foundations and structures of earthly government into the bargain.

In fact, in the eyes of the people, the monarchy was invested with a religious, almost magical character. The monarch, anointed according to a ritual almost 1000 years old, was both priest and king, a being between God and men, capable of working miracles (namely that of healing scrofula). Whoever opposed him became an outlaw and set himself apart from the group, at once heretic and traitor. The proliferation of this breed in the kingdom was felt by gut Catholics to be the assault of a fatal disease upon a healthy body. The apocalyptic tendencies of the thought of the age saw heresy as a sign sent by an avenging God as a warning of worse plagues and evils to come. And the Calvinist 'invasion' was seen as the coming of the dreaded Antichrist, followed by a train of plagues, wars and famines, before Christ himself returned to judge the living and the dead at the last day. Unease, anguish, and intimations of impending doom characterised the reactions of most (though not all) of the Catholics of the time, to the rise of Protestantism.

Protestantism presented them with a world turned upside down. Protestants denied not only the power of the pope, but also the power of the priest to change bread and wine into the body and blood of Christ. They rejected works, masses for the dead, the traffic in relics and indulgences, and the intercession of the saints. To crown it all, they rejected the consoling figure of the Blessed Virgin, the universal mother and sovereign mediatrix, seeing in her simply Mary, an ordinary woman – of course the mother of Christ, but nothing more. Calvinists prayed in French in a bare church devoid of images, took communion (like Catholic priests) under the species of both bread and wine, and retained in their worship only two sacraments – baptism and the eucharist. In the towns and villages their attitudes set them apart from the group, made them different, 'other', strangers in the land whether at the local, regional, or national level.

Alongside its demanding theology, Protestantism imposed an equally demanding social and individual ethic: the daily life of a Huguenot was not that of a Catholic. Huguenots did not observe the Friday or Lenten fasts. They were austere in their dress and deportment, preferring dark and decent clothing. The women eschewed plunging necklines and extravagant dresses. Above all, the Huguenots kept aloof from everyday relaxations such as taverns, dances, cards and dice. Their peculiar behaviour was taken by the traditionally minded as a serious affront. In the hurly-burly of urban life, this austerity seemed utterly intolerable. The word which sprang to the pens of Catholic authors when dealing with Protestants was 'hypocrite'. Florimond de Rémond, a councillor in the Bordeaux Parlement, penned the following wicked caricature of the Huguenot faithful:

> They declare war on the folly, luxury, and debauchery of the world so much in vogue among Catholics. At their meetings and feasts they have Bible readings and sacred songs, above all the metrical Psalms, instead of dances and sackbuts. The women, modest in dress and deportment, present themselves in public like doleful Eves or repentant Magdalenes. . . . The men, who look like death warmed up, seem to have been struck by the Holy Spirit, much like the Baptist preaching in the desert.

The sense of the peculiarity of Huguenot worship and lifestyle, and the perception of the otherness of a group set apart, were sharpened during the first three wars of religion by the taint of treason. The Huguenots came to be seen as the allies of foreigners, and were hated for bringing into the field, against the Catholic armies of the king, the *reiters*, the notorious German mercenaries from the Holy Roman Empire. The *reiters* were credited with nameless horrors, extraordinary sacrileges, and unheard of brutalities. And in their long years of marauding across the kingdom they justified the reputation that went before them. To invite foreign troops onto French soil was, in the eyes of an emergent nationalism, a sacrilege against king and country.

The Protestants were, moreover, seen as rebels who dared to bear arms against their king. In the 13 years preceding the Massacre of Saint Bartholomew they were seen as the troublemakers, not only responsible for the permanent insecurity in which Catholics lived, but also guilty of treason. The people of Paris were shocked to the core by the attempts to kidnap François II at Amboise in 1559 and Charles IX at Meaux in 1567. And they were staggered when Condé, the spirit behind the latter escapade, laid siege to the capital where Charles had taken refuge. Claude Haton, a parish priest in Provins who wrote a chronicle of the internecine conflicts, rarely referred to the Protestants as anything other than 'Huguenot rebels' or 'treacherous admiralists' (i.e. supporters of Admiral Coligny).

We have already touched upon the matter of sacred atrocities, whose numbers were swollen by the iconoclastic efforts of the Protestants. To destroy churches and chapels was to destroy the house of God. To decapitate statues, slash paintings, smash sculptures, break bells and shatter windows was to annihilate the visible symbols which Catholicism set up to link heaven and earth. The Protestant was seen as a blasphemer who dared raise his hand against the sacred. And his actions affected the whole community by rendering it liable to the terrible wrath of a just and jealous God.

The various aspects of Protestant aggression found a curious mirror-image in the words of Catholic preachers. The preachers put into words the conscious and unconscious depths of distress and rage of the Catholic faithful. Often members of religious orders, and thus not tied to a particular parish, they would preach in place of the parish priest on some feast day. More talented and better educated than the parish clergy, they wielded untold influence over the crowds that thronged to hear them. Their language, coarse, colourful, and compelling, fascinated their listeners, who could recognise in the words and images of the preacher the same feelings, reactions, and passions that set them in turmoil. They drank in the words of these rabble-rousers. And for years and years the preachers fulminated against the Huguenots, proclaiming that they had to be exterminated to avert God's terrible vengeance. They heaped abuse on the Protestant leaders Condé and Coligny, and even accused the king and the Queen Mother of favouring heretics or at least of having dealings with them. On several occasions these preachers, whether Jesuits or Dominicans, sparked off the latent violence. The massacres of 1562, 1567 and 1572 were precipitated by the power of the preachers' words. These zealots of 'divine wrath and the end of time'[7] appeared at Troyes and Sens in 1562, and at Paris, Bordeaux and Orléans in 1572, calling on Catholics to slaughter the enemies of divine and human order. The atrocities which the crowds inflicted on the corpses met the felt need for purification, and obeyed the imperative to kill in order to safeguard the divine order of heaven and earth.[8]

This violence was the expression of a profound religious feeling inseparable from a feeling of belonging in a coherent universe which was jeopardised by Protestant 'novelty'. It testified just as much as the labours of the Tridentine bishops to the revival of Catholicism and the strength of the League during the height of the conflicts between 1559 and 1598.

The Origins of the League

Before becoming an organised party machine, the League set down its roots in the critical years 1561–2, when the lightning advance of Protestantism and the tolerant attitude of the government struck fear into Catholic hearts. The Constable Montmorency gathered around himself a group of the most prominent noblemen committed to the defence of the Catholic faith. The 'Triumvirate' of Montmorency, the Duke of Guise, and the Marshal de Saint-André, went on the offensive by withdrawing from Court in March 1561. They were joined by the Duke of Montpensier, the Cardinal of Tournon, the Marshal de Brissac, and Blaise de Monluc. At the lower levels of society, informal associations were springing up among Catholics. These groups were secretive, and evidence about them remains scanty. But at Bordeaux a society for the defence of Catholicism was formed towards the end of 1561; and a secretive group was formed in Toulouse in spring 1562. In the course of 1563 a more aristocratic kind of league grew up around Monluc and the Cardinal of Armagnac. These societies for the elimination of heresy sealed the loyalty of their members with an oath. The movement gathered momentum in 1567–8. At Mâcon, Dijon, Beaune, Bourges, Toulouse and Orléans, Catholics of all classes solemnly bound themselves to defend their faith by force.[9]

This embryonic League was a reaction of spontaneous violence against the heretical foe. Its vocabulary was action, and murderous deeds gave expression to the rejection of Protestantism. In the wake of the Edict of January (1562), which was reckoned too indulgent to the Huguenots, Catholics resorted to murder at Toulouse, Gaillac, Meaux, Troyes, Sens, Tours and Rouen. There were similar massacres at Rouen, Paris and Orléans in 1571 following the excessively generous Peace of Saint-Germain. In 1572, when the Massacre of Saint Bartholomew spread from Paris to other cities, the slaughter assumed apocalyptic dimensions. But in 1572, as in 1562, and in between, the Catholics who killed Protestants saw themselves as purifying society. Killing heretics, stripping their corpses, and dragging them in the dust before flinging them in the water, they were performing the ritual execution of the scapegoat, cleansing away pollution and appeasing divine wrath so as to restore the proper order of things.[10]

Nevertheless, when one sets this apparently mindless violence in its historical context, it becomes clear that it was often a response: partly retaliation against the Huguenots who, at Tours, Orléans, Toulouse, Lyon, Gaillac and elsewhere briefly took possession of towns, indulged in orgies of iconoclasm, and attempted to establish Genevan theocracy; and partly also defiance of a monarch who, in dealing too leniently with his religious enemies, had failed in his duty as Most Christian King.[11] In the massacres which drenched France with blood between August and October 1572, the Catholics who gave themselves up to a murderous frenzy were interpreting the assassination of Coligny and the Huguenot leaders as royal sanction for the wholesale slaughter of heretics. These actions, whether done in opposition or in obedience to a supposed royal policy, represented the political affirmation of Catholic identity and a challenge to the Crown to acknowledge its existence.

In the years 1576–7, the movement took on a more organised, partisan character, leaving spontaneous and periodic violence on the sidelines. The Peace of Beaulieu (also known as the Peace of Monsieur), signed in May 1576 between the Crown and the Protestant allies of the Politiques, marked the end of the Fifth War of Religion. It rehabilitated the victims of the Massacre, authorised Protestant worship, and assigned the Huguenots eight safe havens, among them Péronne in Picardy, where Condé was provincial governor. But Jacques d'Humières, the governor of Péronne, together with the inhabitants of the town, refused to accept this status. A solemn league was sworn between people from all levels of society, its objectives apparently limited for the time being to the defence of religion and the establishment of a national network of supporters bound by oath. However, an appeal to 'neighbouring nations' was not excluded by the spirit of the founders. The organisation, whose members were supposed to keep their membership secret, spread throughout France: in Poitou under the aegis of Louis de La Trémoille, Duke of Thouars; in the Lyonnais under that of François de Mandelot, governor of Lyon; with Tanguy Le Veneur, sire de Carouges, in Normandy; and with the Duke of Montpensier in Brittany. Its leadership in Paris was a little lower on the social scale: the perfume merchant Jean de La Bruyère and his son Mathias, a magistrate. The leaders set out to establish an organisation comparable to that already established by the Huguenots. But, as Emmanuel Le Roy Ladurie and Arlette Jouanna have recently shown, some men used the Catholic cause as a cloak for political protest.[12] This can be seen from the number of nobles who left the ranks of the Alençon's Malcontents in order to join the League.

We have little in the way of official declarations or manifestos issued by the League, but the Estates General of 1576 gave it a remarkable opportunity. Some Huguenot candidates from the nobility found themselves excluded at the elections. And the statements of grievances drawn up by some districts of Lyon, Troyes, Chartres and Provins give an outline of a League programme.[13] It called for religious uniformity in France, the revocation of the Edict of Beaulieu, and the reception of the decrees of Trent. But these demands were mixed with others of a more political nature, criticising the administration of justice, the waste of public money, and the misconduct of soldiers.

When the Estates convened at Blois on 2 December 1576, a document was circulated among the nobles of the Second Estate, with the revealing title *Association faite entre les princes, seigneurs et gentilshommes des bailliages.* It called upon its signatories to swear obedience to a military league directed by a chief and officers chosen by the provincial nobility.[14] Behind the word 'chief' loomed the presence of Henri, Duke of Guise, the glorious victor over the *reiters* at Dormans. Henri III was in no doubt about the threat this posed, and decided to assume the leadership of the movement. He proposed a new formula of association, by which signatories swore to 'devote their goods and their lives to the full implementation of whatever His Majesty decides after listening to the remonstrances of the assembled Estates'.[15] Henri thus killed three birds with one stone: he defused the League movement, whose policies were so threatening to his position, reduced the Estates General to the level of a mere consultative assembly, and managed to shoulder Guise aside.

The Estates General of Blois, as we shall see, were divided on the religious question. If the nobility and the clergy adopted League positions in calling for the revocation of the Edict of Beaulieu and a renewal of war, the Third Estate, agreed as it was on the need for religious unity, was divided between the hawks and those who preferred gentler tactics which would not require further taxation. War would indeed come, because the Huguenots, disturbed by the proceedings at Blois, themselves took the field to open the sixth conflict. But the League was now to lie dormant until 1584.

The League in 1584

The League which reemerged in 1584 on the death of François d'Alençon was of sterner stuff. As Henri III had no sons, the heir presumptive according to the Salic Law was now Henri de Navarre, Prince Bourbon, descended from Robert de Clermont, the son of Saint Louis. Henri III, against the expectations of the hardline Catholics, did not deny his cousin's right to the succession, although he did urge him to convert to the majority religion.

But disquiet, and even anguish, at the thought of a heretic sitting on the throne of the Most Christian King is hardly enough to explain the formidable religious and political movement that developed towards the end of 1584. Henri III had made himself unpopular by his erratic behaviour, his repeated fiscal demands, and his unaccustomed style of government. There was a complete breakdown of understanding between him and his subjects.

Correctly judging the temper of the time, Henri de Guise had no hesitation in assuming the leadership of the League party. Since time immemorial the grandees had availed themselves of the 'right to revolt' when the sovereign was, in their eyes, guilty of tyranny or misgovernment. The enduring and unchanging arguments which served in every age, and – during these troubled times – on every side, to justify barons of either persuasion in taking up arms, fomenting disorder, and bringing misery to the people in the name of fine principles, were poor cloaks for personal ambition. An alliance was formed at Joinville on 31 December 1584, whose simple agenda looked likely to attract widespread support. It was, for the moment, basically religious, aiming at the 'defence and preservation of the Catholic faith', the extirpation of heresy, and the recognition of the old Cardinal of Bourbon, Navarre's uncle, as the heir to the throne. The guiding spirits of the alliance were Henri de Guise, his brothers the Cardinal of Guise and the Duke of Mayenne, and his cousins the Dukes of Aumale and Elboeuf, together with the Dukes of Mercœur (brother of the Duchess Louise of Lorraine who became Queen of France) and Nemours (Louis de Gonzaga).[16] The gathering at Joinville was easily tempted by the 600 000 *écus* of financial aid offered by two representatives of Philip II. But Guise did not stop looking for other foreign alliances, which he obtained from the Duke of Parma (Governor of the Netherlands) as well as from the Emperor and the Duke of Savoy, both of them sons-in-law of Philip II and zealous Catholics. The rest of Europe, except for the King of Scots (son of Mary Stuart, Queen Elizabeth's prisoner), adopted a wait-and-see policy as the old Habsburg–Valois conflict which had kept Christendom in suspense throughout the first half of the century resumed, albeit in a rather roundabout fashion.

In parallel to this decisively noble association, a league was being secretly established in Paris from January 1585. Initially a group of devout Catholics – three churchmen and a squire – panic-stricken at the prospect of a Huguenot succession and the consequent dangers for their faith, it soon spread as its members recruited devout and reliable Catholics among their friends. Subjected to close examination by the founders, these recruits in their turn recruited others, and similar secret societies arose throughout the provinces, not only in towns whose governors were clients of the Guise but also spontaneously elsewhere. The members were bound by oath and a common readiness to risk their lives for their religion. The League drew support from all levels of society, but certain groups were particularly strongly attracted to it: the middling bourgeoisie of public office, the bar, the universities and commerce, and the petty bourgeoisie of tradesmen gave the general tone to the League, but there were local variations. At Rouen the councillors of the Parlement joined the League and, in 1589, risked open rebellion.[17] At Agen, on the other hand, the men (and women) who enrolled came from a more modest background: 14 per cent of labourers and sharecroppers took the solemn oath. A great many clerics came out in favour of the League, with perhaps half of the bishops and a throng of priests and vicars joining. The Church thus largely sided with the League, and in January 1589, after the assassination of the Guises, the Sorbonne sanctioned the alliance of Frenchmen 'against a king who has broken public faith in the assembly of the Estates'. The Parlements, the other great moral authority in the land, remained loyal except for those of Paris, Rouen and Aix.

The League party, at once princely and popular, followed the strategy already developed by Condé and the Protestants to gain support in the provinces and cities. Governors who were related or favourable to the Guises aligned their provinces with the League: Champagne, Burgundy, Brie, Picardy, Berry, Maine and Anjou were all lost to the Crown, as were a large part of Languedoc, the Lyonnais, the Auvergne, the Dauphiné, and Poitou. The process by which they broke with the king was, as in the towns, a gradual one, but the pace quickened after Henri III had the Guises assassinated. The towns represented for the League, as for the Huguenots, privileged space within which they could implement the Christian order to which they aspired. Town councils which were royalist by compulsion, conviction or connection gave way to bodies dominated by League members and operating along Parisian lines: Rouen, Lyon, Marseille, Agen, Toulouse, Orléans, Bourges and Nantes were all gradually secured by the League, forming a sort of loose federation held together by a network of correspondence focused on Paris, the capital of the movement.

It is impossible to set an exact number on the League's membership, which in any case varied considerably over a relatively short period. Crucial events like the death of Alençon, the Day of the Barricades, the murder of the Guises, the murder of Henri III and the accession of Navarre stoked up or damped down passions; and as some people plunged in more deeply, others discreetly disentangled themselves – especially once Henri IV had converted to Catholicism in 1593. The League was undoubtedly a mass movement, but allegiance was paid on an individual basis, and its fortunes fluctuated with events.

The League Programme

In the same way, the faction's policy was made on the run. If the signatories at Joinville in 1584 agreed on some fairly basic aims, the Péronne manifesto issued on 30 March 1585 was already presenting a more sophisticated platform. Worked out in consultation with the Parisian League, it bore, like so many tracts of the time, an expansive title: *Déclarations des causes qui ont mus Monsieur le Cardinal de Bourbon et les pairs, princes et seigneurs, villes et communes catholiques de ce royaume de s'opposer à ceux qui par tous les moyens s'efforcent de subvertir la religion catholique de l'État*. The declaration summarised the now classic religious themes, albeit with new force and violence: Catholics were in danger of persecution at the hands of a Huguenot king; and the Protestants, together with their German allies, were plotting a new civil war. But political themes were also prominent: Henri III's 'mignons', Épernon and Joyeuse, although not specifically named, were accused of cooperating with the heretics, usurping the positions and offices traditionally reserved for the high nobility, and draining the royal treasury. And the king's style of government, seen as autocratic, was subtly attacked. The manifesto prescribed a treatment for these gaping wounds: an end to excessive and burdensome taxation, regular meetings of the Estates General, and the replacement of the 'mignons' by Catherine de Medici in the conduct of affairs.[18]

In the wake of this fundamental manifesto, the League programme was further elaborated in a series of pamphlets, treatises, and declarations issued in response to events. Before the assassination of the Guises, this abundant literature concentrated on the danger posed to the kingdom by a Huguenot succession. In 1586 the Parisian advocate Louis Dorléans replied to those statements by Navarre which held out the prospect of conversion and urged the people to moderation. In his *Avertissement des catholiques anglois aux François catholiques*, Dorléans rebutted Navarre's pretensions to toleration and portrayed for his readers the sufferings of Catholic priests and people in Bourbon Béarn and Tudor England. State and Church were so closely connected that the country could not survive under a Protestant king. Dorléans added his regret that the organisers of Saint Bartholomew's Day had been so pusillanimous as to allow the two Bourbon princes to escape. And the Catholic League had to be ready to call on foreign aid to complete the job, for 'who would not rather be a Spaniard than a Huguenot?'[19]

Like the Protestant pamphleteers after St Bartholomew, the League publicists called authoritarian monarchy into question. While the Protestants, with Henri de Navarre the heir presumptive, now became the champions of an all-powerful Crown, the Leaguers took over their enemies' former arguments, proposing the supervision of the administration by the Estates General and inciting rebellion against a government of favourites who were too lax towards heresy.

The propaganda became frenzied after the murder of the Guises at Blois in 1588, and, if possible, even more so with the accession of Henri IV. The position of the League now crystallised around the concept of tyranny. Henri III was denounced as a tyrant for procuring the murder of his own subjects at a time of peace, for breaking his coronation oath by tolerating heresy in the land, and for laying excessive fiscal burdens on his people. A few months later Henri IV was likewise convicted on the rather different grounds of usurpation: as a Huguenot, his succession was against the religious law of the land. It was a short step from denouncing tyranny to advocating tyrannicide: killing the culprit became a good work, automatically meriting salvation. Jacques Clément, argued an anonymous pamphleteer, had God on his side:

> See the end of the tyrant, which was as wretched as that of the poor friar was blessed. There can be no doubt that this took place by the express permission of God.[20]

However, the League was less united over what means could be used to prevent the establishment of tyranny within the realm. The nobility around the Guises adhered to the traditional view already discussed: the nobility should be accorded their due military and political role, advising the king and governing with him, while the Estates General should be regularly assembled to decide on fiscal, legislative and administrative questions. The popular wing of the League, on the other hand, boldly went for a more radical account of public law. Sovereignty, in this perspective, rested ultimately with the people rather than the king, who simply derived his authority from them. 'Reges a populis esse constitutos', wrote the priest Jean Boucher, adding that *in extremis* the people could do without a monarch. Such arguments inevitably entailed the idea of a contract to explain the transfer of sovereignty. Subjects undertook to obey a king who ruled according to the law of the land, to which he always remained subordinate. Any breach of contract justified resistance and even tyrannicide – the legitimacy of which was amply substantiated in the Bible. Hence there appeared a stream of resistance treatises such as Pierre Du Four L'Évesque's *Mémoire* or Boucher's *De justa Henrici tertii abdicatione.*[21] The pinnacle of the League's theoretical construction was the concept of the people as inspired by God: 'vox populi sit vox Dei'. If the people created kings, then the Salic Law of the succession was void and Henry IV could rightfully be rejected as the heir to the throne. Inspired by God and endowed with the inalienable right to 'resist wicked kings', the people could not govern directly, but did so vicariously through the Estates General, which could control and even elect the king. 'Without the consent of the French people, the king can do nothing of importance.' So the Estates, whose power came (like that of the people who elected them) from God, embodied the State, representing its continuity and standing above the kings whom they elected and supervised. In practice, they dealt with financial and legislative matters and questions of war and peace, and, collaborating with a monarch who was a mere functionary, they excluded all risk of tyranny. The League system would have made France a veritable theocracy, for the French people, the kingmakers themselves, swore 'to believe as the Catholic, Apostolic, and Roman Church believes, and to live and die in that belief', and it was obvious that only the 'Roman, Catholic, and Apostolic religion' would be 'permitted, received, and professed in this realm'.[22] One can see in the pamphlets and sermons of these hardliners the emergence of a wider conception of a world in which Catholics everywhere were brothers united by their common faith, owing obedience primarily to the head of the Universal Church, and only secondarily to a king chosen from amongst their own number. The rhetoric employed earlier in the wars, when the Protestants were denounced as 'bad Frenchmen' on account of their foreign alliances, was now set aside in the face of the necessity for a Catholic international, an open ultramontanism, and an alliance with Spain – the only country capable of defending Catholic values. But this last fact did create some tension within the League, for although they were all dependent on Spanish funding, they did not all adopt an extreme viewpoint. There is a lot to be said for a twofold model of the League: one wing French, Guisard, and aristocratic; the other popular, pro-Spanish, and devoid of any sense of patriotism. The advocate Dorléans, the preacher Boucher, and the 'mad bishop' Guillaume Rose clearly belonged to the latter wing. So too did Louis Morin, sire de Cromé, the presumed author of the famous *Dialogue d'entre le Maheustre et le Manant* (Paris, 1593).[23] This tract denied to the nobility, and especially to that nobility which, together with Mayenne, the brother of the murdered Guises, was preparing to make an accommodation with Navarre, any special role in the theocracy to which the diehard Leaguers aspired. He accused them of conducting a phoney war against the hypocritical convert Bourbon, and of pursuing plunder and profit rather than the cause of the true faith. Such attitudes shocked the Guisard and royalist nobles and made them fear for their privileges, conjuring up spectres of 'a populist State and the establishment of a republic without distinction of rank or quality, and with no difference between noble and base birth'. The theme had been a familiar one since the establishment of the United Provinces of the Midi in 1573, although the latter's supporters had come from more elevated social backgrounds. But for the author of the *Dialogue*, true nobility was earned, and belonged to those who fought for their faith. Similarly, true royalty entailed fighting to defend Church and religion, which ruled out Henri IV because in his heart he remained the heretic he had always been. 'The true heirs to the Crown', said the 'manant' to the 'maheustre' (the lukewarm and politique Catholic), 'are those who are worthy to bear the character of God. If it is God's pleasure to send us a king from the French nation, then may his name be blessed; if from the nation of Lorraine, may his name be blessed. The king's nationality is a matter of complete indifference to us, providing that he is a Catholic imbued with piety and justice, as one coming from the hand of God. We are concerned not with nationality but with religion.' Thus spoke the subversive voice of despair.

The Violence of the League

The politico-religious theories of the League would have been mere utopianism if, like those worked out by the Protestants after Saint-Bartholomew, they had not been put into practice on the ground. Implementation may have been only partial, but it was enough to tear the kingdom apart between 1588 and 1594. The power-base of the League was to some extent provincial, and thus noble, but to a greater extent communal and thus populist. A curious strategy was developed in order to retain the loyalty of towns won by the League and to fan the flames of crusading zeal in their inhabitants. We have already considered the thunder of the pamphlets, some of which were adorned with powerful images for the benefit of the illiterate. Pierre de l'Estoile remarked on them in his *Journal* with the amused and sometimes nervous distaste of the wealthy bourgeois. Preachers took possession of parish pulpits, proclaiming death to the tyrants Henri III and Henri IV, and declaring a holy war against them. Processions of penitents, or of religious confraternities (e.g. the Rosary or the

Blessed Sacrament), or of white-robed believers, constantly wound their way through the streets, uniting the people of God in the symbols of baroque piety.[24] The procession which marched through Paris on 14 May 1590 remains famous to this day thanks to the contemporary engravings which immortalised it. This particular procession was of thanksgiving for the setback Henri IV had received in seeking to take the rebel city via the Faubourg Saint-Martin. The monks and friars of the various orders, clerks, priests, and the bishop of Senlis, 'accompanied by some citizens of the town reputed as zealous Catholics, walked behind an image of the Virgin and the crucified Christ'.[25] The clerics, both secular and religious, bore arms, interspersing prayers and thanksgiving with salvos from their muskets. Such demonstrations unfolded in all the League towns: Philip Benedict has spoken of the people of Rouen under the League as 'penitents as well as militants'.[26]

But Paris remained the model for the rest of the cities in revolt against Henri III and Henri IV. It was the undisputed capital of the League from the Day of the Barricades (12 May 1588), when the secret society of 1585 seized power, and it issued orders, examples, and methods of action. In describing the style of the revolutionary regime, historians have invoked the model of totalitarianism. Certainly the regime's methods were radical. Besides the torrent of written and spoken propaganda and the demonstrations of unity in the streets, one can note the climate of fear which the leaders sought to foster. The violence was more restrained than in the preceding decades, as the Protestants had wisely fled such centres of fanaticism. Instead, it was exemplary, picking out individuals whom the authorities reckoned lukewarm. The murder of President Brisson on 15 November 1591 was such a case, as was the assassination of First President Duranti with his son-in-law Advocate-General Daffis (both of them seen as too faithful to the king) in Toulouse during the summer of 1588. The successive purges of the revolutionary council, the Parlement, and the party itself, the proscriptions, the threats against the suspect, too familiar though they are in our own time, had already been widely used by the factions of Republican Rome. And one must exercise caution in making such comparisons. The pressure exerted by the League leaders had a dimension of which our age has barely a memory, that of refusing absolution to those whom their 'spiritual' directors reckoned too *politique* or too timid in their support of the League.

Thus, towards the close of the sixteenth century, the Catholic Church in France was a complex institution anxious to adapt to the spiritual needs of some of its faithful, to resist, while assimilating them, the demands of some of its more militant members. This was a difficult course to steer in a time of troubles which we vacillate between calling 'wars of religion' and 'civil wars'.

11 The Politiques

Amidst the clamour of Protestants and Catholics, a third party could be heard advocating alternatives to violence and war. This third party is difficult to assess for, quite as much as the papists and Huguenots, its words and deeds hinged on events and were thus prone to variation during the course of the conflict.

Michel de L'Hôpital

Michel de L'Hôpital stands out as a figure of particular importance among the opponents of fanaticism and violence from whatever source.[1] His character merits a little closer examination. Born in 1503 in the Auvergne, the son of a physician and friend of the Constable Charles de Bourbon, who fled the country after the trial of his patron, the young Michel studied law at Padua. After ten years absorbing the culture of law and humanism in Italy, L'Hôpital returned to France to join the Parlement de Paris as a councillor-clerk in 1537. Moving now in the upper echelons of the administration, he was associated with Jean du Bellay (Bishop of Paris) and the Chancellor Antoine du Bourg, as well as with the future Chancellors Pierre Poyet and Olivier. He left his seat in the Parlement to represent the king at the *Grand Jours de Justice* of Moulins (1540), Riom (1542), and Tours (1546–7), and was then sent as ambassador to the prelates gathered at Bologna for the opening sessions of the Council of Trent. On his return to France, even though he reported the hardening of the Church's attitude towards the rise of heresy, he joined the humanist entourage of the Duchess of Berry (and later of Savoy), Marguerite,

319

Henri II's sister. Michel became president of her council and then her chancellor. At about the same time, in 1553, he took office as a *Maître des Requêtes*, and was promoted to First President of the *Chambre des comptes* the following year. These appointments did not keep him from his hobby of writing Latin verse, and he was an associate of the Pléiade and a firm supporter of Ronsard.

It was in March 1560, on the death of Olivier, that L'Hôpital was given charge of the seals as Chancellor. The importance of the post, the foremost office in the land after the kingship itself, goes without saying. It might at first seem surprising that the man known to posterity as the paragon of tolerance should be appointed by the Guise clan which ruled in François II's name, but L'Hôpital had in fact long been a friend of the Cardinal of Lorraine, addressing several Latin epistles to him. The new Chancellor took office at an especially dramatic moment, when the civil wars were brewing and everyone in the corridors of power knew that the powder-keg was about to ignite.

The Chancellor was a major influence over domestic policy from 1560 to 1568, when the second war broke out. But at that point his policy of toleration received such a blow that he was obliged to surrender the seals. Together with Catherine de Medici he sought to give the Protestants political space within the kingdom. To begin with, the Edict of Romorantin (May 1560) seemed hard on the heretics beause it forbade all private or public acts of Reformed worship, and gave jurisdiction over heresy to ecclesiastical courts and the *présidiaux*. But this was a subtle way of out-manoeuvring the Parlements, some of which (notably Paris, Toulouse, Agen and Dijon) were extremely severe on religious dissidents. It was also a skilful move by which L'Hôpital, who liked to keep religion separate from politics, returned the problem of heresy to the Catholic hierarchy and the responsibility for keeping public order to the lower royal judges. It was on his initiative that the Estates General were convened at Orléans in 1560. The representatives of the Third Estate showed enough hostility to the Catholic clergy for the Chancellor to issue in January 1561 a Declaration designed to halt the persecution of Protestants; and then to follow it in July with an amnesty for issues of conscience. The same year saw the Colloquy of Poissy convene at the instigation of the Chancellor and the Queen Mother in an attempt to forge a compromise between the two factions on matters of faith and worship. And in 1562 l'Hôpital signed the famous Edict of January giving Protestants full freedom of conscience and limited freedom of worship. From this time until his retirement in 1568, with the Edicts of Amboise and then in 1568 of Longjumeau (which, although promulgated after his withdrawal from government, essentially repeated the terms of Amboise), he remained faithful to his policy of not driving the Huguenots to despair by excluding them from the French community.

The intellectual foundations of L'Hôpital's policy of toleration (if one can properly speak of toleration with regard to that fanatical age) are far from clear. He no more thought religious diversity good for the country than did any of his contemporaries, even Henri IV, who granted toleration to the Huguenots in 1598 by the Edict of Nantes. However, assessing the balance of forces, and perceiving that the Protestants were numerous and powerful, he thought it prudent to refrain from violent measures against them. And his immersion in a humanist culture impregnated with Erasmian influence made him reluctant to employ force against religious dissidents. 'Force and violence are bestial rather than human. Law derives from the most godlike part of our nature, reason.'[2] On another occasion he remarked, 'The dagger is useless against the soul, and serves only to lose both soul and body.' Like his mentor Erasmus, L'Hôpital would not sanction killing in the name of Christ, the more so as such extreme rigour worked against royal authority, which was L'Hôpital's overriding preoccupation. That authority derived 'from God and the ancient law of the land', and therefore stood above churches and confessions. Thus the Chancellor drew a clear line between politics and religion, not only in his deeds, as we have just seen, but also in his concept of the State. For in his eyes, people 'who will not be Christians' could none the less be French citizens provided that they were submissive and obedient to the king's law.[3] Political unity was thus more important than religious unity for a monarchy. As Catherine de Medici put it, it was essential 'to accommodate ourselves to the times in which we live', and the integrity of the State, embodied in the king, had to be protected at all costs. If the king intervened in religious affairs, it was as the father of the kingdom seeking to pacify his children. The Edict of January was undoubtedly an intervention in ecclesiastical affairs, 'sed de constituenda republica' ('but concerned with ordering the republic').[4] In L'Hôpital's high conception of monarchy, the pious and benevolent king could not, without harming the State which he embodied, execute his subjects over issues which, in the absence of civil disorder, he could, if not sanction, at least tolerate. The Chancellor died a few months after the Massacre of Saint Bartholomew, which struck the fatal blow to his policy of national reconciliation.

In the 1560s many pamphlets and tracts appeared which, analysing the fragmentation of France, echoed L'Hôpital in insisting upon the importance of the monarchical role which the collapse of religious unity had called into question. These texts emphasised that only through a royal monopoly of power could harmony be restored among the people. The *Exhortation aux princes* (1561), sometimes attributed to the historian Étienne Pasquier, urged those in authority to permit the existence of two religions within their domains for the sake of the three main objectives of government: the keeping of the peace, the maintenance of the king in his majesty, and the preservation of the social order.[5] The *Exhortation* aroused considerable interest, influencing Sebastien Castellion's *Conseil à la France désolée* (1562)[6] and Jean Bodin's *Methodus ad facilem historiarum cognitionem* (1566).[7] Jean de Monluc's *Apologie contre certaines calomnies* (1562) was in a similar vein – its author, the Bishop of Valence, was a friend of L'Hôpital – as were the *Brief discours* (1564) and the *Exhortation à la paix* (1568).[8] Compared with the later torrent of League pamphlets, these works appeared in paltry numbers, but their themes had a long future ahead of them. They all emphasised the need for tolerance if the kingdom was not to be torn to pieces. They set the king above religious and ecclesiastical questions, insisting on his duty to preserve the kingdom, his subjects, their families, and his own person. The Protestants were too numerous and too committed to be eliminated easily, argued Monluc, and therefore had to be tolerated. And, as both he and the author of the *Exhortation à la paix* argued, prescinding from doctrinal divisions, the French remained united by their basic Christianity, their shared language, and their allegiance to the king. Foreigners, they added, invited by one or other of the factions, or simply attracted by the instability consequent upon the troubles, wanted nothing more than to intervene and invade what had been but a little while before the finest kingdom in the world. The theme of the sufferings of France was already appearing from the pens of these pamphleteers. The phrases of the tolerant Protestant Castellion echo the famous verses of Ronsard's *Plaintes de la France*, even if the latter did yearn for the elimination of the Huguenots:

Listen well, once flourishing but now tormented France, to what I say. You feel deeply the blows and wounds you receive as your children fall upon each other so mercilessly. You see your towns and villages, your highways and fields, strewn with corpses, your rivers run red with blood, and your air grow foul and noisome.

Malcontents and Politiques

After the Massacre of Saint Batholomew, when first the monarchomach chorus arose on the Huguenot side, and then the Catholic extremists tried to unite against the Protestant Union after 1576, reasonable people grieved over the fragmentation of the realm. The preambles of deeds of association between Protestants and Catholics emphasised the need for understanding between the members of the opposing religions.[9] Toleration – a *de facto* toleration, dictated by circumstances, rather than a spontaneous or principled toleration, but a toleration none the less – prevailed in such provinces as Languedoc, where the two confessions were of roughly equal strength.

A more particular spirit motivated occasional alliances between Catholic and Protestant nobility. Alençon gathered the Malcontents around him on a platform of national unity and the prestige of the kingdom.[10] One could almost believe him were it not for the suspicions inevitably aroused by the spectacle of a young prince with ambitions on the throne at the head of a 'league for the common weal'. The themes developed by Alençon's propagandists – of expanding the kingdom at the expense of the Spanish Netherlands, securing the borders, preventing foreigners from being royal councillors – constituted a platform with widespread appeal. It united thoroughgoing Protestants like François La Noue, Henri de Condé and Philippe Duplessis-Mornay with Catholics like the Montmorency brothers François, Henri and Guillaume, and the jurist Jean Bodin.[11] The civil and religious recognition of a Protestant minority was implicit in the numerous declarations issued by Alençon, Condé, Damville, La Noue, and even Navarre while, until 1576, he remained a prisoner at Court. When the Malcontents went into revolt in 1574, their propaganda laid great stress on establishing civil harmony between the two religions, but, while anxious to defend royal prerogatives which they thought threatened by the Italians on the Council, they called for supervision of the monarchy by the Estates General in order to prevent it lapsing into tyranny. In short, the Malcontents were voicing the traditional grievances of a nobility in opposition to the ruling regime. As so often in these carefully constructed networks of family and clientage, ties of blood or friendship counted for more than religious preferences.

The train of thought of the Politiques was less conventional. Hardly a faction, in that they refused to resort to arms, Michel de L'Hôpital and his pamphleteers in the 1560s argued for toleration under a strong king, and earned from their opponents the pejorative name 'politique' in contrast to the 'dévot' or firm believer. Jacques Charpentier, one of the supporters of the Massacre of Saint Bartholomew, maintained that the Politiques 'respected men rather than God', already hinting at the accusations of atheism which fanatical Catholics were later to heap on them.[12] These moderates, mostly jurists drawn from an intellectual elite of officeholders, sought by an effort of will to raise themselves above fanaticism and to speak the language of reason.

Jean Bodin was the preeminent theorist of the Politiques, even if the theoretical construct he advanced in the *Six livres de la République* (1576) had less immediate impact than the numerous manifestos and declarations poured out by authors more directly involved in events. But Bodin, whose modest career had led him from advocate in Paris to proctor in Laon, for all that he was a great theorist, was by no means isolated from the realities of his time.[13] As we have just seen, he was involved with the Malcontents in 1574, and in 1576 he represented Vermandois at the Estates General of Blois where, confronting the Parisian deputy Versoris, he sought a hearing for the voice of moderation, urging negotiation with the Reformers.[14] Though he found it prudent for a while to join the League, Bodin did not share its extremism. Now, this is hardly the place for an assessment of his achievement as a political theorist, but it is worth picking out certain elements of his writings which assumed significance at a time when the monarchy was being called into question. Bodin claimed to be writing against the doctrines of Machiavelli then current at the French Court, where principles of religion and justice had been forgotten and power was exercised for private gain rather than the common good. Presumably he had Saint Bartholomew in mind. In the same spirit he opposed extremism, whether Catholic or Protestant, advocating the subordination of religion and the Church to the Crown. The State, he maintained, was a coherent entity recognised by all and enforced by the king. Legitimate monarchy differed from tyranny in the respect shown by the sovereign for divine law and the 'various human laws common to all peoples', in a way natural law, the object of monarchy and therefore of the State being the common good. Among human laws, the fundamental laws of the realm – above all the Salic Law – represented an inviolable constitution which maintained the royal succession. A strong and authoritarian sovereign found himself in a position to reject the grievances and petitions of the regions represented in the Estates General or the provincial estates, although Bodin argued that the Estates General were entitled to decide on matters of taxation. The foundation of this political organisation lay not so much in religion (it took little account of the coronation oath or unction) as in human nature and reason, both of them God's gifts.[15] Of course religion remained important, but it had to be uniform and national (i.e. Gallican – Bodin left no room for ultramontanism or notions of Christendom) so that the monarchy might have a free hand to reconcile religious dissidents by compromise. Moreover, Bodin declared in the *Apologie de René Herpin* (1581), the prince had to stay aloof from factions and should never take sides in the quarrels of his subjects.[16] When dissension arose over religious questions, a sovereign concerned for the common good should 'tolerate what he cannot eliminate'. For, he affirmed, abandoning theory for pragmatism, the State would be preserved from anarchy not by a victory of the Catholics over the Protestants but by a cessation of internal conflict. The secularisation and nationalisation of the monarchy were thus Bodin's most novel contributions to political thought in a period when the League was promoting concepts of theocracy and universal Christendom.

In the public sphere, passions were seen as harmful, jeopardising the State and even the monarchy. And, explained Michel de Montaigne, they wrought similar havoc in the hearts of individuals. Montaigne's *Essais*, of which the first two books appeared at Bordeaux in 1580, aroused much more immediate interest than Bodin's works. The tone was of course entirely different: Montaigne,

writing mainly about himself, had no theoretical pretensions even
if he did attain the universal. But if he was shut away in his Périgord
château during the long years of composition, he was by no means
cut off from the things of the world, especially as his apparent
retirement was probably little more than an act put on in anticipation of receiving important official appointments. The fruit of
his reading and of his reflection upon his own times, the *Essais*
were firmly rooted in the Politique *via media*, a still small voice of
calm heard throughout the civil wars. But Montaigne himself was
certainly conservative, detesting 'innovation' and blaming the Protestants for having set the country alight with their new religion
and their new Church. For 'in truth, the best regime for any
nation is that according to which it has always been governed'.
But he was also tolerant, reluctant to treat opinions as truths of
faith, and thus hostile to dogmatism. His suspicion of faction inclined him to moderation. A moderate himself, avoiding any deep
entanglements, he observed wittily, 'I will follow the best side to
the fire, but not into it.' He detested fanaticism of whatever variety.
Princes had to do dirty work and use force where necessary for
the common good, but from 'a man that hath neither charge,
nor express commandment to urge him', only that degree of involvement was required which would not bring down worse
sufferings on him than on others. For his part, Montaigne remained committed to monarchical legitimacy, distancing himself
from both Catholic and Protestant extremism. 'The laws', he wrote
in Book III of the *Essais* (1588), 'have delivered me from much
trouble: they have chosen me a side to follow and appointed me
a master to obey; all other superiority and duty ought to be relative unto that, and be restrained.'[17] Obedience to the laws and
thus to the king led Montaigne to recognise Henri de Navarre as
Henri III's legitimate successor in 1584, and to reject the League
campaign against him. 'But we ought not term duty (as nowadays
we do) a sour rigour and intestine crabbedness, proceeding of
private interest and passion; nor courage, a treacherous and
malicious proceeding.' In his own life, Montaigne certainly did
not aspire to seclusion from the world.[18] He was often entrusted
with diplomatic missions by Henri III, and he also served as mayor
of Bordeaux, thwarting a League plot against his town in 1585
and taking the risk of officially receiving Navarre on 24 October
1587 (when the latter, fresh from his victory at Coutras, was 'on
his way to Béarn to deliver 22 captured flags to the Countess of

Gramont'). If the author of the *Essais* doubted the validity of any opinion held too tenaciously, he nevertheless adhered to the firmly traditional line of 'one faith, one law, one king'. But for him one law and one king took priority over the passionate defence of a Church or faith.

Catholic and Protestant Royalists

The intellectual circle of the Politiques was enlarged when, in the wake of Alençon's death in 1584, the Guises decided on an alliance with Spain. Protestants and Catholics alike had recourse to the same concepts and arguments: they were all 'royal'. The Huguenot Duplessis-Mornay became one of the ablest propagandists of this school of thought, as did the Catholic Pierre Du Belloy, with his *De l'authorité du Roy* (1587).[19] These authors, and a host of others, took up positions already defended by their predecessors in the 1560s and 1570s. They inveighed against internecine conflict and the destruction of France, waxing piteous over their country's sufferings. And they called for that national unity and domestic peace which only a powerful and authoritarian sovereign could guarantee. The State, and thus the king, they agreed, stood above all other considerations. Reason of State and the common good required the separation of religion from politics. 'The State is not within the Church, rather the Church exists within the State', Du Belloy maintained in his *Apologie catholique* of 1585. Authoritarian monarchy also drew support from the Gallicanism current in the world of jurists and lawyers, that was so receptive to Politique ideas. Du Belloy himself went even further towards the laicisation of the State when he went so far as to write that Navarre could cure the King's Evil (exercising the supernatural power granted by God) by the mere fact of his legitimate title according to the law of the succession.

Without going as far as Du Belloy, many authors maintained that only a strong king would be able to impose peace on his subjects.[20] National unity and the peace of the realm rested in his hands alone. The sense of belonging to an entity named France, which was embodied in the person of the king according to the fundamental laws, gripped both Catholic and Protestant Politiques, distancing them from the ultramontane and 'hispanicised' League and keeping them on the side of authoritarian kingship.

The Sense of French Nationhood

When, in August 1589, Henri de Navarre became king according to the Salic Law and the express recognition of his predecessor, the Politique movement was not strong enough to allow him an easy passage to the throne vacated by Henri III's assassination. Indeed, some loyal servants of the last Valois, men hitherto deaf to the siren songs of the League, now joined it, unable to accept a Protestant succession. Such was the case with the Cardinal de Joyeuse. However, there was some rallying to Henri IV among the officeholding classes.[21] As we have seen, officeholders already formed the core of the Politiques. They stood for good order and government, well aware that their careers depended on the continuity of the State. Many of these men were noted jurists, like Antoine Arnauld, Guy Coquille, Étienne Pasquier, and Achille de Harlay, perpetuating the tradition (which dated from Philip the Fair's time) of lawyers as upholders of the royal prerogative come hell or high water. Their number included devout Catholics, and even some Leaguers who dreaded the prolongation of civil war and the succession of a foreigner. Such was the case with the Secretary of State Villeroy and the President Jeannin, who urged Mayenne, the brother of the murdered Guises, to come to an accommodation with Henri IV. They all now recognised the inevitability of religious division within the kingdom, at least in the short term, with the king alone acting as a focus of unity. The royalists developed an ostentatious nationalism. Painting a picture of a devastated kingdom drenched in blood, Guillaume de Vair (a councillor in the Parlement de Paris), and Pierre Pithou (a lawyer and one of the authors of the *Satire Ménippée*) lamented the fate of Paris, which had been prey to the excesses of the League since 1588: 'O Paris, not so much Paris as a den of wild animals, a citadel of Spaniards, Walloons, and Neapolitans, a haven and refuge for thieves'.[22] Others, like the magistrate Étienne Pasquier, tried to count the losses: 1 600 000 men – 50 000 of them gentlemen – had lost their lives in the Wars of Religion. Pride in being French burst through this pity in bitter fulminations against the foreigners called in aid by the League.[23] In 1590, when the League campaign against Henri IV was at its height, the advocate Antoine Arnauld wrote a pamphlet with the unsubtle title *L'Anti-Espagnol*, in which he heaped withering scorn upon the Spaniards as a mongrel people 'half Moor', 'half Jew and half

Saracen'.[24] They sought to conquer France and add it to the tally of their colonies, and they would treat the French as they had treated the indigenous peoples of America, setting them to dig their mines. But, Arnauld resumed, the people of France, a higher and purer race, would not let themselves be enslaved: 'You are not dealing with your Indians here, you will have to face thousands upon thousands of trueborn Frenchmen, who will give you hundreds upon hundreds of battles . . . rather than become Spaniards.'[25]

In any case, France would rise again from the ruins. History showed many examples of States that had risen with fresh vigour after the most terrible disasters, and one needed to go no further than the history of France itself. Though torn into little pieces by the sectional interests of the League, France would prosper once again when united around a legitimate French sovereign. For Henri IV, the 'scion of Saint Louis', 'descended of our own blood', was the rightful king by that most French of laws, the Salic Law. In his Baroque prose, Pierre Pithou forcefully proclaimed his conviction that the first Bourbon, for all that he was a Protestant, was by blood, reason, and nature the true king of the French:

> The king we seek is already given us by nature, born in the true field of the fleurs de lys of France, a true and verdant sprig off the stem of Saint Louis. . . . You can make sceptres and crowns, but you cannot make kings to wear them. You can build a house, but you cannot build a tree or a green branch. Nature must form them in her own time, from the goodness of the soil which fills the trunk with sap.[26]

Many of the Politiques, for whom the Salic Law stood above religious controversy, nevertheless hoped that Navarre would fulfil the half promises of conversion that he had held out to the French since he became heir presumptive in 1584. When his abjuration finally came, in July 1593, it swept away the mental barriers to the succession of a Protestant in a kingdom shot through with Catholic traditions.

In the almost physical, visceral emergence of what was, if not actual patriotism, at least a national sentiment, the Gallicanism in which the officeholding elite was steeped played a fundamental role. Even before August 1589, when Henri IV became king of a fragmentary kingdom, the Politiques had inveighed against papal interference in the temporal affairs of the realm: Sixtus V's bull of excommunication against the two Bourbon princes in September 1585 had aroused a wave of indignation even among hardline Catholics. It was much the same as the reaction of Catherine de Medici, Michel de L'Hôpital, and the Crown officeholders in 1563, when the papacy had claimed the power to depose Jeanne d'Albret from the throne of Navarre and to summon seven French bishops before the Inquisition at Rome on charges of heresy. The jurist Guy Coquille did not baulk at accusing the pope of complicity in Spanish plots to conquer France. Gregory XIV, dismissed in numerous pamphlets as 'that wretched old rabbi', was threatened by Coquille with losing his spiritual rights in France, which he should never have neglected for the sake of meddling in temporal affairs: 'The pope should beware of going to extremes, lest the French should choose themselves a patriarch.'[27]

But it was more than a faction that was striving to reunite France: it was a school of thought. People horrified by iconoclastic excesses, by massacres perpetrated in the name of religion, and by the crimes of a monarchy at bay, emphasised the themes which they hoped would restore order on a basis of hard reality and common sense. They were imbued with the concept of nature, as proposed by Montaigne for the individual or by L'Hôpital, Bodin, and Pithou for the king, in a way which, though perhaps not stoical, was certainly classical and humanist. Their political pragmatism inclined them towards a *de facto* toleration, even if they regarded this more as a compromise than as a moral obligation or philosophical ideal. They relied on the time-honoured values of the Salic Law and Gallicanism as bulwarks against the rising tide of Guisard ambition and clerically manipulated fanaticism.

A powerful but paternal and humane Crown was what they hoped would emerge with renewed vigour from the terrible trials to which it had been subjected.

Henri IV, who, thanks to the Politiques, had ensured the triumph of the Crown, was nevertheless the head of a faction with appetites no less insatiable than those of their adversaries. Luckily for him, and perhaps also for the French people, his hand in the power struggle contained some useful trumps in matters of law and popular appeal. Set in a favourable light by a remarkably well-organised propaganda effort which presented him as the 'fresh and gallant' king, good-natured and trueborn French, he could be seen by his exhausted subjects as a prince sent by Providence to reunite the realm. Strangely enough, the Politiques – gentlemen, lawyers, and intellectuals – though they appealed to abstract and erudite concepts, nevertheless struck a chord in the hearts of their fellow countrymen.

12 Condé's Wars, 1559–70

The real commencement of the protracted troubles now known as the Wars of Religion was Henri II's death on 10 July 1559. The traditional date of 1 March 1562, the date of the massacre at Vassy, was no landmark, except for the fact that at that point Catherine de Medici and Michel de L'Hôpital gave up any hope of reaching a compromise through royal mediation. The real break was Henri II's death. The struggle between noble factions under religious flags over a throne occupied successively by a youth (François II), a child (Charles IX), and then a king first absent and later discredited (Henri III), broke out on that 10 July.

At that point the Guises seized the major posts on the King's Council: they placed their clients in key positions, pursuing a dynastic policy based on their relationship to Mary Stuart, François II's wife. The Montmorency family found themselves squeezed out: not just the Constable and his sons, but even his nephews Gaspard de Coligny (Grand Admiral of France), the Cardinal de Châtillon (Count-Bishop of Beauvais), and François d'Andelot (Colonel of the Infantry). The three Châtillon brothers, sons of Montmorency's sister, were all Protestants. The Guises relieved Montmorency himself of his position as Grand Master of the Household, one of the most prestigious Court offices, and sought to deprive him even of the Governorship of Languedoc. This caused resentments enough, but on a wider front the inflexible policies of the Guises alienated a further section of noble opinion. The soldiers and captains recruited in large numbers by the late king for the war against the Habsburgs had found themselves unemployed after the Treaty of Cateau-Cambrésis. An ordinance of 14 July 1559 announced a reduction in the effective strength of the army. It elicited in response a host of claims from noblemen for pensions and gratuities, which the Cardinal of Guise, as *Surintendant des finances*, brusquely rejected. The Treasury, it must be said, was indeed in a parlous state as a result of the long and costly wars against the Habsburgs. The Crown had been obliged to alienate portions of the royal domain in order to finance the wars, alienations which the Cardinal of Guise revoked as soon as he took office. And the Guises excluded from favour all nobles who had openly espoused Protestantism, above all the powerful Châtillon brothers. They continued the policy of harsh repression inaugurated by Henri II, issuing, in September and November 1559, edicts ordering the destruction of houses where 'conventicles' met and imposing the death penalty on their participants and on those who concealed them. Anne Du Bourg, a Clerk Councillor in the Parlement de Paris, already imprisoned under Henri II for having publicly opposed the persecution of Calvinists, was burned in the Place de Grève on 23 December 1559, despite the hopes in some quarters that the new regime would show clemency.

The Conspiracy of Amboise

The Conspiracy of Amboise, then, was not so much the wild adventure of a few hotheads as the first engagement of the Wars of Religion.[1] The frustrations of noblemen consequent upon the cessation of hostilities and the exclusion from favour of Huguenot noblemen and Montmorency clients, together with the advance of Protestantism, especially among the nobility, created a favourable background for the plot. Its head was Louis de Condé. Its programme, conventionally enough, was to arrest and try the Guises on charges of holding the young king prisoner. Pamphlets denouncing Guise tyranny were circulated, the most explicit of them entitled *Les États de France opprimés par la tyrannie de Guise* ('The Estates of France oppressed by the tyranny of the Guise'), revealing the motivation of the conspiracy. The king, they argued, was too young to govern or to choose his own Council. In such a case the Estates General should intervene to nominate ministers, with the princes of the blood included by right and foreigners (i.e the Guises) excluded altogether. On the other hand, it was important to inform national and international opinion that it

was not just Huguenot noblemen who sought 'to restore the traditional and legitimate government of the realm'.[2] Among the
conspirators were a number of Protestant nobles, but they were
not alone. Pastors such as François de Morel, the minister in Paris,
and men from Geneva, such as Theodore Beza, also took an active part in the plot, although Calvin apparently disapproved. Condé
stayed in the background, leaving the dirty work to the Périgord
gentleman La Renaudie. A group of soldiers recruited outside
the kingdom received orders to head for the Loire valley in order to capture the king and his ministers on 6 March 1560. Incompetent leadership and poor security meant that the plot was
easily foiled by the Guises, who took the king and the Court for
safety to the well-fortified château of Amboise. As the conspirators rolled up in dribs and drabs, royal forces captured them
while their accomplices within the château were clapped in irons.
The remaining attackers were driven off by cannonfire. Rounded
up a little later by the Guise troops, several were slaughtered while
others were bound hand and foot and thrown into the Loire,
and others still were hanged from the portals and battlements of
the castle. Such brutal treatment shocked contemporaries, and
left its mark in the memoirs of some noblemen: Jean de Parthenay-
L'Archevesque, sire de Soubise, overwhelmed by the death of his
friend La Renaudie, went over to Calvinism.

Somewhat disconcerted by the hostile reactions, the Guises
moderated their policy, accepting Michel de L'Hôpital as Chancellor in place of François Olivier. L'Hôpital, of course, published
the Edict of Romorantin in May 1560, giving some respite to the
Huguenots. The Huguenots, encouraged by the progress of Calvinism in Scotland, where Mary of Guise, the Duke's sister, was
unable to keep control, intensified their campaign against the
House of Guise. Pamphlets, leaflets and tracts poured out. The
most violent of them was undoubtedly François Hotman's *L'épitre
envoyée au tigre de la France*. 'Raging tiger! Venomous serpent! Stink-
ing sepulchre! . . . How long will you take advantage of our king's
youth? Is there no end to your inordinate ambition, your imposi-
tions, your embezzlement?' The tone was invariably incisive, revealing the Protestant state of mind. In fact, behind the gentlemen
who took arms in Provence, the Dauphiné and Languedoc, a plot
was afoot to take possession of Lyon. After the setback of Amboise,
Condé was planning to seize power with the aid of the new ecclesiastical institutions of Protestantism. He entered into negotiations

with Germany, Switzerland and England, trying to recruit mercenaries. The second National Synod, held at Poitiers in March 1560, decreed that each synodal province should nominate a noble representative to attend the Court so as to create a counterweight to the Guises. Gentlemen who had fled to Geneva in the aftermath of Amboise now secretly returned to France, heading for provinces where agitation was breaking out. The Huguenot leaders seized control of towns and villages – a strategy developed by Condé and used throughout the first three Wars of Religion. Holding onto these outposts of religious and political resistance, they turned them into autonomous cities, something like Geneva, or the Italian city states under a *podestà*. Nor was the strategy without its logic in the context of the sixteenth-century town, which was often walled and usually governed by a council which enjoyed wide-ranging powers extending into a hinterland occupied by peasants, who worked the land on behalf of the citizens. Provence, the Dauphiné, Guyenne, and even Saintonge were overrun by armed bands led by provincial noblemen, such as Mauvans in Provence, Dupuy-Montbrun in the Dauphiné, Symphorien de Duras in Gascony. Edmée de Maligny led a bold surprise attack on Lyon. The Huguenot troops sacked churches, destroyed the apparatus of Catholic worship, and looted church treasures and plate.

Around the same time, that is from the latter half of 1560 through to 1561, there were widespread peasant revolts against the tithe: in Normandy, around Saint-Lô, in Guyenne (as recorded by Monluc in his *Commentaires*, adding – if this is credible – that they were instigated by Huguenot pastors); and in Saintonge (as recorded by Bernard Palissy), around Nîmes, in the diocese of Auch and elsewhere.[3] These revolts were especially serious in the southern provinces, where the tithe weighed heavily on harvests and the 'gathered churches' of the Reformed faith were thick on the ground.

The Search for Compromise

In the domain of high politics, the assembly of notables which convened at Fontainebleau on 21 August 1560 was an attempt to reestablish consensus at least among the ruling elite. It was a gathering of the high nobility, a sort of enlarged royal Council. Admiral Coligny presented a petition from the persecuted Protestants of Normandy, calling for freedom of conscience and worship.

Jean de Monluc, Bishop of Valence, together with Marillac (Bishop of Vienne) and Morsvilliers (Bishop of Orleans), emphasised that the advance of Calvinism was the fault of the Catholic Church, riddled with abuses and incapable of offering the people spiritual guidance. They called for an assembly of the Estates General and for a national council to reform the Church. More or less veiled criticism of the Guise regime ran through the official statements, while Coligny menacingly announced that he could find 50 000 signatories for the petition he brought. The assembly broke up amid general recognition that a meeting of the Estates General was essential to rally wider support for the monarchy.

An assembly of the Estates was arranged for Orléans in December 1560. The king and his Council installed themselves in the city in November, where, under pressure from the Guises, who were worried by plots, riots, and troop movements, they ordered the arrest of Condé. A special tribunal condemned him to death. But when François II himself died, on 5 December 1560, Parlement and the Estates General appointed Catherine de Medici Regent, as Charles IX was too young to govern.[4] The Guises were ousted from power, and the Estates General remained in session. This was the first gathering of the Estates since 1484, in Charles VIII's reign, before the vast increase in royal authority witnessed under François I and Henri II. The atmosphere was electric. The representatives of the nobility and the Third Estate, some of them Protestants, urged a policy of toleration towards the new religion and called for a thoroughgoing reform of the Church. Despite the desperate appeals of Michel de L'Hôpital for taxes and alienations of church property to cover the 43 million *livres* debt of the Treasury, the deputies refused to vote the necessary supplies, arguing that they were not mandated to do so. The government therefore sent them packing, and ordered a new assembly to gather in a few months' time. The Estates reconvened at Pontoise in August 1561 but with reduced numbers of deputies as, according to a decision taken at Orléans, each order sent but one representative per district. But the financial issue, the reason for the new assembly, was avoided by the Third Estate, whose Speaker reported the fiscal exhaustion of the people through excessive demands. The statement of grievances he brought with him proposed that the royal debt be met by alienations of ecclesiastical property.[5] A programme outlining how the sales could be handled and the yield maximised was produced, showing that the wealth of the Church was not sacrosanct in the eyes of the commons representatives at Pontoise. On the religious question, the commoners again showed themselves in favour of toleration, regarding freedom of conscience as the natural right of the individual: 'The different opinions held by your subjects,' declared the Speaker of the Third Estate, 'proceed from nothing else than their zeal for salvation.'[6]

Catherine de Medici and Michel de L'Hôpital regarded the majority position of the delegates at Orléans and Pontoise as an adequate basis for their policy. The 'contract of Poissy' gave the Treasury a vital shot in the arm just when a certain relaxation of religious tension was getting under way. Among the grandees, Antoine de Bourbon became Lieutenant General of the Realm on 27 March 1561, while his brother Condé was cleared by the Council on 8 March. The Bourbons had thus come to power. By a declaration of January 1562, the gaols were emptied of prisoners of conscience. At the highest levels, preparations were in train for an assembly which would handle religious questions, in response to the demands of the Estates General for the convocation of a national council. While 'papist' attacks on Huguenots shook the kingdom throughout 1561, moderates and Politiques were looking for a compromise between the two religions. And so the Colloquy of Poissy opened on 9 September 1561 with delegates from the Protestant churches facing Catholic theologians and prelates.

This project, of which Catherine de Medici was undoubtedly the instigator, hardly seems extravagant from a twentieth-century viewpoint. On the one hand, the third phase of the Council of Trent had not yet defined dogmas and prescribed rituals with an unprecedented rigour. And on the other, the Peace of Augsburg (1555) in Germany had established, in the wake of the conflict between the German princes, a sort of religious compromise which, even if it horrified a good many people through ruling out a return to religious unity, had at least secured the peoples beyond the Rhine some relief from the tempests unleashed by the Lutheran Reformation. The toleration achieved at Augsburg was the fruit of political necessity rather than principled reflection, but it did put an end – for now – to the problems of the Empire. Finally, in England, Henry VIII had decisively broken with the papacy in 1534, declaring himself Supreme Head of the Church of England and confiscating monastic property; under his daughter

Elizabeth, Anglicanism was on the way to establishing itself as a coherent State religion. The division of the universal Church was thus a fact in Europe. In France, the Crown had disposed of ecclesiastical benefices since 1516 under the Concordat of Bologna, conferring bishoprics and abbeys on whom it chose, with due regard (in theory!) to canon law. It could therefore expect the cooperation of that hierarchy in the formulation of a doctrinal and disciplinary compromise appropriate to the French Church and generally acceptable to the Gallican spirit of the French ruling class. But the Colloquy of Poissy was a setback, as neither the ministers (among them the famous Theodore Beza) nor the prelates (among them the Cardinal of Lorraine) would give an inch on the articles of their faiths, especially not with regard to the Eucharist.

But neither the Regent nor the Chancellor was ready to abandon toleration. Catherine, as we have seen, tried to get from Trent what she had failed to get from Poissy, entrusting her envoys and cardinals with a series of proposals designed to mitigate the doctrinal rigours of both camps. On 17 January 1562, the King's Council confirmed the freedom of conscience already, in practice, acquired by the Huguenots, and granted with it freedom of worship in the suburbs and in private houses. The Edict of January, the 'Magna Carta' of French Protestantism, confirmed its existence as an independent church, and thus gave the seal of legitimacy to the religious division of the realm in the hope of restoring peace.

The regime's hopes were soon shown to be in vain. Foreign nations could not resist the temptation to intervene. On the Catholic side, Spain put pressure on Catherine to stamp out heresy, while Paul IV urged Charles IX to 'spare neither fire nor the sword' in reconciling dissidents to the Church. Geneva for its part despatched platoons of pastors in response to the urgent calls of the nascent churches: 142 were sent in 1561. The spiritual capital of the Huguenots sent in addition bundles of French Bibles, packs of Psalms, and a host of theological, anticlerical, and even political treatises.

Within France the organisation of the Reformed party was perfected in late 1561 and early 1562. Each church was expected to equip, or at least to finance, a horseman. Each synodal province appointed a military commander, each colloquy a colonel, and each church a captain. The framework of an army was thus in place, and the gentlemen who had been demobilised in the wake of Cateau-Cambrésis and frustrated by the military policy of the

Guises, following the grandees such as Condé, Coligny, and even Jeanne d'Albret, could express their discontent and opposition by preparing to take up arms in defence of their religion. At the local level, Huguenots of humbler origin took advantage of the royal decrees of 1561–2 which extended to them first freedom of conscience and then limited freedom of worship, and went on to take over Catholic churches by force. But before celebrating their Genevan rites there, they stripped them of the outward tokens of the old religion.

In the face of what they saw as aggression, the Catholics reacted violently, egged on by preachers who openly decried the Regent and her tolerant religious policy from the pulpits of Paris. A riot broke out at Beauvais in 1561 when the Count-Bishop Odet de Châtillon celebrated a Calvinist communion in his episcopal palace. At the Pré-aux-Clercs in Paris, the students fell on a group of Huguenots in April 1561 and besieged them in the house where they took refuge. Only the intervention of the Provost of Paris prevented a massacre. The Guises tried to ally with the Lutheran princes of Germany, notably the Duke of Württemberg, the better to isolate the French Calvinists; while Montmorency went to Rome to assure the Pope of his total loyalty to the Church.

Vassy and the First War of Religion

The spark awaited with dread by most people (but with anticipation by some) was provided by the massacre perpetrated at Vassy by the troops of the Duke of Guise against some Protestants who had gathered to hear a sermon in a place forbidden under the Edict of January. It took place on 1 March 1562, leaving 23 dead and nearly 100 wounded. Historians have tended to treat this as the official opening of the Wars of Religion, but in fact, as we have seen, they began late in 1559 when the Guises took persecution to new heights and drove the Bourbons onto the defensive.

Welcomed by the Catholics of the Court and the capital, the news of Vassy encouraged Guise to attempt a further coup with the assistance of Montmorency. The royal family was at Fontainebleau on 27 March 1562 when the Duke of Guise arrived with a troop of horse and urged the Regent to return to Paris under their escort, with the king and the Court. Guise knew quite as well as Condé that possession of the king's person was worth 'half of France', and both men were ready to use force to legitimise their faction with that person. Guise's coup forced Condé to go on the offensive, justifying his recourse to arms in the *Déclaration* of 8 April 1562, whose stated aims were the liberation of the king and the Regent from Guise captivity and the enforcement of the Edict of January. But Condé and his noble Protestant followers had in fact been preparing for war, with the support of militant pastors, since the fiasco at Amboise. Throughout 1561 troops had been gathering in the provinces and at Orléans, which had been taken over by the Huguenots and turned into a headquarters of the princely and Protestant cause. Nearly 6000 infantry and 2000 cavalry were there at the beginning of April 1562, while the local churches were preparing to send more, and Coligny's brother François d'Andelot was recruiting *reiters* in Germany.[7]

On the Catholic side the forces were equally ready, although Catherine de Medici was still trying to negotiate with Condé, whom she urged to leave the country with his friends.[8]

The first war was actually fought on two levels: one, which we might call the official, involved confrontations between the regular forces of the Catholics and the Protestants; the other was local and particular, with 'papists' squaring up to Huguenots according to the local rhythms of violence. However, beyond iconoclasm, a mode of action which was fairly rational, not to say educational (aimed as it was at convincing the adherents of the old Church of its errors, abuses, and deviations), on the Protestant side the two planes of intervention formed a coherent whole. Condé, as we know, had since 1560 pursued a plan for taking over the country. As Agrippa d'Aubigné explained, he took over towns in order to create a power block and consolidate his party.[9] For the Huguenots (as later on for the Leaguers), the towns were privileged space, for some a proving ground for the political order advocated by Calvin, for others a traditional space invested anew with the old dreams of communal and mystical solidarity. During the decades of war, the towns were the ground over which the two camps fought both militarily and ideologically, with the countryside remaining largely unmoved by the issues at stake. The peasants, it must be remembered, soon felt an extraordinary weariness with the excesses and exactions of the soldiers of each side, and called a plague on both their houses.

The First War of Religion was entirely typical in the way the towns acted as focuses for both military strategy and religious fanaticism. Condé's plan was largely successful, as, at the local level, he benefited from the spontaneous efforts of Protestant converts determined to conquer their territory for their religion. The civic elites, who were of course inclined to Calvinism, often took advantage of the powers conferred on them by town councils, seeking to exploit municipal liberties – which were always substantial and had hardly been eroded by monarchical authority under François I and Henri II – in order to turn their towns into little Genevas. Some towns rapidly seized by the Huguenots in April and May 1562 were almost as quickly lost again: Rouen, Tours, Blois, Sens, Angers and Beaugency. Elsewhere, in such towns as Toulouse and Bordeaux, Huguenot coups were foiled thanks to the resistance of royal officials in the sovereign courts and committed Catholics at the popular level. And other towns, such as Lyon, Grenoble, Valence, Orléans and Gaillac, were retaken by Catholics after a brief Huguenot occupation. But others still, thanks to a religious consensus among a large part of the inhabitants (sometimes achieved through the expulsion of the Catholics) remained Calvinist, subject to certain nuances consequent upon the application of the various edicts of pacification issued during the troubles: Montauban, La Rochelle, Nîmes, La Charité-sur-Loire, Sancerre, Nérac, Castres, the towns of Béarn, and a host of other centres in the more Protestant regions.

In fact, the Protestants enjoyed runaway success through spring and summer 1562. Towns fell like ripe fruit and entire provinces were won by the swords of Condé's fierce lieutenants. The Rhône valley and the Dauphiné were subdued by the predatory Baron des Adrets. Jacques du Crussol seized towns and territory in Languedoc, as did Symphorien de Duras in Guyenne and Gascony, Paul de Mouvans in Provence, La Rochefoucauld and Pons de Pons in Saintonge, and Montgomery in Normandy. The royalist commanders – Monluc in the south-west, Laurent de Mongiron in the Dauphiné, Tavannes in Burgundy, and Joyeuse in Languedoc – could not withstand this overwhelming assault. But not for long. For the Crown, seeing itself under threat even in areas like Normandy and the Loire valley, where its power was most deeply rooted, managed to break the Huguenot grip. The Constable Montmorency, Antoine de Bourbon and the Duke of Guise directed the military operations. Their first priority was to recover the towns along the Loire. Blois, sacked and pillaged, fell on 4 July; to be followed in August by Bourges, the pivot connecting Condé's base at Orléans with the Midi, where his lieutenants were wreaking havoc. Tavannes was master of the Saône valley by the end of June, while in Poitou Saint-André reoccupied Poitiers. The royal forces were preparing to deal with Orléans when the government learned of the Treaty of Hampton Court made by the Huguenots with Elizabeth I. And on 26 October the Catholic siege of Rouen, in which Antoine de Bourbon met his death, ended in an orgy of rape, murder and looting: the horrors of war were not reserved for conflicts abroad, and were to make frequent appearances during the long years of civil strife.[10]

The Protestant army, reinforced by German *reiters* under François d'Andelot, wheeled around Paris, taking Étampes and Montlhéry and attempting Corbeil on the way, and then made for Normandy in order to rendezvous with the English force. But Montmorency blocked its advance at Dreux. There followed one of the few pitched battles of the war, and a pretty confused one at that. Both Montmorency and Condé were taken prisoner, and Saint-André was killed, leaving Guise the victor: his triumph of 19 December 1562 was celebrated in poems and engravings. Now the sole commander, Guise made for Orléans, which he besieged in early February 1563. But on the eve of the final assault he was assassinated by a Protestant gentleman suspected of being in Coligny's pay.

The death of the Catholic leader marked a hiatus in the military history of the First War of Religion. Catherine de Medici was anxious for peace, though not just any peace: she now had to take account of a Catholic backlash which was not restricted to the King's Council or the clergy. While armed bands ravaged the country in the name of king or Condé, and Protestants tightened their hold on a number of cities, elsewhere Catholic populations were setting upon Huguenot minorities. Need one add that economic conditions were particularly harsh in 1562, explaining the fury and bitterness of the populace? In the Parisian basin prolonged heavy rains prevented the peasants from gathering the harvest, and made the corn germinate on the stalk: grain prices shot up. In the provinces, the price-lists of spring 1562 record incredibly high prices for grain and bread. The poor and even the middling sort went in fear of starvation. Disease broke out in the north, the silent camp-follower of the troops gathered around Orléans and Paris. Hence, 'France was afflicted by the three scourges of God: plague, famine, and civil war.'[11] People were consumed by an anxiety born of fear of the Huguenots, and exacerbated by the problems of everyday existence and the threat of imminent war. Catholic priests fed the flames with spectacular processions of sacred relics and inflammatory sermons against the heretics. Nor were the Huguenot ministers far behind! The air was thick with false rumours (though they could hardly be more disturbing than the truth), which were recorded in crudely illustrated pamphlets and passed on in taverns, markets, and other meeting places. The nerves of the Catholic majority were on edge in these uncertain times, and the figure of the Huguenot presented itself as the culprit which had to be destroyed.

Appalling massacres ensued at Tours, Sens, Troyes, Rouen, Meaux, Toulouse, Gaillac and elsewhere – sometimes in the wake of delivery from a brief Protestant occupation: a tragic foretaste of what was to happen ten years later on the feast of Saint Bartholomew. But spontaneous and irrational though they were, these massacres were generally instigated by higher authority, whether that of priests and preachers, or of royal governors or commanders. In May 1562 it was the preachers of Toulouse who urged their flock, 'Kill and rob them all. We, your fathers, stand surety for you.' And as Denis Crouzet has shown, the triumphal entry of the Duke of Guise into Paris after the massacre at Vassy led to a spate of random killings of individual Huguenots in the city.[12] But a decree issued by the Parlement de Paris on 13 July 1562 (admittedly when hostilities had officially commenced) literally legalised such violence. It put Protestants outside the law and authorised private individuals to punish heretics 'without hindrance, prosecution or interference by the officers of the law'.[13]

At the higher level, the Crown opened negotiations with the imprisoned Condé. The Regent, released from Guise tutelage by the Duke's death, reckoned she was in a position to dictate terms to the Protestants, for she no longer felt at the mercy of a faction and, paradoxically, felt at the same time strengthened by the more or less spontaneous Catholic backlash in the towns and provinces. The Edict of Amboise, signed on 19 March 1563, was on the whole a setback for the Protestant cause.[14] Although freedom of conscience was not violated, freedom of worship was drastically reduced: it was conceded to gentlemen within their households; and to seigneurs with powers of *haute justice* with respect to both their households and their jurisdictions. But humbler Protestants were allowed only one place of worship per bailiwick, and that only in suburban areas. Nevertheless, in towns where the Reformed religion had been practised within the walls until 7 March 1562, it was permitted to continue on condition that no attempt was made to take over churches. Protestant worship was forbidden in Paris and the surrounding area.

The aristocratic character of this edict was obvious to all, except perhaps its beneficiaries. Coligny is said to have reproached Condé bitterly for its terms, and the Genevan authorities certainly did. Here and there, civic elites accused Condé of having betrayed them and their cause, but such discontent reflected not so much the disappointment of their revolutionary hopes of changing the world, as the vitality of a piety frustrated by the restrictions now imposed on its collective expression.

The King Visits His Kingdom

From March 1563 to spring 1567 the kingdom enjoyed a degree of peace. In July 1563 the recapture of Le Havre by Montmorency, with Condé's assistance, healed the wounds inflicted on national pride by the Treaty of Hampton Court. Afterwards, Catherine de Medici took Charles IX to Rouen, a city which symbolised the recent troubles, where the Parlement declared that he had reached the age of majority. From now on the king was a king indeed: henceforth neither faction could justify imposing their will on the Crown on the grounds of his youth. The government now tried to take the country in hand. The Edict of Crémieu, issued in July 1564, put municipal elections under royal supervision, for the Council knew how important control of towns was to the rival factions.[15] A little later, in 1566, an assembly met at Moulins, a sort of royal council supplemented by the Presidents of the Parlements, to discuss questions of justice. The great ordinance drafted by Michel de L'Hôpital in the wake of that meeting reestablished (at least on paper) such prerogatives of the State as had been usurped in the course of the troubles. The cities and their councils were once more placed under royal supervision, and were relieved of civil jurisdiction, retaining only a basic policing function (article 71). Although the ordinance did not enjoy total success, as a number of towns appealed to ancient royal privileges and refused to submit, it at least breached the defences of the civic elites. The Parlements also felt the firm hand of royal authority. The reluctance with which they had registered the Edict of Amboise is well known, as is their general hostility to religious toleration. Their right of remonstrance was now re-defined and restricted, and the registration of edicts became com-pulsory even when the king refused to take account of the grievances of the sovereign courts. Moreover, edicts were to be observed and enforced even if they had not yet been registered. The monarchy thus made its authoritarian aspirations plain, even though it still lacked the means to put them into effect. Urban and provincial governors, recruited from that nobility which had just given free rein to its innate violence and turbulence, were likewise subjected to restraints. They were forbidden to levy taxes without royal warrant, to dispense justice at the expense of royal officials, or to hinder the latter in any way. The *maîtres de requêtes*, loyal agents of the Crown, were to make judicial tours of inspec-tion in order to monitor the performance of the governors, who tended to be transformed in periods of disorder into local magnates.

The financial crisis remained acute, intensified by the arrears of pay owed to the troops, notably to the Swiss infantry hired to deal with Condé. Over and above the financial agreement made between the Crown and the Church at Poissy, the King's Council ordered in May 1563 an alienation of church property worth some 5 million *livres* a year. A further alienation worth 2.5 million *livres* was authorised in 1568 by Pope Paul V, on condition that the revenue go towards waging war on the heretics.[16]

Assisted by Michel de l'Hôpital and the Council, the Regent was making heroic efforts to impose royal authority on sectional interests, efforts which were crowned by the famous tour of the kingdom which the royal family undertook with the Court be-tween 1564 and 1566.[17] The object of the exercise was to present to his subjects the anointed king, who had now attained his ma-jority. Throughout his long peregrination, Charles IX assiduously fulfilled the role of the thaumaturgic king in touching for the 'King's Evil'. The journey was meant to bolster the royal author-ity, which had recently been contested, and it is easy to under-stand why the immense train lingered in the southern provinces, where the Protestants were numerous and political or social cri-sis had reared its head. But could the cracks in the façade be so easily papered over?

The unity which had been damaged by the recent religious conflict could not be rebuilt as easily as the regime hoped. The cult of monarchy was not enough to heal the wounds. The nobility remained characteristically belligerent. So while Huguenots at Court regained their duties and positions, their Catholic counterparts scarcely concealed their distrust for them. Henri d'Anjou (later Henri III) flatly refused to accept Condé as Lieutenant-General of the Realm, and François d'Andelot could not command the loyalty of his Catholic subordinates. Such dissensions could easily end in brawls and murders. The Parlements were reluctant to register the Edict of Amboise, which was therefore not implemented at the grass roots, arguing that religious coexistence was unholy if not impossible. Where Protestants were a minority, the local authorities refused to restore the goods stolen or confiscated from them. And when they gathered for sermons in the suburbs, Catholics pursued them with taunts and blows to break up their meetings. On the other hand, Protestant gentlemen defied the Edict, to keep a tight hold on the church lands and rents they had seized during the war, while sporadic iconoclastic riots continued to break out, as at Pamiers in 1566.

Foreign powers continued to keep their eyes on France. The Pope expressed his despair at the Edict of Amboise, while Philip II of Spain, married as he was to a daughter of Henri II and Catherine, worried about the presence of French Protestantism on the borders of Spain and even more of Flanders, itself torn by religious dissensions since the 1520s. During the famous Bayonne meeting (June–July 1565), the Duke of Alba proposed in Philip's name a Franco-Spanish alliance against the heretics. But Catherine, as far as historians can tell, held back, undertaking merely to seek some remedy for the religious problems. Some months later, the 'iconoclastic fury' broke out in the Netherlands, a wave of ferocious aggression against the outward signs of Catholicism, which left many churches and monasteries in ruins.[18] This storm, in which the Huguenots of France took a close interest, led to the despatch of Alba to the Netherlands at the head of an enormous Spanish force, which marched along the eastern borders of France. Even the French government was disturbed by the presence of this army on its borders, while the French Protestants were terrified. They had not forgotten the secret meeting at Bayonne, and the fears which it had aroused continued to obsess them. They were further troubled by the Swiss mercenaries the Crown hired to shadow Alba's march. Could they be intended for use against the enemy within rather than against the forces headed for the Netherlands? This climate of fear fostered a mutual distrust in the provinces and at the centre which was to dog the French for forty years. From the humblest subject to the highest seigneur, everyone suspected his or her neighbour of dark designs, and too often the riposte preempted the coup.

The Second and Third Wars of Religion

Once again it was the Huguenots who took the initiative by resorting to arms. Condé was no longer the hidden hand, as in the conspiracy of Amboise, and he was actively supported by Coligny, ever more obviously his second in command. They mobilised their troops, levied contributions from the churches, and sent orders throughout the kingdom for a rendezvous in the area of Rosay-en-Brie, where soldiers mainly from the south and west duly gathered. The strategy they pursued underlined again how Protestantism, once transformed into a faction, was exploited for baronial political interests rather than religious objectives. As in the fiasco at Amboise and the more successful coup of the Triumvirate at Fontainebleau, the idea was to seize the king's person and dictate the composition of his Council – in this case, to Huguenot advantage. Condé, characteristically solicitous for his national and international image, published lengthy protestations in both 1567 and 1568, accusing the king of discriminating against the Huguenot nobility and depriving them of the 'degree, estate, and honour' due to their rank.[19] His propaganda demanded an immediate recall of the Estates General, the only institution capable of standing above religious divisions and uniting the country in pursuit of the common good which his forces were ready to promote. The Huguenots at the grass roots complained that these manifestos said nothing about toleration for all, but were concerned only for the aristocracy. But the nobles replied unabashed that the aristocracy mattered more than the common herd because the former exercised the responsibilities of government.

For the civilian populations, the military operations of the second war had the advantage of being short-lived and relatively limited. Forewarned of the Huguenot rendezvous, the Court hurriedly left the château of Monceaux for the more easily defensible town of Meaux, and then headed for Paris with an escort of Swiss mercenaries. Condé's cavalry harried the royal convoy, which only reached Paris thanks to its Swiss escort. The chronicles record the fury of the Regent and the king, who relieved L'Hôpital of the seals now that his policy of toleration had collapsed. Condé's army cut off the capital, which was thus put in danger of famine, while Montmorency sought to break his hold. The result was an indecisive engagement at Saint-Denis on 10 November 1567, significant only as the occasion of the Constable's death. Condé and Coligny, their forces now reinforced by mercenaries under the command of John Casimir (the son of the devoutly Calvinist Elector Palatine), set about besieging Chartres, the granary of Paris, in order to put further pressure on the government. Negotiations were soon under way, and led in March 1568 to the Peace of Longjumeau, which reiterated the provisions of the Edict of Amboise.

Neither Protestants nor Catholics could understand the peace which was so hurriedly agreed between the government and a clique of Huguenot princes. At the grass roots both sides thought the timing bad. Roman Catholics felt overwhelmed by the Protestant tide as they formed leagues and confraternities at the local level and welcomed back into their ranks defectors from the rival church who wished to return to the old faith. Among them were gentlemen who brought their tenantry and peasantry with them, and citizens of towns in which the Huguenot minority was too small to hold out against the hostile population. In the Ile-de-France, Champagne, the Loire valley and Burgundy, the sparks lit by the Calvinist flash-fire of 1559–62 went out. In Normandy, ravaged by war since the start of the troubles, exhaustion and the inconvenience of belonging to a religious and ethical minority disheartened many converts. But in the southern provinces, those of the *langue d'oc* to which Saintonge, Aunis, and southern Poitou had long been closely connected, Protestantism consolidated its position during the second war. A series of towns which the Edict of Amboise had returned to Crown and Church now fell once more under Huguenot control, while further towns also fell into their hands. The 'Michelade' of Nîmes in September 1567, so called because the nobles chose to give battle on Michaelmas (29 September), was tragic proof that the furious hatred of the 'warriors of God' against the adherents and symbols of the 'great Babylon' was far from being assuaged.[20] In the wake of the Peace of Longjumeau, the Huguenot towns complained bitterly that Condé had sold them out. Armed bands, led by gentlemen whom the brief peace had sent back to their estates, resumed their usual habits of pillage and destruction, seizing a village here or a château there. The hinterlands of Montpellier, Montauban and La Rochelle were crawling with soldiers.

It was neither from Condé nor from the banks of the Loire that the signal came for a fresh offensive. It was from the strongly Protestant provinces of the south which looked towards the Queen of Navarre. She had set out from Béarn for La Rochelle in summer 1568, accompanied by a force of Gascon nobles and her son Henri de Navarre. La Rochelle, its security guaranteed by its access to the sea and English support, and its needs for men and money supplied by the abundance of Protestant churches in the surrounding area, was already emerging as one of the symbolic citadels of French Protestantism. When Jeanne d'Albret arrived, she found Condé and Coligny already there, having abandoned their Burgundian châteaux, whose walls offered inadequate protection against the assassin's dagger.

Charles IX and his mother, meanwhile, convinced of the failure of the experiment in toleration, were now bent on harsher measures. Was the murder of the Huguenot leaders conceived then? Their fear of Condé and the Admiral certainly makes it credible. In any case, they were confirmed in their general attitude by the more or less spontaneous demonstrations of Catholic belligerence, and by developments in the Netherlands, where Alba's government had made a holocaust of Flemish iconoclasts and executed two young noblemen of high birth – the counts of Hoorn and Egmont – as an example to the rest. William of Orange himself, heart and soul of the Dutch revolt, had but narrowly escaped the death sentence. In order to deliver a blow at the emerging alliance between the Midi and the House of Albret, Charles and Catherine decided to invoke the ancient feudal law of seisin against the Queen of Navarre. She was stripped of her fiefs as a felonious vassal, and the Parlement of Toulouse was instructed to put this sentence into effect. The king could theoretically do nothing about her sovereign territories of Béarn and Navarre, which were outside French jurisdiction. But he decreed that during her 'captivity' in La Rochelle, they should be occupied by royal troops in order to protect them against foreign invasion. L'Hôpital was no longer at the Council board, and the time for patience and reconciliation was past.

The third war was fought not in the old Capetian heartlands but in the mid-west and the Midi, regions of deep-rooted particularism (was not their adherence to another religion than that of the State proof enough of this?) and traditional loyalty to the d'Albret. The rival armies clashed indecisively south of Poitou in October 1568, and then retired to winter quarters. In spring, royal forces led by the youthful Anjou (assisted by the battle-hardened Marshal Tavannes) inflicted a crushing defeat on the Huguenots under Condé and Coligny at Jarnac. The chroniclers, always on the lookout for heroic or tragic deaths, grieve across the centuries over the fate of Louis de Condé, assassinated against all the laws of chivalry on the express orders of Anjou – whose crime was no better or worse than all the others committed by a noble class theoretically dedicated to the chivalric ideal, but in fact taking full advantage of the opportunities presented by civil and religious conflict. The king's brother thus made himself the second figure in the kingdom, eliminating a political intruder. But the army of the Huguenots was not decimated. Coligny remained, surrounded by the captains and troops of Gascony, Languedoc and Provence. He waited for the *reiters* who were preparing to enter the kingdom from Franche-Comté. But in the second battle, which took place at Moncontour in October, Anjou again got the better of his Huguenot opponents. Coligny, now the leader of the Huguenot faction, tried to repair the damage. Having rebuilt his army in Guyenne and Languedoc, he carried out reprisals in the Toulousan plain and then, after a campaign as terrible for its civilian victims as it was tiring for its perpetrators, headed for La-Charité-sur-Loire, but a few hours by horse from Paris and the centre of royal power. With the capital under threat once more, the seafarers of La Rochelle and the Dutch Sea-Beggars waging an unrestricted war of privateering, and the royal Treasury drained by the recent military operations, Charles IX and his mother simply did not have the resources to follow through the hardline policy on which they had embarked two years earlier. They were obliged to negotiate under pretty unfavourable conditions because Coligny's strategic talents had made up for the setbacks at Jarnac and Moncontour. Nor were they simply military threats that were faced by a Crown which aspired to stand above faction. Was not Henri de Guise on the point of winning the hand of Marguerite de Navarre? The Catholic leaders regarded the prospect of an alliance between the House of Lorraine and the royal family with some satisfaction. But Charles and Catherine would not buy it at any price, seeing very clearly the dangers such a course held for the monarchy, and the Guises found themselves briefly dismissed from Court.

Everything was pointing towards peace, and events in the Netherlands were attracting the attention of the French regime just as those in France had attracted foreign eyes. Representatives of the Protestant faction and the Crown met in the château of Saint-Germain-en-Laye. The Huguenots were granted freedom of conscience, together with freedom of worship in those places where it had been established before the war. In addition, it would be permitted in the suburbs of two cities per district and in the chapels of seigneurs enjoying rights of *haute justice*. As surety for the implementation of the treaty, the Protestants were granted four strongholds for two years: Montauban, La Rochelle, Cognac, and La Charité-sur-Loire.

The edict seemed strange to Catholics, as they did not think the Huguenot faction was strong enough to win such favourable terms. Monluc, who had been campaigning in Guyenne, complained that what the Protestants had lost by the sword they had regained by the pen. Claude Haton, the curate of Provins, by calling and temperament a committed Leaguer, had this to say in his memoirs: 'The peace made with the Admiral and his adherents seemed, and indeed was, highly favourable to the Huguenot cause.' But for two years the kingdom was to enjoy once more a degree of peace.

13 The Massacre of Saint Bartholomew and the Baronial Wars, 1570–84

The massacre of Saint Bartholomew's day was the turning-point of the period. In retrospect, everything beforehand seems to point towards it, and everything afterwards seems to be shaped and determined by what people saw and remembered of that day.

It would undoubtedly be futile to dig too deep in search of its causes. On the eve of the massacre nobody knew that it was about to unfold, for it was unpremeditated. But there is still some point in sketching its background, or at least looking at what floated to the surface of the historical pot in which the ingredients of those days of 'sound and fury' were bubbling and blending together.

The Background of the Massacre

As with the whole course of the wars, one must distinguish two levels of historical experience which, like geological strata, lay one upon the other. In those tense and anxious times, with famine, disease and disorder on all sides, the townsfolk, briefed with biased information, reacted with astonishing vigour and extravagance to the directions they received from the political authorities. It was as though a political amplifier magnified the slightest signal from the centres of power. Rarely were people more responsive to the lead of their superiors. In the midst of the collapse of traditional institutions, their hopes for a remedy to the religious divisions led them to seek on the one hand trusty guides or gurus, and on the other culprits or at least scapegoats.

The Peace of Saint-Germain left the Catholics staggered. The Huguenots returned to the towns they had fled during the second and third wars, recovered their offices, and sought to recover their sequestered goods. Moreover, for the first time they practised their religion in the city centres (previously they had been confined to the suburbs). Their resurgence re-ignited old hatreds, and Catholics set upon Protestants in Dieppe, Rouen, Troyes, Sens, Orange and Paris rather as they had done in 1562. Between spring 1571 and autumn 1573 grain prices rose continually. A similar dislocation had occurred in 1563, and it was worse in 1572–3. The doubling, tripling, or even quadrupling of the price of bread in a matter of months, the result of poor harvests, meant that towns were flooded with desperate refugees from the countryside, and a general malnutrition set nerves on edge and shortened tempers. Unemployment among wage-earners, journeymen and labourers, the inevitable concomitant of urban subsistence crises, filled the streets and the squares with idle men whose tempers were hardly soothed by the oppressive heat of the 1572 summer.

The arrival of Gaspard de Coligny at the Council board in autumn 1571 did not counteract the influence of the Catholic councillors, foremost among them the Duke of Guise, the Cardinal of Lorraine, and Marshal Tavannes. The Court and the Council were preoccupied with two matters in the wake of the Peace of Saint-Germain: at home, the marriage of Henri de Navarre; and abroad, the prospect of French intervention in the Netherlands.

The Netherlands had been in political and religious ferment since the 1560s. Led by William of Nassau, Prince of Orange and governor in Philip II's name of the provinces of Zeeland, Utrecht and Holland, the Calvinists were laying claim to political and religious freedom. Their number included not only nobles, merchants and craftsmen, but also people from the humblest backgrounds – the latter largely responsible for the wave of iconoclasm in summer 1566. There was a certain similarity between the Huguenot faction in France and its Dutch counterpart. They shared the same 'presbyterosynodal' ecclesiastical system and the same party organisation based on a flexible federation of churches, cities and provinces (in the Dutch case, predominantly in the north). Both factions were loyal to a grandee who held a major Crown office, and both deployed the same mixture of political and religious themes in unleashing rebellion. The repressive policies pursued by the Catholic authorities in each country led to convergence between the two Protestant factions. Contacts, meetings and alliances were established between Condé and Coligny on the one side and Orange on the other. Orange sent troops to Coligny's aid during the third conflict, and the seafarers of La Rochelle, Flanders and Holland had cooperated for years in piracy against Spanish shipping in the Atlantic.

In April 1572 the 'Sea Beggars' took possession of the port of Brill and thus gained control of Holland and the coast. Holland then reopened hostilities against Philip II, its provincial estates voting taxes for the rebel army and legislating to introduce religious freedom. Armed resistance to Spanish domination broke out by land and sea. The European powers kept a close watch on this thorn in the side of the Spanish colossus, although the Holy League's victory over the Turkish fleet at Lepanto, on 7 October 1571, confirmed His Catholic Majesty as the leader of the Catholic nations against the Protestants.

In France the Huguenot grandees sought to persuade the king by means of Coligny, their spokesman on the Council, to intervene against Philip in the Netherlands. Sectarian solidarity apart, they realised that a foreign war might heal the divisions which the recent troubles had fomented among the French aristocracy. And it would have the added advantage of resuming, after an interval of ten years of civil war, the expansionist policy which François I and Henri II had so eagerly pursued at the expense of the Habsburgs. Finally, on a more personal level, fighting for the king in a foreign land would erase the bitter memory of divided loyalties that had vexed Huguenot gentlemen since 1559. Even before Coligny proposed an official French intervention to the Council in summer 1572, Protestant gentlemen were preparing to intervene in a private capacity.

On the other main issue of the year, Charles IX and Catherine de Medici were seeking a rapprochement between the ruling house and the house of Bourbon, which had directed hostilities against the Crown for ten years. The marriage between the King's sister Marguerite and Henri de Navarre symbolised the burying of the hatchet. Jeanne d'Albret, mother of the groom, had no objections to a marriage which she thought befitted her son's rank as a prince of the blood, especially as the possibility of this matrimonial alliance had first been raised by Henri II himself. In his view, as in that of Charles and Catherine, it was a matter of tightening the links between the Crown and a powerful feudal dynasty with a large following of clients, vassals and dependants, Protestant or not. There was also the matter of establishing a firmer hold over those provinces of the south- and mid-west which had been largely loyal to the Bourbon cause since the troubles began. And finally, there was the hope of a lasting settlement which would give the people the peace they required, and allow the royal Treasury to recover from the debilitating effects of the recent wars.

The Massacre of Saint Bartholomew

The marriage took place at Paris on 18 August 1572, with the Pope having promised a dispensation for this union of Catholic and Huguenot (though it did not arrive until after the ceremony). But the ingredients which would explode so violently a few days later were already present. The most obvious, and that which detonated the explosion, was the split over foreign policy in both Council and Court. Should France intervene or not in order to assist the Protestant rebels of the Netherlands under William of Orange against the colonial domination of Catholic Spain?

The Protestant nobility, of course, had no doubts. But the arguments for non-intervention were far from negligible. To attack Spain, the champion of European Catholicism, would align France with the Protestant powers of England and Germany and alienate the papacy. It would also give extra weight to the French Protestants in the government and the country as a whole, in effect acknowledging their leadership of foreign policy. The doves therefore included Catherine de Medici and her Italian friends (Nevers, Gondi and Birague) as well as Anjou, Tavannes, and the Guise brothers. Perhaps Charles IX was also of their number, but he was not averse to giving guarded encouragement to the hawks.

The international situation changed suddenly in the course of 1572 when a band of Huguenot nobles, who had gone to the aid of their co-religionists, found themselves besieged in Mons by Alba, the governor of the Netherlands. This focused the issues that faced the French Council. Should they assist the unfortunate soldiers, whom Coligny regarded as the vanguard of a royal army, or should they abandon men whom Catherine saw as mercenaries acting on their own account? The French Protestant troops were cut down near the frontier on 17 July 1572, and letters found on the corpse of their leader, Genlis, proved that Charles IX had promised them his protection. It presented Philip II with a perfect *casus belli*, should he wish to open hostilities with France, a country which in his view was too divided over religion.

The unfolding of the events which made up that State crime and bloody popular pogrom we call the Massacre of Saint Bartholomew are shrouded in shadow.[1] Then as now, camouflage is *de rigueur* in such matters, and there are few enough written sources – apart from the memoirs of those involved in the events, which must always be read with caution.

The marriage between Henri de Navarre and Marguerite de Valois was celebrated amidst spectacular festivities. Four days later, on Friday 22 August, a hidden gunman fired at Gaspard de Châtillon, the Admiral of France. Coligny survived, but who gave the orders for the attempt on his life which sparked off the whole train of events? We know the name of the inept assassin – Maurevert. And we know the owner of the house in which he lay in wait for his victim – a servant of the Guise. Tradition has generally credited Catherine de Medici with responsibility for the bungled murder, but the assassin might just as easily have been in the pay of Alba, Anjou, Guise, or even the Duke of Savoy. The Admiral had plenty of enemies: the Guises, out to revenge the assassination of Duke François; or the Spanish, keen to forestall his plans for intervention in the Netherlands. The violence of the time did not confine itself to pitched battles or mob violence. It also involved, as we have seen, dramatic assassinations of symbolic individuals whose charisma and influence so focused the admiration of one side and the hatred of the other that their elimination represented a defeat for the entire faction with which they were identified.

The Protestant nobility who had come to the capital for the wedding were furious, and threatened dire vengeance against the king and his mother should the attempted murder go unpunished. Panic seized the royal family and the Council, understandably in view of the coups which had been essayed by Protestants and Catholics alike in the preceding decade. Did they perhaps also think that the attempt on Coligny was a Spanish warning against intervention in the Netherlands? At any rate, on the night of 23–4 August it was decided to launch a preemptive strike against the Protestant nobility gathered in Paris. It was a palace coup, the reflex reaction of a regime with its back to the wall, caught between the rival pressures of the Huguenot leaders and the Spanish ambassadors, facing the risks of civil war on the one hand and war with Spain on the other. The point of eliminating the leaders of the Reformed faction was to forestall further religious conflict and to reassure Philip II of French commitment to Catholicism. In 1588, when the Crown was at the mercy of a hardline Catholic faction, Henri III resorted to similar methods to rid himself of the Guise leaders of the League.

Feeling that extreme options were all that was left, the Crown availed itself, amid the confusion, of the policy of extermination advocated by hardline Catholics. In so doing, it unwittingly unleashed an irresistible groundswell of hate which swept the people of Paris into an orgy of slaughter. Paris had nurtured a hatred of the Protestants ever since, in the earliest days of the Reformation, converts had damaged statues of the Virgin in various parts of the city. This hatred had deepened, first as psalms began to ring out from the great Huguenot assemblies like that of Pré-aux-Clercs in 1558, and then during the second conflict as Condé's troops laid siege to the capital. The Parisians had been listening for years, and especially in recent months, to preachers who, experienced in the ways of the word, had stormed against the conciliatory policy of the government, a policy embodied in the 'detestable union' of Henri de Navarre with Marguerite de Valois. The atmosphere in the capital was electric. There was an oppressive, stormy heat, the water in the public fountains was running low, and the town was severely overcrowded. The Court was awash with noblemen in town for the marriage. The survivors of the Protestant expeditionary force to the Netherlands were wandering the streets, and the Huguenot leaders were perhaps already organising a further expedition in aid of William of Orange. The echoes of the revelry in the Louvre, the Tuileries, and the episcopal palace, and the incessant comings and goings around the Court, gave a frenetic tone to the general atmosphere.

On the evening of 23 August the regime called on the urban militia, which shared the general sentiments with regard to the Huguenots, especially as its commander, the former Mayor Claude Marcel, along with many other citizens and militiamen, had profited from the confiscations of Huguenot property during the recent conflicts. The security of their gains was jeopardised by the compulsory restitution required by a clause of the Peace of

Saint-Germain. Restitution was to apply to public office as well as real estate and movable property, provoking enormous resentment and widespread looting in the course of the massacre.

Claude Marcel, accompanied by the incumbent Mayor, was summoned to the Louvre on the evening of 23 August. 1572. They were instructed to take security precautions: to assemble the militia, to seal the gates of the city, and to make fast all ships in order to halt traffic on the Seine. Were these measures taken with a view to eliminating the Huguenot nobility, or simply to forestalling the action which the Council and the royal family feared on their part? It remains one of the many mysteries of those tragic days.

When the urban militia, assembled in the square before the Hôtel-de-Ville, became aware of the killings going on in the Louvre, in the hôtel on the Rue de Béthisy where Coligny was staying with his friends, and in the houses where the noble companions and vassals of Navarre were staying, they concluded that the king was at last fulfilling his obligation to eliminate heretics. This was the signal for which they had waited ten years, official authorisation for cleansing the land of France from the 'pollution' of Protestantism (not to mention venting their frustrations over the confiscations!). The massacre, in the form of a royally sanctioned pogrom, unfolded in horrific murders and a ritualised violence of purification and sacrifice. The witnesses – even Catholics, even hardline Catholics – were horrified. Their mutually corroborative accounts allow us to picture the deeds of a mob aroused to fever pitch by religious fanaticism and economic grievances.

As and when news of the 'Parisian matins' reached the provinces, carnage broke out in other cities where the Huguenot minorities had made their presence all too obvious in the preceding decade. Orléans, Meaux, Bourges, Saumur, Angers, Lyon, Troyes, Rouen, Toulouse, Gaillac and Bordeaux all had their killings, looting, and general settling of scores. 'Saint-Bartholomew was not a day,' wrote Michelet, 'it was a season.'

The body count is hard to assess. The figures suggested by contemporaries ranged from 2000 to 100 000, but they corresponded more to the indignation – or enthusiasm! – of the witnesses than to reality. A conservative estimate might be some 5000 victims across the kingdom as a whole, at least 2000 of them in Paris alone (representing 1 per cent of its population), with some 50 noblemen assassinated in the government operation.

Afterwards, while the killings went on in Paris despite appeals for calm from both the royal and city councils, and despite the measures taken against murderers and looters, the royal family appeared in Parlement on 26 August. Charles IX acknowledged in a declaration issued some days later that 'what has happened was performed on his express orders . . . in order to forestall and frustrate the execution of a wicked and detestable conspiracy devised by the said Admiral . . . and his followers and accomplices'. The king took official responsibility for the coup and lent a cloak of respectability to the popular bloodbath, in what was either an attempt to restore a monarchical authority jeopardised by the atavistic reaction of a people exercising its divine right to punish the heretical authors of cosmic disorder, or else a pathetic affirmation of the Crown's omnipotence. The grim notion of 'raison d'État' arose in these tragic circumstances, justifying the coup and taking responsibility for the fanaticism of the murderers.

The Consequences of the Massacre

Charles IX stuck to his guns, maintaining that the massacre, in punishing the Huguenot conspirators, was a lawful exercise of royal justice. In October he had two survivors of the massacre arrested, tried, and publicly executed: Arnaud de Cavaignes, a Councillor in the Parlement de Paris, and François de Beauvais, sire de Briquemaut. On his orders the Parlement, which sentenced both men to death, also instituted posthumous proceedings against Coligny as the ringleader of the conspiracy. Sentence was duly passed – a second death for the Admiral! – stipulating that his coat of arms should be defaced and his portrait smashed and trodden underfoot by the public hangman, that his goods should be confiscated and his descendants stripped of their noble rank, and that his château of Châtillon-sur-Loing should be razed and the ground on which it stood salted to render it sterile.

The king used similar logic to solve the problem of the Huguenots taken prisoner by Alba or else besieged by him in the fortress of Mons. Charles IX's ambassador in Brussels demanded that the Spanish governor put these 'rebellious subjects' to death. Alba promptly opened negotiations with the besieged, agreed to let them leave Mons with the honours of war, and left them free to return home. But Charles, pursuing the same remorseless logic, instructed the Duke of Longueville to ambush them at the frontier in Picardy. 'Do not permit these factious subjects to reenter my kingdom, but fall upon them', wrote the king. The operation was carried out as planned, and there were few survivors.

Among Huguenots, news of the massacre aroused sheer, horrified amazement. Flight seemed the only option, and once more they left their towns for less dangerous lands: England, Germany, the Netherlands, and above all Switzerland and Geneva. There was also internal migration, as Huguenots from north of the Loire and of Lyon fled to the Midi, and those of Bordeaux headed for Béarn. Nor were the refugees drawn predominantly from the lowest classes, as they had been in the bouts of repression under François I and Henri II. They included gentlemen, lawyers, clerics, scholars, printers and booksellers. But for others, overcome by fear, abjuration seemed the only safe course. Beza lamented the incredible number of defections, which brought joy to the heart of Villars, the king's Lieutenant-General in Guyenne. The American historian Philip Benedict has estimated the number at 3000 – a figure probably too low, but still considerable.[2] Emigration and conversion seriously weakened the Protestant communities, especially those of northern France, of Normandy, Burgundy, and the Loire valley, which had never been thick enough on the ground to establish a coherent and distinctively Huguenot social fabric.

Once the moment of paralysing fear had passed, the Protestants of the mid-west and the Midi organised themselves for resistance. A host of informal gatherings, which took place without the assistance of powerful noblemen (because they had either been killed, or, like Navarre and his cousin Henri de Condé, had been made prisoners at Court and compelled to abjure) laid the foundations of a separate and autonomous State, the United Provinces of the Midi. An assembly at Anduze laid down the constitution of this strange State in February 1573: 'by provision and in expectation of the just will and liberty of the king with the restoration of the good State, public power and authority will be reclaimed, preserved, and exercised by the country according to the advice and deliberations of the Estates'. Sovereignty, then, was transferred from a king seen as a criminal (or as a puppet) to the Estates General (a periodic representative assembly consisting of elected deputies from each province sworn to the Protestant Union). The policy of supervision of the monarchy, at which the Huguenots had aimed for more than ten years, and which their princes of the blood and great nobles had sought to impose in three civil wars, had been exploded by the bloody events of August 1572. Henceforth the Huguenots would form an independent body, a separate State. The Estates General, known by historians as 'political assemblies', assumed the right to appoint a 'Protector' in charge of military affairs, together with a permanent advisory council, a sort of permanent executive. The Protector virtually chose himself: at first it had to be Henri de Condé, son of Louis, who had escaped from Court. And when, in 1576, Navarre escaped in his turn, he took over.

In writing of the United Provinces of the Midi, we have called them a federal republic, because each province enjoyed considerable freedom of action in its internal affairs. Governed by an annually elected chamber, on which depended a permanent general council, each province controlled its own finances, judiciary (with bipartite chambers, and occasionally the royal *présidiaux*, taking the place of the Parlements for the Huguenots) and military organisation. At the local level, the towns and villages, with their hinterlands, preserved their almost autonomous status, which the Valois regime had left largely intact. Civic authorities governed their territories, performing police functions, sometimes dispensing justice, and managing the allocation and collection of royal taxes (now paid to the Protestant Union). To these revenues were added indirect taxes (*aides* and the *gabelle*), the rents of confiscated church property, and the extraordinary contributions levied through the Huguenot churches. The financial administration was in the hands of accountants and receivers at the federal, provincial, and local levels.[3]

Except for the transfer of sovereignty to the elected assembly of the Estates General, the new regime hardly constituted a dramatic break with tradition. The provinces had long possessed their own assemblies, part of the traditional administrative machinery, responsible for allocating and collecting direct taxes on behalf of central government. And urban communities likewise enjoyed their 'liberties'. The political settlement which the Protestants had sought since the outbreak of the troubles, and which they had not been able to secure through influence on the King's Council, was at last achieved in 1573 through the administrative organisation of the regions controlled by the United Provinces of the Midi. But the geography of the federation was none the less a weakness of the Huguenot State. It was a fragmentary agglomeration of towns and regions with strong concentrations of Protestants, but it included pockets of 'peaceable Catholics'. Parts of the Dauphiné, Languedoc, the Cévennes, Guyenne, Saintonge, Aunis, and Angoumois, together with Béarn, were under its jurisdiction, but no entire provinces. So there was a duplication of administrative and fiscal structures in these regions, as there remained men and institutions loyal to the Crown. This in turn added a new dimension of division to the many fractures with which the monarchical structure was already riven.

Another form of resistance to 'tyranny' was the recourse to arms throughout the Midi. Towns closed their gates against the king's representatives, and the provincial gentry, though less prestigious than the nobility which had just been decimated, raised troops and took possession of towns and castles in the Cévennes and Vivarais. The symbolic citadel of this new wave of belligerence was La Rochelle, overflowing with refugees, including a troop of some 50 Huguenot pastors. The port refused entry to Marshal de Biron, sent as governor in the king's name, and appealed to Elizabeth I for aid, offering in exchange sovereignty over Guyenne, 'which from time immemorial has belonged and been subject to you'. The fourth conflict commenced in February 1573, when the royal army laid siege to the rebellious city. Anjou led the siege, during which La Rochelle underwent extremes of religious fervour, defensive zeal, exaltation and deprivation – famine conditions soon prevailed. Repeated assaults in April failed to win the city, which, exhausted and unsupported from the sea as it was, ought certainly to have been taken. It owed its survival first to the political tensions which prevailed in the besiegers' camp, where noble commanders grumbled about Charles IX's machinations, and secondly to the arrival of a messenger with news of Henri d'Anjou's election to the crown of Poland. In the same way, in autumn 1572 and spring 1573, Sancerre had refused to accept a governor sent by the king and had undergone a terrible siege, vigorously prosecuted by Marshal de La Châtre. La Châtre negotiated the surrender of the city in August 1573, sparing the citizens and conceding them freedom of worship. A few days earlier, the government had issued the Edict of Boulogne, recognising the determination of the Protestants of the Midi and the midwest and the consequent danger of a protracted struggle. The edict conceded freedom of conscience, together with freedom of worship, in the cities of La Rochelle, Nîmes, Montauban and

Sancerre, and in the chapels of such seigneurs with powers of *haute justice* as had not abjured. Thus, but a few months after the massacre, the government was forced to accept that the Protestants were still a force to be reckoned with. They were fewer of course – hence this edict was less favourable than that of Saint-Germain three years previously – but still disturbing, seeing that care was being taken to promulgate a treaty which, it was hoped, would sow the seeds of discord among them by discriminating in favour of some towns at the expense of others.

The Dismembered Kingdom

In the years following the massacre, the French Crown reaped the bitter harvest of its efforts to hold the balance between the factions. Having refused to cast in its lot with a faction, it now found itself challenged in principle by the vengeful monarchomach tracts, in sovereignty by the United Provinces of the Midi, and in suzerainty by the rebel 'barons'.

Aristocratic resistance, too often linked with Huguenot guerrilla action, was never short of real or pretended justifications. And it is difficult to distinguish the one from the other, especially in view of the proliferation of declarations, manifestos, addresses, and open letters presenting the good and holy 'causes which have moved' prince so-and-so or duke such-and-such to take arms. The Massacre of Saint Bartholomew, in which a good 50 gentlemen had met a miserable end, undoubtedly inspired among the nobility feelings of solidarity which bridged the confessional divide. Coligny, after all, was a close relative of the Montmorency brothers, both of them good Catholics. But the government remained intransigent. It was quick to execute factious Protestants (Montgomery in 1574 and Montbrun in 1575), and the trusty fellow conspirators of Alençon (La Molle and Coconas in 1574), as well as to imprison two marshals suspected of plotting (Montmorency and Cossé). And at Court a close watch was kept on the princes of the blood – Alençon, Condé and Navarre – who might raise the banner of rebellion. But the nobility entertained growing suspicions of the shady machinations of Catherine de Medici, Charles IX, and then Henri III. The aristocracy, usually so self-confident, was overcome by a neurotic fear of assassination which inspired the romanticised and extravagant speculations of nineteenth-century writers. Damville went in fear of being poisoned by the Queen Mother, and it was said that Birague had suggested strangling the two marshals imprisoned at Vincennes. Under Henri III the factions clashed in the shape of the rival 'mignons' of the king and Alençon, who killed each other with chilling readiness.

Mistrust reached such heights that the pamphlet *Le discours merveilleux* drips with the poison that Catherine probably never used, expressing the resentment and fear of both Protestant and Catholic nobles. This violent diatribe is the intellectual equivalent of the manifestos published by the grandees. All these writings voice the same resentment at the lack of consideration shown by the Crown for the nobility, which of course lived only to serve the king and defend the common good! Thus can one read the claims of a frustrated group. The clearly stated objectives of the rebels included the removal of 'foreigners' from the King's Council – and by now 'foreigners' meant not the Guises, upon whom aristocratic wrath (predominantly Protestant, it is true) had focused in the 1560s, but Italians, friends of Catherine de Medici such as Chancellor Birague, the Duke of Nevers, and the Baron de Retz. They were blamed for the massacre, the financial crisis, and the disintegration of the kingdom. Freedom of conscience and worship were still demanded, for the grandees saw quite clearly that the policy of religious uniformity had collapsed. Yet were not Catholics the companions of Huguenots in these open revolts? Damville, one of the most enterprising of the nobility, ambitious as he was, was undoubtedly of the Politique tendency, like his brothers Montmorency, Thoré, and Méru. But this was not the case with many others, who expressed their discontent a little later by joining the Guisard League. Another refrain taken up by a number of the manifestos was the summoning of the Estates General. In this time of crisis, the myth of the representation of the kingdom through the three orders arose once again as the cure for all ills. One hardly needs to add that the nobles exercised an influence in this assembly out of all proportion to their statistical insignificance in the population as a whole, exploiting it as a vehicle for forcing their claims upon the monarch.

More vaguely, or at least less clearly set down in writing, feudal ambitions reawoke amid the conditions prevailing in the reigns of the last Valois kings. Charles IX, racked with tuberculosis notwithstanding his youth, was visibly failing, and the Court was a mirror of royal wretchedness. He died on 30 May 1574, but Henri d'Anjou, his eventual successor, had left the country the previous autumn in order to take the crown of Poland, and did not return to France until September. In the meantime Catherine de Medici assumed control, but François d'Alençon, as a prince of the blood, was in an excellent position. He focused on his own puny person the hopes or claims of the Protestant and Catholic high nobility, advocating a return to a policy of toleration and aristocratic influence. French intervention against Philip II in the Netherlands was once again a central plank in the platform.

Writing the history of the 1570s is a real challenge in view of the tortuous manoeuvres of leaders – among whom François d'Alençon was typical to the point of caricature – who were constantly making and breaking alliances to suit their own immediate interests. This last remark applies rather less to the Huguenot barons, who inexorably pursued the territorial expansion of the United Provinces of the Midi. But it is therefore essential for the sake of clarity to pick out certain guiding lines amidst the confusion and to try to weave them into a coherent analytical framework.

The Fifth War of Religion (1574–6) saw an alliance of the Catholic Malcontents with the Huguenots against the Crown. The chief figures in the rising were François d'Alençon, the Protestant La Noue, the 'politique' Henri Damville de Montmorency and his brothers, and Henri de Condé, the prince of the blood who had escaped from Court in 1573. Operations commenced in Poitou, Aunis and Saintonge, coordinated by La Noue. Taking advantage of the Mardi Gras festivities, his soldiers, disguised as carnival revellers, surprised a number of towns where the 'full bellied' papists were giving themselves up to 'their customary debauchery'. Around the same time, Montgomery landed at Cotentin and advanced into Normandy. In Languedoc, Damville, in association with the Protestants, seized Montpellier, reached an understanding with Nîmes, and took possession of a number of royal strongholds. Seeking to consolidate his position, he summoned a meeting of the provincial estates of Languedoc in November and December 1574, while Henri III, at that moment in Avignon, summoned other deputies to a similar assembly with a view to levying taxes. Damville, it is true, reckoned that he had a free hand in his viceroyalty of Languedoc, seeing that Catherine, the Regent, had relieved him of his position as Governor in June, transferring it to his uncle the Marquis de Villars. In the Dauphiné, Montbrun and his colleague Lesdigières took Die, Gap, and Embrun, securing communications with Provence, where bands of Protestants and moderate Catholics were squaring up to the royal Lieutenant-General, the Comte de Carcès. In Guyenne and upper Languedoc, Turenne took command for several months in 1575 of a religiously mixed force, before handing it over to Navarre. Finally, eastern France was invaded by massed ranks of *reiters* and *landsknechts* levied by Condé and led by John Casimir.

With the kingdom tossed on the waves of feudal revolt, the regime could deal with little more than the most pressing problems. The Court conspiracy masterminded by Alençon was discovered in May 1574: some conspirators (among them Montmorency and Cossé) were arrested, others executed. Their plan had been to join the Duke of Bouillon at Sedan, a free city, and to take sides with the House of Orange-Nassau. On the military front, the king's army kept La Noue's force in check in the west, while the Duke of Guise halted the first wave of German mercenaries at Dormans in October 1575. But Guise could not contain them, and by December they were camped at Pontoise. Henri III, having arrived in Avignon towards the end of 1574, found himself unable to oppose the marauding bands. He made for Reims, where he was anointed in February 1575, and thence for Paris. Since he lacked the force to overcome his enemies, he had to resort to negotiations, which were conducted on two fronts. The Duke of Alençon was satisfied with an appanage consisting of Anjou, Touraine and Berry, together with the town of La Charité-sur-Loire, which controlled one of the main north–south routes of the kingdom. Dealing with the Protestant and Catholic allies was a longer business. In April 1575 Henri III received in Paris representatives bearing the demands formulated by the political assemblies, Condé and Damville. An agreement was signed at Beaulieu, near Loches, in May 1576.[4] It was highly favourable to the Huguenots, even more so than Saint-Germain. Freedom of conscience and worship were conceded, except that the latter was forbidden in Paris and any place where the Court was in residence. Bipartite chambers of the kind already established in the regions controlled by the United Provinces of the Midi were set up at Poitiers, Montpellier, Grenoble, Bordeaux and (though on paper only) alongside every Parlement. The Huguenots were granted eight safe havens, among them Aigues-Mortes, Beaucaire, Périgueux, Mas-Grenier, Serre (in the Dauphiné), and Seine-La-

Grand-Tour (in Provence). The victims of the Massacre of Saint Bartholomew were rehabilitated, and the most famous of them, the 'late Lord of Châtillon', was restored in all his honours and estates. The widows and children of noble victims were exempted from the obligations of the feudal levy, and their counterparts among the commoners were to be free from the *taille* for six years. The noblemen executed for their Protestant convictions – Montgomery, Montbrun, Cavaignes and Briquemaut – saw their names cleared of all disgrace. Processions celebrating the death of Condé at Jarnac and the Massacre of Saint Bartholomew were banned. The surviving Protestant grandees saw their privileges extended. Condé and Damville retained their governorships, and Henri de Navarre, who, after several unsuccessful attempts, had finally managed to flee the Court's gilded cage, was made Governor of Guyenne, a traditional prerogative of the Kings of Navarre. But it was not enough simply to restore them to their high positions in the State. It was also necessary to indemnify them for having exercised their 'right of revolt'. Alençon was granted an annual pension of 300 000 *livres*, while Navarre, fugitive though he was, was repaid various arrears as well as debts owed to his mother, amounting to some 600 000 *livres*.[5] John Casimir received a pension of 400 000 *livres* a year for providing cannon fodder, besides a lump sum of 6 million *livres* to cover his war expenses and four months' back pay for his soldiers, and to settle his old debts. Reckoning that the money would be slow in coming, he took the *Surintendant des finances*, Bellièvre, back to Heidelberg as a hostage, and left his troops to rampage through Champagne and Burgundy. To round off his hardwon reconciliation with the high nobility, Henri III used one of the articles of the Edict of Beaulieu to announce the imminent summons of the Estates General.

During the following years the Crown experienced a contraction of its authority, though not on the scale of 1574–6. In the north, in Picardy, its authority was challenged by the rise of the League: Péronne, as we have seen, refused to accept Condé as governor. The influence of the Guises spread further in Burgundy and Champagne on the basis of a huge network of noble clients, an agglomeration of lands and lordships which ensured them a large and faithful following, and the firmly Catholic convictions of the people. As Damville moved to distance himself from the Huguenots in Languedoc, the warlords of the two factions kept up the fight. By taking a village here or a fortified house there, descending like vultures on fairs and markets, and holding travellers to ransom, they spread insecurity throughout the province, from the gates of Carcassonne to the edge of the Vivarais. Those towns and villages of the Dauphiné which had joined the United Provinces of the Midi were outside the judicial and administrative reach of the Crown. And Provence was ravaged by the marauding of armed bands under various flags. Some fought in the name of the new royal governor of Susa; others, the 'razés', in the name of Protestants or moderate Catholics; others still, the hardline Catholic 'carcistes', in the name of the Comte de Carcès.

In the south-west, Henri de Navarre skilfully combined his roles as Governor of Guyenne and Protector of the Reformed churches. Having at last escaped, he once more reverted to Calvinism, shrewdly concluding that it would be better to be the leader of a faction than play second or third fiddle in a Court crawling with potential assassins. Oblivious to any conflict between his two responsibilities, and viceroy in all but name, he shut himself away in Guyenne until 1588. But he unflaggingly dinned into national and international audiences the fact that, as a prince of the blood, he had a royal destiny. If, like his cousin Condé, he refused to attend the Estates General convoked in 1576, he nevertheless addressed a masterly letter to the 'Gentlemen gathered in the Estates at Blois', already dangling before them the prospect of his eventual reversion to Catholicism, for 'after the person of my lord the king and Monsieur his brother, I have a greater interest than anyone else in the preservation and restoration of the realm'.[6] None of which prevented him from unleashing the dogs of war whenever he saw fit, whether to satisfy Protestants annoyed at the patchy implementation of the latest edict, or to make a show of force for the benefit of the government and the Guisard League. The sixth and seventh conflicts, in 1576–7 and 1579–80, confused campaigns led by Condé and a temporising Navarre who had no desire to humiliate his 'lord' the king, were brought to a close respectively by the Edicts of Poitiers and Fleix. The Edict of Poitiers, in 1577, went back somewhat on that of Beaulieu, restricting freedom of worship but leaving the Huguenots their eight safe havens and the bipartite chambers. The Edict of Fleix, in 1580, reinforced the safe havens system, increasing their number to fifteen for a period of six years.

The kingdom was exhausted by the incessant calls to arms and their associated ravages: the marauding of the *reiters* in Champagne and Burgundy; and the endemic banditry in Languedoc, against which neither Damville for the Crown, nor Navarre and Châtillon for the Protestant Union, could achieve anything. In 1579 the taking of La Frise by Condé led to the pillaging of the area 'for ten leagues around'.[7] In 1580 the taking of Cahors by Navarre led to a bloodbath. The peasants of the Dauphiné and the population of Romans, worn out by taxation and sick of continuous warfare, rose up in 1579 and 1580 with little other motive than to affirm their existence. The provincial estates of Normandy, Burgundy and Brittany protested against the burden of taxation. Even the usually belligerent Huguenots 'hardly stirred from their houses' during the seventh conflict. But if a degree of peace prevailed for the next five years, France, drained by twenty years of civil war, remained none the less a patchwork of rival authorities.

The State Tries to Keep its Head above Water

Catherine de Medici, Charles IX, and Henri III continued to try to rule the kingdom as best they could. Despite appearances, which contributed to his poor reputation, Henri III, we know, took his royal duties seriously. Almost as much as his father and grandfather before him, he was a legislator. But, like theirs, his laws were too often dead letters. The enormous Ordinance of Blois, which ran to 363 articles and was issued in 1579 after consultation with the Estates General, is altogether typical of his efforts both in the wide range of its concerns and in its ultimate ineffectuality. But even if his legislative activity can often appear rather ridiculous – for example his frequent sumptuary laws or the minutely detailed regulations for his chivalric Order of the Holy Spirit – it at least testified to his determination to govern, to impose the rule of the State. It can be divided into three main areas: political, fiscal, and socio-economic.

Henri III was something of a sedentary king. He liked living in Paris despite the undisguised hostility of its population, and did not share his mother's readiness to grapple with the knotty problems of collective or individual rebellion on the ground in the outlying provinces. Arriving in Lyon on his return from Poland in 1574, Henri set about reorganising his late brother's Council. He reduced it radically to about ten, excluding the Guise brothers.

Instead, it was dominated by experienced administrators who were linked to Catherine de Medici and favourable to religious toleration: Bishop Jean de Monluc, Dufaur de Pibrac, Hurault de Cheverny, Paul de Foix, Bellièvre, Morvilliers, and the brilliant Villeroy. They now enjoyed the title Councillors of State, to distinguish them from the Councillors of the King, a broader title which included all the magistrates of the sovereign courts. The *Conseil d'État*, or Privy Council, dealt indiscriminately with all sorts of government business, but under the leadership of Bellièvre, the *Surintendant des finances*, it seems to have established a sub-committee for financial affairs.[8] However, important matters were discussed by an inner council consisting of the king himself, Catherine de Medici, and the Chancellor René de Birague – joined, after 1578, by Philippe Hurault de Cheverny. While decision-making was increasingly confined to a small informal inner circle, the Court in which the monarchy displayed itself in all its glory was becoming larger and more formal. The nobility, of course, played a full part in Court life, holding more or less important offices in the various households of the king, the queen, Monsieur, or the Queen Mother. Keeping a great nobleman at Court was a guarantee of security for the regime in that era of baronial turmoil. Henri III, deserted by the old nobility, spent his entire reign trying to build up a network of loyal noblemen whom he could trust with household office and military command. It was this counterbalancing role which he conferred on his 'mignons' that so alienated the established noble dynasties. Even the creation of his new chivalric Order of the Holy Spirit was directed towards the same objective of creating a new nobility to protect him against the old. Paradoxically, Henri III governed as an authoritarian sovereign, so jealous of power that he was not prepared to share it except with his closest associates, and yet at the same time as a feudal suzerain, as the premier nobleman in a nobility he sought to renew and to enlarge. The sale of 1000 patents of nobility in 1576, together with the grant of nobility to the municipal magistrates of Paris and, at a higher level, the creation of 11 peer-duchies, showed the king's intention of counterbalancing, perhaps even eliminating, the political authority of the ancient noble houses, especially the House of Guise. An important part of Henri III's legislative activity, around 8 per cent of his output, concerned the nobility in one way or another: a statistic which testifies to the close attention which king and Council devoted to this social group.

Financial problems beset the government because France was living beyond its means. The royal debt was already enormous in 1560, thanks to the unpaid bills remaining from Henri II's foreign wars. It swelled further as troops had to be raised and equipped for use at home. The sums paid or promised to the Malcontents by the Edict of Beaulieu, and those demanded by John Casimir, were more than the Crown could afford. So in 1576 Henri III turned to the Estates General which had been demanded by so many baronial manifestos and popular pamphlets. The deputies, however, refused any increase in direct taxation while continuing to insist on the restoration of religious uniformity. The most effective – and least expensive – means, they argued, would be to bring them back by 'gentle and holy methods', avoiding force and war and their concomitant financial burdens for the people. An assembly of notables which convened at Saint-Germain in 1583 discussed ways to enrich the realm and thus to increase the yield of taxation, especially of those taxes on consumption (the *aides*) whose yields were steadily falling – an index of the poverty into which France was sinking. The assembled dignitaries – princes of the blood, great officers of the Crown, and other senior public officials – advised the king to reorganise the Crown lands (depleted as they were by alienations!), buying them back and renting at good rates those lands still in royal hands. They further recommended a revision of the terms on which the collection of indirect taxes was farmed out, but in the same breath proposed a reduction in taxes as an incentive to industries that brought in gold or foreign currency, together with limits on the import of foreign goods, especially English cloth.

So the financial problem remained insoluble, and once again the Crown turned to the Church. This led to turbulent meetings between the monarchy and the clergy at Melun (1579) and Paris (1580), by which it was agreed that the Church should make regular contributions to the royal budget. The temporalities of the Church, which remained the largest landholder in the kingdom, continued to excite envy; and numerous treatises were published (two of them in 1581) arguing that the confiscation and sale of Church property would solve the State's financial crisis.

The government was forced back upon traditional means. The *taille* was raised to dizzying heights, notwithstanding the protests of the provincial estates. In 1576 the *taille* brought the Treasury about 7 million *livres*, and the government was expecting 18 million in 1588. Even allowing for inflation this was a spectacular increase.[9] It was the same with the *gabelle*, which rose in the same period from 1 million to 3.4 million *livres*. It is not clear how much of this actually reached the royal coffers, what with the political turmoil of the 1570s and the usurpation of Crown revenues by provincial magnates. But in any case the returns were not enough: the royal debt had spiralled to 133 million *livres* by 1588.

The only methods left for replenishing the Treasury were those which historians describe pejoratively as 'expedients'. The first was debasement of the coinage, effected by the Edict of Poitiers in 1577: the golden *écu* or 'sun' was fixed at 3 *livres* and 10 *sous*, and the smallest coins – *douzains, blancs* etc. – were withdrawn, leading to a rise in prices and the impoverishment of the common people, who hardly had any gold coin at their disposal. But by revaluing fine metal upwards, the king made it easier to service his debts. The sale of offices also increased, although the Edict of Blois had reiterated the prohibition on marketing public office. But the Crown was not going to baulk at one more contradiction. Offices were sold in droves in 1577, 1578, 1580, 1581 and 1586, bringing the Treasury fresh revenues, albeit offset by the salaries payable to the new officials.[10] More than 7 per cent of Henri III's legislative activity was concerned with the creation of new offices. He left no stone unturned in replenishing the coffers. He sold letters of mastery to craftsmen without obliging them to fulfil the customary requirements of their trades. He borrowed from individuals (especially Italian bankers) and towns. He seized the rents of the Paris *Hôtel de Ville*. And his raids on that city, as we shall see, were frequent and significant, arousing considerable hostility against him. But above all Henri III put the State even more squarely in the hands of the tax-farmers and their partners. These wealthy people, who individually or collectively (as a company) paid sums to the Crown in advance of the receipts from indirect taxes (*aides, gabelles*, and internal tariffs), provided the necessary lubrication for the royal financial machine, demanding in exchange for their loans State offices or Church benefices. They were by no means all *nouveaux riches* or Italians. The high nobility were not averse to advancing considerable sums against the yields from *aides* or *gabelles*. An entire network thus grew up, within which wealthy commoners rubbed shoulders with titled gentlemen, investing in and profiting from the State. One can quite understand that these lenders – who included the Chancellor Cheverny, d'O (who succeeded Bellièvre as *Surintendant des finances*), and even Henri's favourite Joyeuse – were not prepared to see the collapse of a regime which did so well by them.[11] So they tended to rally in due course to the legitimate claimant Henri IV rather than chance the extremism of the League.

Besides these desperate measures to shore up the Crown's financial situation, Henri III also sought to find solutions to the economic crisis crippling the country. He legislated against the excesses of the soldiery. He introduced numerous regulations for craftsmen, obliging them to join the relevant corporations and to observe trading standards. But this legislation perhaps owed more to the need to keep a close eye on a working population prone to political and social agitation than to a desire to encourage industry, which had suffered untold damage from the political and economic crisis. And his Council made several attempts to encourage trade, granting privileges to the Lyon fairs and to German merchants trading in France, and authorising the export of woollens. 1575 even saw a revival of François I's attempt to standardise weights and measures across the country – some hope.

Some decrees showed a concern for the wretched condition of his subjects, dealing with the establishment of charitable institutions in Paris and the appointment of royal officials to manage them. And in May 1586 he reiterated the provision already introduced in Charles IX's great Ordinance of Moulins, obliging each town to feed its poor in order to cut down vagrancy.

Considering the output of laws, edicts, ordinances and regulations as a whole, one cannot but be struck by their conservative tone. Henri III was not legislatively innovative in the way that François I and Henri II had been. He was simply trying to survive. Finding money, keeping the nobility happy, and keeping the lid on social disorder were – apart from dealing with urgent political problems – the principal objectives of government policy between 1574 and 1589.

14 The 'War of the Three Henries' and the Struggle for Peace under Henri IV, 1584–98

When François d'Alençon died on 10 June 1584, Henri de Navarre found himself, because the reigning king had no sons, heir presumptive according to the Salic Law. Foreseeing the horror of the hardline Catholics at the prospect of a Protestant coming to the throne, Henri III yet again urged his Bourbon cousin to be reconciled to the Church of Rome. But Navarre, aware of the dangers of a too timely conversion, had no wish to alienate the Protestant forces which supported him, and issued a demurrer.

The Revival of the League

The Treaty of Joinville, in December 1584, marked the alliance of the Guises and the League barons with Spain. Three causes were invoked to justify this axis: the 'defence and preservation of the Catholic faith', the extirpation of heresy, and the recognition of the ageing Cardinal of Bourbon as heir should Henri III die without issue.

But there was another threat to the State: the emergence at Paris in early January 1585 of a popular movement organised as a secret society and prepared to seize power within the capital itself. Its central committee, known as the 'Sixteen' (a reference to the 16 'quarters' of Paris) remained throughout the history of the League the symbol of hardcore resistance, no matter who its constituent members were.[1] The League rapidly attracted mem-

bers and sympathisers. The accession of a heretical monarch constituted in the eyes of the Catholic townsfolk, egged on by their
preachers, a sacrilegious enormity which had to be prevented even
at the cost of renewed civil war. The attitude of Henri III, who
did nothing to forestall the eventuality, scandalised hardline Catholics, the more easily in that he had for years been totally discredited in most people's eyes. His desperate attempts to raise
cash by increasing taxes and multiplying judicial and financial
offices helped undermine the support which he had enjoyed from
the capital earlier in the reign. The favours, pensions, and appointments with which he loaded his favourites, such as Épernon
and Joyeuse, carefully enumerated by the pamphleteers dedicated
to the League or in the pay of the Guises, gave great offence to
subjects who were more used to seeing such generosity lavished
upon the scions of ancient families. And the personal behaviour
of the monarch, who flaunted an exhibitionist piety and took
part in flagellant processions, irritated plenty of people who could
not understand the divergence between his private devotion and
his public policy. They wanted him to show the same Catholic
convictions in his public acts as in his private life. But in Paris,
the gap between them was particularly obvious. Henri III had
burdened the capital throughout his reign with incessant financial
demands: a forced loan in 1575, extraordinary annual duties from
1582 to 1587, and shameless exploitation of the *rentes sur l'Hôtel
de Ville*. The creation of new offices alienated the holders of existing offices in the sovereign courts as they saw their birthrights
devalued. The proctors of the Parlement and the Châtelet found
themselves obliged to pay a tax to confirm their positions. Enraged
by this, they went on strike in June 1586: the ordinary courts in
Paris and the surrounding area were crippled, and in July Henri
III had to revoke the edict. The Parisians also had a grandstand
view of the extravagances of the king and his Court. Pierre
L'Estoile's *Journal* records in minute detail the conspicuous consumption and fantastic festivities which served only to irritate further
a city population already alienated from the king.

The eighth conflict broke out at the instigation of the Guises,
to whom the Paris League looked for assistance. Cities and whole
provinces broke away from the Crown: Orléans, Lyon, Dijon,
Picardy, Normandy and Brittany. France was torn to pieces, with
the entire north and centre, together with most of the major
cities, declaring for the League. The Duke of Guise went to

Germany and Switzerland in order to recruit mercenaries, who arrived in April 1585. In Paris the Sixteen were secretly buying arms for their followers. In March 1585 the Péronne Manifesto explained the reasons for the resort to arms, stating the religious and political grievances of the aristocratic and the Parisian wings of the League.

The king and his mother were busy at Court trying to ward off the worst dangers. Somewhat insecure in the capital, they sought to keep control by purging unreliable elements of the urban militia. Catherine took to the road again, meeting Guise at Épernay. Her son provided himself with a bodyguard of 45 Gascons sworn to defend him to the death. But they were short of troops, as the royal forces had mostly defected to the League or the Protestants. So the only way to preserve the State was to make a deal with the more dangerous enemy, in this case the League. The Treaty of Nemours (July 1585), by which the Crown itself in effect subscribed to the League, represented the temporary triumph of the Guises and their followers. It was a bad deal for the Crown, which had to pay off the League mercenaries and heap favours and pensions upon the Guise barons, who also gained in effect their own 'safe havens': Duke Henri obtained Verdun, Toul and Saint-Dizier, three crucial strategic strongholds; Rue was entrusted to Aumale, the castle of Dijon to Mayenne, and both Dinan and Le Conquet to Mercœur. Draconian religious legislation aligned the king for the moment with the hardline Catholics. Protestant worship was forbidden, Protestant ministers were outlawed and ordered to flee the country. The ordinary faithful were given six months to choose between conversion and exile. Huguenot safe havens were to be surrendered, and Huguenots were barred from public office. Navarre was deprived of his right to the succession, and in September 1585 a bull issued by Pope Sixtus V excommunicated the Bourbon princes and thus made them ineligible for the throne. This move caused some consternation in the Politique and Gallican circles of the Parisian officeholders to which Pierre L'Estoile belonged. Protests were made to the king on the grounds that 'princes of France have never been subject to the jurisdiction of the papacy'.

The Battle of Coutras

On the Protestant side, Navarre and Condé were aware of the risks of war. They knew that the Guises, temporarily in control of the king's person and policy, were preparing to throw all their ideological, military and propaganda resources into the fight. So the two Bourbon cousins cast around feverishly for men, money and munitions from abroad. Elizabeth I, less circumspect than usual, because she could foresee that a League victory in France would mean victory also for Philip II, advanced 300 000 *livres* and promised material support. The German princes and the King of Denmark agreed to help the Protestant side. The churches were squeezed once more, and Montauban was turned into a veritable arsenal, while La Rochelle became Navarre's headquarters for future military operations.[2]

The war began in Poitou, where Marshal Biron retook several towns in 1586. Mayenne led a royal army in Guyenne, and Anne de Joyeuse led a force down the east of the Massif Central. Some months later, in 1587, Guise himself was sent to the east to block the path of the *reiters* called in by the Huguenots. The operations were confused, but Catherine and Henri III were still hoping for Navarre's conversion, which would in turn placate the League, whose policies they were obliged for now to follow. The Queen Mother made one last attempt to reach a compromise, travelling south for an interview with Navarre in order to urge him to abjure and thus bring peace to the land. But, like Guise at Épernay in 1585, Navarre made a fool of her, agreeing to a meeting at which he never turned up, sending Turenne in his place. The decisive battle took place down there, where the feudal and religious power of Navarre was most firmly entrenched, and where he knew every inch of the land. At Coutras, on 20 October 1587, the royal force under Joyeuse was cut to pieces. Navarre was chivalrous in victory. He pretended to have fought not à royal army but an army of the League, enemies of both the king and the Protestants. In these troubled times, when even those folk most unshakeable in their convictions looked for signs of heavenly approval, the victory looked like a divine sign which, to the extent that Henri III's authority was not in question, tended to incline Catholic Politiques and Protestant supporters of toleration towards Navarre's case. His propaganda neatly turned the victory into a triumph for the French people. The Leaguers looked at it from another perspective, seeing the hand of God punishing Henri III at the very time when their own leader, Henri de Guise, was winning two crushing victories (in October and again in November) over the *reiters* in Champagne, brilliant victories which have been overshadowed for posterity by Coutras. Henri III's popularity sank to new depths against a background of subsistence crises, crushing taxes and spiralling prices. The people were now profoundly dubious of his ability to lead the country. Nobody could make sense of his tortuous policy, of which the latest twist was to make a treaty with the Swiss mercenaries whom Guise had just trounced, allowing them to return unmolested to their homes. And then he made the Duke of Épernon give only token chase to the Germans, allowing them honourable surrender. There was outrage in the Parisian pulpits over this display of favour to men who had been looting and pillaging the surrounding countryside.

The organisation of the popular wing of the League reaped a rich harvest from this soil. Its membership was verging on 30 000 when the League took over Paris.[3] A paramilitary regime was established (not without similarities to that of the Huguenots in 1561–2) with each quarter of the city commanded by a colonel, assisted by two or three captains. These men led the League's urban militia. A council of around fifteen men was in overall control, and the preachers looked after propaganda. Plans were made to defend the city with a system of barricades, and envoys were sent to establish communications with other League cities.

The Guise princes pressed home their advantage. Aware of Philip II's plan to attack England and rid himself at last of the insolent Protestant Elizabeth Tudor (who allowed her privateers to prey upon Spanish shipping), they sent the Duke of Aumale to Picardy to seize ports and fortresses for the use of the Spanish forces. Henri III, aware of the secret meetings at Paris and of the cooperation between Guise and Philip II, forbade the Duke of Guise to show his face in the capital. In defiance, Guise came to see him in the Louvre on 9 May. At dawn on 12 May, the king brought a regiment of Swiss and French guards into the city, in breach of the city's privilege of providing for its own security. Paris buzzed with rumours about his intentions. The people took up arms and, according to plan, the city was soon a mass of barricades. Neither the Swiss nor the French guards could move. Cut off even from each other, they parleyed and were allowed to withdraw, though they could not avoid a final skirmish in which about 50 Swiss were killed. Isolated in the Louvre, Henri heard the sound of fighting and asked Guise to help him withdraw his troops, whom he had regrouped around the palace. During the night the League tightened its grip on the city. Barricades were placed against the very palace doors, and students, stirred to fever pitch by the preachers, talked of 'getting that bugger the king in the Louvre'. But the bird had flown. Henri had left through the gardens of the Tuileries, abandoning the rebellious city for Chartres.

Paris now organised itself as the League leadership came out into the open. The royalist civic authorities were replaced by magistrates of a tougher stamp, the Bastille was occupied and put under the command of one of the Sixteen, and the captains of the urban militia were replaced by committed Leaguers. But although the leaders of the insurrection, with Guise, wished to impose their policies on the king, they did not seek his destruction. Messengers from the duke and the new Parisian regime reached Henri III at Chartres and assured him of their loyalty if he agreed to their demands. And so, once again reduced to desperation, the last Valois signed the Edict of Union in July 1588, promising to combat and suppress heresy, to refuse to recognise a heretic as his successor, to grant an unconditional amnesty for everyone involved in the Day of the Barricades, and to promulgate the decrees of the Council of Trent. By letters patent of 4 August 1588, Guise was appointed Lieutenant General of the Realm, the Cardinal of Bourbon was recognised as the heir presumptive in default of any sons to the king, and Henri III's old favourites, among them the Duke of Épernon, were discharged from all their offices. In this complete capitulation to the Guise programme, Henri III was advised by his mother and by such ministers as Villeroy, who favoured the hardline Catholic party. But the democratic claims made by the popular League of Paris were completely ignored. The Catholic grandees thus betrayed their rank-and-file support just as their Protestant counterparts had so often done before.[4]

But in August 1588 news of Philip II's worst defeat reached France. The Invincible Armada, the pride of Spain, blessed by the Pope, the hope of zealous Catholics across Europe, had been 'wrecked, ruined, and reduced to nothing', not so much by the English navy as 'by a contrary wind which overwhelmed it'.[5] Henri III breathed again as the Guise hold loosened, for Spanish aid to the League dried up in the wake of this disaster. The king's spirits rose sharply, and in September he dismissed his ministerial team – Villeroy, Cheverny, Bellièvre and the Queen Mother's favourite Secretaries of State, Brulart and Pinart. Did he think that, following Catherine's lead, they had been too submissive to the League barons? Or was he trying to flatter public opinion, ever ready as it was to criticise the holders of high office, and thus to defuse the opposition he could anticipate from the deputies preparing for the Estates General due to convene in Blois in October? Or was it simply a sign that he was still all-powerful, that he could make and break fortunes – a warning to the Guises, to the Leaguers elected to the Estates, and to their supporters in the citys, strongholds, and provinces?

Blois and the Assassination of the Guise Brothers

The assembly which gathered at Blois was far from favourable to authoritarian monarchy. League colours flew not only over the Third Estate but over the other two as well. The Cardinals of Guise and Bourbon presided over the clergy, and Cossé-Brissac, the 'marshal of the League', over the nobility. La Chapelle-Marteau, a member of the secret inner council of the Parisian League who had just been elected Mayor of Paris, was made President of the Third Estate. Despite his misgivings, Henri III was obliged to swear once more to the Edict of Union. The deputies, especially those of the Third Estate, demanded that decisions made by the three orders of the realm assembled in the Estates should have the force of law – an unprecedented challenge to the role of the king as sovereign dispenser of justice. And the demand carried some even more unpleasant implications. Was it not the Estates of France which, like those of Poland, England and Sweden, conferred upon kings the power which they enjoyed? This political dream, sporadically entertained by such assemblies ever since they had first been summoned, thus reopened the old dilemma of the separation of powers and the basis of sovereignty, a dilemma which had been settled for several hundred years in the monarchy's favour. On a more specific issue, the Third Estate was inflexible in its demand that taxes be cut back to their 1576 levels, at the same time insisting that the campaign against the Protestants be renewed. Negotiations followed which resulted in Henri III being voted, for the expenses of his Court and his military operations, an inadequate sum which nobody knew who was going to pay.

The deputies had come to Blois with high expectations, dreaming of a 'reformation of the kingdom', but found themselves arguing every penny with a king obsessed by money. Guise, who looked more and more like the hero, needed to restore the good order to which the League aspired. Guise himself, sensitive to the highly charged atmosphere, exploited the situation, using his influence among those members of the Third Estate favourable to the League and receiving them in his chambers every day. He lost no opportunity to provoke the king and was inventive in finding new ways to humiliate and defy him.

But although Blois was rapidly withdrawing into tragic political seclusion, it was not entirely cut off from the outside world. Couriers brought bad news. The Duke of Savoy, Charles-Emmanuel, had invaded the marquisate of Saluzzo, virtually all that remained of the expansionist dreams of Charles VIII, Louis XII, and François I. The Protestants of Navarre had advanced into Poitou, that battleground of the rival factions; and Niort, Fontenay and Châtellerault had fallen to the Huguenots, who were heading for the Loire. Had Henri III already worked out his plan, encouraged by the proximity of his brother-in-law? Was he already thinking of an alliance with Navarre to regain the towns and provinces which had gone over to the League? After all, the murder of the Guises would be a gesture of reconciliation towards the Huguenots, and the elimination of the League's leaders might well weaken it crucially.[6] Or perhaps he felt so hemmed in that only physical violence could break him free, rather as in 1572 the elimination of the Huguenot nobility had assuaged the government's sense of panic and perhaps reassured Philip II about France's intentions with regard to the Netherlands.

Henri III planned the affair meticulously. He had no intention of letting things get out of hand as they had done in August 1572. His 45-man bodyguard provided the muscle, and the official justification would be that Guise had committed treason and that in such cases the king could sanction expeditious justice without process of law. Henri de Guise, summoned to the king's chamber, was killed on Friday 23 December 1588, and his brother the cardinal was gaoled and killed soon afterwards. Their bodies were burned the next day to prevent the emergence of any cult around their relics.[7] Several League deputies were then arrested during a plenary session of the Estates.

Paris and the Assassination of Henri III

Late on Christmas Eve, news of the execution of the Duke of Guise reached Paris and 'made a 100 000 Leaguers within an hour'.[8] The capital's relations with its sovereign sank to new depths as he became a 'tyrant', a 'villainous Herod'. On 7 January 1589 the Sorbonne sanctioned the union of the French people 'against a king who has violated the public faith in the assembly of the Estates' and declared that his subjects were released from their allegiance. The League broke with the Crown as decisively as the Protestants had done after the Massacre of Saint Bartholomew. But it was hard for a people brought up in the cult of the king as the Lord's Anointed to take this step. It had taken an act of intolerable violence which stigmatised the king as a tyrant to bring things to the point of no return.

A revolutionary organisation comprising various bodies made Paris the head of the League. The Council of the Union, comprising 40 representatives of the three orders and included representatives from the provinces, played a similar role to the 'political assemblies' of the Huguenots. Paris itself was governed by the Sixteen and the local councils in each quarter. There were purges of 'politiques', the 'soft underbelly' of the League, notably at Toulouse (though also at Paris): arrests, exiles, and even murders were carried out on the basis of information received. Mayenne was appointed Lieutenant-General of the State of the Crown of France – a kind of 'Protector' of the hardline Catholics much like Navarre among the Protestants. Hostilities against both royalists and Huguenots were undertaken with the aid of Spanish subsidies, compulsory levies on League towns, and confiscation of the property of those who had fled towns in fear of the inflammatory rhetoric of the preachers. The institutions of royal justice, such as the Parlements, were purged of their moderate personnel but otherwise continued to function in Rouen, Toulouse, Dijon, Aix, and of course Paris.

At Blois, early in January, Henri III dissolved the Estates General, having first released some prisoners. The presidents of the three orders (Renaud de Beaune, Archbishop of Bourges, having replaced the Cardinal of Guise, whose ashes had been cast into the Loire) presented their grievances to the king, and then the deputies returned to their homes replete with emotive memories. The Valois king of a dissolving kingdom had not killed the League by cutting off its head, but he had committed himself to supporting the party which he reckoned less dangerous to his authority – that of Henri de Navarre. Henri III established himself and his Council at Tours, together with a makeshift Parlement staffed by magistrates expelled from Paris. Navarre himself continued his northwards advance, taking towns and strongholds along the way, and met the king at Plessis-les-Tours on 30 April 1589. It was their first meeting for 13 years, and it marked recognition of Navarre's rightful place as first prince of the blood. He was at last able to reconcile his loyalty to the king with his sense of his rank and his responsibilities to his co-religionists. He remained suspicious, for at that time the poisoned cup and the sharpened blade had become commonplace, but he was happy to respond to Henri III's appeal, for the circumstances were from his point of view favourable to a reconciliation. One may recall that on several occasions since 1576 Catherine de Medici and her son had urged Navarre to return to Court. But he had bided his time until the balance of forces put him in a good position to do so. Was the murder of the Guises the sign he had been waiting for? Did his army's untroubled advance to the Loire assure him that he had sufficient backing not to go in permanent fear of an attempt on his life? At any rate, he 'crossed the water committing himself to God', and wept profusely when he greeted the king.

The two kings combined their forces and drew up a plan of campaign. Their aim was to capture Paris, the symbol of the king's downfall, the capital and propaganda centre of the League, from which pamphlets, plans and orders streamed forth to the provinces. Royalists and Huguenots advanced eagerly, brushing aside Mayenne's troops and ravaging the villages around the League's 'Jerusalem'. They converged on Saint-Cloud to prepare the assault planned for 2 or 3 August. But on 1 August the smooth progress of events was cut short by the murderous knife of Jacques Clément.[9]

The War of Henri IV (1589–94)

On 1 August 1589, Henri de Navarre reaped the fruits of a strategy he had pursued with patience, sagacity and determination ever since he fled the Court in 1576. Or was it still a little too soon? Did the assassination of the king mean that the fruit was not yet ripe? What cards did the new king have to play against the League and Catholic Europe? He was at least the legitimate successor according to the Salic Law, and before dying Henri III had made his own Catholic followers recognise him as such. But once their immediate grief was past, these men expected of their new sovereign a deal in which his conversion to the majority religion occupied pride of place. Their word-of-mouth agreement was formalised in the Declaration of 4 August, in which Henri undertook to keep France a Catholic country, to leave his Catholic subjects unmolested in their offices and honours, and to receive instruction in the Catholic faith from 'a good, lawful, and free national or general council'. This was more necessary to reassure such of his ordinary Catholic subjects as were not wholehearted Leaguers than to win over the Catholic grandees, for the latter were easily satisfied by generous patronage. Marshal Biron was made Count of Périgord in return for his support. King in little but name, Henri IV had to pay the price fixed by noble consciences chary at the idea of a heretic on the throne of the Most Christian King. But there were defections: Henri III's favourite, the Duke of Épernon, left in the hope of carving out a principality for himself in Provence; the committed Huguenot La Trémoille had similar intentions in Poitou, assisted by nine battalions of Protestants from Poitou and Saintonge; and the absolutely sincere Louis de L'Hospital, Marquis of Vitry, went over to the League. The combined force which had gathered for the siege of Paris was soon down to half its original strength.

But the first Bourbon was not without support. The United Provinces of the Midi, though their suspicions were aroused by the easy promises of conversion which he scattered broadcast, continued to hold a large part of the south and the mid-west in his name. The Politique royalists rallied behind him in the hope that he would abjure, among them magistrates of the stature of Achille de Harlay, purged by the League from the Parlement de Paris. Many bishops and prelates came out for the new king, together with a few towns: Bordeaux, Châlons, Langres and

Compiègne. Foreign support from England, the German princes, the Calvinists of the Netherlands, and the Venetians (who had gambled upon his success) allowed him to count on men, money and munitions. But two things worked especially in his favour. First there was the underlying solidity of the monarchical structure patiently built up by Louis XII, François I, and Henri II. Shaken by the civil and religious troubles though it was, and weakened by the discrediting of Henri III, the 'royal State' had put down roots that only an earthquake could shift. France and the king were but one entity in the eyes of both lawyers and subjects (or at least those who were not committed Leaguers). Notwithstanding the troubles, there was a settled acceptance of the necessity of government by one man. And thus the beneficiaries of this State, no matter how fragmented it might be, formed a vast interest group: officeholders, nobles, prelates, and moneylenders who had everything to lose by revolution. The cult of monarchy, already tinted with nationalism ('France, the finest kingdom in the world'), could rise above the recent crises, and Henri IV's propaganda machine excelled at stirring that sentiment in the hearts of the French people. Henri's second great advantage was his own character: his charisma, his charm, and his cleverness. In eliminating the Duke of Guise, Henri III had done his successor the best possible good turn, depriving the League of its own charismatic chief, a man who could win people's support for extreme courses. The first Bourbon, a Baroque sovereign and a supreme strategist, playing the lead and setting the tempo, succeeded in weaving the tattered shreds of his kingdom into a coherent ensemble by means of 'Baroque' techniques which amounted to a rationalisation of the practice of politics.[10]

From 4 August 1589 to 17 May 1593, the royalist and League forces were locked in stalemate. The fundamental problem was the king's religion. The League was unshakeable in its opposition to a Protestant succession. On 4 August it formally recognised the Cardinal of Bourbon as King Charles X. Mayenne was his Lieutenant-General, and the Council of the Union was in effect his Council. The Politiques and royalists who had rallied to Henri IV awaited the conversion promised in the Saint-Cloud Declaration, religious conviction and political calculation alike convincing them that the kingdom could never enjoy peace and unity under a Protestant. But Henri could not change his religion overnight without discarding a good many of his trumps: the friendship of the Reformed states of Europe and the support of much of southern and mid-western France. And so, notwithstanding the reiteration at Mantes in July 1591 of his intention to defend the Catholic faith and Gallican liberties of the realm, a certain weariness spread among those who had rallied to him at first. Possible competitors for the French throne sprang up on all sides. Among foreigners, Duke Charles-Emmanuel of Savoy, a grandson of François I on his mother's side, had been intervening in France since 1588 with the aim of expanding his Alpine principality into Provence and the Dauphiné. Charles III, the Duke of Lorraine, who had married Henri II's daughter Claude de France, could also put forward a claim, although his immediate objective was Champagne, which bordered his duchy. And the Infanta Isabella-Clara of Spain, Philip II's daughter by his third wife Elizabeth de Valois, was thus a granddaughter of Henri II, and might be declared Queen of France if she married a French prince (such as the young Duke of Guise). Nor was there any shortage of candidates among the Bourbons, more acceptable under the Salic Law, who might replace Henri IV if he persisted in his Protestantism. Charles X died in May 1590, but Henri's first cousin, Cardinal Charles de Vendôme, became in his turn Cardinal of Bourbon and had a powerful claim. Young, and a member of the King's Council, he was in a position to seek papal dispensation from his vows, which would leave him free to claim the throne and start a family. There were those among the Leaguers of Paris, such as the President Jeannin, who reckoned him a most suitable candidate, and many of the royalists who had rallied to Henri IV agreed with him. The latter also looked favourably on the claim of the Count of Soissons, the brother of Charles de Bourbon-Vendôme, a Catholic son of Louis de Condé, and a young and handsome gentleman who had fought beside Navarre at Coutras. This swarm of potential claimants scared the Politiques, who had a shrewd sense of foreign ambitions on the French Crown, but they also provided a means of putting pressure on the king to change his religion.

The fears of the Politiques were quite justified, as the fragmentation of the realm continued apace. Troops from Lorraine and Savoy invaded Champagne, the Dauphiné, the Rhône valley, and Provence, while Spanish forces responding to Mayenne's appeals for assistance were active in Normandy and around Paris. Paris even saw the day when the Spanish Duke of Feria (Philip II's ambassador) and the Italian Cardinal of Piacenza (the papal legate) openly busied themselves with French affairs. Brittany, under its governor Mercœur, was entirely committed to the League cause, as were large parts of Burgundy and Champagne. In other provinces there was conflict between royalists and the partisans of the League, while in Provence there was a three-cornered fight between Henri IV's supporters, the League, and an army from Savoy. In Languedoc, where Damville stood for the King, the new Duke of Joyeuse led the hardline Catholics of Toulouse. The provincial Parlements at Toulouse, Aix, Rennes, Dijon and Grenoble, staffed by League councillors, dispensed justice and managed the administration in the name of the League. Henri IV, who made Tours his provisional seat of government, duplicated them with courts staffed by his own supporters. In Languedoc there were rival assemblies of the provincial Estates, one consisting of Leaguers, the other of royalists.

These bitter years saw no decisive victories on the battlefield to swing the war one way or the other. In August 1589 Henri IV decided to remain in the north, against the advice of his friends, who advised him to return to his little kingdom in Guyenne. He maintained the blockade of Paris and sought to conquer Normandy, which would open the way for English assistance. The Battle of Arques, in September 1589, indecisive though on the whole favourable to him, guaranteed the fall of Eu and Dieppe, and thus opened the way to the sea. But Paris, the League capital and symbol of resistance to the heretical king, continued to hold out. Only its eventual capture would legitimise him as the successor of Henri III. His army took the suburbs in November, cutting off supplies and thus inducing a famine which the royalists hoped would break the League's spirit. Early in 1590 Normandy began to crumble before the royal attacks as town after town gave up. Resistance in the region around Tours was mopped up, and Vendôme, the ancestral home of the Bourbon dynasty, fell in its turn, reuniting Henri with his ancestors. The campaign became bogged down to the point where both Mayenne and Henri IV were prepared to risk a pitched battle in which the hand of God might allot victory. At Ivry, on 14 March 1590, the king's forces got the better of Mayenne's rather larger army, which was composed largely of Flemings, Germans and Swiss in the pay of Philip II. Philip justified his intervention in terms of 'the imminent danger to the Holy Catholic Church', adding that he was ready to give his own life in order to stamp out heresy in France, and to deliver the rightful king Charles X from the prison in Tours (where Henri IV held him until he died). Victory went to Henri, and his legendary white plume did marvels on the battle-field, on which 6000 League soldiers fell. His propaganda machine cracked up the victory for all it was worth, attributing it of course to divine intervention in his favour: 'It has pleased God', announced the messages he sent to his foreign allies, 'to grant me my dearest wish: to give battle to my enemies . . .'. The official account of the battle, the *Discours véritable sur la victoire*, sounded another theme, that of the king fighting at the head of his valiant French noblemen, who had come to defend 'their king', 'their country', and 'their families and fortunes, which they could see were liable to become the prey of foreigners'. Mayenne lost more than simply the battle. In defeat, his mercenaries did as much harm to his image as those of Condé and Coligny had done to theirs in the 1560s. And the Guise reputation for military prowess suffered so much that in Paris the League preachers hushed up the defeat for a time.

But while things had taken a turn for the better, progress remained slow. The siege of Paris was renewed after Ivry, lasting from April to August. Famine resumed her reign, causing perhaps 30 000 deaths in a population of some 200 000. The Parisians held out, dragooned by a revolutionary government imposing a reign of terror, and driven on by their religious fanaticism. But the stranglehold weakened towards the end of 1590 and in early 1591, and the royal attempts on the city were thwarted. Celebrations of the days of the Escalade (10 September 1590) and the Farines (20 January 1591) joined the Day of the Barricades in the League calendar. Feasts and processions were held to perpetuate the glorious memory – and also to reinforce a solidarity which was beginning to crumble.

Meanwhile, in workmanlike fashion, Henri IV set about recovering the towns around Paris one by one. Chartres and Noyon fell in April and August 1591, and towards the end of September he laid siege unsuccessfully to Rouen. But while in 1592 the Politiques, tired of waiting for his conversion, began to talk of other claimants to the throne, the League too was racked with internal dissension. Mayenne, every inch the haughty noble, was not happy at being controlled by the Council of the Union, and sought to bypass it by keeping a number of matters from it and entrusting them to his own council. In 1592 he sent the long-serving Secretary of State Villeroy, a Leaguer though by no means an extremist, on a mission to Henri IV with a view to negotiating a compromise. But Mayenne, too greedy and too feudal, demanded too much. Moreover, he was playing his hand without taking account of the popular wing of the League – rather as Condé had done in the wake of the first conflict – to such an extent that in 1593 the 'manant' attacked 'this noble bloodsucker who is conspiring with other great families for the overthrow of the preachers and the Sixteen'.[11]

Besides the gulf opening up between Mayenne and the Sixteen, fissures were also appearing within the Parisian League itself. The solidarity of 1588–9, and even 1590, was breaking down under the pressures and privations of the siege. Shut up in their city, the Parisians were increasingly irritated by conditions which were harsh at the best of times and entailed perpetual rationing. The Parlement councillors, officeholders, and wealthy merchants were tired of the restrictions and the excesses. The blockade prevented the elite from trading and from looking after their property outside the walls. They were well aware that their careers and prosperity depended on a monarchy which could bring the country together and restore order. Inclining therefore towards reconciliation with Henri IV, this new class of Politiques, some of them in Paris almost despite themselves, began a pamphlet campaign in his favour within the city walls. Watched, denounced, and exhausted, and kept off balance by the directors of the various councils, they were obliged to temporise. But even among hardcore Leaguers there were some who, like President Brisson (who would pay for it with his life in November 1591), having supported Charles X, were nevertheless prepared to recognise Henri IV if he abjured. Their position was not far removed from that of the Politiques we have just considered. But there remained the zealots, like Boucher, Bussy, and La Chapelle-Marteau, who put religion above all else and would brook no compromise. In agreement with Philip II they advanced the claim of the Infanta Isabella-Clara providing she married a French prince. Suspicious of the Parlement (which they purged), of the nobility, and of the men Mayenne had placed in their militia and their councils, they established a reign of terror in the city. Without wishing to destroy them – for without them the city would fall – Mayenne sought to undermine and thus to control them. Yet for all that, he convoked an Estates General in January 1593, perhaps with the idea of advancing his own claim to the throne. Outraged by Mayenne's audacity, Henri IV accused him of treason: only the king, he maintained, had the right to summon the three estates of the realm. And he extended the charge to all who responded to Mayenne's summons. Oddly enough, the provincial deputies who evaded the Bourbon lookouts and got into Paris, where they were plied with gold by Philip II's agents, were more committed to Spain and the League than their Parisian hosts. The Parisian deputies of the Third Estate adopted a more moderate current of relative hostility to the Spaniard combined with awareness of a French national interest. Their provincial counterparts, on the other hand, demanded the promulgation of the decrees of Trent and asserted the sovereign right of the Estates General to elect the monarch – who need not be French. Such was the bizarre assembly ridiculed by the authors of the *Satire Ménippée*. On the first day, Mayenne announced his own candidature, having done his best to fix the assembly beforehand. He could count on 100 or so deputies, having packed the house with his own clients, moderate Leaguers, and officials from the Parlement and the *Chambre des comptes*, in order to provide a counterweight to the provincial deputies – League extremists in Spanish pay who were favourable to the claims of Isabella-Clara.[12]

Navarre gave proof of his own and his council's political acumen in that same January. From his camp at Suresnes he proposed to the Estates General that their representatives should meet with his to consider ways of resolving the troubles and 'preserving the Catholic religion and the State'. Despite the opposition of the League's hardcore, the increasing exasperation of the Parisian population at their confinement ensured that his proposal was accepted. The conference took place at Suresnes towards the end of April 1593. To protect the negotiators from the danger of an armed coup, a ten-day ceasefire was agreed on 4 May for the area within four leagues around Paris and Suresnes. To their immense relief, the Parisians found themselves free to wander outside the walls. L'Estoile recorded the devotions paid to Our Lady at the shrines around the outskirts.[13] On 17 May Archbishop Renaud de Beaune announced the king's conversion, to the assembly at Suresnes, news which was followed by a three-month extension of the truce. The dramatic gesture which Henri's councillors had prepared left nothing to chance. A gathering of bishops to instruct Henri in the Catholic faith was planned for Mantes on 15 July, and the public ceremony of abjuration or reconciliation (according as it was seen from a Huguenot or a Catholic perspective) was to take place on 25 July. Abandoning vague promises and without waiting for a 'national council', Henri proclaimed his firm intention of returning to the Roman fold. We have already seen the powerful reasons behind his decision. Henri and his councillors (whether Catholic or Protestant) saw no possibility of a military solution with pretenders on every side and the kingdom a prey to the ambitions of Spain, Lorraine, and Savoy. Even among his own entourage, war-weariness was fostering the growth of a party which was beginning to look to the young Cardinal of Bourbon for a solution. But the news of Henri's conversion unleashed the 'dynamic of peace'.[14]

Henri IV and the Compromise of State

From now on the process ran like a well-oiled machine. The rite of passage which turned the turbulent prince of the blood and the Protector of the Reformed churches into the Most Christian King unfolded slowly over two years. But was not this period suitable in the light of the traumas which had been undergone? The protracted rite was punctuated by particular ceremonies: reconciliation with the Roman Church at the Basilica of Saint-Denis on 25 July 1593; the coronation at Chartres (for Reims was still held by the League) on 27 February 1594; the royal entry into the capital early in the morning of 22 March 1594; and finally, to round everything off, the papal absolution granted on 17 September 1595. It was a long and slow journey towards the fullness of sacral sovereignty, an autumnal time during which the doublet of Béarn gave way to the fleur-de-lys of the first Bourbon king, a solitary journey, so often described that the images remain to this day stamped upon the minds of schoolchildren.

After Henri's abjuration, opponents rallied to his cause with almost disconcerting rapidity. It would be tedious to enumerate the towns which opened their gates in the course of 1594 throughout Normandy, Burgundy, Picardy, Champagne, and the Midi. Not all these shifts of allegiance, however, were as spontaneous as they seemed. There was meticulous preparation for the taking of Paris, to forestall possible resistance by the diehard Leaguers.

Pamphlets promised free pardon to the inhabitants, 'even those commonly known as the Sixteen', and the governor was bought off together with several aldermen. The operation had to run like clockwork if bloodshed was to be avoided. Paris, like other cities, was guaranteed a reduction in taxes, preservation of its municipal privileges, prohibition of Protestant worship, retention of its traditional militia, and freedom from royal garrisons. Winning over a town often depended on winning over its governor. In such cases, gifts and promises of money could transform a sincere and committed Leaguer into a good royalist. But a nobleman's honour commanded a high price in those days. Villars-Brancas, the governor of Rouen, promised his allegiance and that of a number of Norman cities in return for appointment as Admiral of France and Governor of the districts of Rouen and Caux, together with 3 million *livres* cash. Marshal Brissac was allowed to remain Governor of Paris, and received 1 695 000 *livres* for handing over the capital. Nor were the Guises far behind. The young Duke of Guise obtained nearly 4 million *livres* and was made Governor of Provence in return for the allegiance of himself, of Reims, and of Champagne. Repurchasing the kingdom from the League nobility certainly cost the Treasury some 32 million *livres*, equivalent to an entire year's income. But this bald statistic takes no account of the offices and appointments conferred or confirmed (Mayenne's had been conferred beforehand), the lucrative positions and the shares in tax revenues to be collected. Long and difficult negotiations, often concluded with veritable treaties (like that of Folembray in 1595, which formalised Mayenne's reconciliation), deals and promises, together with the emergence of a degree of national sentiment, were what rallied the princes and barons behind the Bourbon dynasty. And it remains true that the 'Royal State' was in any case an amalgam of particular interests in which the Crown triumphed to the extent that it could keep a large number of them satisfied. But Henri IV, who had seen enough to leave him pretty sceptical about human nature, was not in the least surprised. When Sully, a Councillor of State and already the specialist in financial affairs, grumbled in 1594 at the sums extorted by the League barons, Henri replied: 'You are foolish to raise so many objections, and you forget the advice you yourself have given me so often . . . to play on the particular interests of all those who are in league . . . on general pretexts.'[15] Machiavelli himself could scarcely have put it better, nor would he have baulked at another of Henri's replies to Sully: 'We will pay whatever it takes to have these things made over to us, because if we had to take them by force, they would cost us ten times as much.'

All the same, even this dearly bought success was far from total, for the League was far from dead. In 1594 Mayenne still controlled Burgundy, and Aumale Picardy. Marseille was ruled by a League dictator, and Mercœur was impregnable in Brittany. Spain was still pouring in money and reinforcing the League remnants through Franche-Comté and the Breton seaports. Nor had the common people as yet all awoken from their theocratic dream. The vast majority wallowed in the luxury of peace, especially as the militants of the League had never represented more than a minority of the towns, but some thought the conversion of the 'Fox of Béarn' a little too quick and easy. Suspicion of a king who many thought remained a heretic at heart condensed on the knives of regicides. In 1593 Pierre Barrière confided to several churchmen his intention of killing the 'tyrant usurper', but having been denounced by an Italian gentleman, he was executed in August. A pupil of the Jesuits named Jean Châtel made an attempt on the king's life in the Louvre itself on 27 December 1594.[16] A searching interrogation convinced the judges that the Jesuits had persuaded him that a deed as meritorious as the slaying of a king unfaithful to God and the Pope would shorten his pain in Purgatory. And after all, Clement VIII had not yet granted Henri absolution. While Châtel suffered the penalty for regicide, the Parlement de Paris showed its Gallican colours by demanding and obtaining the expulsion of the Jesuits from its jurisdiction. And if one recalls that 1594 saw the outbreak of the famous rising of the 'Croquants' ('nobodies'), later known as the 'Tard-Avisés' (the 'wise too late'), one can see that the shattered kingdom was still far from mended.

The declaration of war on Spain in January 1595 was a political master-stroke. At home it discredited such League barons as remained in the field, making them look like traitors to their country as soon as hostilities commenced. The war was a national enterprise reminiscent of the foreign policy of Henri II, an attempt to push the enemy back beyond the frontiers of the realm. On the diplomatic front it provided the allies of France with unarguable evidence that, although now a good Catholic, Henri IV had no intention of grovelling before the old man of the Escorial. It was a tough war, fought on several fronts. A successful engagement at Fontaine-Française, not far from Dijon, was transmuted by the Bourbon propaganda machine into a crushing victory and aroused immense popular enthusiasm: in Jean-Pierre Babelon's words, 'it was the first stirring of the spirit of 1914'.[17] Burgundy was won back for the king, and Mayenne submitted, lured by more than 2.5 million *livres*. But another success at La Fère was offset by a brilliant Spanish coup at Calais. And March 1597 brought catastrophe: Philip II's forces occupied Amiens, near Paris and in the heart of Picardy, a tense province which the League had dominated not long before. An enormous concentration of men and artillery (assembled by Maximilien de Béthune, then Baron de Rosny and later Duke of Sully) forced the Spaniards to abandon the city, and Henri IV made a triumphal entry on 25 September 1597. Then, early in 1598, he set out for Brittany, which was still holding out under Mercœur. The League towns of Brittany duly surrendered, and Mercœur himself offered his allegiance in return for money and honour (his daughter was married off to César de Vendôme, Henri's illegitimate son by Gabrielle d'Estrées). Peace negotiations with Spain began at Vervins in the Vermandois in January that year. Philip II accepted defeat, recognising that his daughter would never occupy the throne of France, that Catholicism would not be the sole religion of that country, and that Brittany, Provence and Picardy would no longer be his. The dream of a universal Habsburg monarchy had been burst like a bubble. The Treaty of Vervins recapitulated the provisions of Cateau-Cambrésis as if 40 years of war, confrontation, pogrom, and assassination had never happened. The tragic period of civil and religious conflict had ended with the restoration of the *status quo* between the two great European powers, except that Spain had had to give back a few towns in Brittany and the north. And Henri IV, secure now in his international role, brought the interlude of war with Spain to a close without any consultation of his allies in England, the Netherlands, Germany and Switzerland.

The Protestants, who with a few exceptions had helped their old Protector to mount the steps to the throne, now hung back because since August 1589 Henri IV had been so concerned to reassure his Catholic subjects by holding out the prospect of his conversion that he seemed to forget that nearly a million of his people were Calvinists. The Edict of Mantes (1591) aimed to reassure the minority, renewing the freedom of conscience and worship granted by earlier edicts. The king's conversion to the majority religion, although approved and even recommended by his Huguenot friends Sully and Duplessis-Mornay, stuck in a good many throats. Agrippa d'Aubigné lamented it in tragic verse. And the understanding between Henri and the Huguenot grandees began to break down as the latter saw their hopes of full recognition frustrated. Henri de La Tour d'Auvergne (Viscount of Turenne and Duke of Bouillon) left the royal army in 1596 together with his troops, in the middle of the hard-fought siege of Amiens. The Huguenots reactivated the federal political structures originally forged in the wake of Saint Bartholomew. The 'political assembly' of Sainte-Foy in 1594 extended the 'Calvinist republic' across the entire kingdom, and there was talk of appointing a new Protector, Maurice of Nassau, the son of William of Orange. In the midst of the war with Spain, the Huguenot nobles discussed with royal representatives the terms of a civil and religious constitution which would integrate Protestants and Protestantism in the machinery of the State. A permanent but peripatetic assembly of nobles, notables and ministers moved between Saumur, Loudun, Châtellerault and Vendôme. Grievances reached such a pitch that a resort to arms was considered (as in the time of Condé), under the command of Bouillon and La Trémoille. But successes against the Spaniards, the recapture of Amiens and the Breton ports, and the opening of peace talks at Vervins, put Henri IV in a commanding position, and his representatives threatened to publish the edict without waiting for the consent of the political assembly. The Edict of Nantes was finally signed in April 1598.[18]

The edict opened with a lengthy preamble expressing the king's wish that all his Protestant subjects would return to the Catholic faith and hinting at the provisional nature of the recognition of two religions within the kingdom. The body of the text comprised 92 public articles, together with 56 secret or 'particular' articles covering individual situations, and a third section of royal warrants providing for the sums the Treasury was to pay to the Protestant organisation. The Huguenots were given full freedom of conscience and were declared legally capable of 'holding any estates, dignities, appointments, or public offices' without having to swear allegiance to Catholicism. Royal offices had been to all intents and purposes closed to Calvinists since Henri III's prohibitive edict of July 1585. [19] There was thus a deep thirst for office among the Huguenots, as among the entire French

bourgeoisie, and in fact the new king had been admitting Protestants to public office since the Edict of Mantes in 1591. The
Parlements had protested strongly, convinced that no heretic could
serve the State and reluctant to share the spoils of office. They
refused to admit Protestants to the sovereign courts or other royal
institutions. Further obstacles were put in the way of Huguenots
eager for office in the aftermath of the Edict of Nantes.

Articles 3 and 5 of the edict concerned freedom of worship.
There was not much room for manoeuvre here, between the
demands of the League cities and barons sick of the sound of
psalm-singing on the one hand, and on the other those of the
Protestants, determined to keep as many places of worship as they
could. Before defining the rights of the minority, the edict stated
that Catholic worship was to be restored wherever it had been
stamped out, and that all confiscated church property was to be
handed back. The Huguenots were permitted to retain their worship wherever it had been established in 1586 and up to the end
of August 1597, and in addition in any other place authorised by
the Edicts of Nérac and Fleix (i.e., in one city, and in the suburbs of another city, per bailiwick). And of course noblemen with
rights of high justice could retain their churches and ministers.
The public practice of the Protestant religion was forbidden in
any city which had made this a condition of surrender to Henri
IV: for example Paris, cathedral cities, and towns in areas dominated by the great League barons.

Besides the rather ungenerous provisions with regard to worship, the Huguenots were given special privileges as a sort of legal
corporation, almost a separate estate of the realm. Some 150 towns,
villages and castles were allocated to them as safe havens, and in
each the king paid for the maintenance of a governor and a Protestant garrison. Special tribunals to judge cases in which a Huguenot was involved were established, as in earlier toleration edicts.
These 'Chambers of the Edict' operated at the Parlements of Paris,
Toulouse, Bordeaux and Grenoble. The Treasury was to maintain Huguenot ministers and cover the expenses of Huguenot
schools and colleges. Article 43 of the secret provisions recognised the existence of the 'political assemblies', providing that
they met only in the presence of a royal judge.

Such then was the Edict of Nantes: a child of circumstance,
the product of a complex interplay of Protestant demands, Catholic
objections, and royal prerogatives, a response to the overriding

need to bring the civil war to an end rather than to any desire for toleration in principle. It remained none the less unique in Europe, for even if rival religions had to coexist in other countries, their coexistence was not defined and guaranteed by legislation. The French monarchy thus asserted one of its fundamental political principles: the rule of law.

The Edict of Nantes had much in common with the earlier documents promulgated under Charles IX and Henri III: the Edicts of January, Saint-Germain, Beaulieu, and Nérac. But the difference was that, coming at the end of 40 years of civil and religious conflict, it seemed definitive to French Catholics (despite the reservations in the preamble), in effect the founding charter of an alternative to the Catholic religion. Even so, Henri IV and his Council had great difficulty in having it registered by the Parlements. On the pretext that the safe havens violated the fundamental law of the inalienability of the kingdom, they refused to publish the edict within their jurisdictions. It took enormous patience and perseverance on the part of the royal commissioners, and even the king himself, to constrain the magistrates of Toulouse by means of a *lit de justice*. Elsewhere, last minute negotiations and concessions were necessary. The Chamber of the Edict at Paris was to have 16 Catholics but only a single Huguenot according to the terms on which the edict was registered in 1599. Toulouse registered the edict in 1600, but Rouen held out until 1609. The resistance of the Parlements was an echo of a deeper malaise, that of the committed Leaguers embittered at having fought so hard for nothing. There were demonstrations in Mans, Tours, and Paris. The assembly of the clergy in 1598 was already calling for the abolition of the Chambers of the Edict and the prohibition of Huguenot synods, their opposition stiffened by Clement VIII's despairing remark on hearing of the edict: 'This is my crucifixion.'

All the old misunderstandings were renewed and exacerbated as the king, who was conscious of the balance of forces and wished, by the law, to be the arbiter between them, clashed with a predominantly Catholic population led by a reinvigorated Church implacably opposed to religious pluralism. It was this tension that brought forth the regicides. And the inevitable compromise led to innumerable problems in implementing the edict on the ground. Commissions consisting of magistrates from both religions were set up to define the Huguenot places of worship, those granted by right of possession, through the mid-west and the Midi; and those granted by concession, towards the middle and north, not to mention those established by seigneurial right, scattered across the realm. More negotiations and deals followed, especially in northern France, where it was necessary to introduce Huguenot worship in places where it had never existed. The King's Council was forever having to intervene and arrange exchanges, modifications and limitations attempting to be an impartial judge – at least until Henri IV was assassinated in 1610.

15 Conclusion

The Wars of Religion did not come to an end with Henri IV's peace, they gradually faded away. But their roots were still in place, and, in the reigns of the first Bourbon and his son, would continue to push forth the shoots of noble rebellions, Huguenot risings, and plots and machinations by the *dévots*, the heirs of the League. But can one still speak of 'Wars of Religion'? The term was hardly ever used by contemporaries, who spoke of civil troubles and conflicts, only adding the adjective religious as a cloak. It was in the nineteenth century that 'Wars of Religion' came into vogue, absolving at a stroke both the Catholics and the Protestants from the charge of political revolt against the monarchy of the last Valois and the first Bourbon.

For, with due respect to those who are enamoured of synthesis, the period of the 'Wars of Religion' breaks down into a succession of particular crises which one might easily call turning-points if Henri IV had not succeeded in bandaging up the wounds – not without cost, nor without risk of them reopening. Might one suggest that French society, faced with the prospect of Leviathan, the rule of the One, broke up in order to resist it better? For forty years and more the 40 000 or 50 000 men of the nobility, from the humblest squire to the haughtiest prince, if not as a whole then at least in large groups, consistently advocated in the face of authoritarian monarchy a return to collective government in which Councils and the Estates General, manned for the most part by the nobility, would be the institutional expression of the aristocratic regime after which they hankered. The religious convictions of some of them, whether Protestant or too rigidly Catholic, excluded them from power at the State level and made them a party, proclaiming to all and sundry 'the reasons which have led us to take up arms'. Thus, in these times of faction, the weakening of royal authority led to a power vacuum which encouraged the emergence of certain charismatic personalities which had been overshadowed and silenced during the reign of the One. Such men as Condé, Guise, Damville, Navarre, and, on a lower level, Coligny, Lesdiguières, Tavannes, Mercœur, Mayenne and Joyeuse, scattered as though from a prism the rays which usually emanated from the king alone, or at least had done so under François I and Henri II.

There was a resurgence of the great baronial predator, a figure almost forgotten since François I and his mother had destroyed the Constable of Bourbon, along with a revival of the provinces, which invested themselves in their leaders, or rather in which the leaders invested through their kinship and clientage networks, their vassals and their servants. The seams which had so recently joined together the tapestry of France were coming apart again. Guyenne, where the cry of 'Long live England' had been heard as recently as 1548 in the *gabelle* revolt, became the lair in which Henri de Navarre shut himself away and prepared to stretch his wings. The Rhône corridor – the Dauphiné and Provence, fragments of ancient Lotharingia – was at once the battleground and the booty over which rival Huguenot and League governors and the Duke of Savoy fought, when the people themselves did not take a hand, as they did in 1579. And Northern France itself was by no means wholeheartedly in the Valois camp. Picardy included Péronne, the birthplace of the first League. And from Condé's time the Protestants had redoubtable bridgeheads in the Loire valley: Orléans briefly, then Saumur and La Charité. Mercœur and the Spanish garrisons were still hanging on in Brittany as late as 1598. Senior State officials knew how dangerous things could get when a prince and his province made common cause against the rule of the centre, so Michel de L'Hôpital and then Birague, the Chancellor of Henri III and Catherine de Medici, sought to reduce as far as they could the powers of the provincial governors, but without success – leaving the task to Richelieu.

The towns played a crucial part in the fragmentation of France. Both Huguenots and Leaguers strove to control municipal institutions and urban space. Both sides regarded the often walled space of the town as ideal for a Christian polity (and the two terms were not so contradictory as they might have seemed), a community of the faithful. The Catholics employed the ceremonies of religious and communal solidarity in the familiar decor of processions, while the Protestants strove to impose the 'political order' tainted with Puritanism which Calvin was trying to establish in Geneva. The economic crisis which brought forth bands of gentlemen brigands and predatory barons drove townsfolk to League fanaticism or Huguenot rigour. The Crown was quite right to multiply officeholders for, even if done partly for financial motives, it thus filled the towns with men who had a vested interest in upholding royal government. And it was with similar aims for control, albeit with but limited success, that the Crown sought to subject free trades to the sworn guild system and to limit the freedom of municipal elections, hoping thus to tighten control of the centres of power.

Leaguers and Huguenots clashed like flints to produce sparks of specific violence which gave a brutal tone to almost half a century's history. However, their modes of political activity were largely the same, and followed traditional baronial and Christian models. The 'Wars of Religion' represented the reaffirmation of diversity in the face of a unifying authority. On the Protestant side, a more arid system of representation exalted the individual as actor and motivator in the group. On the Catholic side, the abundance of signs (exaggerated further in reaction to the Huguenot challenge) led to a social mystique in which the irrational perceived itself as the coherence of an entire and complete system. The two mental universes were radically opposed, but their historical development followed similar – and traditional – paths.

The real victims of social disintegration were the peasants. Victims of the economic crisis which wiped out the middling proprietors and proliferated smallholders, for a brief moment they thought that they might profit from the ecclesiastical alternative offered by Protestantism in delivering them from the burden of the tithe. But the Reformed churches were prompt to disabuse them. After the tithe agitation, the peasants took little interest in the religious debates of the time, their miserable condition rendering them perforce tolerant, except for the great rising of the Croquants in 1594. When occasion arose, they massacred the Catholic or Protestant soldiers who without restraint oppressed them. In this matter too we must revise our terminology, reviving the usage of contemporaries who referred to the 'troubles'. In effect, it was guerrilla warfare rather than outright war that constituted the everyday experience of the French in those decades. Incessant and destructive, it threatened people and property. Any petty captain in a mountain lair could terrorise the countryside for miles around. Omnipresent in the southern provinces, military plunder was less permanent but no less damaging in the North. The *reiters* hired by the Huguenots devastated those parts of eastern France through which they passed in 1570, 1576, 1587 and 1588. And Henri IV's reconquest of France north of the Loire put most of Normandy, the Ile-de-France, Champagne and Picardy under military occupation for almost a decade. From the start of the troubles, war and its accompaniments became the principal causes of economic crisis, upsetting the equilibrium of peasant life, widening the gulf between town and country, and destroying the cohesion of the rural community. But if those who lived on the land certainly paid more dearly in the Midi and the mid-west for living in provinces 'in prey', one can safely say that when the captains and men of war mobilised in 1560, a dark age dawned for all who worked the land.

The Protestants emerged weakened from the troubles that their own existence had in large part sparked off. Reduced in numbers, and reduced in influence through the conversion of gentlemen (a process which accelerated in the following century), they found themselves politically privileged by the Edict of Nantes. But the tendency of the State from Henri IV's time onwards to undermine both estates and corporate bodies left them vulnerable and dependent on the good will of the sovereign. For this reason they remained loyal subjects – at least for a time. But, feeling threatened by the rising tide of the pro-Spanish *dévot* party, they once more took up arms, only to fail finally and decisively in their attempt to become a separate order within the kingdom. The centralising, authoritarian monarchy, however, emerged strengthened from the general challenge with which it had been faced. Always keeping its own head above water – and what violence it sometimes took to avoid being swallowed up by one or other of the parties! – it succeeded also in keeping the notion of the State afloat. This was partly because of the vested interests of that disparate group which profited from the Crown: the nobility, the financial bourgeoisie of tax-farmers and partners, and the officers in the public service. And partly also because François I and Henri II had established bureaucracy so firmly that the aristocratic and communitarian alternatives put forward by both the

League and the Huguenots could no longer satisfy bourgeois or even, to a certain extent, noble aspirations. For the nobles were the leading clients of the State when it set out to wage war, which was why Henri IV shrewdly took his kingdom to war with Spain.

Curiously, amidst the passions that were unleashed, the beneficiaries of the royal State created an ideology for themselves. It was Gallican, for the often bourgeois ideologues had ceased to dream of a united Christendom. It was unitary, because a centralised regime was a precondition of their survival. It was historical, for they could not conceive themselves except in a movement projected across time. And finally, it was rational, for the holding of office (or benefice) in the monarchical machinery of State was evaluated in calculations, negotiations and power relations. This ideology made headway by fits and starts among the French elite, which rallied to the State because its submission 'was connected to their desire to bear the name of the One before any other'.

Notes

Notes to Chapter 1: Peasant Life

1. Michel Mollat, *Genèse médiévale de la France moderne* (Paris, 1977), p. 235.

2. Emmanuel Le Roy Ladurie, *L'État royal: de Louis XI à Henri IV* (Paris, 1987), p. 48.

3. Jean Lartigaut, *Les campagnes du Quercy après la guerre de Cent Ans (vers 1440–vers 1550)* (Toulouse, 1978), p. 83.

4. Emmanuel Le Roy Ladurie, *Paysans du Languedoc* (Paris, 1966), pp. 124–5 and 131.

5. Pierre Chaunu and Richard Gascon, *L'État et la ville, 1450–1660*, in *Histoire économique et sociale de la France*, ed. Fernand Braudel and Ernest Labrousse (Paris, 1977), vol. 1, p. 397.

6. Bernard Chevalier, *Les bonnes villes de France du XIVe au XVIe siècle* (Paris, 1982), p. 39.

7. Alain Croix, *Nantes et le pays nantais au XVIe siècle: étude démographique* (Paris, 1974); Hugues Neveux, *La ville classique* (Paris, 1981; *Histoire de la France urbaine*, ed. Georges Duby, vol. 3), p. 31.

8. Chaunu and Gascon, *L'État et la ville*, p. 407.

9. Jean Jacquart, *La crise rurale en Ile-de-France, 1550–1670* (Paris, 1974), p. 297.

10. Le Roy Ladurie, *Paysans du Languedoc*, pp. 78–79.

11. Gilles Caster, *Le commerce du pastel et de l'épicerie à Toulouse, 1450–1561* (Toulouse, 1962), pp. 41 and 53.

12. Louis Merle, *La métairie et l'évolution agraire de la Gâtine poitevine de la fin du Moyen Age à la Révolution* (Paris, 1958), p. 69.

13. Yvonne Bezard, *La vie rurale dans le sud de la région parisienne de 1450 à 1560* (Paris, 1929), p. 84.

14. Emmanuel Le Roy Ladurie, *Histoire du climat depuis l'an mil*, 2 vols (Paris, 1983).

15. Jacquart, *Crise rurale*; Pierre Goubert, *Beauvais et le Beauvaisis de 1600 à 1730* (Paris, 1960).

16. Claude Haton, *Mémoires contenant le récit des événements accomplis de 1553 à 1587*, ed. Félix Bourquelot, 2 vols (Paris, 1857); Pierre de L'Estoile, *Journal . . . pour le règne d'Henri III (1574–1589)*, ed. Louis-Raymon Lefèvre (Paris, 1943).

17. Madeleine Foisil, *Le Sire de Gouberville: un gentilhomme normand au XVIᵉ siècle* (Paris, 1986).

18. See Merle, *Métairie et l'évolution agraire*.

19. Bezard, *Vie rurale dans la région parisienne*.

20. Yves-Marie Bercé, *Histoire des Croquants* (Paris, 1988), and *Croquants et Nu-pieds* (Collection Archives, Paris, 1974).

21. Le Roy Ladurie, *Paysans du Languedoc*.

22. Emmanuel Le Roy Ladurie, *Le Carnaval de Romans, de la Chandeleur au mercredi des Cendres, 1579–1580* (Paris, 1979). See also Jean Jacquart, 'Immobilisme et catastrophes, 1560–1660', in *Histoire de la France rurale*, ed. Georges Duby and Armand Wallon (Paris, 1975), pp. 34–41.

23. Robert Muchembled, *La sorcière au village* (Collection Archives, Paris, 1979); and Jean Delumeau, *La peur en Occident* (Paris, 1978), chs 11–12.

24. French edition, H. Institoris and J. Sprenger, *Le marteau des sorcières* (Grenoble, 1990).

Notes to Chapter 2: Urban Life

1. Duby (ed.), *Histoire de la France urbaine* vol. 3, pp. 157–163.

2. Frédéric Mauro, *Le XVIᵉ siècle européen: aspects économiques* (Paris, 1966), pp. 213–14.

3. Georges Duby and Armand Wallon (eds), *Histoire de la France rurale* (Paris, 1975), vol. 2.

4. Pierre Jeannin, *Le marchand au XVIᵉ siècle* (Paris, 1957), pp. 92–3.

5. Jacques Bousquet, *Enquête sur les commodités du Rouergue en 1552* (Toulouse, 1969), pp. 109–10.

6. Claude Longeon, *Une province française à la Renaissance* (Saint-Étienne, 1975), pp. 109–17.

7. Lucien Febvre and Henri-Jean Martin, *L'apparition du livre* (Paris, 1971), pp. 260, 266–7, 247–9 and 350.

8. Jean-Pierre Seguin, *L'information en France de Louis XII à Henri II* (Geneva, 1961), p. 51.

9. Hervé Martin, *Le métier de prédicateur en France septentrionale à la fin du Moyen Age, 1350–1520* (Paris, 1988), pp. 615 and 558.

10. André Godin, *Spiritualité franciscaine en Flandres au XVIᵉ siècle: l'homéliaire de Jean Vitrier: texte, étude thématique et sémantique* (Geneva, 1971).

11. Bernard Faivre, 'L'automne du Moyen Age', in *Le théâtre en France*, ed. Jacqueline du Jomaron (Paris, 1988), vol. 1, pp. 58, 60, 63, 72 and 82.

12. Robert Muchembled, *L'invention de l'homme moderne: sensibilités, mœurs et comportements collectifs sous l'Ancien Régime* (Paris, 1988), pp. 205 ff. See also Chaunu and Gascon, *L'État et la ville*, p. 261.

13. Richard Gascon, *Grand commerce et vie urbaine au XVIᵉ siècle: Lyon et ses marchands vers 1520–1580*, 2 vols (Paris, 1971).

14. Henri Hauser, *Ouvriers du temps passé* (Paris, 1909).

15. Natalie Zemon Davis, 'Grève et salut à Lyon', in *Les cultures du peuple* (Paris, 1979); Hauser, *Ouvriers*, ch. 10.

16. Davis, 'Grève et salut', p. 31.

17. Richard Gascon, 'La France du mouvement: les commerces et les villes', in Chaunu and Gascon, *L'État et la ville*, p. 427.

18. Janine Garrisson, *La Saint-Barthélemy* (Brussells, 1987), p. 94.

19. Hauser, *Ouvriers*.

20. Roger Chartier and Hugues Neveux, 'La ville dominante et soumise', in Duby (ed.), *Histoire de la France urbaine*, vol. 3, pp. 214–15.

21. Bercé, *Croquants et Nu-pieds*, p. 33.

22. Chartier and Neveux, 'La ville dominante et soumise', pp. 215–16.

23. Natalie Zemon Davis, 'Assistance, humanisme et hérésie', in *Cultures*, pp. 40–112. See also Jean-Pierre Gutton, *La société et les pauvres: l'exemple de la Généralité de Lyon, 1534–1789* (Paris, 1971); and *La société et les pauvres en Europe, XVIᵉ–XVIIIᵉ siècle* (Paris, 1974), pp. 108–9.

24. Roger Chartier, *Figures de la gueuserie* (Paris, 1982), pp. 11–46; and Bronislaw Geremek, *Truands et misérables dans l'Europe moderne, 1350–1600* (Collection Archives, Paris, 1980).

25. Natalie Zemon Davis, 'Les rites de violence', in *Cultures*, p. 286. The original article was published in *Past and Present*, 59 (1973) under the title 'The Rites of Violence: Religious Riot in Sixteenth-century France'.

Notes to Chapter 3: Passions in France

1. Jacques Le Goff and René Rémond (eds.), *Histoire de la France religieuse* (Paris, 1984), vol. 2, ed. François Lebrun, p. 142.
2. Philippe Ariès, *Essai sur l'histoire de la mort en Occident du Moyen Age à nos jours* (Paris, 1975), pp. 37–41; [English version (tr. Patricia M. Ranum): *Western Attitudes Toward Death: from the Middle Ages to the Present* (Baltimore and London, 1974), ch. 2].
3. Johan Huizinga, *Le déclin du Moyen Age* (Paris, 1967), pp. 235 [Eng. tr. by F. Hopman, *The waning of the Middle Ages* (London: Peregrine, 1975), p. 216].
4. 'Ne faites pas comme infidèles font/Qui estiment par œuvre méritoire/Que paradis justement gagné ont. Si de la foi ne vous coulez parer/Et Dieu vous a en indignation/Courir aux saints serait trop s'égarer. Mais quant à vous, quoi qu'on vous dise ou fasse/Suyez sûre qu'en liberté vous êtes/Si vous avez de Dieu l'amour et la grâce'. The *Dialogue* is not available in English, but there is a useful discussion in Robert D. Cottrell, *The Grammar of Silence: A Reading of Marguerite de Navarre's Poetry* (Washington, D.C., 1986), ch. 3.
5. Pierre Imbart de la Tour, *Les origines de la Réforme* (Melun, 1946), vol. 2, p. 435.
6. Michel Veissière, *L'Évêque Guillaume Briçonnet, 1470–1534* (Provins, 1986), p. 133.
7. André Latreille, Étienne Delaruelle, and Jean-Rémy Palanque, *Histoire du catholicisme en France* (Paris, 1963), vol. 2, p. 147.
8. Latreille et al., *Catholicisme en France*, vol. 2, p. 171.
9. Imbart de la Tour, *Origines*, vol. 2, pp. 489–551.
10. Le Goff and Rémond, *Histoire de la France religieuse*, vol. 2, p. 201.
11. François de Dainville, *Les Jésuites et l'éducation de la société française* (Paris, 1940), p. 21.

Notes to Chapter 4: Charles VIII and Louis XII

1. Yvonne Labande-Mailfert, *Charles VIII* (Paris, 1986), p. 193.
2. Bernard Quilliet, *Louis XII* (Paris, 1986), p. 174.
3. Henri Lemonnier, *Les Guerres d'Italie. La France sous Charles VIII, Louis XII et François I, 1492–1547* (Paris, 1903; *Histoire de la France*, ed. Ernest Lavisse, vol. 5, pt 1), p. 142.
4. Lemonnier, *Guerres d'Italie*, p. 24.
5. Cited by Ivan Cloulas, *Charles VIII et le mirage italien* (Paris, 1986), p. 27.
6. 'L'État des offices'. See Chaunu and Gascon, 'L'État et la ville', p. 193.
7. Labande-Mailfert, *Charles VIII*, pp. 442–3.
8. Roland Mousnier, *La venalité des offices sous Henri IV et Louis XIII* (Paris, 1971), pp. 35 and 39.
9. Roger Doucet, *Les institutions de la France au XVIᵉ siècle* (Paris, 1948), p. 62.
10. Jacques Ellul, *Histoire des institutions de l'époque franque à la Révolution* (Paris, 1962), p. 368.
11. Latreille et al., *Histoire du catholicisme en France*, p. 169.
12. Lemonnier, *Guerres d'Italie*, p. 109.
13. Quilliet, *Louis XII*, p. 352.

Notes to Chapter 5: Foreign Policy

1. Jean Jacquart, *François I* (Paris, 1981).
2. Jean-Luc Dejean, *Marguerite de Navarre* (Paris, 1987).
3. Ivan Cloulas, *Henri II* (Paris, 1985).
4. Jean-Marie Constant, *Les Guise* (Paris, 1984).
5. Jean Jacquart, *Bayard* (Paris, 1987).
6. Ferdinand Lot, *Recherches sur les effectifs des armées françaises, des guerres d'Italie aux guerres de religion* (Paris, 1962), pp. 44–45.
7. Lemonnier, *Guerres d'Italie*, vol. 2, p. 31.
8. Blaise de Monluc, *Commentaires, 1521–1576* (Paris, 1974), pp. 43–4.
9. N. Versoris, *Journal d'un bourgeois de Paris sous François I*, ed. P. Joutard (Paris, 1963), p. 78.
10. Lemonnier, *Guerres d'Italie*, vol. 2, pp. 91–2.

Notes to Chapter 6: Domestic Politics

1. Claude Bontems, Léon Pierre Raybaud, and Jean-Pierre Brancourt, *Le Prince dans la France des XVIe et XVIIe siécles* (Paris, 1975), p. 5.
2. Doucet, *Institutions*, p. 135; Chaunu and Gascon, *L'État et la ville*, p. 82.
3. Jacquart, *François I*, p. 281.
4. Ellul, *Histoire des institutions*, p. 361.
5. Michaud Hélène, *La Grande Chancellerie de France et les écritures royales au XVIe siècle* (Paris, 1967), p. 132.
6. Doucet, *Institutions*, p. 134.
7. Albert Buisson, *Le Chancelier Antoine Duprat* (Paris, 1935).
8. Charles Loyseau, *Cinq livres du droit des offices* (Paris: Langelier, 1610), Book III, ch. 1. In fact, the Bureau was set up in 1523.
9. Roland Mousnier, *État et société sous François Ier et pendant le gouvernment personnnel de Louis XIV* (Paris, 1966–7); Chaunu and Gascon, *L'État et la ville*, pp. 37–9. Mousnier relies on the researches of G. Dupont-Ferrier, *Les officiers royaux de bailliage et sénéchaussées et les institutions monarchiques en France à la fin du Moyen Age* (Paris, 1942).
10. Ellul, *Histoire des institutions*, p. 386.
11. Jean-Richard Bloch, *L'anoblissement au temps de François I* (Paris: PUF, 1934), p. 223–4.
12. Or 'provostship'. The name of these basic jurisdictions varied from region to region: they were called *châtellenies* or *vicomtés* in Normandy, and *vigueries* or *baylies* in the *pays d'oc*.
13. G. Zeller, *Les institutions en France au XVIe siècle* (Paris, 1948), p. 284.
14. Zeller, *Institutions*, p. 290.
15. Chaunu and Gascon, *L'État et la ville*, p. 162.
16. Imbart de la Tour, *Origines de la Réforme*, p. 461.
17. Doucet, *Institutions*, vol. 2, p. 808.
18. Veissière, *Guillaume Briçonnet*, p. 181.
19. Lemonnier, *Guerres d'Italie*, vol. 2, p. 378.
20. Gabriel Audisio, *Les Vaudois du Lubéron: une minorité en Provence* (Gap, 1984).

Notes to Chapter 7: The Monarchy and its Image

1. Lemonnier, *Guerres d'Italie*, vol. 2, p. 206.
2. Jacquart, *François I*, p. 196.
3. Cloulas, *Henri II*, p. 140.
4. Zeller, *Institutions*, p. 108.
5. Norbert Élias, *La société de cour* (Paris, 1974).
6. Lucien Febvre, *Amour sacré, amour profane: autour de l'Heptaméron* (Paris, 1944).
7. Anne-Marie Lecoq, *François Ier imaginaire* (Paris, 1987), p. 367.
8. *Recueil général des anciennes lois françaises depris l'an 420 jusqu'à la Revolution de 1789*, ed. De Crusy, F. A. Isambert and A. J. L. Jourdan (Paris, 1827), vol. 12, pp. 275–6.
9. Jacquart, *François I*, pp. 203–4.
10. *Recueil général*, vol. 12, p. 891.
11. Sylvie Béguin, *L'École de Fontainebleau* (Paris, 1972).
12. Joseph Bédier and Paul Hazard, *La littérature française* (Paris, 1948), vol. 1.
13. Duby, *Histoire de la France urbaine*, pp. 154–7.

Notes to Chapter 8: The People in Power

1. Catherine de Medici has attracted numerous biographers. We have followed Ivan Cloulas, *Catherine de Médicis* (Paris, 1979).
2. *Lettres de Catherine de Médicis*, ed. Hector de la Ferrière and Gustave Baguenault de Puchesse, 10 vols (Paris, 1880–1909).
3. Jean Boutier, Alain Dewerpe, and Daniel Nordman, *Un tour de France royal: le voyage de Charles IX, 1564–1566* (Paris, 1984).
4. The 'razés' were composed of Protestants, with some moderate Catholic support; the 'carcistes' were hardline Catholics led by the Count of Carcès.
5. English accounts, then and to this day, tend to call the port 'Newhaven'.
6. E. Bourassin, *Charles IX* (Paris, 1986).
7. Pierre Chevallier, *Henri III* (Paris, 1985); and Jacqueline Boucher, *La cour de Henri III* (Ouest-France, 1986).
8. Constant, *Les Guise*, p. 123.
9. Alençon has not aroused much interest among historians. See Jean-H. Mariejol, *La Réforme et la Ligue: l'Édit de Nantes (1559–*

1598), vol. 6 of *Histoire de France*, ed. E. Lavisse (Paris, 1904), pp. 167–207.

10. Arlette Jouanna, *Le devoir de révolte: la noblesse française et la gestation de l'État moderne, 1559–1661* (Paris, 1989), p. 35.

11. Nancy Roelker, *Queen of Navarre: Jeanne d'Albret, 1528–1572* (Cambridge, Mass., 1968), which contains useful material on Antoine de Navarre. For the latter, see also Mariejol, *La Réforme et la Ligue*, pp. 27, 28, 40 and 70.

12. Janine Garrisson, *Protestants du Midi, 1559–1598* (Toulouse, 1981), p. 27.

13. Mariejol, *La Réforme et la Ligue*, pp. 13, 14, 61, 62, 68, etc.

14. On the conspiracy of Amboise, see Henri Naef, *La Conjuration d'Amboise* (Geneva, 1922); and Robert Kingdon, *Geneva and the Coming of the Wars of Religion* (Geneva, 1956).

15. *Déclaration faicte par monsieur le Prince de Condé pour montrer les raisons qui l'ont contrainct d'entreprendre la défense de l'authorité du Roy* (No place, 1562).

16. Mariejol, *La Réforme et la Ligue*, p. 97; and Myriam Yardeni, *La conscience nationale en France pendant les guerres de religion* (Paris, 1971), pp. 132–3.

17. Historical writing on Henri de Navarre, the future Henri IV, has been plentiful. The two latest biographies are Jean-Pierre Babelon, *Henri IV* (Paris, 1982) and Janine Garrisson, *Henri IV* (Paris, 1984). [English readers may refer to David Buisseret, *Henry IV* (London, 1984).]

18. On the Triumvirate, see Michel Pernot, *Les Guerres de Religion en France, 1559–1598* (Paris, 1987), pp. 64–6.

19. *Déclaration et protestation par monsieur le maréchal Dampville sur l'occasion pour laquelle il prit les armes pendant l'Union* (13 November 1574).

20. F. Palm, *Politics and Religion in Sixteenth-century France: A Study of the Career of Henry of Montmorency-Damville, Uncrowned King of the South* (Boston, 1927).

21. Constant, *Les Guise*, pp. 231–2.

22. *Journal de Pierre de L'Estoile pour le règne d'Henri III, 1574–1589* (Paris, 1943), p. 610.

23. Pierre Chevallier, *Les régicides* (Paris, 1989), pp. 28–45.

Notes to Chapter 9: The Church and the Protestant Faction

1. Janine Garrisson, *Les Protestants au XVIe siècle* (Paris, 1988), pp. 181–182.
2. Kingdon, *Geneva and the Coming of the Wars of Religion*, pp. 138–9.
3. Garrisson, *Protestants du Midi*, p. 22.
4. Paul Geisendorf, *Le Livre des habitants de Genève*, 1549–1587 2 vols (Geneva, 1957–63).
5. Robert Kingdon, *Myths about the Saint-Bartholomew's Day Massacres, 1572–1576* (Cambridge, Mass. and London, 1988), chs 4, 8, 9 and 11. See also Pierre Mesnard, *L'essor de la philosophie politique* au XVIe siècle (Paris, 1969); and Yardeni, *Conscience nationale*, ch. 5.
6. Pierre Miquel, *Les Guerres de Religion* (Paris, 1980), p. 234.
7. Garrisson, *Henry IV*, p. 136.
8. Denis Crouzet, *Les guerriers de Dieu*, 2 vols (Paris, 1990), vol. 1, pp. 496–7.
9. Garrisson, *Protestants au XVIe siècle*, *p. 58.*

Notes to Chapter 10: The Church and the Catholic Faction

1. Latreille, Delaruelle, and Palanque, *Histoire du catholicisme en France*, vol. 2, p. 238.
2. *Recueil général des anciennes lois françaises*, ed. Isambert, De Crusy and Taillandier, (Paris, 1829), vol. 14, pp. 380 ff.
3. Marc Vénard, 'La grande cassure, 1520–1598', in *Histoire de la France religieuse*, ed. F. Lebrun (Paris, 1988), pp. 298–310.
4. Roger Chartier, Marie-Madeleine Compère, and Julia Dominique, L'éducation en *France du XVIe au XVIIIe siècle* (Paris, 1976), p. 162.
5. Garrisson, *Les Protestants au XVI siècle*, p. 329.
6. Pernot, *Guerres de religion*, pp. 235–6.
7. Crouzet, *Guerriers de Dieu*, vol. 1, pp. 208–9.
8. Garrisson, La Saint-Barthélemy, pp. 12–14.
9. Crouzet, *Guerriers de Dieu*, vol. 1, pp. 379–80.
10. Garrisson, *La Saint-Barthélemy*, p. 124.

11. Crouzet, *Guerriers de Dieu*, vol. 1, p. 479.
12. Le Roy Ladurie, *L'État royal*, p. 272; Jouanna, *Devoir de révolte*, p. 180.
13. Constant, *Les Guise*, pp. 82–3.
14. Constant, *Les Guise*, pp. 84–5.
15. Mariejol, *La Réforme et la Ligue*, p. 177.
16. Constant, *Les Guise*, p. 129.
17. Philip Benedict, *Rouen during the War of Religion* (Cambridge, 1981), p. 182.
18. Constant, *Les Guise*, pp. 132–3.
19. Mariejol, *La Réforme et la Ligue*, p. 253.
20. Cited by Yardeni, *Conscience nationale*, p. 218, note.
21. See in this connection, Élie Barnavi, *Le parti de Dieu* (Louvain, 1980), p. 153.
22. Barnavi, *Parti de Dieu*, pp. 167–8.
23. Louis (or François) Morin, sire de Cromé, *Dialogue d'entre le Maheustre et le Manant*, ed. P. M. Ascoti (Geneva, 1977). See in connection with this pamphlet, Arlette Lebigre, *La révolution des curés: Paris, 1588–1594* (Paris, 1980), pp. 250–2. ['Manant' (literally 'peasant') was a slang term for the Leaguers, while 'maheustre' (soldier, or adventurer) was used to describe Henri IV's supporters.]
24. For these movements, see Crouzet, *Guerriers de Dieu*, vol. 2, pp. 323 ff.
25. Pierre de l'Estoile, *Journal*, vol. 1, p. 46.
26. Benedict, *Rouen*, p. 190.

Notes to Chapter 11: The Politiques

1. Michel de L'Hôpital, a somewhat dated figure on the political scene, has aroused little interest among contemporary historians, who, as befits our times, are more concerned with the extreme aspects of later sixteenth-century history. See the already dated biography by Albert Buisson, *Michel de l'Hospital, 1503–1573* (Paris, 1950). The Chancellor's *Oeuvres complètes* were published by Pierre Duffey (Paris, 1824–5).
2. Buisson, *Michel de L'Hospital*, p. 136.
3. Yardeni, *Conscience nationale*, p. 83.
4. Buisson, *Michel de L'Hospital*, p. 196.

5. Yardeni, *Conscience nationale*, pp. 84–5; and Boutier et al., *Tour de France royale*, p. 175.
6. Edited by Marius Valkhoff (Geneva, 1967).
7. On which, see Jean Touchard, *Histoire des idées politiques* (Paris, 1971), p. 287; and especially Mesnard, *L'essor de la philosophie*, pp. 540–1.
8. See Yardeni, *Conscience nationale*, p. 89; Boutier et al., *Tour de France royale*, p. 175; and Mariejol, *La Réforme et la Ligue*, p. 21.
9. See the *Association passée entre les Catholiques et ceux de la religion réformée* (No place, 1575); on which, see Garrisson, *Protestants du Midi*, p. 190.
10. Jouanna, *Devoir de révolte*, pp. 170–1.
11. Jouanna, *Devoir de révolte*, pp. 172–3.
12. Jouanna, *Devoir de révolte*, p. 167.
13. Mesnard, *L'essor de la philosophie*, pp. 473–546.
14. Mariejol, *La Réforme et la Ligue*, pp. 180–1.
15. Mesnard, *L'essor de la philosophie*, pp. 504–8; and Touchard, *Histoire des idées politiques*, p. 291.
16. Yardeni, *Conscience nationale*, p. 169.
17. Montaigne, *Essais*, ed. Maurice Rat, 3 vols (Paris: Classiques Garnier, 1952), vol. 3, p. 7 [from the essay 'De l'utile et de l'honneste', given here in John Florio's rendering].
18. Crouzet, *Guerriers de Dieu*, vol. 2, pp. 552–3.
19. Yardeni, *Conscience nationale*, pp. 178–9; and Touchard, *Histoire des idées politiques*, p. 284.
20. Crouzet, *Guerriers de Dieu*, vol. 2, p. 557. Crouzet refers to the text by Loys Le Carron, *De la tranquillité d'esprit. Livre singulier*, published in 1588.
21. Marc Vénard, in *Histoire de la France religieuse*, p. 272.
22. The *Satire Ménippée* appeared in 1594, but had circulated in manuscript in Leaguer Paris during 1593. Many rallied to Henri IV thanks to its influence. It was the joint work of a group of Parisian citizens pleased to see, in the decline and fall of the League, the triumph of reason and common sense. The prize piece in it is the *Harangue de M. D'Aubray*, written by Pithou. The general theme of the work is a parody of the Estates General summoned by the League in 1593 to choose a king. See the extracts from the *Harangue in Le Seizième en 10/18* (Paris, 1982), pp. 262–4.
23. Yardeni, *Conscience nationale*, p. 266.

24. Yardeni, *Conscience nationale*, pp. 267–71.
25. Yardeni, *Conscience nationale*, p. 267.
26. Extract from the *Harangue de M. D'Aubray*.
27. Yardeni, *Conscience nationale*, p. 278.

Notes to Chapter 12: Condé's Wars, 1559–70

1. On the conspiracy, see Naef, *La Conjuration d'Amboise*; and Kingdon, *Geneva and the Coming of the Wars of Religion*, ch. 7. See also Jouanna, *Devoir de révolte*, pp. 134–42. For a Catholic gentleman's view of the conspiracy and its suppression, see Anne–Marie Cocula-Vaillières, *Brantôme, amour et gloire au temps des Valois* (Paris, 1986), pp. 72–7.
2. Jouanna, *Devoir de révolte*, p. 141.
3. On the tithe revolts, see Le Roy Ladurie, *Paysans*, p. 382; and Garrisson, *Protestants du Midi*, pp. 162–3.
4. Mariejol, *La Réforme et la Ligue*, p. 46.
5. Pernot, *Guerres de religion*, p. 255.
6. Mariejol, *La Réforme et la Ligue*, pp. 47–50.
7. Garrisson, *Protestants au XVIe siècle*, p. 260.
8. Constant, *Les Guise*, p. 50.
9. Agrippa D'Aubigné, *Histoire universelle* (Paris, 1866–), vol. 1, pp. 14–15.
10. Benedict, *Rouen*, pp. 99–100.
11. Pierre de Paschal, *Journal de ce qui s'est passé en France durant l'année 1562* (Paris, 1950), p. 71.
12. Crouzet, *Guerriers de Dieu*, vol. 1, pp. 412 ff.
13. Paschal, *Journal*, p. 74.
14. Isambert, De Crusy and Taillandier, *Recueil général*, vol. 14, p. 187.
15. Zeller, *Institutions*, p. 45.
16. Pernot, *Guerres de religion*, p. 256.
17. Boutier et al., *Tour de France royal*, passim.
18. Solange Deyon and André Lottin, *Les casseurs de l'été 1566: l'iconoclasme dans le Nord* (Lille, 1987).
19. Jouanna, *Devoir de révolte*, pp. 152–3.
20. Garrisson, *Protestants du Midi*, p. 165.

Notes to Chapter 13: The Massacre of Saint Bartholomew

1. For a recent controversy over responsibility for the massacre, see the articles by Jean-Louis Bourgeon in *Revue d'histoire moderne et contemporaine* (1/1987), *BSHPF* (3/1988), and *Revue historique* (1/1990). See also Crouzet, *Guerriers de Dieu*, vol. 2, ch. 11. For an overview, see Garrisson, *La Saint-Barthélemy*; and for the international context, N. M. Sutherland, *The Massacre of Saint-Bartholomew and the European conflict, 1559–1572* (London, 1973).
2. Benedict, *Rouen*, p. 130.
3. Garrisson, *Protestants du Midi*, vol. 2, chs ii–iii, pp. 177–224.
4. Isambert, de Crusy, and Taillandier, *Recueil général*, p. 291.
5. Miquel, *Guerres de religion*, pp. 315–16.
6. Garrisson, *Henri IV*, p. 121.
7. Pierre L'Estoile, *Journal*, p. 245.
8. Mariejol, *La Réforme et la Ligue*, p. 221.
9. Chaunu and Gascon, *L'État et la ville*, p. 175.
10. Jules Gassot, *Sommaire mémorial (souvenirs), 1555–1625* (Paris, 1934), p. 144.
11. Mariejol, *La Réforme et la Ligue*, p. 236.

Notes to Chapter 14: The 'The War of the Three Henries'

1. On the League, see Lebigre, *Révolution des curés*; Barnavi, *Parti de Dieu*; and Élie Barnavi and Robert Descimon, *La Sainte Ligue: le juge et la potence* (Paris, 1985).
2. Garrisson, *Henry IV*, p. 131.
3. Barnavi, *Parti de Dieu*, p. 78.
4. Lebigre, *Révolution des curés*, pp. 144–5.
5. Pierre L'Estoile, *Journal*, p. 576.
6. Lebigre, *Révolution des curés*, p. 151.
7. Constant, *Les Guise*, p. 18.
8. Cited by Lebigre, *Révolution des curés*, p. 161.
9. Pierre Chevallier, *Les régicides* (Paris, 1989), pp. 27–55.
10. For an interpretation emphasising the Stoic rather than the Baroque in Henri IV's statecraft, see Crouzet, *Guerriers de Dieu*, vol. 2, ch. 20.
11. Miquel, *Guerres de religion*, p. 383.

12. Babelon, *Henri IV*, p. 537.
13. Garrisson, *Henry IV*, p. 249.
14. The phrase is Élie Barnavi's: *Parti de Dieu*, p. 230.
15. Cited by Babelon, *Henri IV*, p. 596.
16. Chevallier, *Régicides*, pp. 125–32.
17. Babelon, *Henri IV*, p. 611.
18. On the edict, see J. Garrisson, *L'Édit de Nantes et sa révocation* (Paris, 1985), ch. 1. See also the stimulating observations of Le Roy Ladurie in his *L'État royal*, p. 294.
19. Mousnier, *Vénalité des offices*, pp. 589–90.

Bibliography

Reference Works and Printed Sources

Agrippa d'Aubigné, *Histoire universelle* (Paris, 1886–1909).

Joseph Bédier and Paul Hazard, *La littérature française*, vol. 1 (Paris, 1948).

Sébastien Castellion, *Conseil à la France désolée*, ed. Marius Valkhoff (Geneva, 1967).

Jules Gassot, *Sommaire mémorial (souvenirs), 1555–1625* (Paris, 1934).

Claude Haton, *Mémoires contenant le récit des événements accomplis de 1553 à 1587*, ed. Félix Bourquelot, 2 vols (Paris, 1857).

Pierre de L'Estoile, *Journal de Pierre de l'Estoile pour le règne d'Henri III, 1574–1589* (Paris, 1943).

Charles Loyseau, *Cinq livres du droit des offices* (Paris, 1610).

Recueil général des anciennes lois françaises depuis l'an 420 jusqu'à la Révolution de 1789, ed. F. A. Isambert *et al.*, 29 vols (Paris, 1822–33).

Political and Institutional History

Alain Boureau, *Le simple corps du roi: l'impossible sacralité des souverains français, XVe–XVIIIe siècle* (Paris, 1988).

Jean Boutier, Alain Dewerpe and David Nordman, *Un tour de France royal: le voyage de Charles IX, 1564–1566* (Paris, 1984).

Pierre Chaunu and Richard Gascon, *L'État et la ville, 1450–1660*, vol. 1 of *Histoire économique et sociale de la France au XVIe siècle*, ed. Fernand Braudel and Ernest Labrousse (Paris, 1977).

Roger Doucet, *Les institutions de la France au XVIe siècle*, 2 vols (Paris, 1948).

Jacques Ellul, *Histoire des institutions de l'époque franque à la Révolution* (Paris, 1962).

La France à la fin du XVe siècle, renouveau et apogée: colloque du Centre d'études supérieures de la Renaissance de Tours, 1983 (Paris, 1985).

Ernest Lavisse (ed.), *Histoire de France*, 9 vols (Paris, 1900–1911).

Henri Lemonnier, *Les Guerres d'Italie: la France sous Charles VIII, Louis XII et François I, 1492–1547* (Paris, 1903), vol. 5 (in 2 parts) of *Histoire de France des origines jusqu'à la Révolution*, ed. Ernest Lavisse.

Emmanuel Le Roy Ladurie, *L'État royal de Louis XI à Henri IV, 1460–1610* (Paris, 1987).

Ferdinand Lot, *Recherches sur les effectifs des armées françaises, des guerres d'Italie aux guerres de religion* (Paris, 1962).

Hélène Michaud, *La Grande Chancellerie de France et les écritures royales au XVIe siècle* (Paris, 1967).

Michel Mollat du Jourdin, *Genèse médiévale de la France moderne* (Paris, 1977).

Roland Mousnier, *État et société sous François Ier et pendant le gouvernement personnel de Louis XIV* (Paris, 1966–67).

Roland Mousnier, *La France de 1494 à 1559*, 2 vols (Paris, 1971).

Roland Mousnier, *La vénalité des offices sous Henri IV et Louis XIII* (Paris, 1971).

Henri Naef, *La conjuration d'Amboise* (Geneva, 1922).

François Olivier-Martin, *L'absolutisme français* (Paris, 1988).

Pierre de Paschal, *Journal de ce qui s'est passé en France durant l'année 1562...* (Paris, 1950).

Gaston Zeller, *Les institutions de la France au XVIe siècle* (Paris, 1948).

Economic and Social History

Yves-Marie Bercé, *Croquants et Nu-Pieds* (Paris, 1974).

Yves-Marie Bercé, *Histoire des Croquants* (Paris, 1988).

Yvonne Bezard, *La vie rurale dans le sud de la région parisienne de 1450 à 1560* (Paris, 1929).

Jean Richard Bloch, *L'anoblissement en France au temps de François Ier* (Paris, 1974).

Guy Bois, *La crise du féodalisme* (Paris, 1981).

Jacques Bousquet, *Enquête sur les commodités du Rouergue en 1552* (Toulouse, 1969).

Gilles Caster, *Le commerce du pastel et de l'épicerie à Touloise de 1450 environ à 1561* (Toulouse, 1962).

Bernard Chevallier, *Les bonnes villes de France au XVIᵉ siècle* (Paris, 1982).

Alain Croix, *Nantes et le Pays nantais au XVIᵉ siècle: étude démographique* (Paris, 1974).

Georges Duby et Armand Wallon (eds), *Histoire de la France rurale*, 4 vols (Paris, 1975–77).

Georges Duby (ed.), *L'histoire de la France urbaine*, 5 vols (Paris, 1980–85).

Richard Gascon, *Grand commerce et vie urbaine au XVI siècle: Lyon et ses marchands, vers 1520–1580*, 2 vols (Paris, 1971).

Bronislaw Geremek, *Truands et misérables dans l'Europe moderne, 1350–1600* (Paris, 1978).

Stéphane Gigon, *La révolte de la gabelle en Guyenne, 1548–1549* (Paris, 1906).

Pierre Goubert, *Beauvais et le Beauvaisis de 1600 à 1730* (Paris, 1960).

Jean-Pierre Gutton, *La société et les pauvres: l'exemple de la Généralité de Lyon, 1534–1789* (Paris, 1971).

Jean-Pierre Gutton, *La société et les pauvres en Europe, XVI–XVIII siècle* (Paris, 1974).

Henri Hauser, *Ouvriers du temps passé* (Paris, 1909).

Jacques Heers, *L'Occident aux XIV et XV siècles: aspects économiques et sociaux* (Paris, 1963).

Jean Jacquart, *La crise rurale en Ile-de-France, 1550–1670* (Paris, 1974).

Pierre Jeannin, *Les marchands au XVIᵉ siècle* (Paris, 1957).

Arlette Jouanna, *Le devoir de révolte: la noblesse française et la gestation de l'État moderne, 1559–1661* (Paris, 1989).

Jean Lartigaut, *Les campagnes de Quercy après la guerre de Cent Ans: vers 1440–vers 1550* (Toulouse, 1978).

Emmanuel Le Roy Ladurie, *Histoire du climat depuis l'ans mil*, 2 vols (Paris, 1983).

Emmanuel Le Roy Ladurie, *Paysans du Languedoc*, 2 vols (Paris, 1966).

Emmanuel Le Roy Ladurie (ed.), *La ville classique, de la Renaissance aux révolutions* (Paris, 1981), vol. 3 of *L'histoire de la France urbaine*, eds Duby and Wallon.

Claude Longeon, *Une province française à la Renaissance: la vie intellectuelle en Forez au XVIe siècle* (Saint-Étienne, 1975).

Frédéric Mauro, *Le XVI siècle européen: aspects économiques* (Paris, 1966).

Louis Merle, *La métairie et l'évolution agraire de la Gatîne poitevine de la fin du Moyen Age à la Révolution* (Paris, 1958).

Philippe Wolff, *Commerces et marchands de Toulouse: vers 1350–vers 1450* (Paris, 1954).

Religious History

Gabriel Audisio, *Les Vaudois de Lubéron: une minorité en Provence, 1450–1560* (Gap, 1984).

Élie Barnavi, *Le Parti de Dieu: étude sociale et politique de la Ligue parisienne, 1585–1594* (Louvain, 1980).

Philip Benedict, *Rouen during the Wars of Religion* (Cambridge, 1981).

Pierre Chaunu, *Église, culture et société: essais sur Réforme et Contre-Réforme, 1517–1620* (Paris, 1981).

Léon Cristiani, *L'Église à l'époque du Concile de Trente,* vol. 17 of *Histoire de l'Église depuis les origines à nos jours,* ed. Augustin Fliche and Victor Martin (Paris, 1948).

Colloque d'histoire religieuse: Lyon, octobre 1963 (Grenoble, 1963).

Courants religieux et Humanisme à la fin du XV et au début du XVI siècle: colloque de Strasbourg, mai 1957 (Paris, 1959).

Lucien Febvre, *Au cœur religieux du XVI siècle* (Paris, 1957).

Janine Garrisson, 'Vers une autre religion et une autre Église? (1534–1598)', *Histoire des protestants en France* (Toulouse, 1977).

Janine Garrisson, *L'Édit de Nantes et sa révocation: histoire d'une intolérance* (Paris, 1985).

Janine Garrisson, *Protestants du Midi, 1559–1598* (Toulouse, 1981).

Janine Garrisson, *La Saint-Barthélemy* (Brussels, 1987).

Janine Garrisson, *Les Protestants au XVI siècle* (Paris, 1988).

Paul Geisendorf, *Le livre des habitants de Genève, 1549–1587,* 2 vols (Genève, 1957–63).

Hérésie et sociétés dans l'Europe pré-industrielle, XIe–XVIIIe siècle: Royaumont, 1962 (Paris, 1968).

Pierre Imbart de la Tour, *Les origines de la Réforme,* vol. 2 (Melun, 1946).

Robert Kingdon, *Geneva and the Coming of the Wars of Religion in France* (Geneva, 1956).

Robert Kingdon, *Myths about the Saint-Bartholomew's Day Massacres, 1572–1576* (Cambridge, Mass. and London, 1988).

André Latreille, Étienne Delaruelle and Jean-Rémy Palanque, *Histoire du catholicisme en France*, vol. 2, *Sous les Rois Très Chrétiens* (Paris, 1963).

Arlette Lebigre, *La révolution des curés: Paris, 1588–1594* (Paris, 1980).

François Lebrun (ed.), *Du christianisme flamboyant à l'aube des lumières: XIV–XVIII siècle* (Paris, 1988), vol. 2 of *Histoire de la France religieuse*, ed. Le Goff and Rémond.

Jacques Le Goff and René Rémond, *Histoire de la France religieuse*, 4 vols (Paris, 1988–92).

Nicole Lemaître, *Le Rouergue flamboyant: le clergé et les paroisses du diocèse de Rodez, 1417–1563* (Paris, 1988).

Émile G. Léonard, *Histoire générale du protestantisme* (Paris, 1961).

Georges Livet, *Les guerres de religion* (Paris, 1962).

Robert Mandrou, 'Pourquoi de réformer?', *Histoire des protestants en France* (Toulouse, 1977).

Henri Martin, *Le métier de prédicateur en France septentrionale à la fin du Moyen Age, 1350–1520* (Paris, 1988).

Pierre Miquel, *Les guerres de religion* (Paris, 1980).

Michel Pernot, *Les guerres de religion en France, 1559–1598* (Paris, 1987).

Les Réformes, enracinement socio-culturel: colloque international d'études humanistes de Tours, 1982 (Paris, 1985).

Réforme et Humanisme: colloque du Centre d'histoire de la Réforme et du protestantisme: Montpellier, 1975 (Montpellier, 1977).

Lucien Romier, *Les origines politiques des guerres de religion*, 2 vols (Paris, 1913).

Joseph Salvini, *Le diocèse de Poitiers à la fin du Moyen Age, 1346–1560* (Fontenay-le-Comte, 1946).

N. M. Sutherland, *The Massacre of Saint-Bartholomew and the European conflict, 1559–1572* (London, 1973).

History of Ideas

Philippe Ariès, *Essais sur l'histoire de la mort en Occident du Moyen Age à nos jours* (Paris, 1975).

Sylvie Béguin (ed.), *L'École de Fontainebleau* (Paris, 1972).

Claude Bontems, Louise Raybaud and Jean-Pierre Brancourt, *Le Prince dans la France des XVI et XVII siècles* (Paris, 1976).

Jacqueline Boucher, *La Cour de Henri III* (Ouest-France, 1983).

Émile Callot, *Doctrines et figures humanistes* (Paris, 1963).

Roger Chartier, Marie-Madeleine Compère and Julia Dominique, *L'Éducation en France du XVI au XVIII siècle* (Paris, 1976).

Denis Crouzet, *Les guerriers de Dieu*, 2 vols (Paris, 1990).

François de Dainville, *Les Jésuites et l'éducation de la société française: la naissance de l'humanisme moderne* (Paris, 1940).

N. Z. Davis, *Les cultures du peuple: rituels, savoirs et résistances au XVI siècle* (Paris, 1979).

Jean Delumeau, *Naissance et affirmation de la Réforme* (Paris, 1965).

Jean Delumeau, *La civilisation de la Renaissance* (Paris, 1967).

Jean Delumeau (ed.), *La mort des pays de Cocagne: comportements collectifs de la Renaissance à l'âge classique* (Paris, 1976).

Jean Delumeau, *La peur en Occident* (Paris, 1978).

Elisabeth L. Eisenstein, *The Printing Revolution in Early Modern Europe* (Cambridge, 1983).

Norbert Élias, *La société de cour* (Paris, 1974).

Bernard Faivre, 'L'automne du Moyen Age', in Jacqueline de Jomaron (ed.), *Le théâtre en France*, vol. 2, *Du Moyen Age à 1789* (Paris, 1988).

Lucien Febvre, *Autour de l'Heptaméron: amour sacré, amour profane* (Paris, 1944).

Lucien Febvre, *Le problème de l'incroyance au XVI siècle: la religion de Rabelais* (Paris, 1947).

Lucien Febvre and Henri-Jean Martin, *L'apparition du livre* (Paris, 1971).

Wallace K. Ferguson, *La Renaissance dans la pensée historique* (Paris, 1950).

John Huizinga, *Le déclin du Moyen Age* (Paris, 1967).

Henry Institoris and Jacques Sprenger, *Le marteau des sorcières* (Grenoble, 1990).

Alexandre Koyré, *Du monde clos à l'univers infini* (Paris, 1962).

Anne-Marie Lecoq, *François Ier imaginaire: symbolique et politique à l'aube de la Renaissance française* (Paris, 1987).

Emmanuel Le Roy Ladurie, *Le Carnaval de Romans: de la Chandeleur au mercredi des cendres, 1579–1580* (Paris, 1979).

Robert Mandrou, *Des humanistes aux hommes de sciences, XVI et XVII siècles* (Paris, 1973).

Pierre Mesnard, *L'Essor de la philosophie politique au XVI siècle* (Paris, 1969).

Louis (or François) Morin, *Dialogue d'entre le Maheustre et le Manant*, ed. P. M. Ascoli (Geneva, 1977).

Robert Muchembled, *Culture populaire et culture des élites dans la France moderne: XV–XVIII siècle* (Paris, 1977).

Robert Muchembled, *La sorcière au village* (Paris, 1979).

Robert Muchembled, *L'invention de l'homme moderne: sensibilités, mœurs et comportements collectifs sous l'Ancien Régime* (Paris, 1988).

Jean Plattard, *La Renaissance des lettres en France de Louis XII à Henry IV* (Paris, 1947).

Augustin Renaudet, *Préréforme et humanisme à Paris pendant les premières guerres d'Italie, 1494–1517* (Paris, 1953).

Fernand Robert, *L'Humanisme: essai de définition* (Paris, 1946).

Jean-Pierre Seguin, *L'Information en France de Louis XII à Henri II* (Geneva, 1961).

Jean Touchard, *Histoire des idées politiques* (Paris, 1971).

Hélène Vedrine, *Les philosophes de la Renaissance* (Paris, 1971).

Biography

Jean-Pierre Babelon, *Henri IV* (Paris, 1982).

Emmanuel Bourassin, *Charles IX* (Paris, 1986).

Albert Buisson, *Le Chancelier Antoine Duprat* (Paris, 1935).

Albert Buisson, *Michel de L'Hospital, 1503–1573* (Paris, 1950).

Pierre Chevallier, *Henri III* (Paris, 1985).

Pierre Chevallier, *Les régicides* (Paris, 1989).

Ivan Cloulas, *Catherine de Médicis* (Paris, 1979).

Ivan Cloulas, *Henri II* (Paris, 1985).

Ivan Cloulas, *Charles VIII et le mirage italien* (Paris, 1986).

Anne-Marie Cocula-Vaillières, *Brantôme: amour et gloire au temps des Valois* (Paris, 1986).

Jean-Marie Constant, *Les Guise* (Paris, 1984).

Jean-Luc Dejean, *Marguerite de Navarre* (Paris, 1987).

Janine Garrisson, *Henry IV* (Paris, 1984).

Léon E. Halkin, *Érasme: sa pensée et son comportement* (Londres, 1988).

Jean Jacquart, *François I* (Paris, 1981).

Jean Jacquart, *Bayard* (Paris, 1987).

Yvonne Labande-Mailfert, *Charles VIII: le vouloir et la destinée* (Paris, 1986).

Étienne de La Boétie, *Discours de la servitude volontaire* (Paris, 1976).

Hector de La Ferrière and Gustave Baguenault de Puchesse, *Lettres de Catherine de Médicis*, 10 vols and index (Paris, 1880–1909).

Blaise de Monluc, *Commentaires, 1521–1576*, ed. P. Courteault (Paris, 1974).

Frank Palm, *Politics and Religion in Sixteenth-century France: A Study of the Career of Henry of Montmorency-Damville, Uncrowned King of the South* (Boston, 1927).

Bernard Quilliet, *Louis XII: père du peuple* (Paris, 1986).

Nancy Roelker, *Jeanne d'Albret, reine de Navarre* (Paris, 1979).

Louis de Santi and Auguste Vidal, *Deux livres de raison, 1517–1550* (Paris, 1896).

Michel Veissière, *L'Évêque Guillaume Briçonnet (1470–1534): contribution à la connaissance de la Réforme catholique à la veille du Concile de Trente* (Provins, 1986).

Nicolas Versoris, *Journal d'un bourgeois de Paris sous François I*, ed. Philippe Joutard (Paris, 1962).

Stephan Zweig, *Érasme: grandeur et décadence d'une idée* (Paris, 1935).

Further reading for English readers

F. J. Baumgartner, *Radical Reactionaries: The Political Thought of the French Catholic League* (Geneva, 1976).

F. J. Baumgartner, *Henri II, King of France, 1547–1559* (Durham, N.C., 1988).

David Buisseret, *Henry IV, King of France* (London, 1984).

Keith Cameron (ed.), *From Valois to Bourbon. Dynasty, State & Society in Early Modern France* (Exeter, 1989).

N. Z. Davis, *Society and Culture in Early Modern France* (Stanford, 1975).

Barbara B. Diefendorf, *Beneath the Cross: Catholics and Huguenots in Sixteenth-century Paris* (New York and Oxford, 1991).

H. O. Evennett, *The Cardinal of Lorraine and the Council of Trent* (Cambridge, 1930).

Lucien Febvre and Henri-Jean Martin, *The Coming of the Book* (London, 1976).

A. N. Galpern, *The Religions of the People in Sixteenth-century Champagne* (Cambridge, Mass., 1976).

Mark Greengrass, *France in the Age of Henri IV* (London, 1984).

Mark Greengrass, *The French Reformation* (Historical Association studies, Oxford, 1987).

R. R. Harding, *Anatomy of a Power Elite: The Provincial Governors in Early Modern France* (New Haven and London, 1978).

Mack P. Holt, *The Duke of Anjou and the Politique Struggle during the Wars of Religion* (Cambridge, 1986).

D. R. Kelley, *The Beginning of Ideology: Consciousness and Society in the French Reformation* (Cambridge, 1981).

R. M. Kingdon, *Geneva and the Consolidation of the French Protestant Movement, 1564–1572* (Geneva, 1967).

R. J. Knecht, *Francis I* (2nd edition, Cambridge, 1994).

R. J. Knecht, *French Renaissance Monarchy: Francis I and Henri II* (Seminar studies in history, London, 1984).

R. J. Knecht, *The French Wars of Religion, 1559–1598* (Seminar studies in history, London, 1989).

Emmanuel Le Roy Ladurie, *The Peasants of Languedoc* (Illinois, 1974).

Emmanuel Le Roy Ladurie, *Carnival: A People's Rising in Romans, 1579–80* (London, 1980).

Emmanuel Le Roy Ladurie, *The Royal State . . . 1460–1610* (Blackwell: History of France, Oxford, 1994).

H. A. Lloyd, *France, the State and the Sixteenth Century* (London, 1983).

I. D. McFarlane, *The Entry of Henri II into Paris, 16 June 1549* (Medieval and Renaissance texts and studies, Binghampton, N.Y., 1982).

J. Russell Major, *Representative Government in Early Modern France* (New Haven and London, 1980).

David Potter, *War and Government in the French Provinces: Picardy 1470–1560* (Cambridge, 1993).

N. Roelker, *Queen of Navarre: Jeanne d'Albret, 1528–1572* (Cambridge, Mass., 1968).

J. H. M. Salmon, *Society in Crisis: France in the Sixteenth Century* (London, 1975).

N. M. Sutherland, *The Huguenot Struggle for Recognition* (New Haven and London, 1980).

M. Wolfe, *The Fiscal System of Renaissance France* (New Haven and London, 1972).

Glossary

Aides   A form of indirect taxation which varied throughout the kingdom in incidence, assessment and collection, but was generally levied upon a region's main product.

Bailiwick   A rendering of the French *bailliage*, a jurisdictional district under a bailiff (*bailli*). In southern France such districts were known as seneschalcies (*sénéchaussées*) and were under seneschals.

'Beautiful sixteenth century'   A rendering of the French '*beau seizième siècle*', a term current among French historians for the period between the end of the Hundred Years War and the beginning of the Wars of Religion (c. 1460–1560).

Bureau des parties casuelles   A department established in 1523 in order to manage the market in royal offices and appointments, presided over by the *Trésorier des parties casuelles*.

Cens   Dues owed in cash or kind to the feudal seigneur, or lord of the manor, by the *censitaire* or villein.

Censitaire   Those who held land from a seigneur (lord of the manor) in return for paying the *cens* and fulfilling various feudal obligations to labour on the lord's demesne land.

Chambre ardente   A special tribunal of the Parlement de Paris established by Henri II in 1547 in order to investigate and prosecute heresy.

Chambre des aides   A sovereign court for litigation over tax disputes.

Chambre des comptes   A sovereign court responsible for auditing royal revenues.

Chambre des enquêtes   One of the constituent tribunals of the Parlement de Paris.

Conseil des affaires   See *Conseil étroit.*

Conseil des finances   The King's Council, or occasionally a select but informal subcommittee of it, deliberating upon financial business.

Conseil des parties   See *Grand Conseil.*

Conseil d'état   The King's Council.

Conseil étroit   The inner ring of the King's Council, comparable to the emerging Privy Council of the Tudors in England, deliberating and deciding upon the highest affairs of State.

Conseil secret   See *Conseil étroit.*

Contrôleur général   A senior financial official (akin to the English Comptroller General), responsible for monitoring and recording cash flows in and out of the *Épargne.*

Cru   A regular supplement to the *taille.*

Devotio moderna   A new form of internalised and individualised piety which originated in the Netherlands in the fifteenth century and spread widely in Europe by the early sixteenth century. It was associated with the Brethren of the Common Life, and is best represented by the pious bestseller, *The Imitation of Christ.*

Duke-Peer   *Duc-pair.* The title of the secular peers of France, an exclusive group of men, in theory restricted to six but occasionally, as under Henri III, more. Along with the six ecclesiastical peers, they took precedence over all others in France after the immediate royal family and princes of the blood.

Élu   The official in charge of an *éléction*, the basic administrative unit for the collection of the *taille*.

Épargne   The new central treasury established in 1523. Its head, the *Trésorier de l'Épargne*, was answerable directly to the king.

Général des finances   A senior official responsible for extraordinary revenues within a region known as a *généralité*.

Généralités   The main regional divisions of the financial administration, whose number was increased from 4 to 16 by François I in 1542.

Gentilhomme de la chambre   See *Valet de chambre*.

Grand Conseil   The King's Council, or increasingly in the sixteenth century a specialised and subordinate part of it, acting in a strictly judicial capacity.

Grand Écuyer   Literally the 'Grand Squire', one of the most senior appointments in the royal household, akin to the Tudor Master of the Horse, responsible for managing the royal stables.

Grand Maître   Or 'Grand Master', the foremost official in the royal household, responsible under the king for every aspect of Court life.

High justice   A rendering of haute justice.

Lettres de jussion   A royal instruction ordering the Parlement to register an edict.

Lit de justice   A personal appearance of the king in the Parlement in order to secure registration of an edict.

Maîtres de requêtes de l'Hôtel   Agents of the King's Council, often also holding office in the Parlement de Paris, responsible to the Chancellor, and employed on a wide range of financial, judicial and administrative business.

Ordinance companies   Armoured cavalry companies manned by the nobility (*gendarmerie*), established by an ordinance of Charles VII.

Pays d'oc   That part of France, roughly south of a line from Poitiers to Lyon, dominated by the dialects of the *langue d'oc*, as opposed to the *langue d'oeil* (which became standard French) spoken in the north.

Présidiaux   A new tier of royal jurisdiction, inferior only to the sovereign courts, introduced in every bailiwick by Henri II.

Président des Enquêtes   Presiding official in the *Chambre des enquêtes.*

Rentes sur l'Hôtel de Ville   Loans raised by the Crown on the security of the revenues of the municipality of Paris.

'Solde des hommes de pied'   A levy introduced by François I in order to tap the wealth of the major towns, which were often exempt from the *taille* or other traditional forms of taxation.

Sovereign courts   Courts which enjoyed a particular royal status because of their direct derivation from the king's court itself. Their principal offices conferred nobility in the first generation on their incumbents. They included not only courts of justice such as the Parlements of Paris, Toulouse etc., but also revenue courts such as the *Chambre des aides* and the *Chambre des comptes.*

Surintendant des finances   An office established under Henri III, with general responsibility for financial affairs.

Taille   The oldest and most important form of direct taxation, assessed in the north on the basis of individual wealth, and in the south on the basis of formal land valuations.

Taillon   A supplementary form of the *taille*, introduced by Henri II.

Trésor de l'Épargne   See *Épargne*.

Trésorier de l'Épargne   See *Épargne*.

Trésoriers de France   Officials in charge of the king's ordinary revenues.

Valet de chambre   A personal attendant of the king, usually of noble or gentle birth, equivalent to the English Gentleman of the Privy Chamber. The new title *Gentilhomme de la chambre* was introduced in 1515 to distinguish the more aristocratic attendants from the other valets.

Index